THE AMERICAN ALPINE JOURNAL

2013

D0354668

[This page] Mike Libecki and Freddie Wilkinson work through bizarre rock formations on the first ascent of Bertha's Tower, Queen Maud Land, Antarctica (p. 248). *Keith Ladzinski*

2013 VOLUME 55 ISSUE 87

CONTENTS

CLIMBS and EXPEDITIONS

362 **BOOK REVIEWS,** EDITED BY DAVID STEVENSON

NEW BOOKS FROM PETER ZUCKERMAN & AMANDA PADOAN, DAMIEN O'BRIEN, GRAHAM RATCLIFFE, RICHARD SALE & EBERHARD JURGALSKI & GEORGE RODWAY, PAT MORROW & SHARON WOOD, JAMES P. SWEENEY, NICHOLAS O'CONNELL, GORDON STAINFORTH, PAT DEAVOLL & CRAIG POTTON, JOE FITSCHEN, AND ANDY KIRKPATRICK

373 **IN MEMORIAM,** EDITED BY DAVID WILKES

REMEMBERING BJØRN-EIVIND ARTUN, BEAN BOWERS, HARVEY CARTER, HERBERT WILLIAM CONN, BILL FORREST, MAURICE HERZOG, BEN HORNE, DALE JOHNSON, ANN DODGE MIDDLETON, ROGER PAYNE, JACK ROBERTS, GIL WEISS, AND MICHAEL J. YBARRA

384 **CLUB ACTIVITIES,** EDITED BY FREDERICK O. JOHNSON

[Back cover photos, clockwise from top left] Angie Payne, Greenland. *Keith Ladzinski;* Kyashar headwall, Nepal. *Yasuhiro Hanatani;* Brad Wilson, Undertow, Mt. Evans, Colorado. *John Lloyd* Matic Obid, Acopan Tepui, Venezuela. *Luka Krajnc*

CORPORATE PARTNERS

SUMMIT PARTNER
patagonia®

BENEFACTOR
Black Diamond®

PATRONS

ARC'TERYX

ASOLO

GUARANTEED
TO KEEP YOU DRY
GORE-TEX®
PRODUCTS
GORE

REI®

THE NORTH FACE®

CAMP
TECHNICAL ADVENTURE EQUIPMENT

[This page]
obert Rauch
n mixed terrain
the upper part
f Los Alcaldes
e Serkhe
hollu, Bolivia
. 214). Chris
larke

The American Alpine Journal, 710 Tenth St. Suite 100, Golden, Colorado 80401
Telephone: (303) 384-0110 Fax: (303) 384-0111
E-mail: aaj@americanalpineclub.org
www.americanalpineclub.org

ISSN: 0065-6925
ISBN: 978-1-933056-79-1
ISBN: (e-book): 978-1-933056-80-7

WE THANK THE FOLLOWING FOR THEIR GENEROUS
FINANCIAL SUPPORT:

GREAT RANGES FELLOWSHIP

Richard Blum
Yvon Chouinard
Anonymous
Ken Ehrhart
Todd Hoffman
David Koch
Peter Metcalf

Anonymous
Mark Richey
Teresa Richey
Cody J Smith
Travis Spitzer
Steven Swenson
Douglas Walker

Douglas Beall
Linda Brown
Jim Edwards
Gerald Gallwas
Clark Gerhardt Jr.
Robert Hall
Sandy Hill
Louis Kasischke
Mark Kroese
Phil Lakin Jr.

George McCown
Amy Meredith
Vanessa O'Brien
David Riggs
Naoe Sakashita
Steve Schwartz
Alan Spielberg
William Straka
Lawrence True

Mr. Warren Adelman
George Basch
Sherman Bull M.D.
Thomas Burch
Mike Collins
James Donini
James Duckworth
Dan Emmett
Ellen Lapham

Jeff Martin
Linda McMillan
James Morrissey
David Olsen
Charles Peck
Wolf Riehle
Bob Street
John (Jed) Williamson
Keegan Young

Larry Arthur
William Atkinson
Steve Barrett
Gail Bates
Laurie Berliner
Tanya Bradby
Wesley Brown

Paul Brunner
Evan Buckland
William Burd
Deirdre Byers
David Byrne Jr.
Robert J. Campbell
Peter Carter

John Catto
Douglas Colwell
Michael Coote
J. Culberson III
Karen Daubert
Stanley Dempsey
Dr. David Dingman

[This page] Searching for a line on Stamprevtinden, Lofoten Islands, Norway. *Jiri Svihalek Collection*

THE AMERICAN ALPINE JOURNAL

Executive Editor
Dougald MacDonald

Senior Editor
Lindsay Griffin

Assistant Editor
Erik Rieger

Art Director
Erik Rieger

Contributing Editors
Frederick O. Johnson, *Club Activities*
David Stevenson, *Book Reviews*
David Wilkes, *In Memoriam*

Illustrators
Jeremy Collins
Tami Knight
Anna Riling (maps)
Andreas Schmidt

Indexers
Ralph Ferrara, Eve Tallman

Translators
Luca Calvi, Sergio Ramirez Carrascal, Peter Jensen-Choi, Tamotsu Nakamura, Joel Peach, Pam Roberts, Marcelo Scanu, Ekaterina Vorotnikova

Regional Contacts
Steve Gruhn, *Alaska*; Drew Brayshaw, Don Serl, and Rapahel Slawinski, *Canada*; Myles Moser and Pullharder Alpine Club, *California*; James Lucas, *Yosemite*; Sevi Bohorquez and Sergio Ramirez Carrascal, *Peru*; Rolando Garibotti, *Patagonia*; Marcelo Scanu, *Argentina*; Damien Gildea, *Antarctica*; Steve Schneider and Daniel Seeliger, *Chile*; Rajesh Gadgil and Harish Kapadia, *India*; Elizabeth Hawley and Richard Salisbury, *Nepal*; Tamotsu Nakamura and Hiroshi Hagiwara (*Japanese climbs*); Peter Jensen-Choi (*Korean climbs*); Anna Piunova, *Russia, Tajikistan,* and *Kyrgyzstan*

With heartfelt thanks to
Christine Blackmon, Claude Gardien, John Heilprin, Craig Hoffman, Phil Hollman, Erik Lambert, Artur Paszczak, Elizabeth Surles, Xia Zhongming, and all *AAJ* donors and supporters

[This page] Walking across the Ruth Glacier during the successful 2012 Tooth Traverse expedition (p. 45). *Camp 4 Collective*

PREFACE

THE MORE THINGS CHANGE...

Last spring two climbers discovered a fun runnel of steep ice on a variation to Mt. Hood's Eliot Glacier. When they posted their ascent on climbing websites, a furious debate erupted, accompanied by the usual Internet chest-thumping. Although there were several issues, it boiled down to this: Was this really a new ice climb, or simply an older route in leaner conditions?

The *AAJ* opted not to investigate—at most, only two or three new pitches were climbed—but in general we would say that exploring the same terrain in different conditions does not make for a new route. Mountains change continuously, and the pace has accelerated with a warming climate. And even when whole pitches fall off or difficult ice runnels appear in place of snow, what rarely changes is the essential path up the peak—the *line*. We may experience the climb in a very different way, but it's still the same line.

Like the mountains and climbs it covers, the *AAJ* also evolves. As you'll see in these pages and on your computer or tablet, we've significantly improved the design, added content in key areas, and built new digital extras. But the core mission of the *AAJ* remains the same: to work with climbers to document the world's most significant climbs in the most authoritative and engaging ways we can.

This is the first full-color edition of the *AAJ* in our 85-year history, and it covers more stories from the mainland United States—which readers requested in our surveys. We've also launched a new website that makes researching and reading old *AAJ* stories easier than ever. Every *AAJ* report since 1929 (some with bonus photos, topos, and maps) is accessible through searches at *aaj. americanalpineclub.org*. In all, we've scanned and digitized more than 30,000 pages of the *American Alpine Journal* and *Accidents in North American Mountaineering*. And this autumn we'll launch our first multi-media stories online, inspired by the pages of the *AAJ*.

None of this would be possible without the *AAJ's* exceptional staff, especially Lindsay Griffin, our one-of-a-kind senior editor, and Erik Rieger, an *AAJ* newcomer who not only edited much of the book but also created its new design. Many, many volunteers also pitched in, from our new In Memoriam editor, David Wilkes, to mapmaker extraordinaire Anna Riling and super-illustrators Jeremy Collins, Tami Knight, and Andreas Schmidt. The list goes on: section editors, regional correspondents, translators, fund-raisers, and too many people to name who worked for countless hours to help prepare our publications for scanning—it truly has been an amazing effort.

As we worked through weekends and late nights to finish this edition, I often consoled myself with the thought that it is precisely the difficulty of its creation that makes the *AAJ* unique—and such a privilege to work on. No one else in the world is as dedicated to documenting the world's climbs. Whatever else changes, that's the route we'll continue to follow.

DOUGALD MACDONALD, *Executive Editor*

The AAJ depends on the AAC.
AND THE AAC DEPENDS ON YOU.

The AAJ is only possible because of thousands of hours invested by the AAC and its volunteers. Please consider supporting the publication of this information by volunteering your time or making a donation to the American Alpine Club.

LODGING   RESCUE   DISCOUNTS   BETA

GRANTS   PUBLICATIONS   COMMUNITY   CONSERVATION

americanalpineclub.org/donate

DETERMINATION

THE FIRST COMPLETE ASCENT OF THE MAZENO RIDGE ON NANGA PARBAT

SANDY ALLAN

We are running on empty. It is 6:12 p.m., late in the day for Rick Allen and I to be on the summit of Nanga Parbat, but that's how it is. We had left base camp almost two weeks earlier with four other climbers, intending to traverse the full Mazeno Ridge. Exhausted, the rest of the team had bailed down the Schell Route from just above Mazeno Gap three days ago. Rick and I decided to press on.

Now we have been wandering above 8,000 meters since 2 p.m., harvesting each small summit as we tried to find the true top in poor visibility. The mist cleared in late afternoon and we climbed up again. I was all but ready to give up, but our years of trust and loyalty to each other provided the spark for Rick to push on in front, one more time, to a high point very near where we'd stood four hours earlier. A peg, a short piece of aluminum, and a length of wire marked the summit.

I'd been on top of Nanga Parbat once before with Rick, in July 2009, crawling about in a strong wind. On that occasion we had climbed the Diamir Face via the Kinshofer Route. We were checking things out, because I was quite certain that if I ever ascended the Mazeno, a fast descent would be vital. Rick and I had each tried the Mazeno before, with Doug Scott and close friends, back in the 1990s. Incredibly, the ridge kept calling me, and to fortify my self-confidence I felt it essential to understand the way off the mountain if my nonsensical yearning to climb the Mazeno endured.

THE MAZENO RIDGE DIVIDES the Diamir and Rupal faces of Nanga Parbat, the ninth-highest mountain in the world. It is 10 to 13 kilometers long—it depends where you measure the beginning. I can assure you it's long, with at least four significant 7,000-meter peaks along the way, inescapable, and then a considerable distance remaining above Mazeno Gap to reach the 8,126-meter summit. Doug Chabot and Steve Swenson made the first traverse of the ridge from August 12 to 18, 2004; they had been acclimatizing for ages before making their attempt, but the effort left them weak and ill. They descended by the Schell Route and graded the Mazeno VI M4 AI3. A two-man German team also traversed the ridge in 2008, but there is little written about it. [*See Climbs and Expeditions for more details.*]

I knew it would not be easy. Many mountaineers, including myself, had hit their heads against this proverbial brick wall, starting in 1979. My pal Voytek Kurtyka and the late Erhard Loretan each tried, and gained no new ground. For us to do the same as everyone else seemed a bit pointless. What remained was to complete the ridge to the summit.

During my frequent expeditions to Nepal, I have climbed with some outstanding Sherpas, and for a long time I had been telling them I had a great route for them. Lhakpa Zarok is one of the best ice climbing Sherpas I have ever seen, and I asked him and a friend to join Rick and me in Pakistan. As usual, cash was in short supply, so I decided to ask Cathy O'Dowd along. She raised lots of funds and was responsible for the web site, networking, and weather reports—things Rick and I are dreadful at and avoid as much as possible.

Cathy lacked confidence about climbing the whole ridge, so we decided to take another Sherpa to climb with her, as she fully expected to turn back early but wanted to see the place. As it turned out, she surpassed her own expectations (which I knew she would), though eventually she and the three Sherpas descended after taking part in one aborted summit attempt. Rick and I would not have been in a position to make the top if not for their outstanding efforts.

And so we were six: Rick, Cathy, Lhakpa Zarok, Lhakpa Nuru, Lhakpa Rangdu, and me as leader. It was a tough call to invite my Nepalese pals rather than Western climbers, as I knew mountain guides who had showed a modicum of interest in my project. But at the end of the day, while my Western friends were outstanding climbers, I had only known them in Alpine surroundings. We had not experienced high-altitude rough times together, so I decided it was not worth the risk.

HAVING SPENT ONE NIGHT AT 6,400 METERS in our acclimatization phase, we embark on the big push on July 2. Weather reports have informed us that we will be climbing into storm conditions about a week away, but we know we are never going to get a weather window long enough for this climb. Our sacks are heavy: eight days of food that could stretch to 10, maybe. So off we go, along the glacier and up onto the first easy slopes.

Two days later, on the morning of July 4, we finally stand high on the ridge and get good views down the other side to the Diamir Glacier, 2,500 meters below us. We can see the tents of teams tackling the Kinshofer Route. I wish them success, hoping they'll climb high on the Kinshofer, our planned descent route, but as it transpires they will only reach Camp 2 and then go home.

It is cold on the ridge—the Lhakpas and Rick wear their down suits all the time; I wear my down parka constantly. Deep, unconsolidated snow and afternoon mist make for slow

[Previous spread] Big packs and a long way to go: Moving across the Mazeno Ridge. *Lhakpa Rangdu Sherpa* [This page] The Mazeno Ridge of Nanga Parbat, Rupal Face to the right. (A) The team acclimatized on the lower ridge before settting off alpine-style. (B) Camp before Mazeno Peak (7,120m), high point of the traverse. (C) The Pinnacles, crux of the traverse. (D) Mazeno Gap, reached on Day 9. (E) After one failed attempt, Allan and Allen summited and descended to the north. (F) The remaining team members descended a variant of the Schell Route. *Doug Scott*

progress, and when views come it seems a ridiculous distance to the summit of Nanga Parbat. It taunts and frustrates our team, some who are probably thinking their leader is a dreamer, and potentially insane!

We are moving alpine style, breaking trail while carrying big sacks, roped into teams of two, taking everything with us. We have more muscle power and more supplies than either of the two teams that have traversed the entire ridge to Mazeno Gap, but even with the outstanding Nepalese we are moving slowly, semi-intentionally, trying to preserve energy in the unconsolidated snow, as we know that we are here for the long haul.

On day four, we are going along well when Lhakpa Nuru, who has traversed under a rock outcrop and is trying to climb a steep snow gully to regain the winding knife-edge, falls some 40 meters after sugar snow collapses under him. Zarok is almost in Nuru's footsteps, with lots of pooled loose rope. The sliding fall goes on until Zarok gets a grip and Nuru stops. With re-ascent difficult, we climb down to him and try to traverse around the snow and rock buttresses, finding an old loop of accessory cord jammed in a crack. Nightfall catches us in a bad place.

We huddle under a rock overhang, the slope below steep enough that a dropped rucksack has a good chance of landing at the foot of the Diamir Glacier. My determination to hack at rocks gets one tent precariously pitched. Rick excavates a natural coffin-shaped cave to share with Rangdu, and Nuru and Zarok curl up half-sitting on an uneven rock ledge. It is a bad night that leads to a short day.

After climbing steeply back to the ridge and on to a col, we bivy again to give everyone time to recover. The next day is our predicted storm day, but we can't get a satellite signal, so have no idea of the updated forecast. What we see suggests high winds. Ahead lie twin peaks, featuring steep mixed ground, narrow exposed ridges, and few camping places. We choose to stay where we are and sit out a storm that, in the end, does not really come. But it is windy—it would be pushy to move!

On the seventh day, we start moving again. The effort remains relentless: wind, deep snow, tricky mixed passages, one peak after another after another. The exposure superb: a traverse in the sky with terrain dropping steeply on either side, spreading out into views of distant peaks. The ridge winds like a serpent's back, decorated with curved cornices poised in frozen waves. We pass our "point of no return" with an awkward, diagonal abseil to descend a rock wall. Should anything go wrong now, retracing our steps would be barely possible; we'd be better off to press on to Mazeno Gap.

On day eight, we cross Mazeno Peak (7,120m), the highest point on the traverse, and the ridge widens. Now we stand at the start of the pinnacles, the last challenge between us and the main massif. From the Chabot and Swenson report, we know this obstacle to be the crux; it took them 13 hours. Yet it looks so straightforward, and I can sense Cathy and the Lhakpas already skipping ahead to summit day. Me, I hold so much respect for the American climbers that I expect a tough time and simply hope for the best.

The next day, July 10, the hours accumulate and the pinnacles seem endless, a crenelated, twisting ridge dropping ever downward, getting narrower and more convoluted as parts of my team get ever more exasperated with it. After 11 hours of climbing, we reach the Mazeno Gap (ca. 6,850m) in the last blush of daylight. Only two other teams have gotten this far. None has gone further.

[This page] View from the Pinnacles to the summit, with the two highest camps marked. (1) First attempt from 7,200m camp by full team on July 12. See Climbs and Expeditions for another view. (2) Allan-Allen route to 7,700m bivouac and summit. After another night at 7,700m, they went down the Kinshofer Route (dashed line). *Lhakpa Rangdu Sherpa*

TIRED, BUT WITH A SENSE OF ACHIEVEMENT, we sleep late before making our way up to a high camp at 7,200 meters. This will do for a bid for the summit at 8,126 meters—it's a tad far, but we could make it. We know we are climbing into a high wind forecast, but food is depleted—one big push to go and perhaps, just perhaps!

We leave at 1 a.m. on day 11, climbing in strong winds. I am tail-end Charley, struggling with my goggles; Nuru is in front. To Rick and Cathy's disappointment, I want to stick to the ridge, seeking a technically cool new line to the summit, instead of traversing lower on the Diamir flank. As daylight expands we arrive spectacularly on top of a subsidiary peak with views to the far western horizon. Sadly this bump is nowhere near the true summit. We are traversing along the exquisite rocky ridgeline that runs between the Rupal and Diamir faces, with awesome exposure. From our bump we are forced to downclimb diagonally over treacherous mixed ground, sugar snow, and loose rock. Nuru is demoralized, and Cathy cold and exhausted.

By 7 a.m., Cathy and Nuru have had enough and they turn back. Rangdu is roped with Zarok, and me with Rick, and we move together on Scottish grade III/IV mixed ground. I wish I had two tools, but in my rush to get to Pakistan I had left my best tools in storage in Chamonix, so I was dependent on our Pakistani stash. We climb steeply up rotten rock and then traverse deep snow to another rock wall, where we find Rangdu and Zarok coming back toward us, wanting to descend. We are already too late, and I so regret being ignorant about this aspect of the mountain.

There is half-hearted talk of another push to the summit during the long traverse

back to our high camp. Then Lhakpa Zarok slips and starts off down the slope; Rangdu tries to hold him but is catapulted off his feet, and they cascade down the face. From where Rick and I are standing, the angle appears to ease before dropping off steeply, but I am beginning to think they may not stop. Finally, after around 300 meters, they come to rest just meters above the steeply dropping seracs of the Diamir face. They stand up and slowly climb the face to rejoin our traverse line.

After 18 hours of climbing, in fading light, we arrive back at our high camp, rejoining Cathy and Nuru. There are almost no supplies left. The decision to descend the next day seems obvious. The Lhakpas and Cathy make it clear they are going down.

I wake up feeling so fine! I want to keep my options open. Zarok and Nuru are almost ready to strike their bivy tents in preparation for their descent. I call through frosted tent fabric to Rick, and he shares my optimism.

Grace and acceptance fill my mind as I watch Cathy and the three amazing Lhakpas head down the Schell Route on that misty enshrouded day. Did I see this coming in my planning stage? Their contribution has been immense. As expedition leader and mountain guide, my sense of duty and accountability is tangible.

Later we learn that, during their descent, they missed the turning off the ridge to the east in the mist and found themselves abseiling into the bowl to the west. Rangdu badly injured his ankle in a fall in the dark, forcing him to spend the night with Cathy under a cliff at the foot of the bowl, exposed to hanging seracs. Early in the morning, an avalanche swept over the tent, but the cliff face protected them, and then, after they reached the safety of the moraine, a second avalanche filled the bowl. Two days after leaving high camp, they reached the road and took Jeeps to Chilas, where they waited in a hotel for us.

After Cathy and the Sherpas depart on July 13, Rick and I rest the remainder of the day. We are left with the satellite phone with a three-quarter battery charge. The forecast is reasonable for four days out. The remaining food generously left for us consists of an almost full packet of digestive biscuits, a serving of porridge, some boiled sweets, and several gas cylinders. Once the others are long gone, I realize that I have not got my own lighter, and they have many. Why did I not remember to take one?

[This page] Climbing through the Pinnacles. *Lhakpa Rangdu Sherpa*

The facts are: We are tired, have little food, and we do not have it in us to repeat our more direct line of the day before and push it to the summit. I am a bit disappointed but accept the realistic option. Our plan is to climb up a bit and then try a rising traverse to the summit pyramid, turning it on the left to join the Kinshofer Route somewhere above 7,500 meters. The tent will be a burden, so we leave that behind and just take sleeping bags. We impulsively leave the sleeping mats as well, as we think we can descend the normally fixed Kinshofer Route in a day.

Light snowfall, wind, and tiny sloughs have erased our tracks on the face from the previous attempt. We make slow work of the traverse. Rocky ribs finger down the face, demanding precise footwork; we use whatever natural protection we can find. We push on, breaking trail in deeper snow. We share leads on a steeper couloir, and I haul myself over a hanging cornice, hoping the debris misses Rick. We begin to recognize features on the Diamir side from our 2009 ascent. It is 5 p.m. and the summit is still far in the distance. Finally, at around 7,700 meters, we dig into a snow bank with our ice axes, move into the cave in the dark, and eat our last biscuits.

On July 15, two weeks after starting the climb, we leave our snow cave early, taking all our possessions with us. We are on the summit plateau by 2 p.m., and eventually find the summit after 6 p.m. Seventeen years after our first attempt on the Mazeno Ridge, we have taken it all the way to the top.

DESCENDING FROM THE SUMMIT, our footsteps are all but obscured with drifting snow. Darkness surrounds us, but experience leads me directly to the cave we'd left that morning. Rick cannot get our remaining lighter to spark, and the half cylinder of gas on the Sumo stove now seems almost extravagant. Fortunately, sleep comes easily.

As we start down the Diamir Face, Rick breaks trail at first, but he is too slow, so I take over for almost the entire day, moving along a seemingly endless downward arc. Mist comes in, and I take a bearing slightly above the traditional Camp 4 on the Kinshofer Route. Rick is behaving out of character, but his work yesterday justifies exhaustion and respect.

No one has climbed Nanga Parbat in two seasons. We are on our own. My concern makes me telephone our agent, Ali, to tell him we are descending the Diamir side, and to send some valley clothes around the mountain with fast porters. I also enquire about our helicopter bond and the potential for rescue if needed.

[This page] Rick Allen looks for the summit as the clouds lift. The two men spent four hours on the summit plateau before finding the true top at 6 p.m. *Sandy Allan*

[This page, left] Sandy Allan at the last bivouac during the descent, above Camp 2 on the Kinshofer Route. *Rick Allen* [This page, right] Rick Allen descending, Day 17. *Sandy Allan*

Rick hears my words and realizes he is the cause of my concern. Digging deep, he seems to get his act together. We carve out another snow cave in unpleasant weather. Rick's energy is wasted as his side of the cave collapses. My excavations are a bit better, and we squeeze ourselves partway in. We try again to get a spark from the stove and lighter, but it is useless.

Day 16: again, no water, no food. We shake off the spindrift, rope up, and move down a steep slope, crusty in places. It is loaded and unstable; Rick triggers an avalanche and rolls as I hold the rope from my solid stance. The slope is perhaps slightly safer now, but we know not to assume! Our options are zero: stay and deteriorate, or keep descending.

We walk the avalanche track until we need to traverse off to one side. Below and to our left is the site of Camp 3. We uncover occasional anchors for fixed ropes, and check them before abseiling hard ice sections. The old ropes are hopelessly frozen; we consume time with 25-meter abseils on our own doubled rope. At dusk, in enveloping mist, we arrive on a ridge above the site of Camp 2. Rick wants to go one way, I the other, and I am sure my memory is correct! There is no snow bank here, so we hack out a ledge, tie ourselves on, and begin a long vigil, sitting in our bags on a few coils of rope. I notice that Rick has not done his vitally important sock change and foot care routine for two or three nights. We are both weak, and I wonder if he is as exhausted and frozen as I think he is.

The weather continues to hold fair as dawn breaks and we move down to the site of Camp 2 on the Kinshofer. We urgently need to hydrate! Rick falls asleep in the sun; I peel off the last of my down layers, changing into my underwear. I awake a slumbering Rick and encourage him to remove his down suit. He does so, and we harness and rope up again. I ask Rick to go in front, as I'm certain that I have the alertness to hold a fall if necessary.

Just above the Kinshofer Wall, we see someone arranging a belay. We descend to greet Marek Holecek, who is soon joined by Djenek Hruby; they are acclimatizing before trying a new line on the Rupal side. Rick is subdued and hardly speaks; I am smiling as I get the Sumo stove set up, making signs to ask for a light. Marek takes off his sack, carefully clips it in, and hands me a lighter and sugar sweets, which I open with my teeth, giving a handful to Rick. They share their flask of tea. My stove is efficient, and soon we have lots of water. Rick coughs and sputters, throwing up the initial hasty drink, but then settles. Marek tells us to use their food and tents at Camp 1, and then they climb on.

Revived somewhat, we launch onto the decaying tangle of fixed ropes on the Kinshofer, using our 50-meter rope to abseil. Then, roped together, we downclimb a huge snow and ice couloir into the night, facing in, kicking front points into ice with semi-frozen toes. Rick keeps stopping and falling asleep. Respectful of our fragility, I am glad to stop too and ease my foot pain. I mentally count seconds into minutes to rest sufficiently, and then encourage Rick to move again, though fearful we'll slip off. I know and trust Rick—he is exceptional—but we are both so wasted!

At 11 p.m. we stumble over avalanche debris and small crevasses until an illuminated tent appears at the foot of the buttress. Three high-altitude porters emerge and embrace us. Incredibly, Ali has mobilized them from their beds in Skardu to Camp 1 on Nanga Parbat in 48 hours. They had moved continually through the night so they could be at the camp to wait for us. The next day, 18 days after we started up the Mazeno Ridge, the porters help us down to base camp, where we drink tea on plastic chairs, sat on nature's carpet of wild flowers.

SUMMARY

First complete ascent of the Mazeno Ridge (west ridge) of Nanga Parbat (8,126m), by Sandy Allan and Rick Allen, July 2–July 19, 2012. The two climbed with Cathy O'Dowd, Lhakpa Nuru, Lhakpa Rangdu, and Lhakpa Zarok to a high point beyond Mazeno Gap. Those four started down the Schell Route on July 13, and Allan and Allen continued to the top, summiting on July 15. They descended the Kinshofer Route on the Diamir Face, reaching base camp on July 19. Read more about the expedition at www.mazenoridge.com. 📷

ABOUT THE AUTHOR

Sandy Allan is an IFMGA/British Mountain Guide (www.teamascent.co.uk), born and brought up in the Scottish Highlands. At the time of their ascent of Nanga Parbat, Allan was 56 and partner Rick Allen was 58. Based in Newtonmore, Allan is a passionate Scottish winter climbing activist.

[This page] Sandy Allan (left) and Rick Allen back in the land of the living. *Sandy Allan*

PILLAR OF THE RISING SUN

AN EPIC NEW ROUTE ON CERRO MURALLÓN IN SOUTHERN PATAGONIA

JEROME SULLIVAN

Chamonix, February 2012. We are four climbers living in a two-room apartment: Lise, Jeremy (a.k.a. Djamel), Pedro, and me. François (a.k.a. Pompon) is always over at our place to play cards or talk about our mountain projects. We spend every free moment climbing together in the Massif du Mont Blanc.

The Cerro Murallón project is born from a conversation with Patagonian veteran Bruno Sourzac, who attempted the east face of the peak in 1999. When I return to the apartment with a photo of the southeast pillar, the team is super motivated. Such an amazing unclimbed line! From then on our daydreams are fed with visions of epic climbing on this sharp-edged pillar, floating in the clouds in a far, far-away land of mineral and ice.

Murallón towers above the Patagonian Ice Cap to the south of the well-traveled peaks of the Chaltén massif. Since 1961, five routes have been climbed on the mountain, and the true summit has been reached only two or three times. [*See Climbs and Expeditions for Cerro Murallón's climbing history.*]

At the beginning of November, after a summer of preparations, the team assembles in Calafate, Argentina. To reach the peak, we must ride a boat across Lago Argentina, and then trek from Refugio Upsala across the Upsala Glacier and up the Cono Glacier. Since we've brought about 300 kilograms of food and gear, this is quite complicated. Our budget is too small to hire porters, and we like the idea of autonomy. We have brought skis and sleds, hoping this will make the approach easier and faster, but we are quickly disillusioned. When we reach the glacier we realize that skiable snow is another 30 kilometers to the north, and in front of us is a maze of chaotic ice. We are going to have to adapt quickly. Instead of shuttling all our supplies to the mountain, we decide to leave two weeks of food on the east bank of the glacier, along with the portaledges and some other gear. With limited food, we won't be able to wait out a long storm and make a good attempt, but we decide to try anyway. If it doesn't work out, we'll come back for the rest of our food and equipment.

Ahead of us is a stretch of glacier 20 kilometers wide. The dips and surges of ice are huge and seem endless. Our haul bags weigh 35 kilograms, and they act as sails—not pushing

[This page, top] Cerro Murallón, with the striking southeast pillar facing the camera. The peak is located far from the well-traveled peaks of the Chaltén massif. Since 1961, Murallón has only seen two or three ascents to the true summit. *Rolando Garibotti* [This page, bottom] Scouting the approach across the broad Upsala Glacier to reach the peak. *Lise Billon*

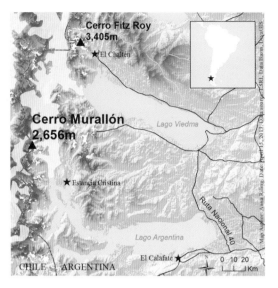

us forward, but rather unbalancing us at precarious moments. Up, down, up again, across, don't fall here, maybe the next bridge to the left, dead-end, turn around. Our progress is very slow. So slow that at some point someone utters the thought that we might not even find a way to the other side. The possibility is quickly discarded as "not an option." We haven't even seen the wall yet!

After 13 hours of "onsight" navigation through this labyrinth of crevasses, Pedro sprains his ankle. We suddenly feel quite far from civilization. If someone gets badly hurt, it will be impossible to carry him back over the knife-edge ridges and through this maze of ice. We decide to stop our frantic race toward the western shore and send scouts to find the easiest way. Finally there's a distant call of "land ahoy," and we manage to make our way safely to a crumbling moraine.

On November 13, five days after leaving Refugio Upsala, with aching feet and painful backs, we finally set foot in base camp. The blackened snow and chaos of rocks aren't very welcoming, but the view of the pillar is incredible. A spine of rock 1,000 meters high, steep and compact, surges from the glacier. The photos we've seen do not live up to the reality. The prow progressively steepens so it seems as if the last third must be overhanging! We spend the next few hours looking through the binoculars and imagining lines. Only one possibility is evident: the very edge of the pillar, dividing the south face, bathed in the sun, from the east face, now in the shade. We can see three distinct sections on the route. The first third is not so steep and has lots of obvious cracks. The second part is steeper gray granite lined with thick veins of white quartz. A crack system seems to run straight though a section of overhangs, leading to the headwall. This last part fills us with doubt. We are here to free climb, and we can't seem to see any lines of weakness.

Two days of storm keep us up locked up in the tents. On the third day we wake to blue skies and finally get to put on climbing shoes. The 15th of November being my birthday, the team gracefully decides to let me go first. The cracks range from offwidth to finger size, and are clean-cut and continuous. We are very eager and make some stupid mistakes; someone drops a climbing shoe, and another forgets his helmet. Anticipating our descent, we hammer in a few pitons and bolts. We put up 300 meters of fixed lines (all the rope we have), and head back down.

[This page] Cerro Murallón (2,656m) rises above the Southern Patagonia Ice Cap, along the Argentina-Chile frontier. *Anna Riling* [Next page] Pedro Angel Galan Diaz pauses on the 22nd pitch (6c) of the southeast pillar, as the rock fades into the fog below. The team experienced a multitude of bad weather, which nearly destroyed their portaledges. *Lise Billon*

[This page] Jeremy Stagnetto and François Poncet enjoy a lighter moment. *Lise Billon*

Jimmy Heredia, our weatherman in El Chaltén, gives us bad news. The upcoming week will be terrible: lots of snow and wind. In any case, an alpine-style ascent seems too risky. We have to go back to get our gear and more food. From our vantage point on the wall, Lise was able to imagine an easier path through the glacier. With little weight, it takes us a single long day of 15 hours to reach the other side again. We retreat to the little Refugio Pascale, where we will rest for the next five days while the storm rages on Cerro Murallón.

We now fully understand the scale of our project: the long and complicated approach, the size and steepness of the wall, and most of all, the terrible weather that afflicts this peak. Murallón's location on the west side of the Southern Patagonian Ice Cap makes it very exposed to Pacific storms. Yet we are now totally engaged in climbing this wall. If we came with doubts, we now have none. During these five rest days, our conversations are mostly about the best strategies to adopt. We imagine every possible situation and debate for hours. Once on the wall, every minute will count! Jimmy finally announces possible good weather coming in another five days.

On November 23 we leave the hut with the portaledges and two more weeks of food. Now that we know the best way through the glacier, we plan on two days to return to base camp. But it's impossible to find the same path again, and it ends up taking three days. When we eventually get there, the snow cave has collapsed. Luckily our gear is buried under the snow and has not been carried away by the wind. We build a wall of snow to protect the tent and put up the portaledges on a big boulder. The coming storm pushes us to be quick, and soon enough the wind and rain come rushing in. The portaledges are slammed up and down, ripping the flies in many places. The tent barely survives.

We are quite doubtful of the forecast for good weather the next day, but at 10 a.m. on November 27 the sun comes out and the wind gradually weakens. By the time we pack up, walk to the wall, and haul our bags to our high point on the pillar, it's 4 a.m. We rest just half an hour and set off again. Good weather is too precious to sleep through! We climb another 150 meters that day. The itinerary is a bit more complicated, as we have to cross a section of overhangs and some black, chossy rock. We finally get to a snowy ledge 350 meters up, where we will set up our last camp under a black protrusion of rock that we call the "Chateau."

Lise, Pedro, and I had rested while Pompon and Djamel led the day before, so now we take over while Pompon and Djamel rest at the Chateau. This is frustrating for them, but they have been climbing 30 hours non-stop and need to recover. The rock is compact and gray, streaked with white veins of quartz and freckled with knobs of diorite. It's like a French pastry! Beautiful cracks lead to a blank slab. On our left a fine vein of quartz seems to traverse toward the south face. What providence, it connects with another crack system. I take a nice fall when a block the size of an oven breaks off, ripping one of the ropes to the core. Apart from this incident, the next 300 meters are enjoyable, following vertical, clean cracks. We can't believe how well things are going! The climbing is sustained between 5.11b and 5.12b, and always well protected. We fix the 300 meters we have just climbed and head back to the Chateau.

Our satellite phone does not work anymore, so we have no information on the weather, on which the success of our expedition largely depends. We decide to move our camp to the other side of the Chateau, where it is better protected from storms coming from the west.

The next day we awake to calm blue skies. We hurriedly get up and start jumaring. Our arrival at the top of the ropes is synchronized with the arrival of damp snow showers and thick fog. But as long as the wind doesn't pick up, we can climb. This may be our last chance. We are 400 meters from the top.

Until now, we have been in doubt about the headwall, because we are not equipped for hard aid climbing. Our relief is huge as we realize the overhanging prow of orange granite is fractured from top to bottom by a perfect crack system. Stunningly, it runs up through a great dihedral and two overhangs. This line is amazing, without a doubt. Meters are gained, slowly but surely. The cracks are running with water, and the "screaming barfies" are almost constant. The leader free climbs, and the others jumar. Pedro does not understand the logic of climbing this way, but we are too cold to put on our wet climbing shoes, and it is now snowing hard. When night comes we are only three pitches from the top, but we are soaked, freezing, and a few centimeters of snow cover everything. We cannot risk spending the night outside. No need to discuss it, we are going down. So close…

We get back to our ledges at 5 a.m. It's now light again, and for the second time during this climb we eat supper and breakfast at the same time. We try to dry our clothes with the stove, a risky technique that leaves the portalege in a flurry of feathers when one of us lets his sleeping bag get a bit too close to the stove.

On December 3, after 40 hours of storm, the sun comes out again and starts melting the snow from our portaledges. In a frenzy of activity, we get ready. We don't have much food left. A 1:30 p.m. we are at the top of the fixed ropes. As usual, the weather quickly changes; clouds come in and snowflakes fly. I

[Next page] Starting the clean-cut corners of the headwall. *Lise Billon*

joke about the "afternoon breeze" that will chase the clouds away, but we are all quite skeptical. Yet half an hour later, the sun is out again. And it will stay clear until we summit.

The cracks we climbed two days earlier are now drier and much more enjoyable. We free everything except a few icy meters that might go at 5.12d/13a. There's no time to work out the moves. By nightfall we have reached our previous high point. It's time to put on the crampons and take out the ice axes. Pompon leads a beautiful mixed pitch on a steep, run-out, ice-plastered corner. When we join him at the belay we are looking at a slightly overhanging wall, nicely decorated with two free-hanging icicles, 1,000 meters off deck. The ice is regularly showered by blasts of spindrift. It's very impressive and quite scary.

I decide to go have a look. After 15 meters and two good pro placements I'm under the spindrift. I put in a cam and engage the steep mixed wall leading to the ice. In the darkness it's hard to find good hooks. I back down to my last cam to look around and suddenly things accelerate. At the belay, Lise sees a snowball with a headlamp inside silently fly past, and then she is yanked into the anchor. The rope is tense, and I'm dangling, head down, five meters below her. I've fallen at least 25 meters. A cam failed—maybe the crack was frozen. I'm fine, but after a quick discussion we decide to wait until dawn before giving it another try. We find a rock wedged in the ice and sit on it to wait for the sun. A foot-tapping, hand-clapping dance starts. It's cold, maybe -20 Celsius, and we are not equipped for such temperatures. We share our last food.

After three or four hours, the sun starts to rise and gives birth to stunning colors. We look up at the ropes hanging from my high point and realize that during my nocturnal fall I cut one of them right to the core. As the sun's rays finally warm up our numb bodies we decide to give it another try. Pompon gears up and starts climbing. The pitch seems so improbable that he doesn't bother to take any ice screws. Little by little, he gains a few meters and discovers a passage that we did not see in the dark. A little tunnel between the ice and the rock allows him to bypass the first overhang. An icy slab gives way to a 20-meter, hanging icicle. The ice is aerated and very steep. He equalizes two bad cams and heads on. This will be his last protection until he reaches the belay 30 meters higher. We heave sighs of relief when we hear him yell that he's off belay.

A last, easy pitch brings us to the top of the pillar, 30 hours after we left the portaledges. We are teary-eyed and incredulous. We don't say much. We just look at each other, each understanding what the others are feeling. After an hour, it's time to go. The summit is perhaps

[This page] Poncet leads the crux ice pitch (WI6 M6). *Lise Billon*

half an hour's walk away, but we don't want to press our luck with the weather, and our goal was always to simply climb the pillar. We start rappelling, laughing and talking about the food we will eat when we get back.

When we are halfway down, my luck changes. As we pull the rope, a microwave-sized rock comes loose and crashes into my shoulder. I am stunned and my vision is blurry. When we reach the portaledges a few hours later, my speech is slurred. But after eating a bit, I seem to recover, to the relief of my friends.

On December 5 we touch ground again. We yell and scream as the tension drops. We still have a long way back, but we are safe and we have realized the project that has been nourishing our dreams for six months. The Pilar del sol Naciente stands proudly behind us.

During the next three days another storm comes in, and when we finally reach the Upsala hut, where we started out 32 days ago, we are soaked, exhausted, and hungry. We have lost about eight kilograms apiece. But tonight we will sleep in a dry place. How luxurious! On the boat back to Calafate, tourists watch wide-eyed as five dirty climbers ravage the pastries offered by the boat company, leaving nothing for them.

Patagonia has changed in the last years. More reliable forecasts and better weather seem to have gotten the better of the "expedition" spirit that still defined the Fitz Roy massif and nearby mountains when Eric Shipton first climbed on Cerro Murallón. But Patagonia still has so many unexplored and uncharted lands, waiting for adventurous souls. From the top of a mountain one sees so many other potential climbs. As one project ends, another hundred take form. And the adventure continues.

SUMMARY

First ascent of the southeast pillar of Cerro Murallón (El Pilar del Sol Naciente, 1,000m, 7b A1 WI6 M6) on the Southern Patagonia Ice Cap, by Lise Billon, Pedro Angel Galan Diaz, François Poncet, Jeremy Stagnetto, and Jerome Sullivan, November 27–December 5, 2012. The route had 32 pitches, of which 30 were climbed all free; the aid sections totaled about 10 meters. The climbers placed 15 bolts, all for belay/rappel anchors, and they rappelled from the top of the pillar without going to the summit. 🔍

ABOUT THE AUTHOR
French-American mountain guide Jerome Sullivan, 29, lives in Chamonix but tries to travel and climb as much as possible.

[This page] Diaz and Stagnetto try to stay warm during the sititng bivy. *Lise Billon*

THE TRIPLE

WORDS
ALEX HONNOLD

ILLUSTRATIONS
ANDREAS SCHMIDT

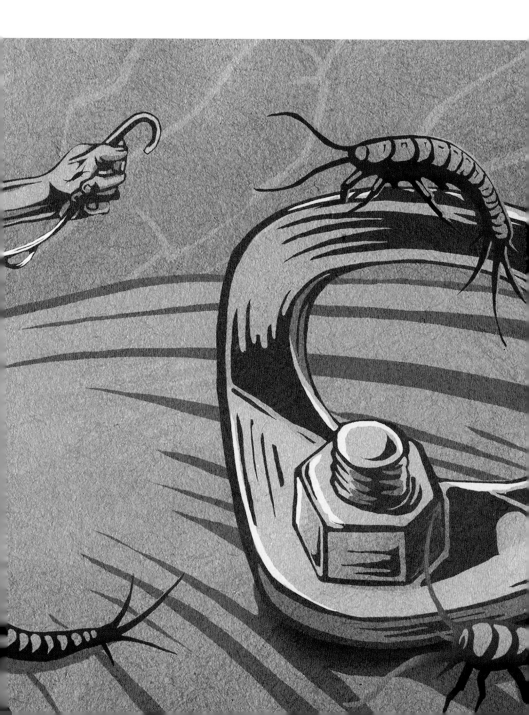

SOLOING WATKINS, EL CAP, AND HALF DOME IN 19 HOURS

Ever since Jim Bridwell, John Long, and Billy Westbay climbed the Nose in a day in May 1975, people have been trying to do bigger and bigger linkups in Yosemite Valley. John Bachar and Peter Croft linked El Capitan and Half Dome in 1986; Timmy O'Neill and Dean Potter added Mt. Watkins 15 years later. The obvious remaining challenges were to climb Yosemite's three largest faces free or solo. Or, I suppose, free solo, but that's for another generation.

I'd thought about both goals since 2010, when I first soloed El Cap and Half Dome in a day. In 2012 all the pieces finally came together: Tommy Caldwell was super-motivated to do the free Triple; it had been a dry winter so the routes weren't seeping; and Hans Florine was psyched to try the Nose speed record. I had partners to practice every part of the linkup.

On May 19, Tommy and I free-climbed the south face of Mt. Watkins, Free Rider on El Capitan, and the Regular Northwest Face on Half Dome in 21 hours 15 minutes, from the base of Watkins to Half Dome's summit. Two and a half weeks later, starting on June 5, I soloed the three walls in about 19 hours. Freeing the Triple gave me a good idea of how tired I would feel 20 hours into the day, and what I would feel comfortable soloing. Overall, freeing it was physically harder, since we had to climb 5.12 pitches after already doing two walls. But soloing it felt a lot more intense, probably because I was just a little on edge the whole time.

[Previous spread] "It had dumped rain the day before, so the first half of Watkins and the Nose were running with water in places. It's 5.10 crack climbing, so not a huge deal, but it made things a little slower and scarier. Up higher on Watkins the silverfish were out of control, just swarming all over everything. They don't bite, but they were getting all over me and made it harder to concentrate."

[Previous page] "When I got to the base of the Nose, I realized I'd forgotten my chalk bag. Thankfully, an aid climber sleeping on Dolt Tower hooked me up. I still remember the sublime feeling of dipping my hand into a completely full chalk bag—after soloing 800 feet of wet cracks in the dark it was blissful to have chalk again. At the Great Roof, I met up with Sean Leary, who was filming. We wound up talking about speed climbing on the Nose (he was then the record holder), chit-chatting about strategies and stuff. It's really nice to have company when soloing through the night. It can be really lonely."

[This page, map] *Watkins*, South Face (19 guidebook pitches). *Time*: 2 hours 20 minutes (new speed record). *El Capitan*, The Nose (31 pitches). *Time*: 6 hours (solo speed record is 5:49, Honnold, 2010). *Half Dome*, Regular Northwest Face (23 pitches). *Time*: 2 hours 55 minutes (solo speed record is 1:22, Honnold, earlier in 2012).

[Gear Notes] "*Watkins*: I used a rope for a pendulum on the first pitch, then threw it down and daisy soloed to the top. I carried two quickdraws, about 10 small cams up to 0.5 Camalot. *El Capitan*: daisies, two draws, roughly a double rack from green C3 to 0.5 C4, and single green and red Camalots. I borrowed a 60m cord, about 7mm, for pendulums and short belays. *Half Dome*: two draws, single set of cams up to about 0.4 Camalot. I have Half Dome pretty wired."

[This page] "After descending from El Cap, Sean Leary and I got a ride over to North Pines campground to wake up my girlfriend and get some food. She gave us a ride to the Mirror Lake trailhead for the Death Slabs approach to Half Dome. Maybe I should have eaten more, because I started to bonk on the approach. It's a pretty brutal hike to do after a big evening of climbing. I sat at the base of Half Dome for quite a while, trying to get motivated. There were two other climbers waiting to get on the route, and we chatted a bit, and eventually I set out. I felt super slow and tired, though it only took 2:50 or so to climb the route, so I guess it wasn't that bad."

ABOUT THE ILLUSTRATOR
Andreas Schmidt, 45, began climbing in the Cascades and now works for Black Diamond in Salt Lake City. These illustrations, he says, are "most influenced by mid-century European travel posters and German expressionist woodcuts."

ABOUT THE AUTHOR
Born in 1985, Alex Honnold has racked up an unparalleled record of free-solo and speed ascents in Yosemite and Zion national parks. He lives in his van.

NEW SPEED RECORD
ON THE NOSE of EL CAPITAN

The Hubers got beat 2:45 ... by Yuji & Hans 2:37

LEARY & POTTER 2:36+ MADE IT HOTTER BUT...

ALEX HONNOLD* & HANS FLORINE 2:23:46
* embarrassed by how MUCH gear Hans took....

FIRE MY ROCKET, ALEX!
USA — NOSE — DUC
Camp 4 over here
cookie down there
SQUAMISH 1761 km
clik clik clik clik

J UNE 17, 2012, my alarm goes off at 0408 hrs at my friend's home in Yosemite West. I have to pack up my 9 & 11 year old kids, wife, Tom Frost & our bivy stuff. The goal is to make a 26 min drive & meet Alex in the meadow at 0450 hrs. RATS we didn't turn the key until 0434 so NO WAY TO MAKE IT. I txt Alex to let him know. Yer runnin' ten minnits LATE? the Horror, the Horror

KWIKKIE HISTORY of FAST NOSE ASCENTS

1st single putsch: 7 DAYS, 1960 TOM FROST, JOE FITSCHEN, ROYAL ROBBINS, CHUCK PRATT
1st 1 DAY Ascent: 1975, Jim BRIDWELL, John LONG, Billy WESTBAY
FAST: 1990: 8hr 6 min Steve SCHNEIDER/Hans FLORINE
FASTER: 1990: 6hr 1 min Andres PUHVEL/Hans FLORINE
FASTER FASTER: 1992 4hr 22 min: Peter CROFT/Hans FLORIN.
Holy doodle! 2002 2:48:58 Yuji HIRAYAMA/Hans FLORINE

ICONIC FOTO OP

Does Hans Florine have a NOSE PROBLEM or duz THE NOSE havva HANS FLORINE problem?

SAFETY First! FUN Second! SPEED third!

BE A CLIMBIN' DemiGod
hairs blowin' in wind!
stern Grimace
No nipple rings
muscles
Six pack
snappy trousers
muscles
Censored! Married!
5.10 hands a thousand feet up
©T.KniAbt 2012

A fter some stretching & gear fiddlin' we get going. It's 0549, Temp is high 70's F. I ask Alex if he's ready to go... Yeah dude. Fer fifteen minz already!

I HAVE 16 cams, 22 quickdraws, 3 long runner with biners & 11 free biners. FIRST LEAD IS 1,600' to the top of BOOT FLAKE.

After about 25 feet up I put in a #1 camalot another 15 feet up I place a 0.4 grey camalot another 10 feet a .75 green camalot. Five feet up I clip a draw to a bashie, 15 feet more a bolt hanger is clipped with a quickdraw. Then it's 30 feet to the anchor where I clip in a long runner

FACT: ONE PIECE O' PRO every 31 feet

I continue up to the last steep 5.9 handcrack climbing & throw in a #1 camalot for pro then continue up to the anchor. I clip a leaver biner on the anchor & yell to Alex to lower me. Alex gets a weighted ride up the 5th class as I head down cleaning the #1 as I pass.

Arriving at the 0.4 I ask Alex to hold me tight & I swing over to the Dolt Hole Cracks and the crowd in the Forest Go NUTS!

DOUBLEHEADER

NEW ROUTES ON K7 AND THE OGRE IN PAKISTAN

KYLE DEMPSTER

"The essence of a climb burns out in the moment of experience." Marko Prezelj's words smoldered in my mind as we chugged up another steep hill en route to base camp on the Choktoi Glacier. *I sure wish it would burn out of my legs.* Fatigue forced me to pause on the dusty path. *Damn it, Kyle, why couldn't you just be content with K7? Why always more?* Even after eating copious amounts of pizza, ice cream, and cake during four sedentary days in Skardu, Hayden looked skinnier than usual as he ground up the same hill. I too felt small after five weeks in Pakistan. *Plug on.*

Five months earlier, Hayden Kennedy and I had agreed on a preposterous plan: climb two 7,000-meter peaks, both via new routes, in one summer in the Karakoram. We dubbed our expedition the Pakistani Doubleheader—alpine gluttony at its finest.

Phase one began in the elegant Charakusa Valley. Hayden and I, along with our friend and Slovenian powerhouse Urban Novak, arrived in early July and began acclimatizing on familiar mountains. In 2011 we had come within 300 meters of the summit on the unclimbed east face of K7 (6,934 meters), before heavy snow forced our descent. We had unfinished business.

At 11 p.m. on July 17, the warmth of the nighttime air encouraged us upward as we climbed familiar terrain. Redpointing an alpine route felt less intense than being on a mountain for the first time. We knew the moves, knew which runnels provided the easiest passage, and, at least until our 2011 high point, we knew what to expect. Through the night, we simul-climbed with ropes coiled in our packs. At 5,800 meters, just as light turned our world to an eerie hue, we arrived at the start of four familiar pitches of steep blue

[**Previous page**] Urban Novak in the lead on the steep ice step of K7's east face. *Hayden Kennedy* [**This page**] The east face of K7 (6,934 meters) from Link Sar. The climb went at AI5 M6 and took 49 hours round-trip. *Jon Griffith*

ice. Hayden led two pitches, making good time on thin ice peppered with granite blobs. Urban quickly dispatched the top two pitches of the intimidating step, Hayden and I followed, and again we were cruising on easier terrain.

The wild card on the upper mountain was conditions. We had heard from other climbers in Skardu that deep snow, from late-spring storms, still remained at higher altitudes in the Karakoram. And at 6,200 meters, a few pitches below our previous high point, the rumors became reality. Our progress stalled as I began digging through deep, unconsolidated snow. From a distance, both our pace and the trough that remained in our wake must have resembled that of a snail. Hours evaporated and clouds formed in the sky. Above our 2011 bivy, steeper ice and rock pitches provided some relief. But it didn't last long, as more deep snow slopes waited higher on the face.

Hayden took a turn at the vertical snow-swimming and led us toward a huge granite corner that appeared to cater well to his phenomenal rock climbing ability. With some effort he scraped up a snow-covered rock slab to the base of the imposing system. After a quick discussion we determined that the daunting corner was impassable. I took the lead and did two pendulums around a corner to the left.

As I started up again, warm snot streamed through my whiskers. The heat from my face melted falling snowflakes into a cold, humid slop. I shuffled my feet on a six-inch-wide ledge, my arms starfishing a blank and imposing bulge of granite. Urban and Hayden hung at the anchor, hoping for the good word that I had found a belay and they could begin to move their cold bodies. Our secret path on K7's east face revealed nothing as I looked around the corner, trying to find a relief from the steep rock. A break from the discomfort. Anything.

"I don't know you guys, this is totally fucked!" I screamed. "It's getting late and I see no place for a bivy! I have no idea where to go, and I think this weather is concerning! Do you think we should bail?" *Bail…bail…bail…* Failure was again on the table. The feeling of exposure crept up my back, swirling with the uncertainty in my mind.

"No way!" Urban shouted. His conviction supreme, he yelled, "This is what we came for! We knew it would be this way! This was our choice and we must keep going!"

Discomfort, the tenuous lead, the exposure—all vanished for a moment. Against my desire, I nearly laughed. From Hayden I heard a faint chuckle. Urban waited for an answer, his face reflecting his anxiety. I searched the granite again for tiny fissures for my picks. My crampons scraped on smooth rock, and I kept moving upward.

We continued well into the night, eventually finding a patch of steep ice where we could chop a narrow seat. After nearly 24 hours on the go we brewed up and dozed against each other's shoulders. A few hours elapsed before the gray bleakness of the morning hour crept back across the sky. Light snowflakes fell as we tried to rally motivation. Urban led the final 200 meters of deep snow to K7's summit. Hayden and I followed in his footsteps.

The rappels took us long into the frigid night, through heavy spindrift. Back at base camp we relaxed in the sun, ate incredible food, and took it all in. K7 had brought us together as friends and partners. The climbing seemed secondary.

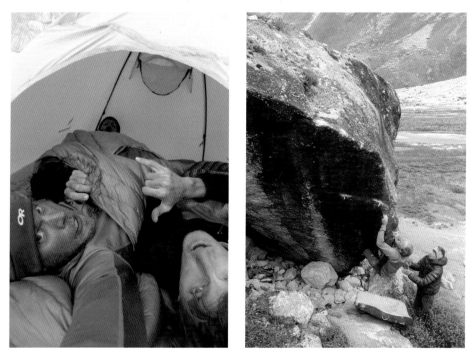

[This page, left] Relaxing before a warm-down climb in the Charakusa. *Kyle Dempster*
[This page, right] Micro-routes in the Charakusa Valley. *Hayden Kennedy*

IN SKARDU WE WATCHED Urban walk through security at the small airport. Saying farewell to our Slovenian friend was sad, but Urban has other talents beyond climbing and had to get back to his Ph.D. work. Hayden and I returned to our hotel and took a nap in a room littered with expedition debris.

Two weeks earlier, while we were still in the Charakusa Valley, we had received a message on our satellite phone that Josh Wharton's partner had bailed, and that Josh was waiting for us at Choktoi base camp. He hoped to try Latok I again after five prior attempts over three years. Hayden and I were open to that idea, or perhaps a new route on one of the Ogre peaks. After another few days of pizza, Magnum Double Chocolate ice cream bars, and complete laziness in Skardu, we left the trailhead at Askole for phase two of our Pakistani Doubleheader. With a group of seven strong porters, we began the four-day approach to the Choktoi Glacier. It felt great to be back in the mountains, but my legs felt weak. Metallica and Iron Maiden raged in our headphones as we wound deeper into the mighty Karakoram.

At base camp we shared hugs, stories, and laughter with Josh and our friend and cook Ghafoor. Josh then gave us newcomers to the Choktoi a tour of one of the most spectacular alpine climbing areas on the planet. Hayden and I gazed up at Latok I while Josh walked us through his proposed route on the north-northwest face. He described his attempts during past years and the reasons they hadn't been successful. He pointed out nuances such as bivy sites, hazards to avoid, and subtleties of the mountain's moods—things that are only visible to climbers who have spent much time on the mountain. The quickest and most probable line of ascent was obvious to him, and he hoped we saw it too.

Unfortunately, Hayden and I saw something else: a large serac hanging high above Josh's proposed route, threatening the lower wall. We felt the route was too dangerous and invited Josh to join us on Ogre II, but he wondered if it might be unclimbable. "I don't need to chalk up another attempt here in the Choktoi," he said. "I want to climb something that we have a chance of sending."

For eight days our surroundings disappeared in thick, white cloud. Invisible, the mountains revealed their presence with thundering avalanches. After five weeks of mild skies in the Charakusa, the storm drove Hayden and I nearly to the point of insanity. Josh, the Choktoi veteran, waited patiently for the bad weather to pass.

[This page] Josh Wharton on the lower southeast face of the Ogre, with the unclimbed north face of Ogre II behind. *Hayden Kennedy*

As the storm dissolved and thickly frosted mountain faces were revealed, decision-making became easier. The north faces of the Ogre II and the Latoks lay under a heavy blanket of snow while the peaks' southern aspects quickly shed the new snow. We decided our best option was the Ogre, following a complex line up the southeast and south faces.

On August 19, exactly one month after summiting K7, we began methodically climbing several thousand feet of 60-degree snow and ice. Kick, punch, breathe, kick, punch, breathe. Why can something so simple at times be so painful? You must meditate.

Unroped, we simul-soloed for several hours, guided by headlamp, the increasing exposure invisible but felt under our feet. At first light we gazed eastward at K2, the Shining Wall of Gasherbrum IV, Masherbrum, and the Crown towering above the Chinese Karakoram. Conditions were perfect, and the morning sun warmed us down to our base layers. By midday we had climbed above and far to the right of several large seracs, and from this safe height we began a long traverse that would unlock the way to the upper route.

Hayden led the key pitch of the traverse: a 55-meter ramp of stacked fragments with no ice or even mud to bond the rock chips together. The pitch made the worst rock in the Canadian Rockies look like dream stone. Hayden's feet skated and sent off showers of kitty litter that fell for thousands of feet to the glacier below. He ripped off microwave-sized blocks that exploded into pieces before making it off the traverse ledge. I looked on in terror as I slowly paid out rope. "I wouldn't question him for a second if he decided to bail," Josh said.

Several hours later, after Josh and I had also battled the choss, we were cruising once again, this time roped together on steeper snowfields. At the base of the overhanging granite headwall that leads to the east summit of the Ogre 1, we found a great tent site and decided to call it a day. We devoured our dehydrated dinners, enjoying the last light of an incredible day of climbing.

We woke to another cloudless day. Josh had been a bit sluggish the previous day and now said he had a headache, but he wanted to continue. Talk ceased and we crawled out of the tent, did a few sun salutations, and were on our way, again climbing unroped on 60-degree ice and snowfields. At about 6,500 meters Hayden and I swapped leads on some tricky leftward mixed pitches. The rock was significantly better than the previous day, but gear remained sparse, and the snow and ice between the rock steps became deeper and less consolidated as we climbed higher.

[This page] Hayden Kennedy negotiates the delicate, chossy 5.9X traverse that unlocked the way to the upper face of the Ogre. *Kyle Dempster*

After a much shorter day, we chopped a narrow tent platform in a small snowfield at about 6,900 meters, and crammed into our tiny tent. Watching Josh climb had left me feeling uneasy, and as he lay in the tent his face appeared swollen and he strained to breathe. Through the night he coughed, even spitting blood at one point. His condition seemed to be stable, but it was obvious he had some level of pulmonary or cerebral edema, and as he snoozed Hayden and I looked at each and wondered what the morning would bring.

When I peered out the tent door, wispy clouds swirled below and around us, while blue skies shined on the southern Karakoram. I had seen this weather before in Pakistan and knew it could go either way. *Heavy snowfall would put us in a very serious situation*, I thought. Hayden said, "We need to decide what we're doing and go for it." Groggily, Josh opened his eyes and said, "I'm worked," and then rolled over in his bag.

I'd like to say our decision to blast to the summit while Josh rested at the tent was difficult. We all understood that life at 7,000 meters is fragile. Maybe Josh's condition would turn severe; maybe Hayden and I wouldn't return from our summit push, leaving Josh stranded; maybe the mountain would take us all. But there was very little discussion of the devastating possibilities.

Perhaps Hayden and I were blinded by the summit and it was dumb for Josh to say, "Go." Surely our decision deserves some level of scrutiny. I know for sure that if Josh had said he needed to go down, Hayden and I would have gone down with him. If either Hayden or I had felt a strong enough conviction that leaving Josh was a bad idea, or that the terrain above was too dangerous, we would have descended. If any of us had felt differently about the circumstances, we would not have made the collective decision that we did. Each moment in the mountains is different, every decision unique, and this one, at that moment, felt

[This page] The Ogre II (left) and the Ogre, with the new route marked (5.9X AI5 M6R). This was only the third ascent of the 7,285-meter peak in 35 years. *Michael Kennedy*

appropriate. Josh would stay in the tent; we left him with the stove, extra food, and an extra sleeping bag. Hayden and I would climb the final 350 meters or so to the 7,285-meter summit of the Ogre and get back to Josh as quickly as possible.

In a beautiful red-granite corner, Hayden and I exchanged leads on several mixed pitches. Eventually we gained a corniced ridgeline that led to another mixed pitch, which accessed the final snowfield. I took the lead and wallowed through waist-deep, very steep snow, remembering Urban's words: *This is what we came for, we must keep going!*

On the pointy summit of the Ogre, Hayden and I stood in warm sunshine and shared an enormous hug. We had nearly completed our Pakistani Doubleheader, and all that remained was a long descent, shepherding a sick friend. Hayden and I had shared everything during our summer in Pakistan: sickness, pain, food, encouragement, fear, a sleeping bag, fatigue, laughter, and joy. K7 and the Ogre seemed irrelevant; the Doubleheader was about friendship.

SUMMARY

New routes on K7 (6,934m) and the Ogre (Baintha Brakk, 7,285m). On K7, Kyle Dempster (U.S.), Hayden Kennedy (U.S.), and Urban Novak (Slovenia) climbed the east face in a 49-hour round trip, summiting in the morning of July 19; they descended by the same route. On the Ogre, Dempster, Kennedy, and Josh Wharton (U.S.) climbed the southeast face above the head of the Choktoi Glacier, and then traversed left to the upper south face. Wharton stayed at their second bivouac while Dempster and Kennedy went to the summit on August 21. During the descent, the team bivied once more. This expedition was funded in part by an AAC Lyman Spitzer Cutting Edge Climbing Award.

ABOUT THE AUTHOR
Kyle Dempster, 30, lives in Salt Lake City, Utah, where he co-owns and manages the Higher Ground Coffee shop.

A version of this story originally appeared, in Spanish, in Desnivel.

[This page] Kennedy leads golden granite at ca 7,000 meters on the Ogre. *Kyle Dempster*

THE TOOTH TRAVERSE

FIVE DAYS ACROSS THE MOOSES TOOTH MASSIF

FREDDIE WILKINSON

There are certain skylines wilder and far more beautiful than the sum of their parts: the Fitz Roy massif in Patagonia, the Aiguilles of Chamonix, and the Trango group in Pakistan. These are places where each mountain seems positioned to complement the next, the ridges and couloirs folding against each other in harmony as if one peak cannot exist without its neighbors. The Mooses Tooth massif in Alaska's Ruth Gorge forms another such skyline.

The Mooses Tooth massif appears more like a long ridge of connected summits than a singular mountain. Indeed, it looks like a jawbone, curved in a subtle horseshoe, each successive point rising in prominence. First there's the Sugar Tooth with its snow-pillow summit, then the canine-shaped Eye Tooth and the gleaming white incisor of the Bear Tooth. Last comes the Mooses Tooth itself, a molar-shaped mountain of bronze buttresses and narrow couloirs, capped by a summit ridge that stretches a mile from its highest point to the west

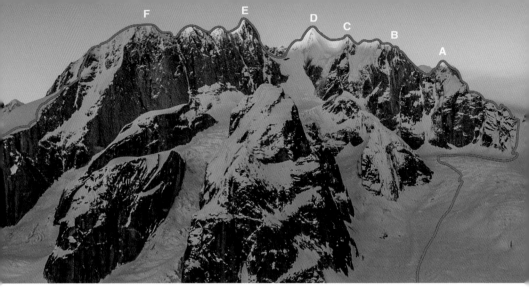

F E D C B A

[Previous page] An aerial photo of Renan Ozturk and Freddie Wilkinson on the summit of the Bear Tooth. *Camp 4 Collective* [This page] The Mooses Tooth massif, showing the Tooth Traverse from right to left: (A) Sugar Tooth, (B) Eye Tooth, (C) Missing Tooth, (D) Bear Tooth, (E) Mooses Tooth, east summit (F) Mooses Tooth, west summit. *Doug Shepherd*

summit. The ridge continues for another mile, dropping steeply to the floor of the gorge.

I can't recall when the idea first popped into my head. Others, I would later learn, dreamed up slightly different iterations of the same concept. I do remember that it began with a photograph, and it came in a heartbeat. I only needed to turn on the light. One second the Tooth Traverse didn't exist. The next, it was the most obvious and beautiful line in the world. All told, I guessed the Tooth Traverse represented five miles of climbing, perhaps 10,000' of elevation gain and loss. To travel it all, from one end to the other, became my dream.

JULY 2009
In the spring of 2009 I hitched a ride to South Boulder to crash for a week at Renan Ozturk and Zack Smith's house. They were planning a trip to the Ruth Gorge that summer. One evening, over beers, between my goofy impressions of velociraptor climbing techniques, I let my tongue wag about how cool it would be to enchain the Tooth massif. Eyes sparked with giddy anticipation.

Six weeks later, Renan and Zack started their trip with a quick repeat of the Cobra Pillar. Afterward, they were stopped below their main objective, the southeast buttress of Mt. Dickey. They turned to their backup plan. It was early July. The nights passed without darkness or freezing temperatures, and the spine of the Tooth Traverse lay mostly exposed in naked rock. Renan and Zack embarked for the traverse in the lightest of styles: Other than a stove, they carried no bivy gear.

Starting at Cavity Gap, a narrow brèche south of the Sugar Tooth, they changed into rock shoes and began simulclimbing. In a mere 12 hours, they onsighted a gendarme-studded new route over the Sugar Tooth, rappelled off the other side, put on their boots and crampons, completed the second ascent of the gargoyled Talkeetna Standard, and reached the summit of the Eye Tooth. From there, they set off across the snow ridge toward the Bear Tooth. Ahead lay massive cornices and steep slopes. The ridge proved to be a slushy mess. They huddled for a brew. It was too risky to continue. They retreated back across the ridge to the summit of the

Eye Tooth and rappelled. Soon after their return to civilization in July 2009, I got an email from Renan. In its entirety, it read: "yo freddie! want to go party of 3 on the traverse some time soon? we love velociraptors!"

May 2010

"Should we take it to the scales?" asked Zack. Mt. Dickey rose like an altar above our camp. Concentric piles of gear stretched in every direction. Zack knelt in the center of it all. In each hand, he held a lightweight bivy jacket. He slowly hefted them in turn. Zack had actually brought a digital scale to base camp to weigh gear. I chuckled. In truth, I cared a lot less about what we brought than I did about getting to know my two partners better.

The biggest question mark was the south face of the Mooses Tooth, a large shield of unclimbed granite that sliced into the sky above the Bear Tooth–Mooses Tooth col. It was Zack's idea that we attempt this section on its own. From the col, the first part looked innocuous enough. Non-threatening flakes breached a sunburned slab into an alcove where the wall steepened. Wearing rock shoes, Zack scurried up the first two pitches. Renan took the lead for what seemed the obvious crux. An hour passed, then two. "Freddie, get up here!" he yelled. Renan lowered to the belay, a gash from his middle finger bleeding profusely. Near the end of the difficulties, he'd tried to place a piton in a shallow flare, only to have a hammer blow ricochet.

I batmanned to his highpoint. The crack pinched down to an unusable seam. After wasting too much time exhausting the alternatives, I cleverly solved the impasse by drilling a bolt. It was the first and only bolt I've placed in the mountains. When I weighted it, the quarter-inch stud flexed mightily. I hooked the pick of my ice axe in the crack above, gave it a few reassuring blows with the other tool, and aided upward toward a belay. My partners quickly joined me, rejuvenated. It hadn't been pretty, but the Bleeder Pitch opened the door to the entire traverse. From the summit, we rappelled Ham and Eggs in only two hours.

After a couple of sun-soaked rest days, we skied toward Cavity Gap, the start of the traverse, with high expectations. We climbed steadily, if not rapidly, toward the summit of the Sugar Tooth. Then Renan slipped, core-shot the rope, and dropped an axe. As the sun dipped and the gorge washed in shadows, we stopped for the night a few hundred feet from the top of the Sugar Tooth. A quietness filled the tent despite the endlessly clear weather. Something was off. In the morning, we rappelled to the start of the Talkeetna Standard and returned to base camp. Our effort felt less like a failure than like a false start. However, after identifying the bodies of two climbers killed in an avalanche the following day, we had little desire for another Tooth Traverse attempt. But there was no question that we'd be back.

March 2011

Just weeks before our scheduled rematch with the Tooth, Renan was skiing and fell, flipped over a short line of cliffs, and pinballed down a tree-spiked face. He was found unconscious. A deep gash peeled back his head to his skull. Zack and I debated going as a team of two without him. We all obsessed over the likelihood that another team might scoop the project from us. I admitted to Zack, "I guess I'd rather do the second ascent of the Tooth Traverse with Renan than the first ascent without him."

In July, Zack wrote to say he was considering going to the Ruth in September without us: *I love you guys but I want to see other people.* Meanwhile, Renan had embarked on a crazy mission to cure himself, and now he felt hurt. I thought Zack's decision was fair, since Renan and I were both leaving on other trips. He was hungry for the line. I understood. "Go for it," I told him. That autumn, the weather was shitty. Zack and his new partner reserved tickets, but they never left Colorado.

May 2012

Anchorage greeted us with gray skies and rain. Our arrival in Talkeetna corresponded with the first flyable weather in a week. Colby Coombs's eyes lit up like a jack-o'-lantern and his lips puckered with sarcastic glee when he saw we'd returned. "It's gonna be some gnarly snow—New Hampsha' style, all right. You're gonna have a fun time, oh, boy!" Over beers and smoldering cigarettes, we talked with one team that had recently returned and heard the worst of it: bottomless snow, sketchy avalanche conditions, impossible corniced ridges. I asked one refugee what aspect might have the most stable conditions. "Hawaii," he responded.

Renan and I tried to counter the reports with a relentless, optimistic plan that bordered on delusion. This year, we hoped to have a helicopter fly by to film us en route—no sponsors or production teams involved, just Renan and I scheming on laptop computers, trying to coordinate a camera and helicopter for a bargain price. Renan's dream was to turn the entire Ruth Gorge into a dolly shot, with us, in the midst of a first ascent, as the subjects, set against one of the most breathtaking vistas we'd ever known. Somehow, this idea had evolved to the point that we both felt the art was as important as the climb.

Zack seemed removed from our banter as he fidgeted with gear. Finally, he broke his silence. His heart was no longer in the Tooth Traverse. He couldn't tell us precisely why. Maybe it was personal. Maybe it was all the talk of helicopters and camera angles. Maybe it was the bad weather, the fear of failure. Maybe he just fell out of love with alpine climbing. There was not much we could say. We hugged him and told him we understood. He told us we had to give the traverse our best effort. A couple of hours later, Renan and I got on a plane for the gorge while Zack boarded an airport shuttle back to Anchorage. Bottled in the overcrowded fuselage, Renan and I soon watched as the pocketed surface of the lower Ruth Glacier slipped past.

Day One: May 17, 2012

Renan and I leave base camp at 4 a.m. It's a relief to be under way. The approach feels shorter than I remember, the glacier's easy curves friendly and familiar. We cache our skis and immediately sink to our knees. I plow a trough to the bergschrund below the Sugar Tooth. In 2009, Zack and Renan climbed over the Sugar Tooth and up the Eye Tooth, hardly ever taking off their rock shoes. In 2010 there were low-angle snowfields, but also dry pitches and plenty of convenient ledges. This year, everything less than 60 degrees is snow.

I punch up a shallow snow feature toward what I recall was an indented slab. Now it's swabbed in verglas with a thin crack I'll have to drytool. I take a breath: the first real move in miles of climbing to come. For a moment, I'm almost crushed by a sense of improbability. The Coffee Glacier slithers away from me past the Broken Tooth. I'm with a great friend at low altitude on a ridge-crest line, with little to hit us. The climbing is tricky but the rock's generally good. We're in no hurry: We have a tent and sleeping bag, a few days' food and fuel. Why not at least go alpine camping? I can think of no other place in the world I'd rather be.

"This is a pain, but it's climbable," I shout to Renan. "We may as well camp for the night on top of the Sugar, and bail the next morning if we have to. This is our vacation, after all." We stop at 5:45 p.m. only a few meters from where we'd bivied two years ago. This snowfield is broad enough that we can unrope for the evening—there's nothing this comfy for many pitches to come.

Day Two

We tiptoe across the summit ridge of the Sugar Tooth at dawn and rappel into the jagged notch at the beginning of the Talkeetna Standard. Thin snowfields and cornices smother the rocky ridge overhead. I glower as I search for an anchor and wait for Renan. Boots and crampons will stay on our feet for a while. Like it or not, the Tooth Traverse is a mixed route this season.

When we bailed two years ago, we'd optimistically cached two days of food and fuel inside a hollow in a rock gendarme here, recorded down to the gel in Zack's meticulous notes. Now, a slight six-foot fin of snow completely covers the ridge. It's fragile enough that I place an extra piece of gear. Renan belays me while I dig. If we don't find that extra fuel canister, it will be another reason to retreat. A half hour passes. I'm almost ready to abandon the effort...and then, there it is.

The next six to eight pitches are a surprise: thin snowfields, pegboard drytooling, and incut slabs. A short chimney bubbles with water ice. And all along, there's just enough gear to keep things reasonable. At the upper headwall, Renan puts on rock shoes. I watch as he puzzles over runout flakes, his movements as deliberate and powerful as those of a praying mantis. We traverse under a dollop cornice and dig another tent site in the deepening twilight blue, one pitch below the summit of the Eye Tooth. It's as if we've unexpectedly caught an updraft, and are just beginning to soar.

[This page, top] Ozturk leading a rock slab in crampons. *Freddie Wilkinson* **[This page, bottom]** Wilkinson rounding a snow ridge. Wilkinson: "Traversing this type of giant terrain is not, strictly speaking, logical—mainly because it involves a lot of transitioning from one style to another, across different mountain mediums: from ice to rock, from rappelling to post-holing. It therefore requires good conditions and time, days of bivouac-enforced commitment, rather than a pure, nonstop, single push." *Renan Ozturk*

DAY THREE

Ahead, the Missing Tooth waits. The surreal architecture of snow, wind, and ridge is both mesmerizing and scary. The Missing Tooth isn't much. Like the Eye and the Sugar, it's more of a bump on a long, serpentine ridge than an independent mountain. The farther we trace our line above the Ruth Gorge, the more I feel as if we're climbing a singular route with its own simplicity, rather than a contrived enchainment. But if it has little geographic importance, this tiny, untouched summit has personal meaning.

A line of sallow cornices leans first one way and then the other, like the individual teeth on a bread knife. The snowpack is translucent, revealing the reddish, toothy granite beneath the mountain's skin. This was Zack and Renan's highpoint from 2009. It's the last truly unknown part of the entire traverse. I downclimb over the first cornice lip, and pause. One foot swings idly in air. I lower myself a little more and, to my surprise, my crampon catches consolidated snow. The sun has baked the mountain into finite, concrete proportions. I shuffle right and begin following the east side of the ridge. We bivy below the summit of the Bear Tooth. The corrugated Coffee Glacier watches far below.

DAY FOUR

Renan and I simulclimb to the summit of the Bear Tooth through an ethereal specter of cascading, cream-colored clouds. Rappelling becomes a time-consuming exercise in one-piece anchors. Finally, we coil the ropes and solo toward the south face of the Mooses Tooth. It's

[This page] Wilkinson traversing the ridge from the Missing Tooth to the Bear Tooth. Wilkinson: "At first, snow climbing is rarely as puckering as you've built it up to be. As you approach a section of ridge, the horizontal space gets compressed, and features look steeper than they really are. But the exposure is guaranteed to be tremendous, protection is always a major concern, and the end of the rope always comes sooner than you're hoping. Then you're both climbing, and you spend most of your time wondering whether you'll be pulled to your death if the other guy falls." *Renan Ozturk*

afternoon when Renan starts up the first rock pitch. He takes off his crampons and hangs his pack. He tries to fudge in more gear. His breaths rattle when he speaks: "I don't know if this will go." For the last week, we've indulged in this mild fantasy that the Tooth Traverse would be possible. Renan's breaths relax, and he makes another move. Now he's swimming up a steep patch of snow. A fall would be inconceivable. I don't let myself relax until I hear the words: "I'm off, Freddie."

I take over the lead for the Bleeder Pitch. The bolt I placed two years ago flexes, once more, under my weight. Shadows deepen, as if Mt. Dickey were reaching across the gorge to grab us. Two more pitches in rock shoes, and then I switch to boots and crampons and head toward the summit ridge. We summit the Mooses Tooth at 11 p.m. I raise my hands, let out a primitive cry, and continue on. Renan follows. The west ridge, our descent route, rolls toward Denali, a narrow strip of snow suspended in the purple-blue twilight sky.

Day Five

It's after midnight when we brew at the top of Ham and Eggs. The mountains are cloaked in a monochrome dusk. There's light enough to carry on. We trudge across the west ridge's curling swales. At first it's easy walking, then we round a dome and a vertical step hovers in the half-light. I cuss my way up it, unable to interpret my footwork in the gloom, scratching and manteling from vertical rock onto punchy snow. We drop steeply toward Shaken Not Stirred. This is the first north-facing terrain we've encountered on the entire traverse. It's impossible to downclimb, so we rappel. More sweat and swear words get us to the top of the gully.

I take the lead again, committing to a blunted crampon point on silky stone and then a long runout across hollow snow. How many pitches like this have we climbed over the past five days? Too many for me to count. We stop and brew the last of our instant coffee near the west summit of the Mooses Tooth. The sun is rising to our left. The morning light singes the ridge crest in sharp relief. From the summit of the Eye Tooth, I can trace our line: I know each cornice, every rock and spine and swirl on this long and whimsical path we've followed. It's probably familiar to more pilots than climbers.

At last, we rappel toward the west shoulder, the long snow ramp that will guide us home. I'm reminded how far we've come, and how far we still have to go.

Summary

First complete ascent of the Tooth Traverse (8,000m, 5.10R M5 A2+) by Renan Ozturk and Freddie Wilkinson, May 17–May 21, 2012, after several years of attempts. During these efforts, the team of Ozturk, Wilkinson, and Zack Smith completed three first ascents—the Sugar Tooth's south ridge, the summit of the Missing Tooth [both *AAJ 2010*], and Swamp Donkey Express on the Mooses Tooth [*AAJ 2011*]. ▤ ▣ ▶

About the Author

Freddie Wilkinson is a New England-based climber, mountain guide, and outdoor writer. He has made numerous first ascents on difficult peaks in Alaska, Patagonia, and the Himalaya.

A version of this story originally appeared in Alpinist 41.

UN MAR DE SUEÑOS

THREE SEASONS OF ATTEMPTS LEAD TO A NEW ROUTE UP THE EAST FACE OF FITZ ROY

JORGE ACKERMANN

It was an idea born from years of climbing in Chaltén, of looking for adventure, of moving fast and light: Michi Lerjen-Demjen and I wanted to climb the east face of Fitz Roy. We started laying plans to attempt the first repeat of the East Pillar (Ferrari-Meles, 1976) in early 2012. But when I told my friend Tincho, a great seaman and adventurer, about this idea, he said that if I wanted to go through the trouble of repeating a route that challenging, *why not open a new route*? Tincho gave me the nudge I needed.

This was around the time the town of El Chaltén was gripped by the whole debate over the bolts on Cerro Torre. Michi and I wanted to open a new route in a way that would leave these mountains pristine, as we believe they should be. We wanted to climb the east face in alpine style, without leaving ropes or bolts behind, so that some of the adventure we experienced would remain for those who followed us.

The Chaltén massif is like Yosemite for us Argentinians. Many of us started big-wall climbing here, and the level of climbing and creativity among Argentinean climbers is very high. In Argentina, climbers like Luciano Fiorenza have opened ingenious and aesthetic lines by the dozen without seeking much exposure from it, and many climbers that come here for the first time are quite surprised by this. We have our own climbing community, our own mountain magazines, and, somehow, this remains unknown to the rest of the world.

In Bariloche, where I grew up, the mountain culture that came with the European settlers remains strong to this day. Refugio Frey, one of the mountain huts near Bariloche, is a hub for climbers and skiers, surrounded by granite spires and only a few hours' walk from town. I got a job at Refugio Frey when I was 16. Peter Lüthi worked there at that time; he was a vibrant character and mentor for many Argentine climbers, and he took me under his wing and transmitted his love for adventure. Here I also met Rolando Garibotti, Luciano and Bicho Fiorenza, and Ramiro Calvo, a group of legendary Argentine mountaineers. From them, I learned to move in the mountains. Their stories made me dream of the Chaltén massif.

[Previous page] Michael Lerjen-Demjen low on the east face. *Jorge Ackermann*

When I was 18, I headed to Chaltén with hand-me-down climbing gear and a few pesos in my pockets. I was ecstatic to finally be there, surrounded by those mythical mountains. I learned to climb big walls—and to climb ice, for that matter. I returned to Chaltén every year and climbed many peaks, and I guess this gave me the tranquility to try new things. Attempting new routes with uncertain outcomes was possible because I had already reached the summits, so the pressure was off, in a sense. I took a liking to the adventure of route finding, of not knowing what comes after the next pitch, of the dynamic that forms in a team when deciding which way is next.

MICHI AND I FIRST CLIMBED TOGETHER on Fitz Roy, on the Supercanaleta, in 2007. Several years later, in December 2011, we guided Fitz Roy together. We worked really well as a team and got our client to the top and back down in 20 hours. It was a blast. Michi went back to Switzerland after guiding, but I called him when I saw that good weather was coming and proposed that we try our new route on Fitz Roy. He came back to Chaltén right away.

Despite all our good intentions and aspirations for greatness, we were naïve about what

[This page] Jorge Ackermann forges up a dihedral toward steeper rock overhead. The lower route was relatively sheltered, so the pair took a chance and approached the face despite a storm. "It was snowing and the wind was howling, but around us the air was still." *Michael Lerjen-Demjen*

lay ahead. In the pictures of our proposed route the cracks looked big—lots of offwidths, we thought. Once on the route, we realized that these offwidths were in fact razor-thin cracks. This was disappointing since we had left most of the small gear behind to leave room for our big cams.

While we were taking our No. 4s for a stroll up Fitz Roy, the sun blazed and rocks flew down the face all around us. Thankfully, the route is so steep that the rocks cleared the whole wall before hitting the glacier. The conditions that season were surreal. Patagonia is renowned for the harshness of its storms, and now it was the *good* weather making things difficult. Many accidents occurred in the days before our climb, and Michi and I joined the rescue parties. In the aftermath, we both were going through some mind games.

After eight pitches of thin cracks—artificial climbing, plain hard—we decided to retreat. We joked that it would be easier with ice on the route. "We should come back in winter," we said. What a crazy idea: no one around, no tragedy except for

maybe our own, no controversies, no rocks falling—the more we thought about it, the better it seemed.

In July 2012, I picked up Michi in Calafate and we headed to Chaltén across the frozen *estepa*. I had never been to Chaltén in winter, and I had no idea what to expect. The hills around town were covered with a dusting of snow. It was quiet. Apart from the handful of people who live in Chaltén year-round and a few construction workers from the north, there was no one around. It was great to have the tranquility to focus on the task at hand. We needed peace and quiet to face the challenges ahead.

Despite the serenity we felt in town, the conditions proved difficult. The first time we brought gear up to our base camp at Paso Superior, two meters of loose snow lay on the ground and the going was rough (although the ski down was unreal). The second time we went up, the snow had turned to ice. We spent four days on the wall and made it only five pitches higher than we had in the summer, despite all the extra gear we had and our knowledge of the route. We retreated before some bad weather came in.

This winter attempt was tough, but it was probably the best climbing experience I've had in Patagonia. We were all alone, and it felt like what Patagonia must have been like 50 years earlier. In fact, it was such a good trip that we decided to give the route another try, but this

[This page] The author relaxes at a small but welcome bivy ledge. *Jorge Ackermann*

time in summer, since the winter conditions didn't turn out to be all that helpful after all.

I MET MICHI AGAIN IN NOVEMBER. One more attempt, and that was it. We had spent a lot of time together in 2012, and we felt very solid. During our first weather window, we reached Paso Superior only to realize the wall was in worse condition than we had seen it in winter, and the ropes we had cached were gone. We felt like it was over. We came back to town, and after a fair amount of sulking we pulled ourselves together and waited for the next good weather window, which came three days later.

In winter, we had figured out that the lower part of the route was sheltered enough that it could be climbed in bad weather, so we took our chance when only a few days of good weather appeared in the forecast. We approached the face under stormy conditions. Once on the wall, it was snowing and the wind was howling, but around us the air was still. What are the chances to be climbing in such conditions in Patagonia? With every pitch we reached higher ground. It felt like cheating. Finally, we were *moving*.

We spent that night on the Ledge of Hope, a name we'd coined from far below, while scoping the route, when it appeared the ground above the ledge might be easier. Here, we found very little comfort but much hope for the climbing ahead. The chimney we'd been dreading since we first saw it during our winter attempt—a gaping flake that we feared might be unprotectable—turned out to have a fist crack in the back.

[This page] Ackermann en route. *Michael Lerjen-Demjen* **[Next page]** Approaching the east face in winter 2012. Un Mar de Sueños (1,200m) lies mostly to the left of the Ferrari-Meles East Pillar (1976). *Michael Lerjen-Demjen*

[This page] Nearing the glacier after a long night of rappelling the Ferrari-Meles route on the East Pillar. The climbers expected to find old rappel anchors but were forced to build most of their own. *Michael Lerjen-Demjen*

After 40 meters of relatively easy climbing we emerged back onto the face. Above, a really thin crack, about 20 meters long, disappeared into a blank dihedral. But again we were lucky: An amazing orange dike led over toward more inviting dihedrals to the right. After some free climbing, some hooking, and a big pendulum, we reached the dihedrals with big grins on our faces. We had studied this part of the wall so intensely in our pictures—I couldn't believe we were finally there.

Now the cracks were deeper, and though the climbing was not actually easier, our minds relaxed knowing we had good gear. At around 10 p.m., we reached the second ledge on the climb. We felt grateful for that small bit of horizontal space, knowing we wouldn't have to sleep hanging in our backpacks. After cleaning the ice off the ledge, making water, and eating our polenta, we finally went to sleep at 1 a.m.

The next morning, when I looked down from our small ledge, I realized I could still see the first pitch of the climb—it's rare in Chaltén to find a climb this steep from the bottom to the top. We started climbing again with the sun on our backs. The wall became less vertical, and the terrain grew easier. When we joined the Ferrari-Meles route, we decided to leave some gear on a ledge so we could reach the summit faster. This was a huge mistake. As we advanced, the wall became very steep again, and we had just left behind our aid gear. But we pulled through. After six pitches on the Ferrari-Meles, we decided to look for better rock and easier terrain further right. The rock got better, but easy climbing remained to be found. After five more pitches of challenging but fun mixed climbing we topped out just 50 meters from the summit.

I had never felt so happy on a summit before. I'd been transfixed by this climb for three seasons, and we had succeeded without leaving any bolts or using any fixed ropes. The exhilaration of the summit was short-lived, however; we had to get down. And now we had to descend the East Pillar to retrieve the gear we had left there. It felt sketchy to go down that way, but we were curious about this unrepeated climb. We had heard there was a ton of abandoned gear on the route, and we expected to find fixed anchors all the way down, but in the end we discovered only three rappel stations. We had to build our own rappel anchors the entire way as we continued down through the night. It was vertical, and we prayed at each rappel that our ropes would not get caught. We reached the base of the route at 6 a.m., after 24 hours on the move.

Only as we walked toward Paso Superior in a daze could we look back at the wall and understand that our dream had come true. We had gone up this massive wall, this sea of granite, *un mar de sueños*.

Summary

First ascent of Un Mar de Sueños ("A Sea of Dreams," 1,200m, 7a A3 M4) on the east face of Fitz Roy, by Jorge Ackermann (Argentina) and Michael Lerjen-Demjen (Switzerland), November 14–17, 2012. The two climbed 23 pitches to the left of the East Pillar route (Ferrari-Meles, 1976), then joined that route for six pitches, and then broke right for five more pitches to reach the top. They bivouacked twice en route and then rappelled the East Pillar through the night to descend.

About the Author

Jorge Ackermann, 26, grew up in Bariloche, Argentina, but now resides in Canada for much of the year. "My passion is to climb and discover new climbing spots, but I need to discon-nect from the climbing world from time to time," he says. "I work as a car-penter in the off-season, and I really enjoy working with wood and resolv-ing building problems."

[This page] Lerjen-Demjen (left) and Ackermann (right) on the summit of Fitz Roy. *Jorge Ackermann*

GROUND UP

AN OLD-SCHOOL EFFORT IN YOSEMITE VALLEY

MIKEY SCHAEFER

DAY 0. FALL 2010
Most climbers who flip through the Yosemite guidebook give Mother Earth (VI 5.12a A4) only a cursory glance. It's a route that could define the word obscure in Yosemite Valley, yet anyone who has spent days on El Cap has gazed at Mother Earth for hours upon hours. It takes a proud line up the 2,200-foot western margin of the north face apron of Middle Cathedral Rock. An even prouder group of seminal Yosemite climbers (Chapman, Kauk, Long) established the route the year before I was born in 1978. I thought it might make a great free climb, or just a fine repeat, and with little effort I convinced Jeff Johnson to take a look at the lower pitches.

We ventured up discontinuous cracks and face features. The climbing was stout and brilliant. As we moved upward, Middle Cathedral continued to reveal itself. At each belay I scrutinized the massive flanks of granite to my left and right, looking for other signs of passage. Off to the right I could barely make out the unlikely line of the Smith-Crawford, another route that has always piqued my curiosity. But even more captivating was the uncharted sea of golden rock to my left.

I was introduced to establishing new routes by Jim Yoder, one of the most active first ascensionists in Washington state. Before I was even old enough to drive, Jim taught me the basics of route selection and bolt placement. I tagged along as he and a small crew inspected, cleaned, and equipped routes for others to enjoy. They would often spend all weekend doing this—barely climbing for themselves. At the time it was hard for me to understand this kind of motivation and dedication. To me it seemed like an odd and thankless act. But without a doubt it made a lasting impression.

DAY 47. MID-SEPTEMBER 2012
Thankfully, for once, there is no one here. No one to witness my explosion of frustration. No one to see me kick and scream at the wall. No one to see me completely defeated. The walls of Middle and Lower Cathedral are the only ones to bear witness, and they stand as silent as statues of iron and gold. They are indifferent and offer no sympathy (which I have never expected from them). I'm alone in a war of attrition that I rarely feel I'm winning. The war is internal and I can only defeat myself.

I've never been one to set goals. My biggest projects most often start accidentally and

[Next page] Pitch 16 (5.10), the only true crack climbing pitch on the route. *John Dickey*

innocently, but then seem to grow out of control. An idea evolves into a goal, becomes an obsession, and finishes as an affliction. This route, this war, this affliction is no different. This tendency is possibly one of the greatest traits I have as a climber, as well as one of my biggest downfalls as a person.

DAY 14. JUNE 2011

This isn't what I signed up for. The plan wasn't to solo this thing. My feet ache and my calves scream as I slowly raise the hammer above my head. *Tap. Tap. Tap.* The bit bounces off the granite. My heart bounces in my chest, but it's more like *thump. Thump. THUMP!* Then I'm soaring through the air, hand drill in my left hand and hammer in my right. Thirty feet later the rope comes taut, and the Gri-Gri attached to my harness catches me. This *really* wasn't the plan.

Before Jeff and I had even finished rappelling from our exploratory mission up Mother Earth back in 2010, we had hatched a plan to come back the next day and venture into the unmapped sea of granite to the left of Mother Earth and the Smith-Crawford. Calling it a plan was a stretch—most plans involve research, a desired outcome, and execution. We decided to just start at the bottom of a 2,000-foot cliff and go climbing. Pretty simple, really. After 14 days of effort spread out over two seasons, I managed to establish eight pitches. Unfortunately, Jeff injured his shoulder at the beginning of the second season, which left me to my own devices.

DAY 23. EARLY JULY 2011

I shoulder my pack, slide shut the door of my van, and head up the gentle 20-minute approach

[This page] The north face of Middle Cathedral Rock, showing Father Time. *Mikey Schaefer*

to the base. But I only make it a short distance before stopping. I'm struggling to find the motivation to work on the route today. Something is telling me not to go. Internal frustration sets in, but I don't fight it. Back in the van, I head toward Tuolumne and a much-needed break and some socializing. I give myself a three-day vacation.

DAY 24. EARLY JULY 2011
Renewed after my short break, I charge up the trail. Head down, music turned up. I hardly notice my surroundings. I'm determined to finish another pitch today, and my jumars efficiently slide up the rope as the ground slowly drops away. I look up for the first time and notice something weird: One of my fixed ropes dangles oddly from the anchor above. The rope has been chopped in half. Thoughts race: *Did someone sabotage my ropes? Was it rockfall?* With no way to continue, I retreat down my nylon highway, trying to piece together what happened. At the base I find a small, fresh-looking block and then another, larger block.

Curiosity leads me east along the base of the wall. Fifty feet from the start of my ropes, I stand on a small rise and see the rest of the north face apron, completely devastated. Dump-truck loads of fresh rockfall are strewn across the base. The sight makes me sick to my stomach. I could have been climbing when this happened. I have nearly 1,500 feet of rope and a whole rack of gear on the wall, but as I head down the trail I wonder if I'll ever come back.

DAY 25. MAY 2012
Nearly a year after the rockfall, I'm ready to return. Ready might not even be the word—it's more of a need. I clear my schedule as much as possible, turning down jobs that would advance my career, fatten my wallet, and take me to Mt. Everest, Morocco, and other faraway places. I need to be in Yosemite and finish what I started. At the base of Middle Cathedral, I attach a Mini Traxion to my old rope and start up again, tagging 800 feet of new line to replace the damaged cords.

DAY 30. MAY 2012
I've learned to break everything into manageable sections and routines. I find that timing myself helps with the motivation. Forty-five minutes for the first 1,000 feet of jumaring. Then a 15-minute break. Then one hour for the remaining 800 feet of steeper jugging. The whole process becomes automated, and I try to focus on the immediate task, not letting myself become overwhelmed or lonely. Today is a workday, no *real* climbing. I've hand-drilled close to 100 bolts for this route. Most of them start out as 1/4" by 1 1/4" bolts, and they all need to be upgraded to 3/8" bolts for free-climbing. At a minimum of 30 minutes a bolt, I'm looking at 50 hours of drilling on this line. I'm hoping to replace 10 bolts today.

[This page] Josh Huckaby (left) and the author simul-drilling on pitch two. *Jeff Johnson*

Day 35. June 2012

Progress continues glacially. Ground-up, self-belayed climbing is anything but fast. It's easy to look over my shoulder at El Cap and question my choices. With its simple access, trail to the top, tick marks, pre-stashed camps, move-by-move beta, and daily Internet reports, El Cap has turned into the ultimate granite playground. There's little glory to be found on the other side of the Valley, but I crave the unknown, the untrodden, and the possibility of failure. Middle Cathedral offers heavy doses of all three.

When I return to the Valley and people ask how the route is going, I can tell they wonder what I'm doing up there. Some joke that I must be installing the longest bolt ladder in Yosemite. Others ask why I'd bother with such chossy rock. It's easier to agree with them than to explain. Occasionally people ask why I even bother climbing ground-up. I respond that I honestly never considered an alternative. One of the fundamental joys and challenges I find in climbing is to start at the bottom of a wall and try to get to the top. If I had opted to carry 2,200 feet of rope to the top of Middle Cathedral and start rappelling, I would have cheated myself out of a great opportunity to fail. And without a great opportunity to fail, I would have no chance at a great success.

Day 40. Fall 2012

One hundred feet of moderate climbing leads to manzanita bushes, sandy slopes, and the top. Along with Jeff, who is healthy again and back on the team, I scramble to the summit. There were so many days that I deeply doubted this would happen, and now the top is more a relief than it is a cause for celebration. Regardless what happens next, the route is at one stage of completion. But the project is still far from finished. Numerous pitches required aid, and the ultimate goal is to free-climb them all, some of which might be beyond my ability. I'm not sure if I'm actually getting any closer.

Day 50. Late Fall 2012

There was a time when I loathed project climbing, mostly because I didn't understand it. The process initially appears to be one of simplification and narrow-mindedness, with the sole goal of chasing higher grades. Without a doubt this mentality exists, but it is far from the only aspect of redpointing. During every hike up the trail, every trip up my fixed ropes, and every attempt to lead the crux pitches, my experience grows and becomes more acute. I've learned to take joy in knowing the route so intimately. Simple things such as knowing which rock will roll under my foot on the approach, or telling the time from the shadow that Middle Cathedral casts across El Cap Meadow. Or knowing that if my hips shift slightly to the left and my right heel turns in too much I can't hold the right-hand pinch long enough to move my left hand. These things can't be understood without an investment of time and commitment. And the more I invest the more I gain.

Day 55. Late Fall 2012

It's the fifth day of my free attempt, and time is running out. I have a flight out of Fresno and weeklong job starting in two days, and then a month's work in the Middle East right after that. It's hard to remain positive. I haven't managed to free any of the three crux pitches, and no amount of effort or desire may change that. Two of the cruxes, "The Index 11d" and "The Athletic 12c" are within reason, but "The Boulder Problem" still seems far out of reach. I've

[This page, left] Exhaustion. Frustration. Rain. *John Dickey* **[This page, right]** Staring down the Boulder Problem (5.13) on pitch 13. *John Dickey*

given it well over 50 attempts in the last two months, and I wouldn't be surprised if it takes 50 more for me to do it.

My friend James Lucas has been my regular belayer on my free attempt, and he does his best to keep me from going crazy with bad jokes and abundant stoke. As I repeatedly fall off the Boulder Problem, he urges, "Come on, Mikey, come on!" He has a belief in me that I no longer have in myself. Another try. Then another. I inch closer but come up short again. We head up to the last crux pitch, the Index 11d, a sequence of insecure smears, subtle backsteps, and thin liebacks. I do much better on this pitch and almost manage a clean ascent. My second go is even better. The thought of actually sending helps with morale.

Back in the portaledge I weigh my options. I *should* be rappelling tomorrow and calling it quits, but I'm concerned that if I don't finish the route this season it may never happen. The climb has already stressed my relationship to the breaking point, and disregard for my photography career isn't wise. The choice is obvious, though. I call my client and cancel the next shoot. Thankfully the producer is a climber and understands my desires. I've just bought myself another week.

Day 57

Success in climbing is a complex web of many variables: the properties of the rock, atmospheric conditions, equipment, preparation, knowledge, strength, motivation, and belief. Now, 1,600 feet off the Valley floor and seven days into my planned five-day ascent, I have little ability to control anything except my motivation and belief, and hardly a fragment of these remains. But until nothing is left I have to keep trying. Trying to get my foot to stick, believing I can reach the next hold. Burn after burn I explode out of the corner of the Index 11d. Again I match feet, backstep, slide my shoulder up the corner, match feet again, push harder—and this time I reach farther. My tips take purchase, as does my belief.

Day 58

One single hard move remains. One shitty gaston I can't hold. I've fallen off this move more than a 100 times already. In what is surely a final move of desperation, I slightly change my sequence. A nominal shift of my hand unlocks the move, and again I reach farther. Joy and

satisfaction completely overwhelm me. The Boulder Problem is laid to rest. Things fall into place, and I make quick work of the Athletic 12c. Tomorrow, all I need to do is struggle up the last few pitches, which I know I will.

Day 59

There is a weird emotional vacuum after reaching the summit. For the last two years Middle Cathedral has been my muse and my foe. It provided challenge and commitment that I struggle to find in other parts of my life. I learned to thrive off the pressure and the possibility of failure. And now, as I lay here for one final evening in my portaledge, it's hard not to wish the experience would continue.

Just before going to sleep I get a text from Tommy Caldwell, saying congratulations and asking about the route. He's interested in checking it out with Jonathan Siegrest. I don't even know how to respond.

When I get down to the Valley, I swing by their campsite to give them the details, and I'm genuinely shocked when they say they want to go up right away. The only problem is that I still haven't cleaned up the route. Most of my fixed ropes and directionals are still in place, so I set my alarm and made a plan to jug ahead of them, cleaning the ropes as they climb. I go to bed worrying about what those guys will think. Will they fly right up the route? Or does it warrant the fight I had to give it?

Day 61

From my perch up on the fixed lines, I have a bird's eye view of Tommy tick-tacking up the small, perfectly sculpted holds on the first hard pitch of the lower slab. When he reaches me at the belay, he has a grin from ear to ear. He and Jonathan make quick work of the next pitches, and then slow as the wall kicks up into the crux leads at two-thirds height. Jonathan fights for the onsight on the Boulder Problem but falls after committing to the wrong sequence. As I finish rappelling, I look up and see Tommy and Jonathan's headlamps click on. They are battling it out on the final crux, giving it everything they've got. It makes me happy to see that my muse and foe may live on.

Summary

First ascent of Father Time (VI 5.13b) on Middle Cathedral Rock, Yosemite Valley, California, by Mikey Schaefer. After a ground-up ascent that spanned 60 days of effort over three years, Schaefer finished redpointing all 20 pitches on October 18, 2012. 🔍

About the Author

Raised in Washington state but now living in central Oregon, Mikey Schaefer is a professional photographer and widely traveled climber. In 2013 he completed another longstanding goal: new routes on each of the seven major summits of the Fitz Roy massif skyline in Patagonia. During 2009 he put up another new route on Middle Cathedral, Border Country (IV 5.12), with Jeremy Collins and Dana Drummond.

[Previous page] Latching the jug on the Boulder Problem. Schaefer originally thought the pitch might be 5.13+, but a new sequence brought it down to "about 5.13b." *Jeff Johnson*

CHANGE

THE MENTAL GAME BEHIND THE WORLD'S FIRST 9B+

ADAM ONDRA

I enjoy climbing as much as anything in the world. I indulge in that beautiful upward movement, feeling the breeze and trying to be creative and become a part of the wall. It is enormous fun. But I also love setting goals for myself. The challenge. Trying as hard as I can despite multiple failures. In climbing, I can have both.

Since I started climbing, my passion for moving on rock has never changed. And new challenges have never ceased to appear. Nevertheless, the challenges have changed over time. In the past, I wasn't much into putting up first ascents. School limited my free time, so whenever I got the chance to go abroad I preferred to climb instead of bolting. Except for a couple of climbs at my home area, I had never opened a significant route. This changed when I finished school last May. I couldn't wait to visit an unknown crag, poorly developed and with enormous potential for extreme new routes.

This is why I decided to go to Norway. I had heard so much about this beautiful country, and I became even more motivated when I saw a picture of the cave at Flatanger. Instantly, I understood that this place was not to be missed. We packed our stuff in early summer and headed north—an unusual direction for a Czech climber. It was about 10 days before we got to Flatanger, and driving the last 30 kilometers was exciting. I was a little afraid the cave would disappoint me. But at first glance, the doubts diminished. I knew I'd found the place for bolting an ultimate project. I stared into the endless sea of light granitic gneiss as if it were the best TV program on Earth. It took some time to decide which was the perfect line, and in the meantime I did a couple of onsights and made the first ascent of a Magnus Midtbø project, Thor's Hammer (9a+/5.15a). Then it was time to bolt.

It is hard work bolting from the ground up through 55 meters of constantly overhanging terrain. I aided with hooks, Camalots, and 6mm bolts—one can never be sure whether these will pop off. But after two days the line was completed. The enormous advantage of this rock is that there were no loose flakes, and the surface was absolutely free of dust and moss. Finding such a steep cave with solid holds all the way is almost impossible on limestone; nowadays most of the hard-core routes tend to be reinforced with glue, or else the route would change with every ascent. Flatanger was different.

[Next page] Adam Ondra does the last hard move of the crux of the second pitch on Change. Still 20 meters to go! During the redpoint, he linked the two pitches. *Petr Pavlicek*

[This page] The line of Change (9b+) in Flatanger's enormous Hanshalleren cave. The circle marks Ondra, climbing near the end of the first pitch. *Petr Pavlicek*

It was not clear whether the route was possible, especially because I found the lower boulder problem absolutely heinous. But searching for sequences, being creative, is one of the most interesting parts of climbing. And creativity paid off. The easiest way through the lower crux is one of the craziest sequences I have ever come up with. I started by kicking my right foot way out and making a long reach into an almost non-existent gaston in the seam below a roof. Then I turned the roof into a dihedral by bringing my left foot up, desperately, just below my left hand. I grabbed an intermediate with my left hand in order to bring my left foot even higher, dropped my knee and bent my spine as much as I could—all the while crimping desperately on a terrible gaston with my left—and stabbed my left hand into a two-finger pocket. It took me a long time to figure this out, and I am quite confident it is the easiest way through this section. Nevertheless, it still felt extremely difficult.

The route was beating me up. Three moves in the crux and I couldn't catch a breath. My back was sore, and the skin on my fingers was thin. But I made some good progress, and on the sixth day of work I sent the first pitch, which resolves 8b climbing into an 8B+ boulder problem. After about 20 meters, there is an anchor in a kind of dihedral where the rock is almost vertical. You can press onto both sides, releasing your hands while crouching under a little roof, pushing your head into the ceiling. Here I planned to rest before linking into the second pitch, obviously without making a belay in the middle.

I thought the first pitch was 9a+ (5.15a), and with a 25-meter, continuous 9a following it, I believed the whole route would be hard 9b. The ascent seemed within a reach, a question of a couple of days. But the more I tried it, the more I understood how difficult the first pitch was. I was unable to link that pitch again, even though I felt stronger at the bottom. Eventually I told myself I needed to quit, go home, train sufficiently, and return with full power.

Back home I began training power endurance for the World Championships in Paris, doing 30- to 40-move laps on a bouldering wall. At the same time, this was exactly what I needed for my project in Norway. I also did some pure power training on the campus board, and occasional shoulder-power workouts for that special move on the first pitch.

Mentally I was still in Flatanger. I couldn't stop thinking about the route. Even though I was training for the World Championships, I thought mostly about what would follow after the comp. In late September, we packed our car and headed north again. I was in shape, I had regained motivation, I thought it would go quickly. But not everything goes according to plan. The moves didn't feel any easier, the holds were humid, and my confidence was kicked down. Nevertheless, after a couple of days, I was back in the game and finally I repeated the first pitch cleanly. I had never climbed the whole second pitch, only six moves in—most times I would save myself for the next day. After linking the first pitch for the second time and resting beside the anchor, I slipped off a heel-hook in the crux traverse of the second pitch. But my mind was calm. I saw it was climbable.

Over the next few days, though, the route suddenly didn't seem doable anymore. Some days the rock felt humid, but then cool days with wind came and still it felt desperate. I couldn't understand it. I would be perfectly rested, warmed up, the wind would be blowing,

[This page, top] Ondra does the dirty work, bolting the second pitch. *Petr Pavlicek* [This page, bottom] In the middle of the crux boulder problem, itself around V14. *Petr Pavlicek*

and I couldn't hold onto the rock. My self-confidence froze at the point of zero, my mind overwhelmed with doubts. Did I even enjoy this? Why was I doing it? Wouldn't it just better to go climb something easier? Every day started with hope but ended with more doubts. It was like going into a factory from 8 to 4. I even started to plan another trip; I needed some change.

I still believed I could do the climb, but I had to find the day when everything clicked: power, conditions, mental strength, and luck. The last two factors are closely interdependent. Luck is something you can influence a lot. On a route like Change, when you have only two goes a day, it is super-difficult to stay calm and focused. You need to climb everything as efficiently as possible, which can mean taking risks with your feet and how hard you grip the holds, which can lead to numerous errors. If these errors happen, doubt may enter your mind, making it impossible to climb at your limit. But at the same time, you can't over-grip to prevent errors or you'll never have enough strength to finish the route. It's a vicious circle. Mental strength is the key; luck might be the consequence.

During one rest day, a horrendous wind came up. I stared through the window at the leaves of the trees being blown away, with the blue fjord in the background, and all of a sudden I felt happy. I had an irrational feeling that the next day would be it. I couldn't sleep that night, listening to the wind—I felt a mixture of calm and nervousness.

The morning began as usual: oatmeal, green tea, jogging. That irrational feeling came over me again as we were approaching the cave, and my warm-up felt exceptionally good. As I set off, I felt strong, flowing through the first meters and entering the crux. I made a slight mistake, placing a foot one centimeter too far to the left, but held on. After clipping the first anchor, I stayed in the no-hand rest for a long time. Here, the crux is not getting distracted. You've got plenty of time to think about failure. And from this relaxed mode, you need to switch immediately into fighting mode.

[This page] Ondra on the second-pitch crux traverse. *This page and next: Petr Pavlicek*

The second crux is traversing the lip of a roof by compressing and heel-hooking very flat holds, followed by big reaches on crimps above. I did everything with perfection, but I was getting pumped, and the closer I was to the next rest the more desperate I felt. When a jug appeared in my hand, I couldn't catch a breath—another 20 meters of solid 8b+ remained. The game was on. I tried desperately to de-pump my forearms in the rests and sprint through the easier sections. The higher I got, the better the rests were, but still I felt more desperate. Four meters below the anchor I made the only mistake on the upper route—falling off flashed through my mind, and I surprised myself as I latched the final jug. After 26 minutes of climbing, this incredible route was free, as was I. I felt too tired and thirsty to realize what I had just done.

I had been thinking about the grade for a long time. While attempting the climb, I didn't admit that it could be 9b+. But the longer I tried it, the more desperate it felt. I had done all of my 9b routes way faster than this climb. And Change actually fit my style pretty well. I had never had a nemesis like this. It drained me, frustrated me multiple times, but the patience paid off and the whole process came to a beautiful ending. With slight hesitation, I am proposing the grade of 9b+, as it seems reasonable to me.

It is privilege to be among those such as Wolfgang Güllich, Ben Moon, or Alexander Huber who established one of the first routes of a new grade. I sometimes wondered what drove Wolfgang or Ben to keep trying routes that were rumored to be impossible, over and over again, training for them specifically and succeeding eventually. What audacity! But now I am getting the hang of it myself.

I am the kind of guy who is never satisfied. As soon as I finish a project, I want to climb another. It is endless. It is not a question of pushing the limits of sport climbing; it is about pushing my own limits. And with first ascents it is even more motivating. Take a look around—you might find your own line. Clean it, treat it well, and have fun climbing. You will make something for many climbers to enjoy, but most of all you will find out how great the process of first ascents can be.

SUMMARY

First ascent of Change (9b+/5.15c) in the Hanshalleren cave near Flatanger, Norway, by Adam Ondra. After five weeks of attempts spread over two visits to Norway, Ondra redpointed the pitch on October 4, 2012. 📷 ▶

ABOUT THE AUTHOR

Adam Ondra, 20, is a professional rock climber who grew up in Brno, Czech Republic, where he began climbing at age 6. In February 2013 he completed the first ascent of La Dura Dura in Spain and graded it 9b+, saying it was harder than Change, but also reaffirming his belief that his route in Norway was the world's first 9b+.

NO MYSTERY NO ADVENTURE

NEW FRIENDS AND NEW ROUTES IN EAST GREENLAND

MIKE LIBECKI AND ANGIE PAYNE

""Libecki! I have never been so fucking scared in my life!" Ethan Pringle's yell from 80 feet above startled me to attention. I'd been lost in the view of electric-blue icebergs floating in the sea a mile away. We were 1,500 feet up—not even halfway—on a sheer granite tower above a remote fjord on Greenland's east coast. Around us, spear-tipped summits stabbed into thick, gray-pink clouds.

We had already been moving 14 hours, and I'd begun to think this route might take longer than the 48 hours we'd planned for our nonstop push. Suffering seemed a sure thing. Ethan has just danced through a spectacular, pinky-sized 5.12 crack, making it look like 5.9. He yelled again: "…But I am having so much fun! I've never been so psyched!"

At that moment, I knew we'd not only climb this tower, we also were going to have a great time doing it. Ethan and I had only met once before this team-of-strangers expedition. We had never shared a rope. At base camp were two other members of our team, Angie Payne and Keith Ladzinksi, who also were strangers to me. Coming here together was not our idea….

I FIRST MET ETHAN PRINGLE, a leading U.S. sport climber and boulderer, at a marketing meeting in California at the headquarters of Mountain Hardwear, one of our mutual sponsors. We were there to discuss a project where climbers with diverse skills and strengths would join forces somewhere remote among steep rock peaks. My job would be to take younger climbers who were crushing in their respective climbing genres and bring them on a Libecki-style expedition. It sounded fun. And who could resist another trip, paid in full, to go somewhere beautiful and do first ascents? However, I would not be following three unofficial rules for expeditions: 1) Go with friends. 2) Go with friends. 3) Go with friends.

On expeditions into deep wilderness, emotions are laid bare. People get scared or lonely or frustrated. Team dynamics can go in any direction. Neither Angie Payne, one of the

[Next page] Angie Payne, spotted by Ethan Pringle, on Richard Keil (V9). In back is Daddy's Tower, which Mike Libecki was soloing at that moment, via the left skyline. *Keith Ladzinski*

world's top female boulderers, nor Ethan had ever been on a remote climbing expedition. Photographer Keith Ladzinski had been plenty of wild places, but I had never met him either. He was there to capture the beauty and adventure of climbing in the remote fjords of east Greenland. But would he also witness a dramatic meltdown? Or would this be the beginning of new friendships and great success? Always an optimist, I truly believed the latter. I have always said, "Without mystery there is no adventure." On this trip it was more like, "Without strangers there is no adventure."

We met up in Iceland. I arrived directly from a solo expedition to Franz Josef Land, Russia, where I narrowly avoided being killed by falling rock. Ethan came from Norway after completing a new 5.14 project. Angie arrived fresh from bouldering competitions in the States. Keith came with Angie after finishing one of his award-winning films. This would be my seventh expedition to Greenland. For me it was going to a second home, for them a strange and unknown land.

At the end of our two-hour flight to Kulusuk on Greenland's east coast, the pilot pulled up at the last minute, unable to see the wet tarmac through the rain and clouds. Our stomachs dropped like we were riding a roller coaster, but I could see this was no laughing matter for Angie. She was already way out of her comfort zone. When we finally arrived in the Inuit town of Tasiilaq, bright red, yellow, and blue houses were surrounded by a cobalt blue ocean and snow-white icebergs. Wisps of gray fog slithered by, adding to the fairy-tale scene. Dozens of Greenlandic huskies stood barking by abandoned fishing boats when we stepped off the helicopter. I smelled the familiar scent of seal blood—the dogs were being fed their favorite meal.

Soon we were at my friend Hans Christian Florian Sorensen's house. A surgeon and key contact for many expeditions, he is one of Greenland's heroes. We soon learned that excessive ice and rough seas would prevent us from going where I had hoped. But Hans Christian suggested another possibility, a fjord lined by granite towers that he had seen the previous summer. None of the most prominent towers had been climbed. We sipped hot coffee and looked at maps and photos in Hans Christian's living room, where walrus skulls and narwhal horns three and four meters long provided the decorations. Ethan's mouth literally hung

[This page, top] Libecki and team study maps at Hans Christian Florian Sorensen's home in Tasiilaq. *Keith Ladzinski* [This page, bottom] On guard for icebergs. *Keith Ladzinski*

open. "That wall is freaking huge!" he exclaimed. Angie spotted beautiful boulders in Hans Christian's photos, and scooted her chair over to the computer for a closer look.

We hired a fisherman to take us north to the fjords in a 22-foot boat, dodging icebergs as we moved up the coast. Ten hours later we were near our destination, but fog had settled like wrapping paper around the towers. Unsure where to land, we probed for icebergs with the boat's spotlight as we tried to find a place to drop anchor and wait for the fog to lift.

Gray. Rain. Wind and waves. The captain fired up the engine, and half an hour later we could see towers through wispy layers of fog. We unloaded our bags on a granite slab as the mist turned into pouring rain. Soon we were soaked as we scouted the spongy ground for a suitable base camp. Purple flowers glowed from bright green moss dotted with shiny dew diamonds. We were surrounded by huge granite towers, our tents crowded by boulders the size of small homes. The sharp needle of first-ascent longing pricked into my veins.

After setting up our cooking tent and crafting a stone-tabled kitchen, we settled around a stove and hot coffee with a touch of whiskey. This was perfect—the weather forced us to be tentbound and get to know each other better. We sipped steaming drinks, listened to raindrop drum beats, and talked about life and all the unclimbed rock that waited somewhere out in the mist. For the first time I could feel real camaraderie flowing among the team.

By the second morning the rain had slowed, and Angie made it clear that she wanted to focus on bouldering. But I wanted to get her tied in for a big first ascent, to feel the glory of standing on a high summit. The previous day, after we came ashore, I had hiked to the base of the most prominent tower in the cirque. A proud father who always misses his daughter on expeditions, I called it Daddy's Tower. A system of splitter cracks and corners went directly up the steepest, longest part of the northeast face. It was over 3,500 feet tall. Just as I was about to walk down in the rain, Ethan showed up.

"Do you think we can climb that line?" Ethan said, gazing up at the tower. "Dude, that is huge!"

"That is the best line here, maybe the best I have seen in all of Greenland," I said. "We are definitely going to climb that route."

But first I wanted to climb as a team, and I suggested we try the long but seemingly straightforward ridge left of the main face. We packed up for two days, and a three-hour hike brought us to a bivy site on a patch of green grass and lavender flowers, 1,000 feet above the ocean. Vanilla glaciers wound down the mountainsides across the fjord, and massive icebergs drifted in gray-turquoise ocean. I could smell the fresh scent of rain. The team was beaming.

The next morning, we had to cross a half-mile-wide glacier to reach the tower's base. Mazes of 40-foot-deep, five-foot-wide crevasses crisscrossed the bare ice like tiger stripes. I feel comfortable on these dry glaciers; the crevasses seemed to me like welcome smiles. To Angie they were like frowns of doom. "This is insane! Is this safe?!" she yelled. Small stones and dirt had sunk into the glacier's surface, leaving spiky points of ice that worked like grip tape on a skateboard. I assured Angie the glacier was quite safe to cross, even without crampons.

The drizzle turned to light rain. We made it across the glacier and started up a steep talus slope of loose, geometric puzzle pieces. Angie was nearly paralyzed with fear as we picked our way up the gully. "Are we going to die in here? I am *not* psyched right now!" Then, just as we started to harness up, pouring rain shut us down.

During the descent, Keith and I began trundling boulders down the slippery slopes, simply for the childish pleasure of it. We kept finding bigger and bigger boulders to send crashing down. As the two of us heaved a huge boulder, Keith slipped and tumbled head over heels. He soon came to a stop, but it could have been very ugly. Angie shouted, "What the fuck, guys? This is too dangerous!" We walked back to camp in silence. Angie went back to her tent and cried, her emotions raw. By evening, hot chocolate mixed with whiskey had us all smiling again, laughing over the events of the last two days. But for me the taste of defeat lingered—I badly wanted the first ascent of that gigantic tower.

The following morning revealed bluebird skies, freshly cleaned by the rain. I was up early making coffee. Our conversation quickly led to the hunt for sweet new boulders. Not for me, though—my thoughts were on a completely different wavelength.

"Hey guys, I'm going to run back up to that route we got rained off and try to solo it. I can be up and back in a day." I said this casually, hoping no one would mind if I took off for a bit. But Ethan said, "Dude! Libecki, are you crazy?" Angie chimed in, "You *are* nuts. Are you serious?" Eventually they came around. An hour later I left with a rope, a bit of pro, Clif Bars and water, my Year of the Dragon mask, and my iPod rocking to a live Grateful Dead concert from 1977, fueling my psyche. I sang out loud to the rocks and icebergs, "Fire, fire on the mountain…there's a dragon with matches that's loose on the town…"

The route was not difficult, mostly 5.6 and 5.7, but I dragged the rope behind me in case it got too scary. More than halfway up, I had to stop and consider the next section for about 20 minutes. Above was steep, flaky rock for about 400 feet. The last time I'd free soloed anything remotely dangerous was the same day Derek Hersey fell to his death from the Steck-Salathe in Yosemite Valley, back in May of 1993. Free soloing gives me the chills, especially now that I am a father. Still, it appeared manageable. I had been in similar positions many times before, and felt I could make the right call. I thought of Angie and her intimidation the previous day. Like her, I've had to overcome fear throughout the years. I still do on every expedition. I've just found ways to make friends with fear—fear keeps me safe. I started up a set of triple cracks and climbed steadily but cautiously until I could pull on to a good ledge below a fourth-class ridge, full of adrenaline. Back on easy ground, I pulled up the rope and headed for the top.

WHILE I WAS SOLOING THE TOWER, Angie, Ethan, and Keith explored a dreamland of Arctic bouldering. Angie writes:

I had no desire to go back and climb that tower with Mike, but I did have a new respect for his drive and his skill. Although I experience climbing in a very different way than he does, I saw in him a hunger to climb, and I could relate to that. I was still physically and emotionally exhausted from our team outing the day before, but Mike's psych was invigorating. There was a granite playground at our fingertips, so Ethan, Keith, and I set out to see what we could accomplish.

For the most part, I've bouldered existing problems. Clean boulders with chalked lines present concrete challenges that I can wrap my mind around. In Greenland, I felt like a beginner all over again. Finding the best boulders, spotting the lines, chalking holds, and unlocking the movement—it was a process I'd rarely experienced in its entirety.

Ethan had a knack for finding the good rock, so I followed his lead the first day. We quickly realized that the boulders further up the hill were cleaner than those near camp. But this perk came at the cost of my feeling out of place and vulnerable again. The talus was loose underfoot, threatening to crush my toes with every step. The sounds of rockfall punctuated the serene setting.

Then we came upon a perfect, cottage-sized boulder. And for the first time in my 17 years of climbing, I saw a line, chalked it up, and completed a real first ascent: *The Legend of Hans Christian.* Ethan quickly followed suit and established *Richard Keil* on the same boulder.

We continued exploring in the shadow of the tower that Mike was soloing, communicating with him intermittently via hand-held radios. Ethan and I were experiencing the rock in a drastically different way than Mike was, but we were all climbing, and something about that fact was uniquely motivating. Ethan found the gem of the area on a sweeping, 35-degree overhang of fine-grained granite. He worked on the main line for about half an hour and was set to try the problem again when Mike radioed from the top of the tower. Through Keith's longest telephoto lens, we could just see him on top, waving his arms in the air. Ethan sent *Shipwreck* (V11) on his next try. "It was one of my proudest boulder first ascents ever," he said later.

When Mike returned to camp, he and Ethan began planning their new route on the front side of Daddy's Tower. I planned to sit this one out, and so I set out to establish more boulders, sometimes alone, sometimes with Keith doubling as photographer and spotter. I was finally hitting my stride, and everything was falling into a familiar rhythm as I completed lap after lap on a hilltop boulder overlooking the iceberg-dotted ocean. And then, suddenly, I was rocketing through the air toward two poorly placed pads, with no spotter and the reality that any rescue could be days away. In that terrifying moment, I gained a new understanding of the word "remote." Luck was on my side, though, and I hobbled away bruised but not broken.

Before departing for Greenland, I'd been dead-set on establishing new boulder problems: perfect rock with perfect lines. I'd make a perfect little list of first ascents to bring home. Thinking about the trip nearly a year later, it would be a gross disservice to reduce it to a list of names and grades. Greenland was a journey of individuals through emotions and experiences, surrounded by a mind-blowing landscape. I had never seen as much raw beauty as I saw in Greenland—the kind beauty that is laced with volatility and unpredictability, the kind that makes one feel small and insignificant. It's no wonder I was intimidated.

As the purple-black of the late August Arctic night threw its blanket over the fjord, Ethan and I sat side by side on a small ledge with a bivy sack spread over us like a quilt. It was

[This page] Payne on *Cowboy Toast* (V6). To the left is *Roger Johnson* (V8), the code phrase Libecki planned to radio if he got in trouble while soloing. *Keith Ladzinski*

[This page, top] Ataatap Tower (a.k.a. Daddy's Tower). (1) Dragon's Back (Libecki). (2) Coronis (Bunn-Royer). (3) Built Fjord Tough (Libecki-Pringle). See Climbs and Expeditions for more. *Hans Christian Florian Sorensen* [This page, bottom] Libecki leading on Daddy's Tower and bivying with Pringle (right). *Ethan Pringle*

just dark enough to reveal the northern lights slithering green and blue across the darkened heavens. Their beauty was so fantastic, I don't remember feeling the freezing cold. Then they were gone. Shivering, teeth chattering like cartoon characters, we waited for the sun to rescue us with its warmth. This was Ethan's first bivy. I farted a couple times under the bivy sack. "Mike, seriously, please fart again," he said from deep inside the bunched hood of his parka. "It was so warm for a second." Finally it got so cold we just decided to keep moving.

We were close to 2,000 feet up, maybe 30 hours into our push. With all the teetering blocks we had encountered, I knew it would be very dangerous to rappel the route. "Dude, do you think we should keep going?" Ethan asked. His curious, sideways smile, arched brows, and wide eyes showed both psyche and serious concern. He was relying on my judgment. I assured him, "Yeah man, we might suffer a bit, but sometimes going fast just means we have to keep moving. We just need to keep going up." He smiled, buzzing with enthusiasm, as I re-racked and started up a golden corner.

Later, Ethan cruised a run-out, bouldery 5.11+ pitch and began setting an anchor 60 meters above. He yelled and I looked up and saw an object flying directly at me. I don't remember making the decision—I just reached up and caught the bullet coming toward me. It was Ethan's ascender. A moment later my hand was burning in pain. I got out the first-aid kit: a skinny roll of old medical tape. I couldn't close my two middle fingers, but I taped them together and jugged up to Ethan. He spewed apologies, but I actually found it kind of cool that I'd caught his ascender from 60 meters up. With no time to lose, I suggested he keep leading and I would jug fast behind him.

Ethan was fired up, and renewed strength swept over both of us. The next dozen hours were a blur. Night came again—the northern lights failed to impress us this time. We were tired but still moving, yearning for the top. A few hours after the second sunrise on this push, we found ourselves on the summit, above a sea of clouds. We celebrated with a hug. Ethan told me this wall was "by far the most meaningful piece of rock" he'd ever climbed. Sixty-two hours after starting our push, we staggered into base camp and hugged Angie and Keith.

Expeditions are like short-term marriages. Sometimes they go bad, but when they're good, they may create friendships that last a lifetime. Ethan and Angie's willingness to dive into first ascents and wilderness exploration reminded me of my own first expeditions. I saw their eyes light up with inspiration and fear from Greenland's raw beauty and unpredictable power. I was inspired by their physical and mental strength. Even though we'd been thrown together as strangers, this was far more than a marriage of convenience. I feel honored to have been on such a journey with these climbers, and even more honored to call them my friends.

Summary

First ascent of Ataatap Tower ("Daddy's or Father's Tower"), near Kangertitivatsiaq Fjord in east Greenland, via the south-west ridge (Dragon's Back, 5.8), free solo by Mike Libecki. First ascent of Built Fjord Tough (3,500', V 5.12 A2) on the northeast face of Daddy's Tower, by Mike Libecki and Ethan Pringle. The two fixed 600 feet of rope and then climbed the rest of the route in 52 hours, with a brief sitting bivouac; all but 15 feet was led free. Pringle and Angie Payne also established numerous boulder problems up to V11.

About the Author
Mike Libecki has a goal to survive 100 expeditions by the time he is 100 years old. As of May 2013, he had 60 years and 53 expeditions to go.

LOOK OUT! DANGER!

A PLEA FOR RESTRAINT IN THE FISHER TOWERS OF UTAH

STEVE "CRUSHER" BARTLETT

I dreamed I was in the Fisher Towers, walking on a ledge a couple of hundred feet up. I kept stumbling into pieces of angle iron bolted to the rock. These were, I realized, anchors. Peering below, I saw what seemed to be climbs every few feet—each defined by a vertical procession of broken cables, bent pitons, and half-fallen-out bolts. Somehow, I knew each climb had a name and a history. Yet they were so close to each other, so alike, they had no meaning.

As I woke, I wondered what the dream reflected of my recent experiences in the Fisher Towers. I've climbed around the deserts of southern Utah for almost 30 years, and I've always felt there was a reasonable consensus about ethics on new desert climbs, about conforming to the rock and leaving an enjoyable challenge for the next party. Last spring, while hiking around the Fisher Towers, I was confronted with a new route that shattered that assumption: the ugliest aid climb I've ever seen, a line of fresh holes and new-but-decaying hardware on the Titan. During the same hike, another new route caught my eye: Far subtler, it forged a graceful arc up the east face of Kingfisher. Both routes were established by the same team: David "Pelut" Palmada and Esther Ollé, from Catalonia in northern Spain. Why did these two routes appear so different from existing climbs, and from each other? What was going on?

In the Spanish magazine *Desnivel*, Palmada suggested that his August 2009 route on the Titan, Oju, Peligru! ("Look Out, Danger!") might be the hardest aid climb in the world. For comparison, he used his earlier ascent of Jim Beyer's Intifada, on Cottontail Tower in the Fishers, originally rated A6. The Spanish Mountaineering Federation (FEDME) awarded Palmada its 2009 award for big-wall climbing, with a prize of 2,000 euros, for the "proposed A6+" route. This was followed the next year by a prize of 2,500 euros for Palmada's first ascent, with Josep Esquirol, of a 1,400-meter big wall on Baffin island. At home, Palmada is an enthusiastic and respected member of a small but energized aid-climbing fraternity.

Mystified by these climbs, I decided to repeat Hot-Parad-Ice, Palmada's August 2012 route on the Kingfisher. In March 2013, I found myself roping up under a pitch that looked right at the limit of possibility. Something that *might* be feasible. Small hints of weaknesses

[This page] The Fisher Towers, with 50 years of aid-climbing history, are one of the last places in the United States where new nailing routes are still being put up. *Steve Bartlett*

emerged and shyly vanished. Which side of feasible would it be? Sheer genius? Contrived and trenched? I gently tapped a No. 1 Pecker into a tiny seam and stepped up.

CUTLER SANDSTONE USUALLY FORMS bland slopes, lost in the vast space of the Colorado Plateau. But in the Fisher Towers, the Cutler has weathered into a riotous labyrinth of gothic cathedrals and castles, dark and foreboding, with fantastic, convoluted buttresses and flutes. There are five major formations and myriad smaller ones.

In 1962, Layton Kor, Huntley Ingalls, and George Hurley climbed the largest tower, the Titan. Kor, who led every pitch, freed what could be freed, used pitons where there were cracks, and placed bolts where the cracks ran out. Soon after, Harvey Carter summited the other four big formations: Kingfisher, Echo Tower, Cottontail, and the Oracle. In the 1960s, just reaching these summits was seen as challenge enough.

During the 1970s climbers began looking for harder routes with few bolts. One person took this as far as it could be taken: Jim Beyer. From 1976 to 1989, climbing solo, he created a singular, spectacular legacy: 14 new routes, most of which were of unprecedented difficulty. His early lines followed big, natural features. Next he was drawn to the spaces in between. Sometimes these held seams that could be nailed—if only just—but sometimes the features ran out.

Beyer wanted to keep the bolt count low and the seriousness high, so, notably on World's End (1987) and Intifada (1988), where the rock did not yield "natural" placements, he drilled shallow holes and hammered copperheads into the resulting slots. Such "trenched" placements were quick to place; they held body weight but not long falls.

In Yosemite Valley, Jim Bridwell and Peter Mayfield had experimented with one or two such trenched placements during the first ascents of Zenyatta Mondatta and Aurora, in 1981. At the time, Bridwell and Mayfield kept quiet about what they had done, understanding that it may have crossed a line, beyond an honest attempt to take on the natural challenge of the rock. Or perhaps, by playing with it, they *defined* this line. In 2006, Mayfield wrote at Supertopo, "If you are good, you know when artistry turns to a travesty and you take the other path."

A new generation in Yosemite, including Walt Shipley, Steve Gerberding, and John Middendorf, rejected trenching. If there were no cracks or other natural features that could be pitoned, headed, hooked, or free-climbed, they believed a bolt or rivet should be installed. In the softer Fisher Towers rock, trenched placements deteriorated fast from erosion and repeated use, requiring subsequent parties to carry a drill. Which led to another problem: Because a drill was needed to maintain these placements, the drill might, by accident or design, be used on previously natural placements as well.

I'm in awe of Beyer's résumé of hard routes in the Fisher Towers. But not his trenching. On a first ascent, my partners and I strive to leave a route that can be enjoyed by others, without forcing them to drill. A route where we conform to the natural challenge presented by the rock, leaving solid bolts where no placements are to be had. And, fortunately, new lines in this style keep getting put up in the Fisher Towers.

In 1996, with nine ascents of the big Fisher Towers via existing climbs under my belt, I decided to attempt a new route on the enormous west face of the Oracle, with Chip Wilson. I geared up, free-climbed to a ledge 15 off the ground, and placed a Birdbeak. Above was a vast, vertical ocean. I could not bring myself to step up onto that piton. I came down, Chip declined to try, and we walked away.

A year later I returned with Dave Levine. We spent hours staring at the cliff with binoculars from different angles and at different times of day. For a new route to be worth doing, it has to have a low bolt count, and that means the line has to have mostly continuous cracks. After studying the face, we finally saw the full line. This time I stepped up with confidence on the first Birdbeak, placed another, stepped up again, and kept going. Our line, Beaking in Tongues, was a first-ascent dream: We placed bolts at the belays, but otherwise followed seams and cracks for seven independent pitches.

Of course, we have it easier today than Beyer did. In 1989, just as Beyer stopped climbing in the Fishers, John Middendorf's A5 Adventures began selling the Birdbeak. This tiny piton had a nifty drooped-pick design, like a minuscule ice axe. With Birdbeaks (and the more recent Peckers and Tomahawks), previously unusable seams like those on the Oracle were now open for business.

In 2007, Jeremy Aslaksen did the fourth ascent of Beaking in Tongues, 10 years after the first. He reported that the route had held up well. "We couldn't even see where the original placements were, let alone find widened slots," he said.

Aslaksen and Paul Gagner have established most of the recent hard new routes on the big Fisher Towers. Their campaign began on the east side of Kingfisher, with a long sequence of Peckers in a crack system that was mostly hidden by a mud curtain. How many Peckers? Aslaksen recalls, "24? More? Most were kind of A-frame style, when you have two or three teeth into the rock and the base is balanced on a nubbin below. Only good for a bit of a downward pull." Gagner calls Weird Science (A4) his favorite Fisher Towers route "because of how improbable it was, and because it came together with minimal drilling."

In March 2010 they started up a route on the Titan. Gagner, hiking near the tower, pulled a huge boulder onto his foot, crushing his toes. A week later, Aslaksen, at home in Albuquerque, pulled a boulder onto *his* toes. Not until August did the pair reassemble in the Fishers to finish the climb, Gimp Warfare (5.9 A3). In September 2011 they completed Trick of the Tail (5.10+ A3), which meanders up the enormous, heavily corrugated west face of Cottontail. On a roll, a few months later Gagner led the serious first pitch of a new route on the Oracle, working up sloping 5.10 ledges right of Beaking in Tongues to access an excellent crack system. In April 2013 they completed another new line on the Kingfisher, this time on the west face [*see Climbs and Expeditions.*]

All of these routes ranged between A2 and A4. In this context, Palmada's unrepeated, supposedly A6+ route on the Titan was an anomaly. Had a pair of European climbers, under the noses of the locals, found a line that was harder than any existing Fisher Tower climb?

In the spring of 2012, Oju, Peligru! on the Titan was repeated by Richard Jensen, a highly experienced aid climber who also had repeated Beyer's Intifada. He wrote an extensive blog about the experience (*www.conclusivesystems.com/danger/*). Did he tell a tale of struggle and fear, of admiration and respect? Not at all. Jensen suggested a rating of A3, at best, and claimed that Oju, Peligru! was a "completely manufactured 'route,' with virtually every placement requiring drilling."

Jensen found trenched heads of aluminum and lead, and wood dowels stacked against tiny pitons in trenched holes. Unsustainable, unpleasant. Presumably, these are techniques that work well for aid climbs on pocketed Spanish limestone. But could they be transferred successfully to the Titan's blank sandstone? No, they could not.

During his ascent, Jensen made an odd decision. Rather than struggle with the flared holes and rotting fixed heads Palmada had placed, he drilled new bolts alongside them. Adding bolts during a second ascent would normally be regarded as poor style, but Jensen asserted that Palmada and Ollé had been "methodical and calculating," and what he encountered was not "climbing." As such, he felt no obligation to use their placements.

Jensen's blog includes a video of the belay atop Palmada's first pitch, touted by the first-ascent team as an anchor from equalized hooks, followed immediately by hard, serious climbing—thus the proposed A6+ rating. The video shows that the three hooks in question were seated in drilled holes. Palmada's own video shows the rightmost hook being cleaned with multiple blows from a hammer—more solid and secure than the word "hook" usually suggests. Several other placements, perhaps drilled, were used at this belay, and it appears that the placements immediately following this belay were trenched into blank rock, making the seriousness rather contrived. Jensen skipped this belay entirely during his ascent, continuing

[This page] David Palmada and Esther Ollé at the "A6+" belay of Oju, Peligru! *David Palmada*

to an anchor in a good crack 170 feet off the ground. But Jensen's "second ascent" was equally contrived, and did not conform to the challenge left by the first ascent.

In an interview with the magazine *Desnivel*, Palmada said he based his style and rating on what he found on Intifada: "Yeah, Intifada for me is the WAY!" But Intifada had extensive drilling and chiseling, perhaps more than any other route in the Fisher Towers.

What do other Fisher Tower climbers have to say about such tactics? Paul Gagner said, "I've never trenched a head," and that if there are no natural placement options, your only choices were to "drill a hole or to bail." Gagner and Aslaksen did exactly that when the second pitch of a line they attempted on the east side of the Oracle proved to have no crack to follow. They retreated rather than manufacture placements or drill an excessive bolt ladder.

Duane Raleigh, responsible for two new routes on the Titan, both unrepeated, said, "I've only ever nailed or nutted conventionally, or placed a bolt—not counting lasso tosses or hooking with an ice axe, which in my mind is fair." He added, "I've always believed that rivets,

[This page, left] (A) Palmada's first fixed heads on Oju, Peligru! on the Titan. (B) Richard Jensen's bolt, presumably placed for a self-belay anchor. (C) Tomahawk placed by the author with small rock while standing on the ground, leaving him wondering why any of Palmada's placements were needed. [This page, top right] Fixed head on Hot-Parad-Ice. [This page, bottom right] Beak hole pounded into blank rock. *Steve Bartlett (all photos)*

trenching, and any sort of technique that didn't leave a solid, repeatable placement didn't have a place in the Fisher Towers."

WHEN CHIP WILSON AND I REPEATED Hot-Parad-Ice in March, we found it immensely enjoyable. The first pitch, in particular, is a superb, heads-up affair, wandering up a subtle groove for 130 feet. About four or five fixed alumi-heads poked out of tiny, trenched holes. (Since Palmada seldom reached farther than 18 inches between his placements, these were easily bypassed.) The first solid placements are in a tiny dihedral about 50 or 60 feet up. Compared with his route on the Titan, Palmada's second new route in the Fisher Towers was a vast improvement.

But Hot-Parad-Ice was still seriously flawed: It featured Pecker placements in blank rock. I emailed Palmada and asked how he made these holes. He replied: "Where sections are blank, what I do is look for the softer rock, trying various places with a sharp Pecker, and where it starts to sink easily because the rock is not as strong, I finish nailing there."

Is looking for an area of "softer rock" and pounding a Pecker into it a viable part of the game? Aslaksen said, "You're still drilling a hole, but you're using Birdbeaks. A beak's a drill if you whale on it enough times. It's utterly manufactured." For me and, I think, for every other local Fisher Tower first ascensionist of the last 25 years, the line between "artistry and travesty" is defined by whether the rock offers a weakness, a crack or seam, or a pocket—a *placement*.

In the early 1950s, Jerry Gallwas was a pioneer of forging pitons that were harder than the soft-iron versions that had been available for decades. He chose not to make his steel *too* hard. "You want a certain amount of malleability, or else you just destroy the rock," he told me in 2007. Birdbeaks, Peckers, and Tomahawks are no harder than other chrome-moly pitons, but they are designed with such a tiny, sharp tip that they can, sometimes, be pounded directly into desert rock. But this is not "placing" a piton. It's using a piton to drill a hole. If there's a hole, it should be filled with a bolt or rivet.

Climbing in the Fisher Towers is a free-for-all, as it should be. Climbers from Utah, California, Catalonia, Estonia—all over the world—are free to do what they want. But with this freedom comes a responsibility to understand the ethics and expectations of the locals, who have learned to work with the soft sandstone to create fine, sustainable climbs. It pains me to write a critical article like this. If I try to dictate how others should climb, I'm contradicting and denying the very freedom that attracted me to climbing in the first place. And, yet, it pains me even more to see the travesty that is, or was, Oju, Peligru!

In the year 2013, drilling large numbers of holes to create a route—whether by hand or power drill, chisel, or Pecker—is no longer acceptable. Bolt ladders went out of favor in the late 1960s. Trenching with a drill went out of favor in the 1990s. Trenching with Peckers? We can do better. And if we can't, we should walk away.

ABOUT THE AUTHOR
Steve "Crusher" Bartlett has been climbing for nearly 40 years, in the U.K., Europe, Mexico, Canada, and Morocco. His favorite place, by far, is the Southwest desert, where he has climbed about 150 towers, including 30 first ascents. His coffee-table history book Desert Towers *(2010) was a finalist at the Banff Mountain Festival and the Kendal Mountain Festival.*

Joel Peach and George Urioste provided translation assistance with this article.

LIFE ESSENCE

FIVE JOURNEYS TO NORTHWEST CANADA'S VAMPIRE PEAKS

PAT GOODMAN

The de Havilland DHC-2 Beaver floatplane slowly spiraled downward, aiming for a tiny, emerald-green lake. The contrast between spruce trees and glacial ice formed a defining line between the harsh forested wilderness and rugged mountainscape of the Northwest Territories. On touchdown a small but unmistakable message, assembled from duct tape and sleeping bag insulation, became visible on the shoreline: "HELP."

It was early August 1999. Brad Jackson, Nan Darkis, and I had traveled from Colorado to visit the remote Vampire Peaks. We had been inspired by a 1998 *Climbing* magazine article that presented amazing images and promised loads of free climbing potential on 1,000- to 2,500-foot granite walls. Our pilot, Warren LaFave, owner of Kluane Airways, had assured us that our team was only the fourth he had ever flown there. The third team, which he had dropped off just two and a half weeks earlier, was still in the Vamps, and he had not heard a peep from them.

Debris was strewn a hundred feet in either direction from our tie-up on shore. Torn-apart food cans, tattered wrappers, fuel canisters with bite marks, and ripped clothing littered the otherwise serene tundra landscape of dwarf shrubs, sedges, mosses, and lichens. But the climbers were alright. Their unprotected cache by the lake had been ravaged by a grizzly while they were climbing, and they had spent eight days scavenging the remnants for sustenance and searching for the radio that went missing during the incursion. Had our team not showed up, with 12 more days before their scheduled pick-up, those fellas might not have fared too well.

[This page] Hank Jones at sunset on the Fortress during Goodman's second trip to the Vampire Spires. On that trip, in 2003, Jones and Goodman freed Cornerstone (V 5.10 A2) with some variations: You Enjoy Myself (1,800', V 5.12). *Pat Goodman* [Previous page] The Fortress, wreathed in clouds. *Pat Goodman*

The Vampire Peaks, part of Nahanni National Park, are located in the Logan Mountains, a sub-range of the Mackenzie Mountains, summer home of woodland caribou, mountain goats, Dall sheep, and bears. These rugged peaks were shaped by the last ice age, and are some of the highest in the Northwest Territories. Mt. Sir James MacBrien (9,052'), the second-highest summit in the range, is a formidable highpoint at the apex of a long rock ridge forming the Lotus Flower Tower and Parrot Beak in the well-known Cirque of the Unclimbables. Twenty-five miles to the south of the Cirque stands the tallest peak in the Northwest Territories, Mt. Nirvana (9,098'), home to several easy fifth-class routes and a collection of 2,000-foot walls, possibly only having one established route [*AAJ 1966, 2001*]. Fifteen miles northwest of the Cirque are the Vampire Peaks.

Perhaps the biggest attraction in the Vampires has been the stunning collection of granite spires flanking the southern aspect of Mt. Appler (8,569'). Soaring like high-rise buildings, this trio of columns, known as the Vampire Spires, comprises Vampire Spire (990'), the Canine (600'), and the Fortress (1,500'). Each has a distinctive fang-like summit, with the Vamp and the Fortress side by side and the Canine tucked behind. Two miles east of the Spires is the Phoenix, a 2,600-foot wall on the northeastern aspect of a multi-buttressed, unnamed ca 8,530-foot massif. The Vampire Peaks also host half a dozen other impressive granite features, some still unclimbed. Moraine Hill (8,838'), five miles to the south of the Vampire Spires, has an impressive assembly of south-facing walls and at least one established mountaineering route. A mile to the north of the Spires is a big, possibly unclimbed granite peak dubbed "The Warlock" (ca 8,316'), which also has a formidable south-facing big wall. Vague reports suggest many of the prominent peaks with were climbed by fourth-class routes in the early to mid-1900s. The first difficult rock route was recorded by Mike Benge, Jeff Hollenbaugh, and Greg Epperson in 1994, when they made the first ascent of the Vampire Spire via the Infusion (V 5.11 A2+).

My first outing to the Vampires, back in 1999, was blessed with warm, dry weather and yielded several new aid routes as well as the second ascent of Vampire Spire and loads of bouldering. Thus began my fascination with this remote area. The well-featured granite is black, gray, and gold and peppered with profusions of knobs and big feldspar crystals. The cracks tend to be undulating and slightly flared, with a side of grass, though the steeper terrain yields splitter corners and flawless crack systems. This collection of boulders, walls, and jagged peaks became my sanctuary, an alpine climbing haven without the hassle of overseas flights, remote and free from the carnivals of hype and crowding.

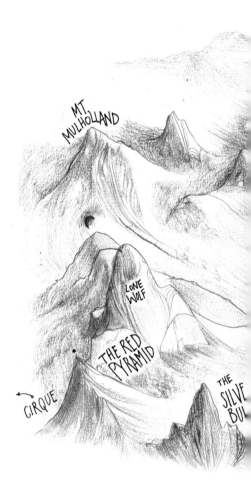

I RETURNED TO THE VAMPIRE SPIRES in August 2003, with Hank Jones, to attempt the first free ascent of the Fortress via the route Cornerstone (V 5.10 A2), first climbed by Matt Childers and Cogie Reed in July 1998. This route follows an incredible series of corners and straight-in cracks that just scream "free me." As with the other two spires, the premier wall on the Fortress is the south face. Five hundred feet of splitter dihedral, a big multi-tiered ledge, 400 feet of even more splitter dihedral, another big ledge, 350 feet of straight-in cracks splitting a headwall, a really big ledge, 250 feet of corners and chimney, and the summit—that's the Cornerstone in a nutshell.

Our first attempt after a rainy, tent-bound week revealed incredibly clean crack climbing and a big unknown: Following features right of the Cornerstone, someone had installed a heavily bolted route up to two-thirds height of the wall. But who? Warren LaFave had assured us that nobody else had flown into the Spires since my previous trip. This "new" line followed an incomplete, five-pitch route started by John Young in 1998, and then climbed several new pitches before joining Cornerstone at the top of pitch seven. The bolt count was approximately 27 (¼-inch Petzl self-drives) with anchors every 25 meters. We later learned Kurt Albert and three other German climbers had paddled from near the Tungsten Mine, following the Little Nahanni (class IV) and South Nahanni rivers to access the Vampire Peaks "by fair means." They spent approximately eight days in the area, establishing this route (VIII+) on what they called Vampire Peak. They then went on to climb the Lotus Flower Tower in the Cirque before

floating 150 miles by the Nahanni out to Blackstone Territorial Park.

Our trip that year was a rough one for weather. Out of 24 days, we spent only five actually rock climbing. But four days before our chopper ride out, the skies cleared and the fluffy white stuff on all the mountaintops quickly began to melt. In a manic, disaster-style, 26-hour effort, we managed to free the Cornerstone with some variations. Our 12-pitch route (You Enjoy Myself, 1,800', V 5.12) followed the original line up fantastic corner systems for six pitches. Then we diverged to the right and climbed a nice, flared crack system to the top of the headwall. For the last pitches, we climbed left of the Cornerstone, skipping a short rappel the first-ascent team had used, and accessed a more straightforward crack system to reach the summit, completing the formation's second ascent and first free climb.

[This page] The Vampire Peaks, as interpreted by Jeremy Collins in his expedition sketch-book. Several of the formations have had different names over the years. *Jeremy Collins*

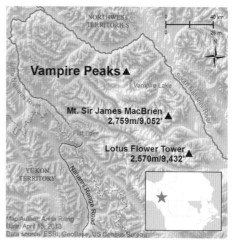

[This page, left] Scoping the approach down the Little Nahanni River. *James Q Martin*
[This page, map] The Vampire Peaks are not far from the relatively popular Cirque of the Unclimbables. *Anna Riling*

NOT EVEN A FULL YEAR PASSED before Hank and I were 30 hours deep into the northbound ramble, bound again for Vampire granite. With at least that many hours still to drive, we got word that a group of three from Flagstaff also was planning a trip to the Vamps. Nothing worse than feeling like somebody's going to swipe your project, but our stoke was undampened. We met the other group at Kluane Airways' plush Inconnu Lodge and shared the cost of the helicopter ride into the Vamps. They were planning an aid climb, and Hank and I had free-climbing ambitions, and so our two groups coexisted harmoniously in this alpine haven.

This time our goal was the first free ascents of the Vampire Spire and the Phoenix—the two proudest features in the area still without free climbs. We thought was the best-looking contender for a classic free route on Vampire Spire followed the tallest stretch of wall; Hank and I dubbed it the Coffin, after the shape of a large alcove at two-thirds height. We had climbed the first few pitches in the rain the year before while working a thin nailing route. (The three climbers from Flagstaff finished this aid route, calling it Nosferatu, V 5.9 A2+.) On the Coffin, after a couple of hundred feet, straight-in cracks funneled into a big shaft, barely narrow enough to stem across, for several pitches. Mixed crack and face climbing then led toward a big roof. Up to this point, our route had followed good, dry rock with difficulties around 5.11+. The pitch leading to the roof was to die for—flared fingers in a steep corner that slowly opened up into what looked to be 5.12 liebacking—but it was soaked. After aiding up to the roof through the cold wetness, I could see a shimmer of blue ice back in the bowels, loads of it, the cold heart of a Vampire. A "fun" 5.11 fist folly out the left side of the roof brought us to two wide crack pitches and the summit. The Coffin (310m, V 5.11 A2) will have to wait for hell to warm over for a free ascent.

With less than a week left in camp, the two of us searched for an alternative free line up the spire. Our attention turned to a finger-sized splitter 100 feet to the left of the Coffin's initial pitches. This crack went up 210 feet to a ledge, then wandered up less than vertical terrain, before moving around to the north side of the spire for several hundred feet. On these last pitches we found an incredible overhanging fist crack followed by a steep offwidth—lucky for us, a hidden jug rail inside the maw kept this stretch under 5.12. The glory pitch was a 5.9 corner crack laser-cut by God and broken only by the spike of the Vampire's pointed summit. We named our route Dark Side (1,000', IV 5.11+); this marked the first free ascent and the first one-day ascent of the Vampire Spire.

A few years passed, and my incomplete project to do the first free ascents of the three most prominent features in the Vampire Peaks gnawed at me. Another NWT vacation was in order. At this point, coughing up another $7,000 to go "free" climbing in the wet, albeit beautiful, north country was becoming a little outrageous, considering it costs about the same to visit the Charakusa Valley in Pakistan. But I needed another dose of Vampire tranquility.

In the interest of cutting costs, I investigated the approach used by the Germans. The paddle-verus-chopper savings are huge if you have the time, and the added adventure is priceless. It seemed the best strategy would be to paddle/hike in, then hike/fly out. You could save more and not use any air support by following the South Nahanni out to Blackstone, as the Germans did, but the added river time and car shuttle costs are considerable. In 2006, once again, Hank and I stuffed into the cab of his red truck. In the back, our familiar tools for adventure were tucked away in haul bags and duffels, along with one new addition: a raft.

The Little Nahanni starts from Flat Lakes and is accessible by truck via the Nahanni

[This page] Pat Goodman bouldering the Caribou Crack, near the Phoenix Wall. The new route Phreenix climbs the prominent buttress on the left. *James Q Martin*

Range Road. Its cold waters begin as a shallow, 50-foot-wide creek meandering around small islands and oxbows, and through tight forests of stunted spruce and willow. The mountains are rugged, with loose and variegated sedimentary layers of sandstone and limestone folded into colorful, mineral-rich striations. After several miles, tributaries raise the volume and the bumper-car ride turns into class IV whitewater. Big drops and tight wave trains through narrow canyons make up at least a third of the 50-mile float trip. Once the clear, fast water converges with the slower, dark green water of the South Nahanni, the game goes from paddling for life in the torrents to paddling for warmth and speed in the flats. Four days on the water gets one to a gravel bar by the drainage below the Vamps. Hiking from the river is no easy task; tight forests lead to shrubbery and slick, tundra-covered talus; it takes two days to hike about eight miles up the steep drainage to Vampire Lake and the northern terminus of Moraine Hill Glacier.

It was a bad season in 2006. Incessant drizzle soaked the 2,600-foot wall of the Phoenix. Above the wall, a snow- and ice-covered ridgeline guarded what we believed to be a virgin summit. On a pleasant day we attempted the northwest rib of the mountain in a desperate attempt to summit the peak. We climbed loose 5.8 for 1,800 feet before being stymied by ice-covered rock. The terrain we'd covered to that point was undesirable for retreat, and to the north and the south the ridge dropped a thousand vertical feet into unknown and unpleasant territory. With our ropes uncoiled, nearly committed to an epic rappel from off the north side, we heard a faint hum. Slowly growing in magnitude, the hum became a whirlwind of helicopter blades and airflow. Mr. LaFave was in the house—he buzzed by close enough for us to make eye contact, and Hank dismissively waved him in for a landing. LaFave soared away, out of sight, and we chuckled at the prospect of jumping from our tiny perch into the small aircraft. Moments later, with no warning, the blast from circling helicopter blades about blew me over. A skid bounced

[This page] Pat Goodman leading the sixth pitch of the Phreenix. *James Q Martin*

around on the rock's edge, the door popped open, and Warren gestured for us to "get the fuck in!" And so ended our first Phoenix adventure, with no summit and thus no conclusion.

IN 2012, WITH THE HELP from the Copp/Dash Inspire Award, Jeff Achey, Jeremy Collins, James Q Martin, and I laid plans for another go at the Phoenix. Jeff, Q, and I paddled in. We worked it out so Jeremy would helicopter in with our remaining gear and meet us in base camp below the Phoenix, four days after we left Flat Lake; these tactics kept us light on the river and saved us from the grueling hike.

The Phoenix had been named in 1998 by Matt Childers, Harrison Shull, and John Young, the first team to climb the huge northeast face. They followed a direct line up the steepest part of the golden wall and called their route Freebird (VI 5.10 A2+). Since then Tyler Stracker and Matt Christie had added an incomplete line right of Freebird, following somewhat incipient features for four to five pitches before gaining splitter cracks and corners that flow to the top— they made it up nine, very long pitches before being thwarted by bad weather, and called their line After School Special (A.S.S.), V 5.10+ A2+. In 2004, Jasmin Caton and Amelia Patterson climbed A.S.S. up to Smurfagetti Ledge, a terraced ledge system, and then joined Freebird; they were forced to retreat several hundred feet from the top, and they called their variation Wallflowers (VI 5.10 A2).

I'd seen enough of the Phoenix to know that *the* free line would loosely follow A.S.S. up the proudest part of the wall, so we focused our attention there. Pitch four proved to be the headiest section, after which we left A.S.S and followed our noses up virgin rock, uncovering several fantastic crack climbing pitches. In four days we climbed seven pitches, freeing them all, and we placed only one protection bolt. Two days of drizzle forced a rest day, followed by a day of hauling supplies up fixed lines to our highpoint.

We rejoined A.S.S. on our eighth pitch, which involved a delicate 5.11 traverse into "Yo

[This page] Goodman on pitch seven, the Dixie Crystal Corner overhead. *James Q Martin*

Momma's Got a Wide Crack"—a rope-stretching odyssey of five-inch bliss, made casual by big features inside the crack. That dropped us off at a nice, flat ledge below the five-star, 5.10+ "Dixie Crystal Corner" pitch: 200 feet of perfectly cut, 90-degree corner. A nondescript 5.8 section brought us to Smurfagetti Ledge, where we spent a cold, wet night. In late August the nights last only five hours but get minutes shorter with each passing day.

Above our bivy we climbed up and right, following a steep, flared hand crack (5.11-) into a big, right-facing dihedral feature. We followed the dihedral for a long pitch, passing the A.S.S. highpoint, and then climbed virgin terrain into some wild chimneys. At the top of pitch 14 we joined Freebird and reached the Wallflowers highpoint. The remaining four pitches followed convoluted chimneys and corners with difficulties around mid-5.10. At the top of the wall we found a small cairn containing a register signed by the Childers party. Our entry was the second—we had successfully free-climbed the wall, onsighting all but three pitches out of 18, with our efforts spread out over six days. Every pitch was led and followed free. We used fixed lines to the top of pitch seven before committing to the wall.

Our next objective lay approximately a quarter-mile away and at least 1,000 feet higher: the real summit. What in years past had been an icy snowfield was on that day a somewhat casual romp up dry ridgeline, with very little snow travel. We stashed the pointless ice gear we had carried up the wall and cruised up the ridge to make the peak's first recorded ascent. After high-fives and an all-night rap session, we got back to camp around 7 a.m., 46 hours after leaving. The Phreenix (VI 5.11) is by no means a cutting-edge free climb, but without a doubt this rig is a modern-day classic.

I do not know who named the Vampire Peaks, but to me the name sparks a feeling of mystery and enigma. During the second ascent of Vampire Spire, I distinctly heard an ensemble of "voices" in my head, resounding like ballroom chatter for well over 15 hours. At first I attributed this to dehydration, but both of my companions later spoke of experiencing the same phenomenon. Maybe it was something else. All great mountain ranges have a spirit. In the Vamps it's born from supernatural legends of vanishing tribes and dismembered prospectors, from nearby place names like Deadmen Valley and Headless Creek, and from the ghostly mist that wreathes granite spires rising unexpectedly out of a land of rivers and lush forests. It's that spirit that sets the Vampires apart from any other climbing destination on Earth—and that keeps calling me back.

SUMMARY

An account of five expeditions to the Vampire Peaks in Northwest Territories, Canada, culminating in the first free ascents of Vampire Spire, the Fortress, and, in 2012, the Phoenix Wall. Jeff Achey, Jeremy Collins, Pat Goodman, and James Q Martin climbed the Phreenix (VI 5.11, 18 pitches) and summited the previously unclimbed Peak ca 8,350' in August 2012. 🔍

ABOUT THE AUTHOR
Pat Goodman, 35, developed his obsessive appetite for vertical adventure on the crumbling flanks of Shiprock, near his hometown of Farmington, New Mexico, at age 16. Since then he has sampled the vertical wilds of China, India, Pakistan, Venezuela, Canada, Mexico, and Europe. He owns a hardwood flooring business in Fayetteville, West Virginia.

HIMJUNG STYLE

THE FIRST ASCENT OF A REMOTE 7,000-METER PEAK IN NEPAL

AHN CHI-YOUNG

Himjung is located north of Annapurna and Manaslu in the Peri Himal range, and is nestled between Himlung Himal and the Nemjung peaks, surrounded by numerous 6,000-meter peaks with large glaciers and difficult approaches. Despite having been opened by the Nepali government in 2002, the 7,092-meter peak has been somewhat mysterious until now, not just to the Korean alpine community, but to the alpine world in general.

We had little information on how to reach the Himjung base camp, and simply relied on our map of the region and the locals of nearby Phugaon village to find our way. The journey from Kathmandu took 23 days. From the village of Besisahar, we hired a seven-donkey caravan to carry our 450 kilograms of gear and supplies. Base camp was roughly 16 kilometers straight up the Pangri Glacier. When we arrived on September 29, we were able to find traces of what appeared to be the base camps of two Japanese expeditions led by Osamu Tanabe (Gyajikang, *AAJ 1995*, and Nemjung, *AAJ 2010*). Here, Kim Chang-ho and I pitched our tents.

Measuring a direct line on our map, Himjung's southwest face appeared to be roughly eight kilometers from base camp; however, negotiating the moraine, glacial terrain, and the enormous, crevasse-laden ice plateau below Himjung and Nemjung added about four kilometers to the approach.

On October 4, we went out to inspect the wall and carry a load of gear and provisions up to advanced base camp. After passing through about three hours worth of moraine and lower glacier terrain, a 150-meter, boulder-filled couloir, and then more glacial terrain, we reached the midsection of the main glacier. We continued up the glacier to get a better view of our route. On this day, the weather was good, but

[This page] Ahn Chi-young leading steep rock on the second pitch of Himjung's southwest face. *Kim Chang-ho*

sharp winds above smeared thin clouds across the sky, which seemed to be a sure sign of the Himalayan jet stream and winter season to come.

At 4 p.m. we were still slowly making our way through the rough confines of moraine and crevassed glacier. Realizing it would still take us much more time to reach the foot of the mountain, we decided to pitch our two-man tent for the night, using a shovel and ice axes to cut out a site among the fragmented rock and ice. The next day, October 5, we carefully crossed over jumbled and dizzying crevasses to advance to the upper section of the glacier. After two more hours of scrambling through a large snow basin, we probed the area where we would commence our climb, pitched the tent, and headed all the way back down to base camp.

Up until now things had more or less gone as planned. However, our intended route—up to the col between Himjung and Nemjung, then up the southwest ridge and southwest face to the summit and back the same way—now seemed much less efficient and safe than we'd hoped, because of a long row of rock pinnacles along the southwest ridge. Instead we opted for a more direct route up the southwest face.

After four days of rest at base camp, on October 9 we headed back up. This time it took us only a day to reach our bivy site (6,050m), where we packed up the two-man tent for the climb and replaced it with a three-man tent. We carefully chose our gear for the route, which included a 7mm, 50-meter Dyneema rope and a 6mm, 50-meter Kevlar rope. We planned to start climbing in the dark hours of morning, but that night the weather was not promising, with wind and snow throughout. Clouds and fog made visibility difficult at best, and we decided to wait things out inside our tent.

We were up by 10 the following morning, and the weather seemed to have cleared a

bit. As we prepared our gear we listened for falling rocks, trying to figure out the safest line. Finally the fog lifted enough that we could climb. "Let's get on with it!" we shouted. The lower section of Himjung's southwest face is mostly rock, and I began climbing with a tense body and racing heart, but gradually I regained my normal climbing composure and left the initial onslaught of emotions behind. The cracks were jammed with ice and snow, which made placing pro difficult. During our third pitch the fog returned, and as the visibility narrowed the difficulty of the climbing increased. By 2 p.m., frustrated but unable to continue, we retreated to our bivy site.

On October 11 we were up by 5, stirring up some Korean bean paste with veggies, yak meat, and alpha-meal protein drink. After reorganizing our gear to reduce even more volume and weight, we started out again, hoping for better weather. We zigzagged across the glacier basin to the wall, where we stepped into our crampons and I headed up again.

Although the average angle of the wall was about 80°, there were several overhangs to pass, but this time we found much better protection, using a lot of knifeblades and small cams. At one section, a wall of thin, fragile ice forced us left onto mixed ground. Occasional brief volleys of whizzing rocks passed by overhead, but the weather was improving. I had to sweep a lot of snow off the rock to find the right holds, and the gradual soaking of my gloves had become a worry, but luckily this was only a marginal concern in the end.

On the fourth pitch we encountered blue ice that was as hard as the front points we struggled to punch into it. This section ran to the end of the sixth pitch, and knowing it could rob us of an enormous amount of strength and energy, we tried to climb quickly. We had to use a lot of ice screws because we could not get them in deep enough, and we made our belay

anchors in a rock wall on the left. Once we overcame this testy section of ice, we sped through the seventh pitch of mixed hard snow and rock, and then continued up a slope of hard snow. The wall was so calm and silent we could only hear the sounds of our breathing and the echoes of hammer on pitons.

A large cornice and wall of black and ash-gray rock wall guarded the way to the summit ridge. We planned to take a line that passed to the right of the cornice and followed hard snow up the middle of the rock wall. On the 13th pitch, only about a 60° slope, I heard the sound of falling rock from far above and peeked up to see a huge

[This page] Peaks above the Pangri Glacier. (A) Himlung Himal (7,126m), northwest ridge (Japanese route, 1992). (B) Himjung (7,092m), southwest face (Korean route, 2012). (C) Nemjung (7,140m), west face (Japanese route, 2009). *Kim Chang-ho*

boulder headed straight for me. As the boulder hit the face above and fractured into pieces, I scurried in a panic about eight meters to my left to find some semblance of shelter and stuck my face into the wall, just as five half-body-size chunks whizzed by on both sides. An onslaught of smaller rocks pelted me and my pack, impossible to dodge. When the rope was struck, I felt certain it would yank me off the face. Afterward, I couldn't believe I was alive and essentially unharmed. I looked down at Chang-ho, who had been able to take shelter behind rocks at the anchor. "Are you okay?" I asked. He replied with a simple, "Yes," and we started climbing again with no need to say any more.

The wind blew, but now the skies were clear. To reduce our weight for this climb, we'd left our radios at the bivy site and we had to shout our signals. At times we used rope signals or just sensed from experience what the other person was doing.

We had planned to set camp just below a large cornice in the middle of the main wall; however the angle was very steep, and cutting out a platform would have been too exhausting and time consuming. We continued around to the right of the cornice, across an ice wall, and up an ice column to reach the cornice top, hoping to pitch camp there, but the position was not safe and so we continued upward.

Above the 14th pitch, Chang-ho took over the lead, and we simul-climbed about 300 meters above the cornice, until we spotted a long, horizontal crevasse. Here, at 6,770 meters, we pitched our two-man tent in a 1.5-meter-high cave. We were able to anchor our tent to four snow pickets and stomp down snow for a platform, but we couldn't pitch the tent too deeply because of the unknown void inside the cave. There was only room for one person outside the tent, and we had to stay constantly attentive so as to not fall. A few snow showers slid our way along with a few falling rocks, but this site protected us very well. We melted icicles from the ceiling of the cave for water and could finally eat. The panoramic view included Manaslu, Annapurna, and Dhaulagiri, and gazing up the face we could see a faint

[This page, top] Snow climbing on the upper southwest face. *Kim Chang-ho* [This page, bottom] Ahn leads the steep first pitch of the route. *Kim Chang-ho*

indication of a saddle in the ridgeline.

The sun warmed our tent in late afternoon, and we soothed our exhausted bodies with a one-hour nap. Chang-ho and I cooked our freeze-dried rice and yak meat with Korean bean paste, and prepared ourselves for the night as the temperatures plunged. With a single sleeping bag to share, we shivered in discomfort as the winds raged outside and frost lined the thin tent walls. We were committed to each other, our single sleeping bag, and our will. We tried to sleep, curled up back to back to feed off each other's warmth, but to no avail. At 5 a.m., we boiled a basic soup and split a chocolate bar for breakfast. Space was tight, so Chang-ho went outside to gear up while I got dressed piece by piece inside.

By six o'clock we were off, with Chang-ho leading as we simul-climbed 25 meters apart. The dawn was bright, but no sunlight reached us yet, and it was extremely cold. For about 30 minutes I felt a nasty freezing pain in my left hand, and I put on a heavier glove only for that hand. I could hear Chang-ho's heavy breathing just ahead. From the ridge stretching up to the summit we could look past Himlung Himal to Ratna Chuli (7,128m) and other Himalayan peaks spread out to the north. Wind blew down the mountain into our faces. Just one pitch before the summit, we drank some warm water and divided another chocolate bar to eat.

Chang-ho handed the lead to me and prepared for the final belay. I postholed up to the summit, taking huge breaths, and finally straddled the knife-ridge top at 9:05 a.m. I hammered my axe into the summit snow and belayed Chang-ho up, and we cheered and embraced like little kids.

Summary

First ascent of Himjung (7,092m) by Ahn Chi-young and Kim Chang-ho (South Korea) via the southwest face, October 11-13, 2012. The difficulties were rated 5.10+ WI4 M6. They descended by the same route.

About the Climbers

Ahn Chi-young began his Himalayan climbing with the first ascent of the southwest face of Lobuje West (6,145m) in Nepal in 2005. A climbing instructor and guide, he has since joined many expeditions. Earlier in 2012 he climbed a new route on Teke-Tor in Kyrgyzstan with members of the Corean Alpine Club (see report elsewhere in this AAJ.) Kim Chang-ho has climbed new routes in the Hindu Kush, Karakoram, and Himalaya, and has summited 13 of the 8,000-meter peaks without the aid of oxygen. He is the director of the Korean Student Alpine Federation and Seoul City University Alpine Club. For their first ascent of Himjung, Ahn and Kim received the seventh annual Asian Piolet d'Or.

Translated from Korean by Peter Jensen-Choi.

[This page] A preclimb puja ceremony for Kim Chang-ho (left) and Ahn Chi-young at base camp. *Kim Chang-ho*

RECON:
REVELATIONS

GREAT OBJECTIVES IN ALASKA'S
FORGOTTEN MOUNTAINS

CLINT HELANDER

Deep in the southwest corner of Alaska, the Revelation Mountains, like their biblical namesake, comprise the final chapter of the Alaska Range. These magnificent peaks are the last major folds of earth to rise above the western lowlands that stretch for hundreds of miles to the Bering Sea. Unlike most of the Alaska Range, the Revelations are entirely hidden from any road or city.

This seldom-visited corner of Alaska holds only whispers of history and still offers truly exploratory alpine climbing. The few who have ventured to the Revelations have left with an experience that marks a major milestone in their lives.

GEOGRAPHY

LIKE THE KICHATNA SPIRES 70 miles northeast, some Revelation peaks boast 3,000- to 4,500-foot granite walls, but these are tamed by more veins of ice and passages of snow. Most peaks resemble larger versions of the north and central Cascades in Washington state—the Enchantments on mega-steroids. Storms bred in the Gulf of Alaska hit the Revelations first and with little warning. Large low-pressure systems may mire over the range, bringing long periods of horrendous winds and heavy precipitation. On the rare clear and windless day, the Revelations rival any of Alaska's mightier alpine playgrounds.

[Previous page] Looking southwest from Apocalypse, past Jason Stuckey, to the head of the Revelation Glacier. At left: Golgotha (8,940'). Center: Hydra (ca 7,800'). Right: Angel (9,265') *Clint Helander* **[This page]** Hesperus (9,828') from Apocalypse. *Clint Helander*

Etched by the Big River to the north, the Stony River to the east, and the Swift River to the south, the Revelations contain 13 peaks over 9,000 feet and more than 35 peaks over 8,000 feet. Rock quality ranges from superb crystalline granite to mile-high mounds of frozen dirt.

The Revelations' highest peak is 9,828-foot Mt. Hesperus. Rising more than 7,000 feet from the Big River, this "Matterhorn of Alaska" is the northernmost peak in the main spine of the Revelations. During an attempt on the mountain in 1981, Fred Beckey found "snow and rock conditions intolerable" (*AAJ 1983*). The mountain has only been climbed once.

Where Hesperus resembles a 7,000-foot cairn of decomposing shale, with pockets of pale

[This page, map] A. Hesperus B. Apocalypse C. Dike Peak (unclimbed) D. Pyramid Peak (unclimbed) E. Four Horsemen F. Century G. Sentry H. Golgotha I. Hydra J. Angel K. Seraph (unclimbed) L. Vanishing Pinnacle M. Sylph N. Cherub O. South Buttress P. Patmos Q. Babel Tower (8,365', unclimbed). R. Exodus S. Medusa T. Ice Pyramid U. Mausolus V. Pirate Peak W. Peak 9,304' (unclimbed) X. Jezebel Y. Titanic Z. Peak 9,076' SLO: Hartman Glacier, area of 2012 Slovenian expediton (see Climbs and Expeditions). *Anna Riling.*

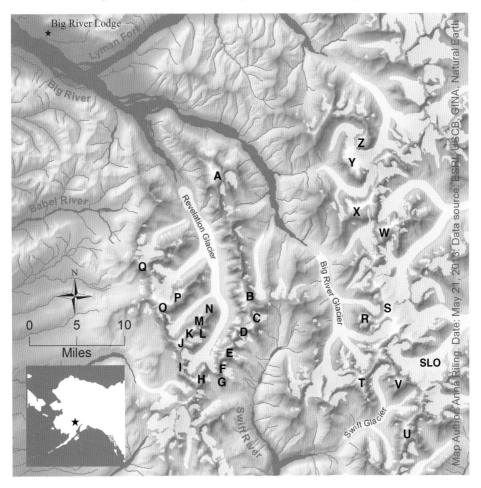

granite slabs, rock quality improves dramatically further south, where a line of wild, unnamed 7,000- and 8,000-foot peaks rises and falls in steady rhythm. These summits feature stunning xenoliths of quartz sandwiched between layers of fractured granodiorite. Large dikes cut down many of these peaks, often sporting enticing Ham and Eggs–style routes waiting to be plucked. The Apocalypse (9,345') holds numerous 3,000-plus-foot granite walls supporting the mountain's snowy crown. Peaks encompassing the rapidly receding, half-mile-wide Revelation Glacier, like the Angel (9,260'), Golgotha (8,940'), and the Four Horsemen (8,600'), contain the range's major pockets of immaculate granite.

East of the main spine, significant mountains are separated by expansive glaciers. Among the most inspiring are the Ice Pyramid (9,250'), Mt. Mausolus (9,170'), and Pirate Peak (9,005'). All of these have seen only a single ascent and contain some of the finest rock and ice lines in the range. The Ice Pyramid's southwest ridge is reminiscent of the southwest ridge of Peak 11,300 in the Central Alaska Range. The Mausoleum (*AAJ 2012*) on Mausolus' 4,500-foot west face contains more than 2,500 feet of continuous technical ice in a narrow slot between alluring and unclimbed granite buttresses. To the northeast, a group of massive 9,000' peaks rises above the Big River. Several have been ascended from the north, but their impressive southern faces remain untouched.

Many summits are blocked by ridgelines stacked with seemingly impassible gendarmes and bomb-bay voids. Sinuous couloirs occasionally funnel down otherwise sheer rock faces. There has been limited activity by world-class skiers, but low snow volume in the Revelations favors technical alpine routes. Select peaks have big-wall climbing possibilities.

HISTORY

THE REVELATIONS WERE FIRST EXPLORED in 1967 by David Roberts and fellow Harvard Mountaineering Club members George and Rick Millikan, Matt Hale, and Ned Fetcher. Art Davidson, who was still recovering from frostbite after making the first winter ascent of Denali, rounded out the crew. The team made six serious attempts on the south ridge of the Angel, but atrocious bouts of wind and freezing rain drove them to the verge of hypothermia, defeating their efforts again and again. "During that summer," Roberts wrote in a 2011 *Climbing* magazine article, "we endured the most fiendish weather I would encounter on 13 Alaskan expeditions."

Various team members climbed and named many peaks during their astonishing 52-day expedition (*AAJ 1968*), but none succeeded in climbing the Angel. On one of the final days, Hale and Roberts climbed to their highpoint in record time, intending only to retrieve the final scraps of gear left on the route. The siren summit pulled them higher than they had ever reached on any attempt. With only one ice axe, and no crampons or bivy gear, they were unprepared for a full-on summit bid. With anguishing reluctance, they descended on that perfect day when the summit was within their grasp.

The Revelations went unvisited by climbers for nearly 15 years. True to form, Fred Beckey caught wind of the area and attempted Hesperus in 1981. Deterred by poor rock quality, he set his sights on the craggy ice and rock peaks several miles to the east. "Facing us was a major granite rock wall, a climbing opportunity we did not have the time to undertake," he wrote in the *AAJ*. Navigating around the base of the south face, they made Mt. Titanic's (9,300+') first ascent via a snow and ice route on the east face. In 1981, Pete Sennhauser and

[This page, top] The unclimbed southeast faces of the North Horseman (ca 8,400 feet, left) and Pyramid Peak (8,572 feet, behind right), showing potential for good rock climbs. Three of the Four Horsemen have been climbed. The North Horseman has not. *Clint Helander* [This page, right] The 3,400-foot west face of unclimbed Pyramid Peak. The author made two attempts on the obvious ice line but was stopped by overhanging snow mushrooms. A massive WI6 pillar hangs 2,000 feet up the route. *Clint Helander*

Janet Smalley climbed Jezebel (9,620'), the range's second tallest peak. In 1983, Dick Flaharty of Fairbanks and friends spent 10 days on the central wall of Apocalypse, making it 1,500 feet up before encountering a band of poor rock.

On their third attempt, via three different routes, Alaskans Karl Swanson and Stephen Spalding, and New Zealander Justin Lesueur, made the first and only ascent of Hesperus in 1985 (*AAJ 1986*). That same year, Greg Collins, Tom Walter, and friends quietly amassed a handful of bold and prolific first ascents at the head of the Revelation Glacier. Among those was the Angel, via a difficult route on the southeast buttress that required several pitches of challenging rock climbing. Their ascent went unreported for several years (*AAJ 1988*). There are unconfirmed tales that a second team climbed their same route, thinking they were making the Angel's first ascent. Rumors say they found a rappel sling high on the route and were more than a little displeased. Further details are lacking. Such is the mystique of the Revelation Mountains.

The range lay mostly dormant for the next decade. Sporadic accounts of good climbing and poor weather can be found in the *AAJ* through the early 2000s. But even though every other range in Alaska saw frequent activity during this time, somehow the Revelations stayed largely off the climbing radar.

Between 2008 and 2013, the author made yearly expeditions to the Revelations, claiming five first ascents of mountains and several other routes on seldom-explored peaks. In that time only one other climbing team has visited the range (*see Climbs and Expeditions*).

While many of the most prominent peaks have now been climbed, few have seen second ascents. Many obvious lines on shorter yet still incredible peaks have yet to be explored. Dozens of 8,000-foot peaks have never been attempted.

[This page, top] The unclimbed north face of Golgotha, seen from the Angel during the first complete ascent of the Angel's south ridge, the route attempted six times by David Roberts and party in 1967. *Clint Helander* [This page, bottom] The 3,400-foot east face of Golgotha. Clint Helander and Ben Trocki attempted the direct route up an ice couloir splitting the face in 2012, but were driven off by spindrift. Instead, they completed the first ascent of the 8,940-foot peak via the ice ramp to the southeast face on the left. *Clint Helander*

WHEN TO CLIMB

THE BEST TIMES TO CLIMB in the Revelations are from mid-March through July. Before mid-March, it is not uncommon to see temperatures remain well below –40°F. Sometime between late March and early April, the jet stream shifts and a noticeable temperature change occurs. Combined with the increasingly long days (nearly 18 hours of usable light in early April), this makes for very climbable weather in shaded gullies where ice is prevalent. March through April usually has long periods of high pressure.

After mid-April, most steep ice chutes and narrow couloirs become gutters that scream with rockfall and run with wet slush avalanches. By mid-May, the weather is warm enough to experience fully enjoyable rock climbing. By June and July, most of the snow is gone and the warmer temperatures bring inconsistent weather. Long periods of wind and precipitation can be expected. That said, midsummer conditions can be phenomenal.

GETTING THERE

GETTING TO THE REVELATIONS is neither easy nor cheap. As of 2013, the average rate per person is between $900 and $1,300 from Anchorage or Talkeetna. The two best options for flights in to the Revelations are Rob Jones of R&R Guide Services in Anchorage, and Talkeetna Air Taxi several hours north. Jones flies straight to the Revelations from Anchorage and has a tremendous lodge, the Big River Lodge, within sight of Mt. Hesperus. Even if he cannot fly you in to the mountains, he can almost always access his lodge and watch the weather from there. As a pilot, he knows the range better than anyone. If flying with Jones, it is an easy and incredibly enjoyable (not to mention cheaper) walk or ski from base camp on any of the glaciers to his lodge. Leave the heavy gear on the glacier for Jones to pick up, and casually trek out in one or two days. Walking the 18 to 35 miles to the mountains from his lodge with food and gear would be less enjoyable. Talkeetna Air Taxi has bigger airplanes, but is farther from the Revelations, which could make it harder to predict local weather and modify plans. If going with more than two people, Talkeetna Air Taxi is the best bet.

Climate change is rapidly impacting the narrow glaciers in the Revelations. The overall volume of ice on many glaciers, including the Revelation Glacier, is steadily decreasing. More and more large boulders are strewn over the ice, limiting potential landing areas. Likewise, melt-water channels seem to run lateral to the glacier in many areas, making late-season landings on bare ice increasingly problematic. Landings on most glaciers in all seasons are still possible, but conditions are likely to change more in the coming decades. Numerous river bars facilitate late-season landings by small planes equipped with tundra tires, but this may increase the approach distance and difficulty for certain objectives. Helicopter landings are allowed in the area, but the flight from either Anchorage or Talkeetna would be exorbitant.

While the Revelations lack the massive expanse of the central Alaska Range, solitude is nearly guaranteed and adventure is out there. This remote and wild range inspires unparalleled possibilities for new cutting-edge climbs as well as modern classics. A chance for true exploration and a direct confrontation with untamed wilderness promises to exist in this beautiful corner of Alaska for years to come. Those willing to embrace the mysterious spirit of the Revelations will find it well worth the journey.

ABOUT THE AUTHOR
Clint Helander, 28, migrated to Anchorage from Seattle when he was 18, and his passion for climbing began with friends and mentors at the University of Alaska Outdoor Club. He has made six expeditions to the Revelation Mountains, most recently the first ascent of Apocalypse with Jason Stuckey in April 2013.

[Previous page, top] The west face of Apocalypse. The first ascent of the peak in April 2013 (A Cold Day in Hell, 4,400', AI5, Helander-Stuckey) followed a partially hidden ice line in right center. In 1983, a team climbed 1,500 feet up the central rock buttress. In 1985, Karl Swanson attempted to solo the ice line left of the buttress, reaching the upper snowfield. [Previous page, bottom] Mt. Hesperus has only been climbed once, via the ca 7,000-foot west face, seen here from Rob Jones' lodge. [This page, top left] West face of unclimbed 7,000' peak between Hesperus and Apocalypse, with ca 3,000 feet of relief. [This page, top right] The 4,000-foot east face of South Buttress (9,345'). This beautiful peak has excellent granite and has seen only one ascent, via a couloir on the south face. [This page, bottom] Although Hesperus is known for rotten rock, ice lines may offer possibilities. Shown here: the unclimbed northeast face (at least 5,000 feet). *All photos: Clint Helander*

[This page, top] Peak 8,301', an attractive, unclimbed snow and ice peak at the head of the Swift Glacier, near Mt. Mausolus. The vertical relief of this face is about 2,800 feet. *Clint Helander* [This page, bottom] The 3,000-foot-plus southwest face of unclimbed Peak 9,304', east of the Big River Glacier. *Clint Helander*

[This page, top] The ca 3,600-foot northwest face of Jezebel (9,650'), the Grandes Jorasses of Alaska. This peak has seen two ascents, one via the Ice Schooner route, near the left skyline (*AAJ 2001*) and the first ascent by a couloir on the southeast face (*AAJ 1982*). *Clint Helander* [This page, bottom] The unclimbed, ca 3,700-foot north face of Titanic (ca 9,300'). Fred Beckey and team made the peak's only ascent in 1981 via the east face. *Clint Helander*

CLIMBS AND EXPEDITIONS

2013

UNITED STATES—LOWER 48

WASHINGTON

NORTH CASCADES

Big Kangaroo, south face, Walkabout. In winter of 2004, the Big Kangaroo wall was burned into my memory. The golden, sheer, 850' face is not like any other wall in this area. The glacier-sculpted southern cirque had left a broad cathedral-like remnant—the central wall as the main prize. Until now, the plumb line contained only a history of ungratified desires and few attempts. The first 600' consists of either vertical or overhanging rock guarded by crackless, monolithic granite, seams that lead to nowhere, and large roofs.

In August 2012, I rallied Mike Pond, Matt VanBein, David Elder, and Jon Schrock for an attempt. The complete ascent would take three days and multiple combinations from our group.

We established the first two pitches on day one. Mike led a fabulous splitter layback off the deck, and I competed a pitch involving tensioning and seven bolts to reach the main crack (A1), which we later freed at 5.11. On day two, Jon lead a heady pitch with bird beaks, hooks, and tipped-out cams to the base of the large roof system (175', A2), which we coined the Kangaroofs. From here, Jon and I tried to pendulum right, but the cracks turned to seams, and we failed on that go.

On day three, Jon, Dave, and I pulled our ropes and started fresh with a clear vision of where the line needed to go; we saw no need for the drill above the roofs. Jon and I re-led pitches one through three to the high point. Dave took the fourth pitch, ascending a corner in the roof. With 400' of air below him, he pulled two RPs and whipped into space but rallied to finish a brilliant lead (A2). I aided out the next roof (A2) only to blow a placement as well, fall past the belay, and core-shot the rope. At dusk, Dave and I finally finished the lower wall.

Above, the upper wall would break down to free climbing. The remaining cracks, dihedrals,

---

[Previous spread] Brad Wilson leading pitch one on the first free ascent of Undertow (IV 5.11+), Black Wall, Mt. Evans, Colorado. See page 142 for the report. *John Lloyd*

and chimneys went slow but steady, and we topped out the wall at 2 a.m. on August 19. Not seeing a clear way off the summit, we spooned at an open bivy on coiled ropes at ca 8,300' and descended the Beckey-Tate in the morning.

Our nine-pitch route, Walkabout (850', IV 5.11 A2), was established ground-up. We used a mechanized drill on the first three pitches, leaving bolted anchors and seven protection bolts. After that, it's natural gear to the top. For the climbers, it was *questing* in every sense of the term. 📷

MARK ALLEN, *AAC*

Big Kangaroo, south face, Skinny Start; Going Down Under. On July 27, Mike Pond and Matt VanBein climbed a three-pitch variation 30m right of the Kearney-Thomas route, which they called Skinny Start (850', III 5.11). The two climbed solid granite splitters and left-facing corners (5.10+) before heading slightly left into a right-facing corner that eased off into an easy crack system. From here, they trended left and joined the Kearney-Thomas line. The two finished with a 5.11 fingers variation and

[This page, top] The south face of Big Kangaroo, showing: (1) Walkabout (IV 5.11 A2), (2) Beckey-Tate (III 5.8), (3) Quadroon Crack (5.10), (4) Going Down Under (III 5.11c), (5) Kearney-Thomas (III 5.11), and (6) Skinny Start (III 5.11). *Mark Allen* [This page, bottom] Mike Pond leading pitch one of Walkabout. *Mark Allen*

topped out the wall.

In August, after climbing a nearby one-pitch wonder, Dave Elder, Mike Pond, and Matt VanBein started as for the Beckey-Tate route and climbed five pitches of new terrain. Beginning on a broken ledge system, the team traversed hard right across overlaps to reach a big ledge at the base of a beautiful open-book corner. They climbed two classic, clean corners—the second through a burly bulge (5.11c)—before continuing up slabs and exiting via a wide crack with poor rock to a belay below a big roof. They bypassed the roof via easy cracks to the top of the wall, establishing Going Down Under (850', III 5.11c). 📷

MARK ALLEN, *AAC*

Half Moon, northwest face, Butter Face. In July I returned to the Half Moon massif (located near the Liberty Bell group and Washington Pass) with Tino Villanueva to attempt a new route on a prow-like feature on the northwest face, leading to the highest point on the ridge. We completed the route sans bolts, ground-up, and onsight in five hours. The 900' line is sustained at 5.10. From a distance the route is beautiful: direct to the high point, minimal traversing, steep rock, and vertical fractures; however, while each pitch had sections of great climbing, they also contained sections of poor, crumbly rock—hence the name Butter Face (7 pitches, III 5.10+ R).

Both this climb and my other ascent on Half Moon's northwest face, Diggin' for Dreams [*AAJ* 2012], provide sections of great climbing interspersed with questionable rock and run-outs. With room for a couple of other independent lines, plenty of adventure exists on this steep 900' wall. My partners and I have been fortunate enough to keep the lines bolt-free and do them ground-up. If you are solid at the 5.11 grade come check 'em out—it's only a two-hour hike! 📷

ALAN ROUSSEAU, *AAC*

STUART RANGE

Aasgard Sentinel, The Valkyrie. The granite walls and peaks of the Stuart Range have seen prodigious new route activity in the last few years, with the rock generally excellent and often studded with knobs and fins when the cracks peter out. After climbing the north ridge of Mt. Stuart in June with Graham Zimmerman and Scott Bennett, we had intended to repeat a neo-classic of the area, Acid Baby, which climbs a 300m tower looming above Aasgard Pass. As we post-holed up from Colchuck

[This page] Northwest aspect of the Half Moon massif. (1) Butterface (III 5.10+ R). (2) Northwest Face (Beckey). (3) Lunar Rubble (Kearney). (4) Diggin' For Dreams (IV 5.11 R). *Mike Pond*

Lake, I realized my one ascent of the route had left me with almost no recollection of where Acid Baby went, but I had remembered a long dihedral to the left. Scott and Graham were happy to try something new, so we began up a slab 40m to left of Acid Baby.

We generally followed a left-facing corner system, which yielded five pitches of 5.10 climbing before joining Acid Baby for its remarkable finish—a hand-traverse along a knife-edge prow. The crux came high on the second pitch, where Scott's onsight of a steep corner was briefly halted as he changed footwear mid-pitch, thus nearly, but not quite, leading all the hardest pitches in tennis shoes. The route was quickly repeated by several friends and neighbors from Leavenworth, with generally positive reviews: The Valkyrie (300m, 5.10).

BLAKE HERRINGTON, AAC

Colchuck Balanced Rock, west face, first winter ascent. In late January 2012, Nathan Farr and I likely made the first winter ascent of the west face (300m, 5.11+) of Colchuck Balanced Rock (8,200') in the Stuart Range. We approached on skis for the first four miles, then followed a well-established boot-pack for four miles to Colchuck Lake. With potential avalanche concern, we eventually settled on the traditional summer option, which follows a steepening gully starting near the lake's southwest edge. We spent a cold evening nursing our flickering stove in the cirque below the face, and began climbing the next morning with one set of tools, one set of aiders, one set of jumars, and some oversized rock shoes. The route is generally very steep and features long sections of crack climbing. Even with gloved hands and big socks on, these pitches were fairly easy to lead. The most difficult moments came early on the climb, as the occasional easy mantel or 5.8 slab move (in summer) tended to be covered in sugar snow or verglas. The sun came out as we brushed snow off holds of the final slab pitch, illuminating Mt. Stuart and Dragontail Peak with orange winter light.

BLAKE HERRINGTON, AAC

Colchuck Balanced Rock, Accendo Lunae, new variation. Scott Bennett, Graham Zimmerman, and I climbed a new variation on Colchuck Balanced Rock (8,200'), which connects the start and crux of Let it Burn with the end and crux of the west face. From a narrow ledge atop Let it Burn's fifth pitch, we moved right and found a steep, off-sized splitter leading to a sloping belay ledge in a tight corner. The second new pitch followed a thin crack and flare past a square-cut roof and a final thin-hand crack to join the west face beneath its crux roof. Accendo Lunae (1,000 5.12-) is Latin for "illuminating of burning moon," as none of the trio had a headlamp for the final pitch and descent.

BLAKE HERRINGTON, AAC

[This page] Asgard Sentinel, showing the new route, the Valkyrie (left), and Acid Baby (right). Five of the six pitches on the Valkyrie are 5.10. *Blake Herrington*

OREGON

Elkhorns and Wallowas, new route potential. A review of past *AAJs* reveals only a smattering of new alpine routes in Oregon, all on Cascades volcanoes. Yet the largest walls of granite and limestone in Oregon lie to the east of the state's rain divide. Tucked away in the glacial cirques of the Wallowas and Elkhorns of eastern Oregon are large walls and alpine crags waiting to be climbed. The 1,200' limestone cliff above Eagle Creek, the 700' alpine granite Benthos Buttress above Birch Creek, and a 600' granite face above Traverse Lake, among others, beckon for new routes.

In a one-day trip Peter Mullins and I traveled to the Elkhorn Mountains, just west of the Wallowas, to climb a clean 350' cliff on the eastern rib of Van Patten Butte. Unfortunately, the crack systems that seemed obvious from a mile away turned out to be flaring water grooves. We found bolts on the second pitch of this three-pitch climb, and so hope to shed light on this previously undocumented route.

On another trip, Nathan Leichty and I traveled to a possibly unclimbed 600' granite face above Traverse Lake in the southwestern Wallowas. We chose the central dihedral as our goal for a weekend. After five miles of hiking and 3,000' of elevation gain, we reached the crag above the lake. The granite looked similar to that found in the Enchantments or North Cascades. The first pitch was meandering and a little sandy. Unfortunately, an injury on the harder second pitch forced us to bail.

With so much seemingly untapped climbing potential in northeastern Oregon, I hope others make the trek to these isolated and beautiful cliffs. 📷

MATTHEW C. MORRISS, *AAC*

CALIFORNIA

YOSEMITE NATIONAL PARK

Summary: new routes, major linkups, and speed ascents. In addition to the routes described in more detail in this section, as well as Mikey Schaefer's Father Time route on Middle Cathedral [*see feature article in this AAJ*], there are a few other significant new routes to report from Yosemite Valley in 2012.

Luis "Lucho" Rivera and Dan McDevitt free-climbed Romulan Freebird (10 pitches, V 5.12b/c) on Fifi Buttress, across from the Leaning Tower. McDevitt first established the route as an aid climb in 1999. The free version is described as a harder version of the Rostrum, with thin and sustained 5.12 cracks.

Additionally, Alex Honnold set out to free the 1,550' west face of the Leaning Tower, freeing the lower portion of the wall directly via a hard slab he called A Gift From Wyoming (550', 3 pitches, 5.13c), in honor of the late Todd Skinner, who originally projected the upper west face. The upper portion, a potential free version of the aid route Jesus Built My Hotrod, is estimated at hard 5.14 or even 5.15 and awaits a successful redpoint.

Alex Honnold and Tommy Caldwell completed the first free one-day ascent of the "Yosemite Triple," which linked the south face of Mt. Watkins, Freerider on El Capitan, and the Regular Northwest Face on Half Dome—about 7,000' vertical—in a combined time of 21:15 from the base of Mt. Watkins to the summit of Half Dome. Subsequently, Honnold repeated the one-day linkup solo, employing minimal aid, substituting the Nose for Free Rider on El Capitan. [*See feature story in this*

AAJ.] The elapsed time was approximately 18 hours 55 minutes.

Honnold and Hans Florine also set a new speed record on the Nose of El Capitan at 2:23:46, breaking the previous record of 2:36:45 set by Dean Potter and Sean Leary in 2010. [*See feature story in this* AAJ.) Honnold remarked, "I think it could go sub–two hours someday with a lot of cardio [training] and a little less safety."

ERIK RIEGER. *from information provided by* JAMES LUCAS *and various sources*

Liberty Cap, southwest face, Bad Moon Rising. In early October, Steve Bosque, Ezra Allee, and I established an eight-pitch variation to Harding's southwest face route on Liberty Cap. Bad Moon Rising (14 pitches, V 5.8 A2) begins 50' to the right of the massive corner system that makes up the southwest face route, in a parallel system—equally impressive yet overlooked.

After an initial bolt ladder, the route follows these right-facing corners for half of the wall. Around halfway we tamed an intimidating roof via a friendly crack that cuts through the ceiling, followed by an airy belay over the lip. The following pitch was short but very steep, following a featureless corner. Unfortunately, what we'd hoped would continue to be usable features above this point turned out to be an illusion. Often, the corners on Liberty Cap look blank but actually take beaks and heads. However, these next pitches were different; we were at a crossroad.

We opted not to continue straight up, as it would have needed heavy manufacturing, which we were not into. Thankfully, while scoping, we'd noticed a horizontal crack that we could use to exit onto the Harding route. We placed our seventh belay at the start of the "Crack of God," a splitter half-inch crack that shoots 100 feet dead left into the middle of the sixth pitch corner of the Harding route. This pitch was classic, ending with a natural belay on a perch.

The finishing pitches of the Harding route were adventurous, especially while hauling a massive kit. Six days were needed to complete the route, after fixing four pitches. We drilled and filled 35 holes (including one 3/8" bolt at each belay); we did not drill any bathooks, but rather used rivets and bolts for progression when necessary, as we care about the longevity of the route.

Did we free climb up there? Some, but this was 90 percent aid for us, due to the difficulty of the pitches. We have, however, had free climbing in mind while new-routing on Liberty Cap, as the lines are damn near built for classic free climbing. A 5.12 climber would absolutely eat up the huge

[This page] Bad Moon Rising on the southwest face of Liberty Cap. As of May 2013, Cedar Wright and Lucho Rivera had redpointed every pitch but not freed the route in a push. *Joe Hornof*

corner: 800' of 0.5"–1" cracks, mostly all clean on cams. It's all there for the right suitor.

[*Editor's note: As of May 2013, Cedar Wright and Lucho Rivera had redpointed each pitch of the route, but it awaits a ground-up free ascent. Wright believes the route will be one of the best free climbs in Yosemite when completed.*]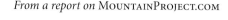

JOSH MUCCI

TUOLUMNE MEADOWS

Fairview Dome, The Arsonist. Erik Anderson and Bob Jensen added a route on the north side of Fairview Dome, left of Burning Down the House. The Arsonist (III 5.11) climbs six new pitches of sustained edging and smearing. Easier ground for several pitches leads to the top.

From a report on MOUNTAINPROJECT.COM

SIERRA NEVADA

Complete Palisade Traverse, first winter ascent. Jediah Porter and I were only acquaintances when, by complete accident, we crossed paths on the Evolution Traverse in August 2011. We made plans to attempt the Evolution Traverse during the winter of 2012; however, our climb was foiled by an optimistic disregard for the weather forecast. The successful first winter ascent of that route followed only a few days later by three climbers from the Pullharder collective. Inspired by their accomplishment, we decided that if we had failed at our first objective we should probably pick something harder.

On February 26, 2013, we left the Big Pine Creek trailhead at 6 a.m. with 30lb. packs, hoping to complete the first winter ascent of the complete Palisade Traverse in five days. A seven-mile, 5,000' hike put us at Southfork Pass, the start of the climbing. The next eight miles included 5.9 rock, steep snow and low-angle ice without crampons, and loads of classic climbing with incredible exposure. The ridge includes six 14,000' peaks, many 13,000' peaks, and scads of shorter peaks and towers.

Though the climbing on the Palisade Crest (a mile-long concentration of 12 peaks in the southern half of the traverse) was not particularly difficult, our pace was the slowest through that section. We bivied four times: on the summit of Middle Palisade, the base of Mt. Williams

[This page] Ian McEleney on the first winter ascent of the complete Palisade Traverse. Likely the longest technical climb in the Lower 48, the Palisade Traverse (not to be confused with the much shorter Thunderbolt to Sill traverse) runs from Southfork Pass to Bishop Pass. *Jediah Porter*

(immediately south of the Palisade Crest), Scimitar Pass, and halfway down the northwest ridge of Thunderbolt Peak. We returned to my truck on the evening of March 2, four days and 16 hours after leaving.

The main challenges of the traverse were moving efficiently over the terrain and staying as fit and healthy as possible. Free-soloing the whole route in boots, while possible, was more risk than we wanted to take on. We used the rope sparingly but strategically, and found that some sections were dispatched more quickly with the mental comfort of a belay. We brought a small tent to ensure a good night's sleep, and always took a brief water and food break every hour, with a real lunch break daily to melt more water. This also gave us time to dry our boots and sleeping bags in the sun and wind.

The complete Palisade Traverse (VI 5.9) is probably the longest technical route in the Lower 48, and yet has seen fewer than 10 complete ascents since the first ascent in 1979. Until more locals start heading from the front-country to the hills, or alpinists from other areas notice the pearls here, we few will continue to have this amazing alpine playground to ourselves.

IAN McELENEY

Mt. Langley, New Army Buttress, Better Red Than Dead. Each time I awoke during the night, I'd turn my head toward the towering black void outlined by the tail of the Milky Way. My partner, Jan Roestel, and I had just finished a recon on the first pitch of an unclimbed feature in the southernmost cirque of Mt. Langley (36°29' N, 118°14' W). Loose blocks, vegetation-filled cracks, and popping crystal knobs led to a ledge system and the start of what looked to be some serious climbing. The closer we got to the main corner, the more the wall seemed to crest over our heads like an angular, Escheresque wave. The dizzying corners gave way to serious doubts: Cache the gear and rap so we could get a quick start in the morning, or come back another day with aiders, hammers, and pins? *No, we're here, and it's only about 800 feet. We'll cache and rap.*

The morning of August 16 was bright, warm, and silent over High Lake, reflecting a pure Sierra morning when summer makes way for fall. During the short trudge up to our dangling rope, I looked up; the light was different. The wall almost seemed welcoming. The vertigo was gone, and only the hard work remained. Still focused on our line, I yelled over my shoulder, "We got this one!" We called the route Better Red Than Dead (800', III 5.11- R), and it took us six hours to complete.

JEFF MAHONEY, *AAC*

Luoma Peak, Ducky's Wild Ride; Cyclorama Wall, Netherworld; new route potential. The year I was born (1979), Galen Rowell established the first and only line on the mythical Cyclorama Wall (Peak 12,860'). His write-up in the 1980 *AAJ*, where he called the wall "every bit as impressive as the Diamond on Longs Peak," inspired me to make the 20-mile slog to see if there was either more potential for new lines or potential to free his route—if I could find it. New to the deep Sierra, Jenny Luoma and I scouted Rowell's approach description online, with a guidebook in hand.

On June 30 we were following in his footsteps. As usual, the altitude devastated me, exacerbated by a solid cold. We moved slowly but surely through Southfork Pass and Mather Pass, then cut west through an unnamed pass, which was solid fourth class, to drop into the valley south of Amphitheater Lake. The next day, having spied a spectacular unnamed rock face on the southeast

end of the Amphitheater Lake basin, we decided to gun for a first ascent as opposed to pushing through to the Cyclorama Wall. We managed to put up an approximately 1,000' new line on Peak 12,610', which I'm naming Luoma Peak.

Starting at the toe of the formation, we wrapped around to the right, finishing on the summit block. The first pitch climbed a corner; the second climbed a pitch of perfect splitter fingers and hands (both 5.10-). Three easier pitches followed obvious ledge systems up and right. From there, we chose a crack system leading directly toward the summit, containing two more 5.10 pitches, including one of overhanging hands (5.10d). Having brought the Pullharder mascot, a rubber ducky, we named our new route Ducky's Wild Ride (IV 5.10d).

The area north of Amphitheater Lake seems to have vast potential for first ascents, including a Cyclorama-looking wall with what appeared to be higher-quality rock. The rest of our trip involved scouting the Cyclorama Wall, which looked very difficult to free climb. We established a new climb on the east arête of the wall instead: Netherworld (III 5.10a R). We ended our excursion in an unnamed pass between the Amphitheater Lake basin and the Dumbbell Lakes basin, due west of Luoma Peak, where Jenny tried her first traditional lead up a very beautiful unclimbed arête. We named it Jenny's Training Day (II 5.6). 🔳

JOSH HIGGINS, *AAC*

Mt. Chamberlin, new routes. An excellent trip to Mt. Chamberlin in 2010 left Chris Brown, Jimmy Haden, Mike Pennings, and I pining for more. So in late July 2011, we reconvened for another trip to the alpine playground surrounding the Crabtree Lakes, this time armed with bacon, steak, beer, and whiskey, courtesy of a mule train. Nothing fuels adventure like a little swine-in-the-'pine.

On the first day, Chris and I headed for the western buttress, which has interesting patterns on its east-facing prow. I wheezed and thrutched my way to a sketchy hanging belay about 150' up a steep corner. (Turns out the climbing was just hard.) Continuing up the corner, Chris encountered guillotine flakes that threatened to trundle down on my tethered position, so he aided left across incipient cracks into an alcove. I followed free, just barely. Unfortunately, the alcove proved inescapable, with overhanging walls on all sides, so we bailed.

On the ground, we had a perfect view of Mike and Jimmy doing battle high on the mountain. They had made their way up the lower wall and over to a crack we dubbed the Wingsuit Splitter for a gold splotch resembling a BASE jumper we'd seen buzzing the northeast face earlier. This attractive

[This page] Ducky's Wild Ride on Luoma Peak. The approximately 1,000' line was climbed en route to the mythical Cyclorama Wall, climbed by Galen Rowell in 1979. *Josh Higgins*

fissure led to another splitter crack a pitch or two higher. Eventually Mike tensioned left to another crack and ran the rope out to a nice ledge, and Jimmy followed free. Another clean but burly 5.10 pitch and some easier terrain took them to the top. They named the route Beanstalk (V 5.11+ A0) in memory of their friend Bean Bowers. "If it's not hands it's fingers; if it's not fingers it's hands," said Mike [of the Wingsuit Splitter].

We hoped to climb the route too; however, watching Mike and Jimmy wrestle with the crack above the Wingsuit Splitter gave us pause. We planned to climb Beanstalk to the upper splitter, then exit via the north face route instead (V 5.10 A2, 1983). We'd figure out how to deal with the aid climbing when we got up there. The first few pitches of Beanstalk were incredible: A 70m pitch of varied 5.11, an amazing rising traverse with just enough protection, and a chossy chimney gained the top of a pillar. From there, I downclimbed a series of flakes to the Wingsuit Splitter. A lone cam was the only protection. I hemmed and hawed across the flakes, then finally committed, lunging for the bottom of the splitter. I latched it for a second, then ripped off and whipped back to the belay, slicing my finger. Next try, I made it over to the splitter and continued up. Mike was right: sweet fingers and hands on golden granite right in the middle of a huge wall—*classic!* Another pitch brought us to a ledge where Mike and Jimmy moved left. We continued straight up into the north face route. Some dicey climbing past a bolt placed by the first-ascent party led us to the aid climbing. I took a left here and managed a difficult crack switch, avoiding the wide cracks and aid on the north face. Another 5.10 pitch followed by easier right-trending cracks and we were on top. We called our variation Great Northern Beans (V 5.11+).

The next day, Mike and Jimmy climbed a line just right of their 2001 route, Asleep at the Wheel (V 5.12-). The thin crack they were aiming for turned out to be a figment of their imagination. Fortunately, it was surrounded by 5.8 knobs, and they made the top without further incident. They report that the new route, Reckless Driving (V 5.12), is even harder than Asleep at the Wheel.

After a rest day, Chris and I climbed the first six pitches of our 2010 line Safety First (IV 5.10)

[This page] Mike Pennings leading Asleep at the Wheel, one of many fine routes on the buttresses comprising Mt. Chamberlin. *Chris Brown*

to reach the base of a 150' freestanding tower perched on Chamberlin's west ridge. Chris traversed a dicey face (5.9) to reach a ledge near the base of the tower, then jammed two physical pitches of hands and fists to tag the summit. We slung the top of the spire and rapped into the notch behind it, then traversed toward the descent gully. The Bean Pole Variation (V 5.10+) adds a few more short pitches to Safety First. 🔍

JOSH FINKELSTEIN, *AAC*

Merriam Peak, west face, Dr. Bear Love. In July 2012, Casey Zak and Luke Stefurak established a four-pitch route, Dr. Bear Love (800', III 5.11a C1) on Merriam Peak, located in the Royce Lakes Basin outside of Pine Creek. The route climbs a clean crack system on the west aspect of the buttress, right of the two Croft-Rands routes established in 2011 [*AAJ 2012*]. Stefurak and Zak believe the route is potentially free-climbable at 5.12 or 5.13. More info at MountainProject.com.

Compiled from information by LUKE STEFURAK

Day Needle, BCB On The Prow; Keeler Needle, Blood of the Monkey. In summer 2011 and 2012, Amy Ness and I established two new routes on the needles of the Mt. Whitney massif. The first route is on Day Needle: BCB On The Prow (15 pitches, VI 5.10 A1). We initially sieged the first four pitches (500') of this route over a period of two weeks in summer 2011, reaching a high point over a massive roof, where we found thin seams and blank slab above. We retreated, but soon afterward returned to make the final push from our high point, which totaled four days and three nights. We went as light as possible: a single sleeping bag, no stove, and five gallons of water. We placed a total of 12 bolts (six for protection), and fixed 11 pitons (two for a pendulum to a very small bivy ledge atop pitch four). Pitch six contains a button-head rivet ladder with one piton (A1). The seventh and eleventh pitches are incredibly overhanging and clean. And the tenth pitch contains 70m of the best high-altitude crack climbing I have done thus far.

The route is now equipped for an all-free ascent with some wild crack climbing. Pitch three is not easy: Exciting moves past two button-heads will bring you to a 30' horizontal traverse between two pitons. This leads to an incredible finger crack to finish this 70m pitch. The giant roof on pitch four will prove to be the crux of the free ascent, as well as the blank slab on pitch six. We encountered no signs of previous ascent until pitch 14, where we found a homemade bong and 1/4" hanger, as well as a homemade nut above a massive chockstone when we intersected the John Vawter route.

Our second route ascends Keeler Needle: Blood of the Monkey (16 pitches, VI 5.12). Beginning in late May 2012, we went capsule-style over 10 days and nine nights for an all-free ascent. At times we had to rappel back down several hundred feet to redpoint certain pitches. We hauled 72 pounds of water, a whole lot of equipment, and were completely self-supported. We feel this is a very proud and climbable line.

The first five pitches of the route jump between Australopithecus (a.k.a. Southern Monkey, VI 5.9 A3) and the Lowe Route (V 5.9 A3). It also briefly links back into Southern Monkey at the end of pitch nine and the start of the tenth-pitch headwall. We fixed two knifeblade pitons on Jeff Lowe and John Wieland's route at pitch four, which we linked from Southern Monkey, and dubbed the Upside-Down Screamer Traverse. Outside of those two pitons, we fixed nothing else on existing routes. A total of 15 bolts (12 button-heads and three 3/8") were placed on the new pitches: seven for protection, eight for anchors. Three knifeblade pitons were also left behind.

[This page] Day Needle (left), showing BCB on the Prow, and Keeler Needle (right), showing Blood of the Monkey, major new routes and link-ups on the Mt. Whitney massif. Moser recommends BCB on the Prow for an all-free attempt. *Myles Moser*

Some highlights pitches from the route include: the Great White Shield (originally C2 on Southern Monkey, now 5.11), the Upside-Down Screamer Traverse (A2 hooking, now 5.10c), and Lowe's Splitter (5.10), which has perfect locks and splitter jams for 180'. Pitch seven starts with a cool wide section, leading to an arête on the left and a massive north-facing dihedral on the right. Two button-heads protect this wild arête, followed by an exciting traverse to a piton (5.11). This sets the climber up for the crux eighth pitch: a slightly overhanging, well-protected 100' crack (5.12). Pitches 10 and 11 were by far the most impressive part of the route. This headwall is very blank and overhung, yet the pitches went at a fairly moderate grade: Pitch 10 climbs through a ledge system, slowly petering out at a hanging belay (5.11); pitch 11 climbs the Red Explosion Dike Traverse, which has incredible moves through red huecos, including underclings, jugs, and side-pulls on the steepest part of the headwall (5.11d). 📷 🔍

MYLES MOSER, *AAC*

Lone Pine Peak, new routes. On Lone Pine Peak, Amy Ness and I completed three new routes, a previously unrecorded route, and also a first free ascent. The first new route was Full Quiver (14 pitches, IV 5.9+ R). This route ascends the Three Arrows formation, which lies on the east side of Lone Pine Peak, and is comprised of not three but actually four towers. Prior to our ascent, Fred Beckey had the only existing route on the formation. Amy and I began just above the toe of the buttress on the left side of the formation, ascending mixed terrain on knobs, slabs, and gendarmes. Our goal was to hit every tower on the ridge via whatever viable means. There was some good rock, bad rock, and run-outs, and the adventure of climbing 14 pitches of untraveled terrain in the quickest way possible during a sunny winter day was unforgettable. The snow at the base made the approach a lot easier, too.

On the south side of Lone Pine Peak, Amy and I established Pertergio Dieythno (III 5.9). This is the obvious white fin that protrudes off the south side as seen from the Stone House. We began at the cleanest part of the rock and rode the arête the whole way. Beautiful white-pink granite, perfect cracks, bulletproof red patina, roofs, chicken-heads, and exposed knob traverses comprise the eight fantastic pitches to the summit. No fixed protection was left behind.

Next up was the Serrated Ridge (10 pitches, IV 5.9+), also on the south side of the Lone Pine Peak. The route starts behind the Summer Ridge Route and in front of the Czech Pillar. Intent on a first ascent, we were surprised to find fixed protection: first a hex, then some nuts, then bolts on the arête. We believe this to be a second ascent of an unrecorded route, possibly climbed by Fred Beckey or Galen Rowell. Either way, this superb route should be noted and is highly recommended.

The third and longest route Amy and I climbed was Windhorse (21 pitches, V 5.11 or 5.10 A3, Binder-Holland, 1999) on the south side of Lone Pine Peak. Located deep in the Turtle Creek drainage, we began our climb as an attempt for the first winter ascent of this long, hard route, but it soon turned into a six-day push for the first free ascent. Mild winter weather allowed us to climb comfortably on the rock, yet melt snow for water. After freeing a section of hooking (A3) through a beautiful dihedral, we were able to find an alternate path to free a tension traverse. A memorable 5.10 offwidth squeeze, a three-pitch dihedral, and a 13-year-old can of Sapporo left in a crack remain the most vivid memories of this awesome climb.

The final route we completed was on the northeast ridge of Lone Pine Peak: the Northeast Arête (8 pitches, III 5.9+). This striking arête can be seen from the town of Lone Pine. It is a fantastic adventure route, which contains great exposure toward the final portion. We established the route

[This page, left] South side of Lone Pine Peak showing routes (left to right): The Forgotten Ridge, The Serrated Ridge, and Pertergio Dieythno. *Myles Moser* [This page, right] Three Arrows, showing Full Quiver, only the second known route on the formation. *Myles Moser*

in a day with no fixed protection. Once finishing the main difficulties, one can continue 300' up the northeast ridge for a mega day or descend the west side to the slopes below. 📷 🔍

— Myles Moser, *AAC*

Peak 3,986, The Forgotten Ridge. Amy Ness and I made the first ascent of the Forgotten Ridge (V 5.10 R), which follows a massive spiraling ridgeline on the southeast aspect of Peak 3,986. We climbed the ridge over two straight days, hauling one bag. We fixed no pitons or bolts and stretched every pitch as far as we could with a 70m rope, making for really long leads. After pitch 11 we divided the load between two bags and simul-climbed the remaining 800' to the summit. A majority of the route was 5.9, but it contained three pitches of 5.10. Pitch 2 gets an "R" rating due to a long runout on knobs and chicken heads past a roof. While approaching the wall, the route may appear to shrink. It has not. It will only grow and grow in amazement while you climb. 📷 🔍

— Myles Moser, *AAC*

Lone Pine Peak, south face, Mountain Devil Dike. In August, Brad Wilson and Dulcinea Groff established a six-pitch route on the south face of Lone Pine Peak: Mountain Devil Dike (900', III 5.12d). The route begins on the first two pitches of the Michael Strassman Memorial Route and then climbs four new pitches (5.10–5.12) up a prominent dike on the face. More info at MountainProject. com.

Compiled from information by Brad Wilson

Whitney Portal Buttress, The Never Ending Story; El Segundo area, new routes. In 2011 and 2012, I completed five new routes on the Whitney Portal Buttress and surrounding walls with various partners. The longest of these is the Never Ending Story (12 pitches, V 5.12 or 5.11 A0) on the Whitney Portal Buttress proper. On the first attempt of this route, Amy Ness, Paul Lebouisue, and I spent six days and five nights on the wall, climbing capsule-style. We had to bail 400' from the summit due to lack of supplies and hardware. Amy and I returned later for another four-day push to finish the route. During that time we experienced wind so strong it was able lift up our portaledge.

[This page] A close-up of the Forgotten Ridge, a massive new route on Peak 3,986, which is a prominent point on the south side of Lone Pine Peak. *Myles Moser*

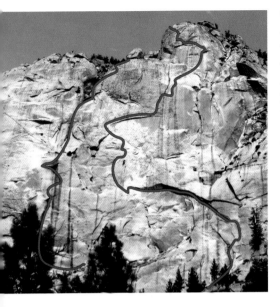

This route, which contains some of the best crack climbing on the Portal Buttress, follows the massive arch above the only giant pine on the wall. It then dances around, grabbing the most aesthetic features, with eight pitches of perfect cracks and four pitches of slab. The 5.12 crux comes at the end of pitch 10—a full 70m slab. The desperate slab crux can make for a big winger, but it can be bypassed with a lasso to a roof. The climbing up to that point is mostly 5.10–5.11.

Next up, Neil Woodruff and I took on a massive divide in the center of Whitney Portal Buttress, which can only be called "The Butt Crack." Neil and I spent four days on the wall to reach this chasm. During that time we experienced spectacular waterfalls and thunderous skies. The second pitch involved a very stout 5.11 lieback to a button-head ladder with mandatory free moves between the rivets. The next pitch also went at 5.11. The gem pitches were inside the wide upper crack. Full on hand-and-foot-bridging spanned the seven-foot gap and made for a wild and airy scenario. From here, we had to leap from one massive chockstone to another, and yet another, which brought us to the final chockstone boulder crux, which exits the large chasm (5.11). Two more pitches led to the top of the central tower just below a massive block, completing Skid Marks (8 pitches, IV 5.11 A0).

The next three routes were climbed on walls adjacent to the Portal Buttress. High in the northeast corner of the canyon, and up behind El Segundo Buttress, is a prominent pillar with cracks that run clean and true. I made the first ascent of this route with Phil Bircheff and later returned with Amy Ness to free the entire climb, calling the route Pillar Altisimo (6 pitches, 5.11)

Pitch one is the crux, with two bolts protecting a wide trough (5.11). Pitch two, the Dulcimer Pitch, is wildly exposed, and the third pitch is the highlight, with two parallel cracks that run for 120' with sinker 5.9 jams. After this, the route follows the obvious crack system (5.7–5.8) to a ramp with bushes on the west face, where it climbs a broken dike to the spire summit. Five rappels down the east side take one to the base.

To the right of Pillar Altisimo, on the far eastern arête, Amy Ness, Phil Bircheff, and I established Altisimo Arête (5 pitches, III 5.10c). The climb begins in a gully, moving east with some third-class scrambling to the start. A 5.5 crack goes to a ledge with a small pine. The second pitch is marked by a fixed piton and passes a giant roof to the right. Knifeblades were used to protect around the roof for the crux (5.10c) on the first ascent. The third and fourth pitches are very clean and memorable splitter cracks, and the route finishes with a short pitch and mantel onto the summit block. Subsequent parties should bring a small rack of knifeblade pitons and a hammer, or a drill, to make the route properly equipped.

[This page] Skid Marks (left) and Never Ending Story (right), new routes on the Whitney Portal Buttress. *Myles Moser*

To the left of Pillar Altisimo and to the right of Moonstone Buttress, Amy Ness and I climbed a massive four-pitch dihedral, which we called Sombra De La Luna (6 pitches, 5.11). The climb starts in a large flake system (5.9) and reaches a brushy ledge. From the ledge, the corner above offers consistent 5.10–5.11 climbing. The third-pitch corner blanks out and forces the climber onto the face before regaining the upper dihedral. We turned the dihedral on the left, which brought us onto the face below an arching corner. Exciting slab and knob climbing eventually brought us to an offwidth with a perfect belay. From the anchor, the sixth pitch moves up and right through a small roof, past a bolt, and into a left-trending arch with one final airy move into a wide crack. After reaching the summit block, we dubbed the last pitch the Shadow of the Moon and then rappelled down Apollo 13. The climb required six protection bolts, six anchor bolts, and three pitons to complete. 📷 🔍

MYLES MOSER, AAC

Mt. Russell, southeast face, new route. The southeast face of Mt. Russell is a looming triangular wall above Upper Boyscout Lake in the Mt. Whitney region. On September 4, Amy Ness, Phil Bircheff, and I climbed a new route on the face via a clean corner system. The route begins just left of a massive corner (which may have been climbed by an unknown party), under a very obvious red corner 150' up. The first pitch climbs to the red corner, and the second follows it for a full 60m. Two more 5.9 pitches are followed by easy fifth-class terrain, which gains the east ridge and eventually the summit, making for a big day out. While the route has a long approach from Upper Boyscout Lake, it is quite worth it (III 5.9).

MYLES MOSER, AAC

KINGS CANYON & SEQUOIA NATIONAL PARKS

The Fortress, The Siege. In fall 2012, Daniel Jeffcoach, Vitaliy Musiyenko, and Tom Ruddy established a new route, The Siege (1,000', IV 5.10c A0), on a formation known as the Fortress. This wall is located in Sequoia National Park, six miles from Paradise Ridge trailhead at an elevation of ca 7,693'. The team noted no known history of other routes on the wall and said potential exists for more climbs.

From a report at MOUNTAINPROJECT.COM

[This page] A new route on Mt. Russell's southeast face, at an accesible length and grade. *Myles Moser*

[This page, left] The Valkyrie on Angel Wings' main wall. The 17-pitch 5.12 route required over a decade of attempts to complete. *Brandon Thau* [This page, right] Shaun Reed leading the fourth pitch of Astro-Gil, a new 11-pitch 5.11 route on Tehipite Dome. *Scotty Nelson*

Tehipite Dome, southeast face, Astro-Gil. In September, Shaun Reed, Brad Wilson, and I spent two weeks establishing a new route on Tehipite Dome in Kings Canyon National Park. The route, Astro-Gil (1,700', IV 5.11), ascends the previously unclimbed southeast face up bullet stone. We had splitter weather and saw no people except for a group of Sierra Club hikers. We named this route after our friends Gil Weiss and Ben Horne, who perished during the descent from Paclaraju Oeste in the Cordillera Blanca, Peru, after establishing a new route. *Vamos a la cumbre!* 📷 🔍

SCOTTY NELSON, *Pullharder Alpine Club*

Angel Wings, Valkyrie. On September 3, 2012, Dave Nettle, Peter Croft, Greg Epperson, and I completed the first free route on the main wall of Angel Wings, located in Sequoia National Park. Valkyrie (V 5.12) is the product of over a decade of attempts while enduring injuries, dead-end crack systems, base-camp thieves, late-melting snowpack, and season-ending storms. Each successive trip to the wall pushed the route a little higher, until finally we made a breakthrough on the ninth pitch and the route flowed free to the top. Due to the complexity of the natural features on Angel Wings, we made at least three wrong turns before the free line was found.

Our first-ascent push was made from the ground up. Dave and Peter had trail-blazed new ground up to pitch 13. When I showed up a few days later, we decided to complete the route in a one-day push, unsure of the final pitches above. Peter and I started from the ground and both freed each pitch (except for one 5.12 crux, which I aided through). Greg Epperson jugged beside us taking photos. Once reaching pitch 13, Dave and Peter navigated and freed, onsight, the last four pitches to the top. Greg and I followed behind, shuttling gear to the summit. By sunset we were back in camp and celebrating.

This exquisite route is comprised of 17 pitches, with only two under 5.10 in difficulty. It begins at the lowest point of the wall and parallels the Steck route up to "Upper Bearpaw Meadow," a 45-degree, sloping grassy ledge. From there, the route cuts out right and up an exposed arête for another 1,000'. The route is characterized by linking crack systems with face climbing cruxes. There is some fixed gear on the route—all bolts were drilled, excruciatingly, by hand, and there is one fixed pin. The belays all the way up to pitch 13 have one or more bolts; after that, it's natural gear to the top. A 16-mile approach and every granite climbing technique are required to ascend this backcountry wall. 📷 🔍

BRANDON THAU

NEVADA

RED ROCK CANYON NATIONAL CONSERVATION AREA

Cactus Flower Tower, Blood on the Tracks; Mt. Wilson, Cactus Connection. In early April 2012, Chris Weidner and I linked up up two of the biggest peaks in Red Rock, in a day, both via new routes climbed onsight. We began in the crack system 100m to the left of the Warrior on Cactus Flower Tower and climbed 120m before veering right to the next dihedral system. The climbing was varied and never harder than 5.9, with generally good rock and protection: Blood on the Tracks (300m, 5.9). We joined the Warrior atop its final pitch, then scrambled the final fourth-class terrain to the summit.

From there, we downclimbed and rappelled to the col between Cactus Flower Tower and the Aeolian Wall on Mt. Wilson. Beginning just south of the col, we climbed 100m of excellent cracks to the shoulder of Mt. Wilson. The crux was a splitter fingers-to-hands pitch straight out of Indian Creek. From the shoulder of Mt. Wilson, we scrambled up stepped terrain to the summit. This finish up Mt. Wilson is consistent with the grade and quality of the Warrior, and would be a logical extension to that climb after summiting the tower: Cactus Connection (100m, 5.11). Even the famous, highly visible features of Red Rock still hold potential for boltless, ground-up adventures! 📷

BLAKE HERRINGTON, *AAC*

[This page] Blake Herrington leading Cactus Connection, Mt. Wilson, the second new route of the day, established after climbing Blood on the Tracks on Cactus Flower Tower, a satellite summit of Wilson. Both new routes were climbed onsight without bolts or pins. *Chris Weidner*

ARIZONA

GRAND CANYON NATIONAL PARK

Zoroaster Temple, southeast face. In April 2012, Mathieu Brown and Zach Harrison climbed a five-pitch, "stellar and demanding" route up the southeast face of Zoroaster, the well-known formation near the bottom of the Grand Canyon. The new route (520', III 5.10 C1) ascends a large corner/ramp at the south end of the face on mostly good rock. The first-ascent party used aid on pitches two through four. Two protection bolts were placed. In April 2013, Harrison and Alwyne Butler returned to Zoroaster to attempt an all-free ascent. They freed the second and fourth pitches, at 5.11 and 5.11+, respectively. However, the third pitch still required two clean-aid moves. 📷

From information supplied by ZACH HARRISON

BLACK MOUNTAINS

Bloody Butte, The Coke Bottle, Tower of Kor, Bighorn Tower. I was fortunate to spend some time visiting with Layton Kor at his home in Kingman, Arizona, in the last few years before he died on April 21, 2013. While Layton was still healthy enough, we were able to get out climbing. On a trip to western Arizona in April 2009, with Ed Webster and Dennis Jump, we teamed up to make the first ascent of a small tower in the volcanic Black Mountains, which we called Bloody Butte, a.k.a. Kor's Kastle. This was the last first ascent of a desert tower that Layton was able to make. He led the first pitch (5.7 A1), pounding pitons for pro and three blades for an anchor.

Layton told me about another tower that he had discovered farther south in the Mt.

[This page, top] The southeast face of Zoroaster Temple in the Grand Canyon, showing the new five-pitch route. *Zach Harrison* [This page, bottom] Bighorn Tower (left) and Tower of Kor in the Mt. Nutt Wilderness Area. Layton Kor climbed three pitches on the ca 350' Tower of Kor (a.k.a. Coke Bottle) in 2011, his last attempt on a major desert first ascent before he died in April 2013. *Stewart Green*

Nutt Wilderness Area, which he dubbed the Coke Bottle for its appearance from the highway above Bullhead City. In April 2011 he joined Dennis and me for an attempt on the 350-foot tower. After a day of driving and hiking around the desert to find the best approach, we climbed three pitches in 90°F temperatures before bailing. Layton was excited to see a big Mojave rattlesnake during our hike out.

I returned the following winter with Dennis Jump and Brian Shelton, and on February 8, 2012, made the first ascent via a circuitous six-pitch route we called Hard Kor (III 5.8 C1 or 5.10-). As we stood on the summit under azure skies, we decided to call it Tower of Kor to honor a great climber and friend. That evening, over a celebratory steak dinner in Kingman, Layton wistfully told me, "That's the first tower that I've discovered and didn't make its first ascent."

Next to the Tower of Kor, and separated by a deep gash, is an even taller tower. Although several climbers had asked for beta on climbing Tower of Kor, we resisted giving out information before we had a chance to return. On February 7, 2013, Brian Shelton, Dr. Bill Springer, and I climbed the nearly 500-foot tower via a seven-pitch route (III 5.8 C1 or 5.10-) that shared Hard Kor's first three pitches. Brian suggested we call it Bighorn Tower for the herd of sheep we saw earlier in the day, effortlessly scampering up an almost vertical gully opposite our route. 🖸

STEWART GREEN, *USA*

IDAHO

LOST RIVER RANGE

Mt. Idaho, east face, new routes. In August 2012, two routes were established on the previously unclimbed east face of Mt. Idaho (12,065'). They both go more or less up the center of the diamond-shaped face. Kevin Hansen and Wes Collins completed the first ascent of the face via the Mountaineer's Route (III 5.8). Their route starts to the left of the massive chimney at the base and continues up to the overhanging upper headwall, where it escapes left into a steep gully. During their ascent, Kevin noticed a series of cracks and features that went directly up the center of the face that looked fun. When he mentioned this possibility, I jumped at the chance to return with him.

Kevin and I started on a right-angling crack from the base of the chimney (5.9). Some easier terrain (5.6) took us to the headwall, which we climbed via a faint, overhanging water streak about 15' right of the prominent white triangle in the center of the face (5.10a). Another long pitch of moderate terrain (5.7)

[This page] Mountaineer's Route (left) and the East Face Direct (right), the first known routes on Mt. Idaho's nearly 1,000' east face. *Cory Harelson*

took us to the base of the imposing and overhanging headwall. From there we climbed up a slightly less steep notch where there are two facing corners about 20' apart. Kevin climbed the left-facing corner and, after excavating a lot of dirt and rocks from the crack in the middle of the crux, managed to pull through, climbing to the top of the face (5.10b/c). We called the route the East Face Direct (III 5.10b/c) and climbed it in five rope-stretching 70m pitches, with a bit of simul-climbing. 📷

CORY HARELSON, *AAC*

UTAH

WASATCH RANGE

Lone Peak Cirque, Summit Wall, The Wonderette. Over a handful of weekends from June to August 2012, I tricked three unsuspecting victims into making the 5,000' vertical trek up to Lone Peak Cirque to establish a new route we called the Wonderette (500', 5.12). The idea for the route was hatched in 2011 when my friend Louis Arcvalo and I supported SLC superstar "Sick" Nik Berry while he worked out the moves on the Wonderwall, which he eventually freed at 5.13c R. I couldn't touch Wonderwall's crux moves on toprope, and it blows my mind that Nik committed to them way above Peckers, small knifeblades, and micro-cams. While on belay duty, Louis and I noticed a way to sneak around this crux pitch. Above, we saw an exit pitch avoiding the original route's 5.8 finish, a lichen-shellacked chimney featuring all sizes of wedged block missiles aimed right at the belay ledge.

The next summer, with promises of summit glory, I solicited some help from Louis, Rob Duncan, and Brad Barlage. With so much arête climbing, we knew we were going to have to place some bolts—so we did. I was not taught to climb using what I call "suss and fuss" tactics, but for a number of reasons (time, safety, route quality, etc.) we quickly decided that rap-bolting would be the best way to put up the route. Rob and I ended up hand-drilling a total of nine protection bolts (and no anchor bolts) in about 270' of climbing. The four-pitch Wonderette follows the first one and a half pitches of the Undone Book (old-school 5.9R), traverses right into the opening dihedral of the Wonderwall proper (5.11+), then busts left to an arête via a boulder problem (5.12), and finally follows another arête up to the summit blocks (5.11-). Much of the climbing is exposed and airy face and thin-crack climbing in the 5.10+/5.11- range. Often, you've got one hand slapped around the edge with hundreds of feet of exposure below. 📷

ARI MENITOVE, *Salt Lake City*

[This page] The Wonderette, a major new variation on the Summit Wall in Lone Peak Cirque. The route sports a healthy amount of airy arête climbing. *Ari Menitove*

CASTLE VALLEY

Castleton Tower, southeast face, Ivory Tower. On October 22, 2012, Chris Kalous freed a wild new route, Ivory Tower (110m, 5.13b) on southeastern Utah's iconic Castleton Tower. Ivory Tower climbs four long pitches up a sharp arête and face on the southeast spine of Castleton, to the right of the famed Kor-Ingalls Route. It ends atop the Arrowhead, a huge flake, just below the summit. Most of the climbing is bolt-protected, but there are substantial crack-climbing sections as well. In addition to the crux second pitch (5.13b), the route has three 5.12 pitches, which had been redpointed earlier by Sam Lightner Jr., who also reconnoitered and bolted the line. During Kalous' successful ascent with Lightner on October 22, Kalous followed the first and third pitch free, and led the crux second pitch and the fourth pitch.

Compiled from information on CLIMBING.COM

Mystery Towers, Citadel, The Mugacki Variation. In October 2012, Fisher Towers veterans Joe Forrester and Jeremy Aslaksen climbed a new variation to the Forrest-Briggs route on the Citadel: the Mugacki Variation (V 5.3 A2+). The route starts at the southernmost base of the tower and avoids the original bolt ladders on the first three pitches of the Forrest-Briggs by climbing challenging, shallow seams, via beaks and cams, for two rope-stretching pitches. From there, they joined the Forrest-Briggs to the summit. The two did not place any bolts on lead, but did leave a two-bolt anchor atop the first pitch.

Compiled from information provided by JOE FORRESTER, *AAC*

Fisher Towers, The Oracle, Beak to the Future. In the fall of 2009, Jeremy Aslaksen and I climbed a new route on the south face of Kingfisher in the Fisher Towers. We called the route Weird Science [*AAJ 2010*] and made a pact to see if we could do new routes on all five of the main Fisher Towers. In the fall of 2010 we completed a new route on the Titan that we called Gimp Warfare, and then a few months later a new route on Echo Tower called Sidewinder [*AAJ 2011*]. Then, in the spring of 2011, we found a wild line on Cottontail Tower that we called Trick of the Tail [*AAJ 2012*]. All that was left was a route on the Oracle.

The Oracle had two routes: Fantasia, a wild free and aid route, and Beaking in Tongues, a cool, all-natural aid line. We had scoped both sides of the Oracle, and in the spring of 2012 settled on a route on the backside. Jeremy led the first pitch, which came together nicely. A few weeks later we were back at it, only to discover that the cracks we were hoping to use on the second pitch were nonexistent. Instead of drilling a long bolt ladder, we pulled our gear and bailed.

Fast-forward to November 2012: The Oracle was still on my mind, and I was convinced there was a way to connect to a system high on the face right of Beaking in Tongues. The first pitch started with a boulder problem off the ground, an exposed traverse, and a few Peckers in a seam before launching into a long traverse right to a few bolts, free climbing, and a short bolt ladder to a belay. The second pitch started with a short bolt ladder and then followed Pecker seams to another belay ledge. The third pitch, the Mud Shield, was the money pitch. After a few holes off the belay it followed a long, singular Pecker-sized crack up a sweeping, steep headwall. The final pitch on the headwall involved a "take-everything-off" squeeze-slot, and landed us just below a V-shaped notch on the ridge. From there, a pitch straight left and then up got us to another belay 20' below the start of Fantasia's last-pitch bolt ladder, which we followed to the top. The final two days on route had been frigid, with snow and wind. But it was worth it, as the summit culminated our goal of a new route on every major Fisher Tower: Beak to the Future (700', 5.10 A3+). 📷

PAUL GAGNER, *AAC*

MONTANA

Hairpin Brow Buttress, Classy Girls. Ben Hoiness and Brooks Munyer found a fine four-pitch line on a possibly unclimbed granite buttress above Hairpin Lake in the Hell Roaring Plateau area of the Absaroka-Beartooth Wilderness Area. Classy Girls (5.11a/b) takes a line of cracks up the left side of the buttress, with mostly good rock. The wall appears to hold potential for other difficult routes.

From information supplied by BROOKS MUNYER

WYOMING

GRAND TETON NATIONAL PARK

Grand Teton, southwest face, Bean's Wall of Shining Storms. In good weather, the southwest face of the Grand Teton shines in the last rays of evening light. In bad weather, the fetch that allows this nice light also allows storms to crash into the exposed and overhanging walls. The Tetons' best rock is here, at the top of the range. Between the past efforts of Pownall-Gilkey and Beyer-Hartman lies a beautiful path with steep, clean rock, good protection, and classic ambience.

I started this route many years ago. Ryan Hokanson and I were chased down from the overhanging second pitch by a furious summer storm. Then, the late Bean Bowers and I found a way around this pitch and made it to the steep fourth-pitch corner, where a similar storm attacked us. As if we were strapped to the mast

[This page, top] Classy Girls on the Hairpin Brow Buttress, Absaroka-Beartooth Wilderness Area. It's the first route known route on the wall, with plenty of potential remaining. *Ben Hoiness* [This page, bottom] Bean's Wall of Shining Storms, located high on the Grand Teton's southwest face. The difficult seven-pitch route is dedicated to the late Bean Bowers. *Greg Collins*

in a hurricane, we waited it out. When storm had just passed—the hail and graupel melted, the rock dried—another one struck us. Now in stormy darkness, Bean and I bounced down the very overhanging wall beneath us on a single rope. For years it was difficult to find climbers willing to hike 2,000m to approach this new high-mountain route, which is only warm enough to climb in the afternoon. In summer 2011, Dan Corn and I climbed the fourth pitch, but time and work forced us to traverse off and back down to the valley.

Hans Johnstone and I have been new-routing for years; some of our routes are memorials to fallen friends, and some of these new routes were made with Bean. The route to this point had been excellent, and we knew the ground above would be even better. We made finishing the route a priority. The summer of 2012 was virtually storm-free, so in two days we beaked upward to equip the fifth and sixth pitches with the necessary bolts and pins. And, finally, on July 26, we redpointed the whole route with no falls, in one day from the valley, creating our best and most rewarding new route yet: Bean's Shining Wall of Storms (7 pitches, V 5.12-).

GREG COLLINS, *AAC*

WIND RIVER RANGE

Cirque of the Towers, Warbonnet Peak, new routes. In summer of 2012, Nathan Brown and partners Jonathan Foster and Tony Spainhour established two new routes on left side of Warbonnet Peak in the Cirque of the Towers. [*Brown and Foster established an additional route on the same aspect of Warbonnet in 2011: Weather or Not (750', III 5.10)*]. The first route, War Paint (1,000', IV 5.11 C0), begins right of Weather Or Not and left of Seams and Dreams in an obvious low-angle corner. From there, the route climbs clean splitter cracks, knobs, and corners for 10 pitches, with one short section of aid on the steep seventh pitch. The second route, Drop of a Hat (700', III 5.11b/c), climbs the first two pitches of Weather or Not, then branches left to climb four pitches of cracks directly up the headwall.

Compiled from information by NATHAN BROWN *and* MOUNTAINPROJECT.COM

Sundance Pinnacle, north face. Matt Hartman and Jake Tipton climbed a possible new route on the north side of this prominent buttress along the approach to the Cirque of the Towers. The two climbed the left side of the north face in five pitches (III 5.11a/b C1), and after a bail sling at the top of the 5.9 first pitch they believe they were on previously unclimbed ground. The remaining four pitches were all 5.10 or harder, with a marginally protected 5.11 seam on the third pitch. The first-ascent team suggest the crux fourth pitch would go at 5.12 with some cleaning.

Compiled from a report by MATT HARTMAN *and* MOUNTAINPROJECT.COM

COLORADO

BLACK CANYON OF THE GUNNISON

South Rim, Big Island area, Black Cloud. In the summer of 2012, Chris Righter and I were lured into establishing a new route on Wild Bill's Wall, a relatively unexplored and unclimbed part of the canyon. After an initial recon, we decided upon an unclimbed section of rock approximately 1,600' tall. Unfortunately, the continuous crack systems were up high, and the bottom of the wall was guarded by face climbing with no natural protection. We regrettably decided that we would have to tackle this adventure from the top down; however, the top of this route is not in a convenient location like those elsewhere in the canyon, but on Big Island, which is separated by a 70-meter-deep gash near the parking at Cross Fissures Overlook. Only after rappelling from the South Rim and climbing our way to the top of the island could we establish fixed lines on the route.

After much trundling of large, loose blocks from the crack systems, core-shot ropes, frustration and dehydration, a wild new line began to unveil itself. We encountered unparalleled stone and, as with all Black Canyon routes, a short section that was extremely friable. The route wanders up from the river through well-protected face moves, dihedrals, and bomber jams of all sizes. Each pitch required a little something from the leader as the moves became committing and the exposure increased. However, we were always rewarded with a ledge system at the belays. The route remains sustained until pitch eight, where we traversed up some easier terrain to climb the final roof and headwall dihedral. From the top, one must rappel into the gully and then climb up one more scramble before a one-minute walk back to the car.

In all, our new route Black Cloud (1,600', IV 5.12- PG) contains 11 long pitches of classic Black Canyon climbing. This is sure to become a regularly climbed route in the Black once word gets out about its quality.

ROB PIZEM, *AAC*

South Rim, The Quota. Jeff Popko and Chris Righter put up a six-pitch route, the Quota (750', 5.12a), below the Cedar Point lookout. The crux second pitch avoids a loose chimney with bolt-protected face climbing, and then turns a huge roof.

From information supplied by JEFF POPKO *and* CHRIS RIGHTER

North Rim, new routes. In April 2012, Jonathan Schaffer and partners established two new routes along the North Rim. The first, Cloak Dagger (III 5.10c, Schaffer-Zeilman), takes an independent line right of Comic Relief. Starting on the Comic Relief ledge, the route climbs six pitches (mostly 5.9-5.10), with the crux third-pitch corner (5.10+) said to be of very high quality. The second route, Locals' Route (IV 5.11+ R, Schaffer-Rees-Zeilman), climbs the backside of the Great White Wall via a massive right-facing dihedral for 10 pitches, eventually intersecting with the Tourist Route to the top of the rim. The crux fourth pitch (5.11+ R), freed by Schaffer, climbs a long, thin corner past intermittent gear and a lone bolt, which lead to committing moves below a roof and a striking hand-to-offwidth crack above. More info at MountainProject.com.

Compiled from information by VIC ZEILMAN *and* MOUNTAINPROJECT.COM

SAN JUAN MOUNTAINS

Camp Bird Road, various ascents. The Camp Bird Road area above Ouray, famous for climbs such as the Ribbon, Bird Brain Boulevard, Talisman, and countless others, has seen a recent burgeoning of bold new mixed climbs. In January 2011, Steve House and Hayden Kennedy established Desperado

(800', III M6 R/X), which begins in a prominent orange cleft left of the Ribbon and climbs four long pitches of thin ice and steep, runout rock. House and Kennedy partnered again in January 2012, establishing an additional climb on the Ribbon Buttress, the House-Kennedy Chimney (800', III M6 R), which tackles a steep wall approximately halfway between Bird Brain Boulevard and Racing Stripes, via overhangs and a prominent right-facing corner on the final pitch.

Three more new routes were climbed in December 2012. Bryan Gilmore and Jim Turner established Dirty Minds (800', III 5.9 M6 R), just left of the House-Kennedy Chimney. Dirty Minds ascends obvious corners, trending right toward a left-facing corner on a large pillar high on the wall. Phil Wortman and Erik Wellborn established Tasty Talks (1,400', 5.8 M5 R) on a large buttress downriver from the Ribbon, above and left of Fall Creek. And, lastly, Noah McKelvin and Jason Maki established Wake Up Call (900', IV M5+ R), which follows a major chimney system two buttresses downriver from the Ribbon. 📷 🔍

ERIK RIEGER, *from information provided by* HAYDEN KENNEDY *and* MOUNTAINPROJECT.COM

ROCKY MOUNTAIN NATIONAL PARK

Longs Peak, The Diamond, Waterhole #3, first free ascent. Waterhole #3 was the first route to be put up solo on the Diamond (Walker, 1971). I first attempted to free the route in 2011, going ground-up, onsight. It looked like there were small cracks on the route that would take gear, but I kept climbing higher and higher to false shadows and seams with no openings (150', 5.10 X). I eventually reached a massive roof that wouldn't be possible to reverse once I went over it and bailed. My partner, Lukas Hill, never wanted to come back, but for some weird reason I did.

I returned in 2012, threw down a massive static line from the top of the Diamond, and spent an entire day cleaning the route. I Mini-Traxioned the route, doing all the moves, and soon gave up my cleaning efforts because it was too miserable hanging out in the route's namesake waterfall, by myself, 1,000' off of the ground. I convinced my friend Jeff Duran to come out and belay me. He said he would try and follow the route clean, but after watching rock rain down on the first pitch, he became content to jug.

The route starts by going through a waterfall and then climbing up behind it. You pop through the waterfall at various times on the wall, getting totally soaked. At one point, it started to rain on us, which I didn't even realize until the thunder began and I saw a storm surrounding us. I think there's a natural spring above this side of the Diamond. The water seems to just come right

[This page] Dirty Minds (left) and the House-Kennedy Chimney (right). These two routes, like the other new routes established on Camp Bird Road, ascend mostly pure rock. *Hayden Kennedy*

out of the mountain. As for the climb, it's the worst route I've done on the Diamond, and probably even in the park (6 pitches, 800', 5.11+ X). I don't recommend it to anyone. I love adventure, but sometimes there are adventures just not meant to go on, you know what I mean?

Jason Haas, AAC

Mt. Evans, Black Wall, Undertow, first free ascent. In the spring of 2010, Will Butler took me to the Black Wall on Mt. Evans to show me the old aid line Undertow (IV 5.10 A4). When we rapped in, I couldn't believe this gorgeous dihedral system in the middle of the Black Wall had never been freed. The rock is stellar, the approach almost nonexistent, and the line seemed obvious. While we originally thought we would add some sort of bolted variation around the A4 roof, a more natural line presented itself. Later in the season, though, I realized why the climb was never freed: The alpine moss at the top of the wall acts like a sponge, dripping water down the final pitch.

After two seasons of cleaning the route, replacing bolts, and fighting wetness in the later part of the alpine season, I was finally able to free this amazing line with Brad Wilson on June 23, 2012, with both leader and follower freeing every pitch. The majority of the route follows the original aid line, except for a half-pitch that completely avoids the A4 roof traverse. Instead, the free variation follows a wide-hands layback out the other side of the roof, before cutting back underneath another massive roof to a spectacular hanging belay on the arête. Every pitch is high quality and very sustained, with at least four pitches clocking in at 5.11 or 5.11+ (6 pitches, IV 5.11+). 📷

Shaun Reed

Mt. Evans, The Tan Buttresses, various ascents; The Black Wall, The Rainbow Highway, various ascents; Mt. Warren, various ascents. In 2008, Josh Thompson and Glen Griscom put up the first route on the slightly chossy-looking buttresses just north of the Black Wall, known as the Tan Buttresses. They called their route Noth'n but a Good Time (400', II 5.11- R). Later that summer, after deciding that climbing to the right of Roofer Madness was a little cold for September, Steve Su, Jonny Copp, and I retreated to the relative warmth of the Tan Buttresses and discovered they were so featured that all one needs to new-route is a regular rock rack and a little bit of creativity. In the ensuing years, I managed to drag various people out to climb a number of ill-planned new routes. Meanwhile, Josh Thompson put some effort into equipping, cleaning, and sending the high-quality Fallen Angel (330', II 5.11+) with Josh Wharton. Recently, a few other groups have discovered the joy of new-routing on the Tan Buttresses. At present, there are 15, four to six-pitch routes ranging from 5.8 to 5.12, with the majority in the 5.10 to 5.11 range.

During my obsession with the Tan Buttresses, I noticed there were some unclimbed dihedrals on the right side of the Black Wall. In June of 2010, Josh Finkelstein and I did the shorter, right-hand dihedral: The Ant Farm (500', III 5.10+ R). A month later, Josh Thompson, Doug Haller, and I climbed the left-hand dihedral, finding great features and lots of vegetation: The Emerald Highway (700', III 5.10+). Afterward, Josh was intrigued by features to the left of the dihedral, so, two years later, we returned to have a look at them on rappel. While we were disappointed by the features that Josh had initially noticed, we were amazed by a series of thin cracks and chicken heads that continue 400' above the top of the hard climbing in the dihedral. A couple of days of route preparation produced a very nice climb with six or seven pitches of 5.10. A violent thunderstorm on the last pitch produced a spectacular rainbow on the hike out: Rainbow Highway (800', III 5.10+).

[This page] The Black Wall with approximate lines of (1) Undertow, (2) Rainbow Highway, (3) Emerald Highway, (4) Ant Farm. The popular Good Evans is left of Undertow. *Dougald MacDonald*

Additionally, in 2009, several people made the long walk to the large northwest buttress of Mt. Warren, located down-valley from the Black Wall cirque, and climbed several long, fun mixed ice and rock routes. In the summer of 2012, Chris Sheridan and Andy Grauch explored the rock climbing potential on this buttress and found several routes up to 800' in length. The most notable of these appears to be Highrise Buttress Left (800', III 5.10+). 📷 🔍

BENJAMIN COLLETT, *AAC*

NORTH CAROLINA

Laurel Knob, new routes. Laurel Knob, a 1,200' dome in the Cashiers Valley, saw a boom in 2012 with four new routes, all 700–1,000' in length and 5.11 or harder. Brad Wilson, Mike Fischesser, and Joe Lovenshimer established two routes. The first, Fathom Escape Hatch (875', III 5.11 A2), starts right of Cruising With the Top Down, and climbs seven pitches up a water groove. The second, Steep in the Teacups of Laurel (935', 5.12d), starts between Hone Ranger and Have Not Need, ascending a steep water groove through bulges and some mandatory runouts. To date, it is one of the hardest routes established at Laurel Knob.

Nathan Brown and partners established the other two routes. The first, High & Dry (700', 5.11-), begins between Dolphin Graveyard and Stemming Laurel in a vegetated right-facing corner; from there, it climbs a high-quality face through two steeper sections, with high-friction rock throughout. The last route, Dike Hike–Monster Groove (1,000', 5.11a), begins downhill from Groover on an old project, which it follows for two pitches before ascending four more pitches up the tallest part of the wall. As the name suggests, the lower half follows a huge dike, while the upper follows a huge groove. All four routes employ a mix of gear and bolts, with some sizeable runouts, which is common style for the cliff.

ERIK RIEGER, *from information by* BRAD WILSON *and* NATHAN BROWN

ALASKA

DELTA RANGE

White Princess, west face, Maiden Voyage. On April 22, Chad Diesinger, Kennan Jeannet, and I climbed a new route on White Princess (9,800'). White Princess is located six miles up the Castner Glacier and three miles up the M'Ladies Branch. The approach gains almost 3,000'.

We approached during the day and bivouacked below the west face. Our proposed route was threatened by seracs on either side near the summit, so we planned to start climbing early and access the obvious snow ramp low in the central part of the face. Leaving camp shortly after 1 a.m.,

it took us three hours to reach the base of the route. Once on the ramp, we climbed stable snow unroped until the upper slopes, which held hidden crevasses, some steeper sections, and an exposed snow ridge. We reached the summit at 10:30 a.m. and descended the west ridge by downclimbing, taking 12 hours round-trip. We called the route Maiden Voyage (3,000', 70°). The west face had seen one other recorded ascent by a team in the '70s, who climbed the snow and ice face to the right of our line. See *Scree* February 2013 for our full story. ◉

Jason Stuckey

CENTRAL ALASKA RANGE

Denali National Park and Preserve summary. The 2012 climbing season marked the 20,000th time Denali's summit was reached. The number of climbers has increased from less than 500 per year prior to 1980 to about 1,200 a year today. This year on Denali, 498 climbers out of 1,223 reached the summit. (In 2011, 687 reached the summit.) Foraker saw a summit-less season, with only six total climbers making attempts.

Sadly, there were six climber fatalities within park boundaries, in addition to numerous other injuries or illnesses that required intervention by NPS rangers and volunteers. Four of the deaths occurred in June from a fatal avalanche on Motorcycle Hill (ca 11,200') on Denali's West Buttress

[This page] The west face of White Princess, showing Maiden Voyage. *Galen Vansant*

route. Meanwhile, the Mislow-Swanson Denali Pro Award was given to climbers Ben Smith and Bernie Babcock for facilitating the potentially life-saving rescue of a climber injured on the route Shaken, Not Stirred (Mooses Tooth) when a rappel anchor failed.

In 2013, Denali National Park and Preserve will be commemorating the centennial anniversary of the first ascent of Denali via the Muldrow Glacier route. In mid-September, a "Sustainable Summits" conference will be held in Talkeetna, planned and organized by the American Alpine Club and Denali National Park, with help from other organizations. We hope that, working together, we can find long-term solutions to help secure another 100 years of climbing on Denali and other mountains around the world. The complete Mountaineering Summary can be found at www.nps.gov/dena/planyourvisit/summaryreports.htm. More information about Sustainable Summits can be found at www.americanalpineclub.org/p/sustainable_summits. [*Editor's note: Just before press time, this Sustainable Summits conference was postponed until July 21–24, 2014.*]

Summarized from the DENALI NATIONAL PARK AND PRESERVE
ANNUAL MOUNTAINEERING SUMMARY–2012

Mt. Hunter, north buttress, Sympathy Variant. Choi Suk-mun, Moon Sung-wook, and I reached the top of Mt. Hunter on May 21 by a variation of Deprivation, the Sympathy Variant (VI AI6 R A2+). Our original plan was to climb a completely independent route just left of Deprivation, but we were stopped by the collapse of a huge ice pillar eight pitches up, near the first ice band. This pillar is at about the same height as "The Prow" on the Moonflower route. We reached the ice pillar by way of a 50m overhanging traverse (A2+). The pillar was wide but thin and sublimated; despite the conditions we kept climbing. However, while Choi was leading, the pillar suddenly fell. Fortunately, the terrain was overhanging, so none of us was injured.

We retreated, and three days later we began climbing toward our previous high point. We climbed the exact same route until two pitches below the collapsed ice pillar, where we traversed right to reach the first ice band on Deprivation. After passing this ice band we began to look for unclimbed terrain, and took our route through a rock band to the right. The ice conditions in this section were terrible and contained unstable

[This page] Mt. Hunter's north buttress. (1) Sympathy Variant. (1a) First attempt. (2) Deprivation (Backes-Twight, 1994). *An Jong-*

belay stances (AI6 R). Once reaching the second ice band, we joined Deprivation again and bivouacked at the entrance to the third ice band. From here, we climbed a ramp that connected us to the Bibler-Klewin route, where we spent a night in the cornice bivouac after passing through the "Bibler Come Again Exit." There was heavy snow on the final snowfields, and it took us many hours to reach the summit, forcing us to spend a second night in the cornice bivouac. After 30 rappels down the Moonflower, we arrived back on the glacier the following day. 📷

AN JONG-NEUNG, *Korea*

Mt. Hunter, north buttress, first solo ascent, no summit. In late May, I made the first solo ascent to the top of the Mount Hunter's north buttress in 15 hours from the bergschrund, but failed to reach the summit. I began climbing on the bottom right margin of the north buttress, climbing diagonally left across the first ice band to join Deprivation, which I followed through the second rock band. From there, I joined a line slightly left of the Bjornberg-Ireland route, which I climbed directly to the cornice atop the north buttress. I continued toward the summit but descended from a plateau ca 100m from the top due to exhaustion, clumsiness, and concern about my descent. I downclimbed to the cornice and rappelled the Bibler-Klewin with a group of four Koreans.

COLIN HALEY, *Seattle, AAC*

Mooses Tooth, east face, Magic Mushrooms; Bear Tooth, east face, Bear Skin. The French Federation of Alpine Clubs (FFCAM) initiated this expedition as part of a dedicated training program to help young climbers in their 20s reach a high level of excellence in alpinism. This expedition to Alaska was the conclusion of a two-year training program. Six climbers joined the final expedition to Alaska together with two guides: Christophe Moulin, the leader of the expedition, and me.

Our team arrived in Talkeetna on March 23. We took a scenic flight over the Buckskin Glacier and the Ruth Glacier to check snow and ice conditions on different mountain faces. We opted to go for the Buckskin Glacier, from which we thought we might be able to open new routes on the Mooses Tooth and Bear Tooth. On the following days the weather conditions were poor, but on March 26 Paul Roderick was able to drop us on the glacier. He was quite surprised by the amount of bread we brought to base camp—forgetting that the French love bread! We dedicated the first day to the installation of our base camp, and the second to a ski recon of the faces. From that point on we divided the team into two groups. Christophe would climb with Estelle Dall'Agnol, Max Bonniot,

[This page] Moon Sung-wook leading pitch five of the Sympathy Variant. The Prow is visible above left. *An Jong-neung*

and Robin Revest, and I would climb with Jérémy Stagnetto, Romain Jennequin, and Simon Remy.

The wind blew hard on the spur where we were camped, and temperatures were very cold (–4°F). During the rest of the week, the weather was partly cloudy with snow on two days. On March 29, after a final check of their bags, Christophe's team decided to start directly up their objective on the east face of the Moose's Tooth. They planned to climb to the right of There's a Moose Loose About This Hoose (Bracey-Helliker, 2008) and expected to reach the summit in five days, with one day to return to base camp. For safety reasons, they brought an extra day of food, which proved useful since they finally reached base camp after seven days of intense climbing.

The first part of their climb consisted of a steep gully, which contained difficulties up to 90° with a section of M6 and A3. Sometimes they had to use bolts at the belays. On day five, they reached the northeast ridge, from which they had a direct view of the summit. It wasn't far, but a gigantic serac blocked access to the top. They first tried to go directly up the ridge, but the climbing proved too complicated. Finally, Christophe's team decided, after much risk assessment, to cross the snowfield below the serac and climb to the summit on the far side. [*Editor's note: In 2008, Jon Bracey and Matt Helliker had decided to stop their climb at this point (AAJ 2009)*]. Christophe and his team went as fast as they could to minimize the risk. The crossing turned out to be shorter than expected, and they finally reached the summit in deep, fresh snow. Their final summit push took seven hours. It was Christophe's second time on the summit, after climbing it from the Root Canal. They called the route Magic Mushrooms (1,500m, ED 90° M6 A3), after the snow conditions, and descended the same route.

Meanwhile, our team was eager to finish our own route on the east face of the Bear Tooth.

[This page, left] The east face of the Mooses Tooth, showing Magic Mushrooms. The Bracey-Helliker attempt (2008) took the deep groove to the left. *Frédéric Gentet* **[This page, right]** East face of the Bear Tooth, showing Bear Skin, with its thinly iced slabs visible down low. *Frédéric Gentet*

We had already fixed six pitches up a gully—just left of a massive, clean pillar—during the other team's ascent. The climbing consisted of thin ice slabs covering a steep rock face. We spent two long days going back and forth from base camp to the face, preparing for our big attempt. The weather was sunny and still very cold when we left for our final push. We hoped to exit the gully in three full days. During our second day on the wall, we decided to leave our heavy equipment at the bivouac. We knew that we had only two days of good weather remaining and wanted to be as light as possible so that we could exit the gully by nightfall. After 18 hours of climbing, though, it was already midnight, and we sadly accepted that we would not make it. We were frozen, the technical difficulties were very demanding, and the night climbing made any further progress impossible. We were truly disappointed to descend after two bivouacs and 900m of climbing.

Upon returning to base camp, we thought it would be impossible to return to our line on the Bear Tooth. There were too many runouts, and the barely-there ice in the gully had been severely damaged by the four of us. The decision to pull our fixed lines seemed to make it final. However, four feet of snow fell in the following two days. The snowfall gave us some time to think calmly and recharge. Eventually, we decided to return to our line. It would be "Kiss or Kill." The line was really worth it.

The next day we left camp at 3 a.m. with four days of food. Motivated, we surmounted the first ice slabs before midday. The weather forecast suggested temperatures around −20°F, but the actual temperature was closer to 35°F, generating a decomposition of the gully. Again, doubt was cast; we had to wait almost three hours before we could restart climbing. We reached the bivouac at midnight. It was too small for a tent, resulting in a short and uncomfortable night. We started climbing again by 4 a.m., and by the end of the day we finally reached the shoulder. While searching for a bivouac location, I released a monster avalanche by breaking a cornice, stirring all of our emotions. On the summit wall, we followed a very logical diagonal line up a gully. To exit the gully, we were forced to make a hole in the cornice with our shovels. On the ridge, there were still difficult sections to climb, and I was quite surprised after I fell on one section. We needed the entire day to reach the summit from the base of the summit wall. Once on top, our emotions were intense, and we shouted loudly in celebration of our win: Bear Skin (1,350m, ED+ WI6+ M5 A1). We began our descent at 9 p.m., admiring the northern lights most of the way down.

FRÉDÉRIC GENTET, *translated by Nicolas Brunel*

Mt. Bradley, The Sum of Its Parts; Heavy Mettle. Silas Rossi and I established two new climbs on Mt. Bradley (9,104'). The first, completed on April 17, was a 49-hour camp-to-camp effort that resulted in the Sum of Its Parts (4,000', Alaska Grade V AI6 M7 A2). The route climbs Bradley's southern aspect via an obvious large cleft just right of the Gift (Blitz-House-Twight, 1998). Our line begins on a steep ice ramp that leads into a beautiful mixed corner capped by a roof at ca 800'. Mixed climbing to M7 and some creative aid out the roof allowed us to gain a major chimney system that continues the full height of the wall. The climb meets the west ridge just 300' below the summit. Our descent lasted through the night, after a faulty stove added to the appeal of an immediate return to base camp.

The quality of the climbing was exceptional and offered many varied challenges. The Sum of Its Parts was climbed in 28 pitches, with a brilliant rope-stretching finish that we dubbed "The Mind Shaft" due to its straightforward appearance but mentally jarring exit. One of the climb's defining sections was climbing the left wall of a wild chimney for 500' at AI6 (mandatory AI5+ R). These

[This page, left] The south aspect of Mt. Bradley, showing the Sum of Its Parts. *Peter Doucette*
[This page, right] The northeast aspect of Mt. Bradley, showing Heavy Mettle. Both routes follow sustained "s'nice" with difficult mixed climbing. *Peter Doucette*

pitches involved overhanging "s'nice," nearly show-stopping anchor difficulties, and a fair number of exclamations by both of us on lead.

Ample rest, a fresh foot of snow, and casual days of ski touring affirmed our intentions on an impossible-to-miss line of ice that we'd stared at from camp since our arrival. On April 25, we clicked into our skis at 2 a.m. to approach the striking line with plans to beat the early morning sun on the lower portion. This line is located on the north side of Bradley's east ridge. Heavy Mettle (4,600', Alaska Grade V WI5+R M6 A0) begins by ascending the major couloir through short bands of rock (M6) between the prominent east ridge and Welcome to Alaska (Charon-Faure-Moulin-Ponson, 2002).

From high in the couloir we traversed left into a large corner system just below half-height on the wall. Our route follows this corner for 1,800' of "s'nice" and water ice spackled into the back of the corner, eventually joining the east ridge at ca. 8,300', about 800' below Bradley's summit. Upon meeting the ridge we continued up and over the summit by what we felt was the path of least resistance. This included one rappel to cross a gap in the ridge and avoid large cornices. After descending the ridgeline toward the Bradley-Wake col, we post-holed for eight hours toward our Ruth Gorge camp, which reaffirmed our belief that skiing is a far superior method of travel, no matter how rewarding the line of post-holes looks over your shoulder. We arrived back in base camp 43.5 hours after starting (including a three-hour rest stop).

Both new routes are sustained in quality. An incredible stretch of good weather and a deep desire to make the most of our first trip to the Ruth Gorge contributed to great outcomes. Silas

and I are extremely grateful for the support of our sponsors, friends, and climbing community for making this trip possible. ▶

PETER DOUCETTE, *UIAGM*

Mt. Dickey, northeast face, No Such Thing as a Bargain Promise. For me, the story of Mt. Dickey started in 2009, when Doug Shepherd took a chance and agreed to a Ruth Gorge trip with a complete stranger: me. I first met Doug in the Seattle Airport, en route to Anchorage; he was easy to spot standing in line at Starbucks wearing his double boots. I introduced myself, and six days later we had ticked off two Ruth Gorge classics and laid the foundation for one of my great climbing partnerships. More importantly, for me, this trip set the Alaska hook that is still firmly planted; I return as often as other obligations allow.

In spring 2010, I returned to the Ruth Gorge with Dylan Johnson. We spotted a line on Mt. Dickey's northeast face during our ski recon the first day. Unfortunately, a prevailing cloud layer sat firmly parked at ca 8,000', preventing us from seeing the critical exit from the 5,000' face. We decided to place a safer bet and opted for a "first mash-up" on Mt. Bradley's southeast face, linking parts of Season of the Sun with the east buttress via some new terrain. Following a rest day, we blasted up Ham and Eggs on the Mooses Tooth. In addition to an enjoyable day out, Dylan and I were rewarded with a full view of the Mt. Dickey line, where it appeared that steep snow slopes funneled into a deep chimney and, more importantly, climbed left of the serac overhanging the northeast face. We snapped photos and made plans to return the following year.

Unfortunately, when 2011 rolled around, work conspired against me and our attempt was shelved. It might have been a blessing in disguise as 2011 was a very dry year for Alaska and the lower pitches likely would have been impassable. In 2012, a solid, early-season weather window presented itself. Dylan was unavailable but encouraged me to give it a try if I could find a partner; Doug Shepherd and I were sandwiched into a plane a few days later. Paul Roderick was kind enough to "fly slow," and we were able to scope out several possible lines en route to camp on March 30. We settled on trying the Dickey line.

On April 1 we launched. We crossed the bergschrund at 7 a.m. and were immediately faced with challenging terrain. Thin ice, vertical to overhanging s'nice, and snow mushrooms made for slow progress and minimal gear-placement options. Doug, just off a long winter of writing his

[This page] The northeast face of Mt. Dickey, showing No Such Thing as a Bargain Promise. Frieh and Shepherd climbed the line over two days, during a four-day trip to the Ruth Gorge. *John Frieh*

thesis and numerous three-day weekends of ice climbing, fired off pitch after pitch despite minimal protection. I took over and hammered out a long section of technical wallowing before nightfall. We were forced to chop a bivy ledge and settle in for a chilly night of spooning. Our best efforts over a full day produced only 3,000' of climbing. We both wondered if we would be able to finish the following day before our food ran out.

On day two, we started climbing with the hope of the chimney exit above. But we discovered enormous snow mushrooms choking the chimney system. Rather than bail, we opted to traverse north around the northeast ridge, hoping for a different exit off the face. A 30m rappel (A0) deposited us in a runnel system splitting the north aspect of the northeast ridge. We followed this up to the serac that overhangs the true north face, nicknamed "Walmart" [Stover, *AAJ 2005*]. After a brief food, water, and psych-up break while still sheltered from Walmart, we blasted two quick pitches through the serac onto the summit slopes. After some trudging, we reached the summit around 8 p.m., 37 hours after crossing the bergschrund, completing No Such Thing as a Bargain Promise (5,000', VI WI5 R M6 A0). We descended the west ridge, and around 1 a.m. on April 3 we reached our camp back on the Ruth Glacier. Later that morning Paul Roderick brought us back to Talkeetna, making for a brief four days in the range. 📷

JOHN FRIEH, *AAC*

Peak 747, Kuriositeten, second ascent; Americans Go Walking, first ascent. In April, Matt Barela, Mike Pond, and I climbed Kuriositeten (800m, AI5 M3+) on the east face of Peak 747, between Mt. Bradley and Mt. Dickey, which we believe is the third ascent [*AAJ 2009*]. On our descent we found a striking blue ice line that rose right out of 747 Pass. It did not appear to be very long, but, wow, was it impressive!

The next day and a half brought two feet of snow with high winds. We hunkered down in base camp and gave the snow a day to settle before Mike Pond and I headed back up 747 Pass toward the ice line, breaking trail through waist-deep snow. We found the snow stable enough to continue up the route, which consisted of three 60m pitches of great blue ice in the WI3+ to WI4 range. After topping out the ice, we exited the face to the right below a large cornice, and then followed the ridge to the summit of Peak 747, which took another 45 minutes. We named the line Americans Go Walking (II+ WI4) since we, like most others on their first trip to the Ruth, spent more time walking around looking for things to climb than actually climbing.

We believe this is a great route for unstable snow conditions, parties climbing the west face of Mt. Dickey, or those looking for a less serious route with high-quality ice. It is on par with classic ice lines like Pinnacle Gully on Mt. Washington. We descended the route with one snow bollard and two V-threads, completing a 10-hour round-trip from base camp. 📷

ALAN ROUSSEAU, *AAC*

Mt. Wake, south face, The Cook Inlet. Sometime during the spring of 2012, Jess Roskelley tracked me down through mutual friends and asked what resources I used for spotting weather windows for climbing in Alaska. Considering Jess had just spent weeks on the Kahiltna earlier that spring, mostly waiting for good weather to arrive, I didn't blame him. Unfortunately, the method isn't that simple, at least not yet, so I offered to call him to climb the next time I saw a weather window. He quickly agreed.

Months passed before a window finally opened in southeast Alaska in early October. (*See Mt. Burkett report below.*) Late-fall weather windows are extremely rare, so I was amazed when a second one appeared a few weeks later. I called Jess, and, fortunately, he was available. A day later, we were headed north for my second Alaska trip in two weeks.

Paul Roderick was waiting for us when we rolled into town on October 21. Paul has been instrumental in all of my "smash and grab" trips in the Central Alaska Range, with up-to-date conditions and a flexible schedule. We quickly packed up, and Paul dropped us on the Ruth Glacier below Mt. Dickey around 4 p.m. We did a quick tour in the remaining sunlight, scoping out some possible objectives before settling on the south face of Mt. Wake.

The following morning, October 22, we got a sport climber's alpine start due to what little sun Alaska gets this time of year. We crossed the 'schrund at 9 a.m. and made slow but steady progress up to the Johnson-Wake col. We bypassed the crux serac on the climbers' right with a few pitches of AI4 and 100 percent premium Ruth Gorge "cracker jack" granite mixed climbing. From the col we climbed through some mixed bands (M4) to reach the summit of Wake shortly before sunset, completing the Cook Inlet (4,500', IV AI4 M4). Nine hours of daylight is as short as it sounds.

We retraced our steps to the col in the dark and took a coffee/Perpetuem brew stop before continuing the descent into the night. Minus my near-miss crevasse fall, unroped, it was largely uneventful. We reached our skis around midnight, 15 hours round-trip, and opted for a nap before the ski back to base camp. [*Frieh made the second ascent of the Cook Inlet in April 2013, with Daniel Harro, finding "a little more involved" ice and mixed climbing.*]

JOHN FRIEH, *AAC*

KICHATNA MOUNTAINS

Tatina Spire, Mt. Neveragain, various summits and possible first ascents. The Equipe Nationale d'Alpinisme Masculine is a group of young climbers selected by the FFME to learn the skills of high-level alpinism over a three-year period, culminating in an expediton project. Our team of Philippe Batoux, Thomas Vialletet, Jonathan Crison, Olivier François, Sebastien Brugalla, Dimitri Munoz, Helias Millerioux, Zsolt Ozstian, and me represent the 16th advancement of this group. For our expedition project, we chose the Kichatnas, as they appeared wild and ripe for exploration, especially in early season.

On March 9, we established our base camp in the middle of the Tatina Glacier, affording us a

[This page] Mt. Neveragain: Oups, I Did It Again! (left) and I'm Comin' Again (right), two routes established on the French expedition. *Antoine Pecher*

magical playground. On March 10, half of our team went to the south end of Tatina Glacier to have a closer look at the beautiful north face of North Triple Peak, while the others attempted what appeared to be perfect melted snow runnels on the east face of the aptly named Flattop Peak. For both teams, the enthusiasm was short-lived. Triple Peak was full of snow and huge cornices, and the perfect-looking runnels on Flattop were only powder snow over rock.

On the 11th, we split into three teams and headed in different directions. Dimitri, Helias, and Zsolt attempted a big gully just left of Mt. Jeffers' north summit. The climbing was serious with scary, runout sections on very thin ice, and they were forced to bail below the summit. Philippe and Thomas found a nice *apéritif* on the west side of Tatina Glacier: a big snow slope with mixed climbing. The route reached a rocky summit, possibly unclimbed before. They suggested naming the summit "Pointe Olive" in memory of our friend and teammate Olivier Bernade, and named the climb Alaska Warm Way (800m, 3R M5). Meanwhile, Jonathan, Olivier, and I spotted a perfect gully heading up to a nice summit. The 800m climb was easy, mostly 40° to 60° snow, with a short section of vertical ice and two big chockstones that provided some M5 climbing. By the time we all returned to base camp, we were already thinking about the next day's projects.

On March 12, Philippe, Thomas, and Seb left for the right side of the east face of Tatina Spire, where some very thin gullies looked attractive at the top of the face. But, once again, what they expected to be ice was revealed to be inconsistent snow. They were forced to climb on the rock, and bailed due to lack of protection. The same day, Jonathan, Olivier, and I headed for a mostly rocky line on the southwest face of Mt. Jeffers' south peak. We found some old gear in the middle of the climb—likely the Fitschen-Raymond-Robbins route (1969). About half of our route deviated from the original line, and the climb was enjoyable, with nice featured granite, some scary belays, unreliable flakes, and, again, astounding views from the top (800m, 6b M5 A2).

According to our weather report, March 14 was supposed to be the last day of sun, so we all left camp highly motivated. Philippe, Thomas, and Sebastien are definitely not ardent hikers; they chose to explore an evident gully just above camp, on the west part of the glacier. Their new route alternates boring deep powder sections with interesting mixed climbing. As the weather changed, the wind increased and they sometimes felt like they were climbing in a large ventilator, so they named their route Vive le Vent (800m, 4 M5+). In the next valley to the south, still on the west side of the glacier, Dimitri, Helias, and Zsolt reached the top of Tatina Spire. A long snow gully brought them to a notch before climbing up the mixed west ridge to summit. They named the route Arête Bernade (800m, WI3 M5). Jonathan, Olivier, and I went into a parallel valley further to the south, where we climbed a very nice gully with perfect steep, *couik* snow, followed by moderate ground that

[This page] Antoine Pecher on the steep first pitch of I'm Comin' Again. *Oliver François*

led us to the top of Mt. Neveragain. We didn't
see any gear on the route, and did not see any
information about previous ascents. We named
the route I'm Comin' Again (800m, WI5+). No
doubt, in the Alps this route would become a *"classique."*

The next four days reminded us that we were in the Kichatnas: bad weather, snow, wind,
and a lot of time to maintain our new American-size bellies. On March 18, though, the weather
improved, and on the following day we left camp with high ambitions. Philippe and Seb went back
to the east face of Tatina Spire, but this time a bit farther on the right. We called them the Russians,
as they attacked a direct line up the middle of the steepest part of the face! It looked hard, but they
found the way. After two days of climbing, they fixed three pitches of high-level aid and mixed
climbing. The route above looked awesome, but the weather deteriorated so they descended. During
this time, Jonathan, Oliver, and I started a new project on the huge west face of Mt. Jeffers. We fixed
the first 200m: a pleasant line of mixed climbing with a run-out pitch masterfully lead by "Air" Olive.
A portion of the route reminded us of the Eiger's "God Traverse," which brought us to the foot of an
amazing line heading straight to the north summit of Mt. Jeffers. With a bad weather forecast for the
coming days, we decided to bail and try this king line during a better window.

On March 20, Jonathan, Oliver, and I returned to Mt. Neveragain, where we spotted a
nice gully to the left of our previous route. It was mostly solid snow, but we faced the strange
experience of climbing vertical, unconsolidated powder. This new route joined its right twin sister
at the top of the steepest part. But, being French—read: cowards and lazy—we didn't go back to
the summit, and by an easy traverse we descended to the right. We called the route Oups, I Did It
Again! (400m, WI5).

The next three days were classic, bad Kichatna weather. We had only two remaining days
to finish our projects. On March 24 and 25, Philippe, Seb, and Thomas finished their king line on

[This page, left] Tatina Spire, showing Directe Française, the hardest route established by the
French team. *Antoine Pecher* [This page, right] Sebastien Brugalla leading the A3 pitch of the
Directe Française. *Phillipe Batoux*

Tatina Spire with beautiful, hard, and airy mixed climbing, followed by powder snow over smooth granite slabs. They reached the east *antecime* of Tatina for what they called the Directe Française (700m, 5R M7 A3); no doubt, this is the hardest line our team established during our trip. Jonathan, Oliver, and I faced uncertain weather on our own project, and the collapse of a big snow mushroom a few meters away caused us to bail from our final attempt on Mt. Jeffers. On March 26, the planes of Talkeetna Air Taxi arrived for our rendezvous, bringing us back with all our garbage, dreams, and souvenirs of this amazing and wild place. 🗂 📷 ▶

ANTOINE PECHER, *France*

Middle Triple Peak, northwest pillar, Hard Arteries. It started on a sun-soaked crag near home, when Twid Turner asked, "Dave, do you fancy getting strapped onto a new route in Alaska in a few weeks? My partner has just dropped out. I have some funding, loads of kit already there, and the new route potential is crazy."

Twid and I arrived in Alaska after the usual airport shenanigans, but before we knew it, we were on our way to Talkeetna, blurry-eyed, with a month's food and climbing kit. We arrived in the "drinking town with a climbing problem," and spent five days there before I began to dream of an easier life in the mountains. Eventually a fly-window appeared, and we had five minutes to haul-ass and make our flight to the Kichatna Spires.

My usual approach to climbing peaks is to go alpine-style, packing everything I need for a safe multi-day trip, then halving the load and accepting that once you start you just cannot stop. But after five days of snowstorms, the avalanche risk was high, so Twid's approach of, "Come on, lad, let's

[This page, left] David Gladwin leading on Middle Triple Peak. *Twid Turner* [This page, right] Hard Arteries on Middle Triple Peak. The rock pillar had mostly solid, splitter cracks. *David Gladwin*

just get strapped onto something and suffer," really paid off as we suffered our way up inch-by-inch while other parties in the Alaska Range continued to get shut down.

The climb started with 500m of snow and ice, that led via a precarious traverse to the base of a superb pillar, topped by amazing snow ridges. We chose a direct line linking perfect cracks and icy corners via steep aid and mixed climbing. We named the line Hard Arteries (1,000m, Scottish V A3) after the lads Stu Inchley and Kim Ladiges, who joined us for the climb and withstood a diet of pure butter during our six-day effort. I have no doubt that the majority of this line could be free-climbed in ideal conditions, as it takes on beautiful soaring cracks, which were unfortunately plastered with snow and ice. 📄 📷

DAVID GLADWIN, *U.K.*

REVELATION MOUNTAINS

Golgotha, east face; The Angel, south ridge. During late March and early April, Ben Trocki and I established two climbs at the head of the Revelation Glacier—the first ascent of Golgotha and a new route on the Angel, making the second ascent to that peak's summit.

From base camp, Golgotha (8,940') presents few climbable options; however, a recon several years earlier unveiled several potential routes on its 3,700' east face. Ben and I focused on a shaft that cleaves the east face like the crease of an open book, never more than two meters wide. On our first attempt, we were cast out by spindrift and deteriorating weather. However, before returning to base camp we decided to salvage our attempt and traversed up a couloir that wraps around to the southwest face. Several moderate pitches (5.7) were made harder by 80mph gusts that threatened to rip us from the mountain. However, the summit was within our grasp, so we continued upward as the blizzard welded our eyes shut with ice. After tagging the summit, we retraced our steps and descended the couloir, reaching our advanced camp after 17 hours on the go.

Upon returning to base camp we found our four-season tent smashed and our Mega-Mid buried with our shovels inside. We spent the next hour digging with a pot, and after repairing the tent and kitchen we vigorously fortified camp. Massive walls did little to buffer the wind so, as any good Doomsday-prepper would do, we went subterranean. The cave was made inhabitable only by the numerous Playboy vixens that adorned the walls. Luckily the weather improved and we never hunkered in the cramped cave for long.

Our next objective was the Angel (9,265'), first tried in 1967 by David Roberts and fellow members of the Harvard Mountaineering Club, who failed despite numerous attempts on the south ridge [*see feature article in this* AAJ]. The peak was not climbed until 1985, when Greg Collins and Tom Walter ascended the southeast buttress. In 2010 I made an attempt on the south ridge with Seth Holden, but we bailed from well below Roberts and Hale's highpoint.

On April 3, Ben and I left camp at 2 a.m. and soon arrived at the notch between Hydra Peak and the Angel. We then began climbing one of the most high-quality routes I have ever done. We simul-climbed much of the route, pitching out eight to 10 technical leads. We quickly reached my 2010 highpoint beneath a major gendarme that resembles a falcon looking west. Here, we made a rappel, traversed left, and climbed a tedious mixed pitch to bypass the Falcon Gendarme. More mixed pitches (5.8) led to the snow traverse that stopped Roberts and Hale in 1967. A snow-covered slab with minimal protection gained the crest, where we traversed exposed cornices. Above, on a diamond-shaped face, Ben took an obvious weakness on the left and we simul-climbed to the

summit. From below the top, we rappelled into the southwest couloir and downclimbed the gash in two hours. We then ascended to the col between the Angel and Hydra, and skied back to camp 21 hours after leaving.

On our last day, we casually made the third ascent of the Vanishing Pinnacle, finding the original anchor from 1967. I pulled out two of the Swiss-made pitons and returned one to David Roberts. 📷

CLINT HELANDER, <i>Alaska, AAC</i>

Revelation Mountains, various ascents. In April our team of Bor Sumrada, Bostjan Virc, Dusan Huc, Grega Azman, Janez Rutar, Matej Pobezin, Urban Iglic, Valentina Mravlje, Ziga Fujan, and myself had an active vacation in a little-visited part of the Revelation Mountains, where—based on talks with a veteran of the area, Clint Helander, as well as other resources and publications—we believe to have climbed a dozen new peaks and routes.

On April 12 we flew to the southern tributary glacier of the remote Hartman Glacier in the eastern part of the Revelation Mountains, northeast of Mt. Mausolus. We landed in 30cm of fresh powder snow and, after looking at the surroundings, immediately realized we were in a mountaineer's heaven. There was 280cm of snow atop glacier ice, which allowed us to dig underground tunnels, a food cache, and kitchen area for bad weather. To our knowledge, all of the nearby mountains were unclimbed, except for Pirate Peak (9,005').

We had four perfectly sunny days, but the weather was mainly overcast with a common pattern of snowstorms in the morning, improvement in the afternoon, and blue skies from 4 p.m. until sunset. We quickly adapted and seized all but three days out of 16 spent on the glacier. Overall, we climbed 11 peaks via 12 new routes, in addition to a number of ski descents and speed-flying flights. The following climbs were the hardest and required pitched climbing on technical terrain: Freeapproved Spitz, southwest buttress (600m, M4 40-70°, Azman-Cokl); Freeapproved Peak (2,709m), Final Frontier (1,100m, V 3/4, Azman-Cokl); and Windy Peak (2,350m), Sleepwalker (700m, V 4 M5, Azman-Cokl-Sumrada). The rest of our climbs were easier mountaineering ascents on ridges, couloirs, and gullies, not requiring pitched climbing.

The area offers first-class mixed climbing on perfect granite, as well many great and exposed

[This page] Slovenian climbers traverse a ridge in the southeastern corner of the Revelation Mountains. The Hartman Glacier area appears to contain much potential for rock and mixed climbing, though generally on somewhat smaller peaks than elsewhere in the range. *Anze Cokl*

ski descents. The only hindrance seems to be the weather and snow quality. We generally found unconsolidated snow at this time; however, some areas were very dry, and some steeper spindrift lines contained hard névé. 🔍 📷

ANZE COKL, *Slovenia*

TALKEETNA MOUNTAINS

Eeffoc Java Peak and other summits. In May, James Kesterson, Paul Muscat, Joe Stock, and Glenn Wilson made first recorded ascents of a few snowy 7,000-8,000' peaks from the Sheep River Glacier in the Talkeetna Mountains. They landed on the glacier southwest of Point 7,820', 1.25 miles south of Chickaloon Pass, and set up a base camp at ca 6,850', from where they made all of their climbs. Java Peak (8,000') and White Knight Peak (8,450', first climbed in 1995) are probably the most notable, and the area seems to offer good mountaineering and ski-mountaineering potential. See *Scree* July 2012 for a full report.

From information supplied by JOE STOCK *and* STEVEN GRUHN

CHUGACH MOUNTAINS

Heritage Point, new route, B Wright Dak. In spring 2012, Josh Varney and partners established a new route on the seldom-climbed Heritage Wall, which is reached along the southwest side of the north fork of the Eagle River, in the western Chugach Mountains. The 3,900', triangular-shaped wall is located on the north aspect of Polar Bear Peak (6,614') and tops out at Heritage Point (ca 4,640'). The three climbers bivied below the wall before starting up the face via a thinly iced and mixed gully. After a bivy, they continued climbing the next morning, topping out the wall in the dark. They called their route B Wright Dak. John Kelley and Dan Petrus put up the first route on this massive, Scottish-like wall [*AAJ 2005*]. ▶

From information supplied by JOSH VARNEY *and* STEVEN GRUHN

Goodlata Peak, first ascent. In March, Jay Claus, Ben Gray, Ruedi Homberger, Andrew McLean, and Eli Potter made the first ascent of the prominent Goodlata Peak (8,166'), which lies between the east and west forks of the Chakina River, and is one of the few named peaks in the region. The team landed on the east fork of the Chakina and used skis for most of the ascent and descent, before flying out the same day.

From information suppplied by ANDREW McLEAN, RUEDI HOMBERGER *and* STEVEN GRUHN

Mt. Steller second ascent, northwest ridge variation. On April 22, Jason Buttrick, Jay Claus, Paul Claus, Ruedi Homberger, and I climbed and skied Mt. Steller (10,515'). This was the peak's second ascent after first being climbed over a 10-day period in 1992 [Jacobs-Anderson-Bowling-Wesson, *AAJ 1993*].

Mt. Steller is the high point of Waxell Ridge, an isolated and convoluted mass sandwiched between the Bagley Icefield and the Bering Glacier. While not particularly high in elevation, its

relative stature provides staggering views. To the south it falls over 8,000' to the Bering Glacier and, within a few miles, the Gulf of Alaska. Its nearest higher neighbor is over 20 miles away. In a landslide in 2005 an estimated 65 million cubic yards of ice and rock calved off the southern face of the peak. It reverberated with the equivalent of a magnitude 3.8 earthquake, and the debris tumbled eight miles out onto the glacier. Seismic stations around the world felt it; Paul and Ruedi were the first people to see the aftermath, only hours afterward.

Our route began at ca 7,000' on the north flanks of the horseshoe-shaped massif that makes up Steller. We started on a spur left of the first-ascent route. From base camp, we ascended a direct line to join the northwest ridge. The ridge is a ski mountaineer's dream: massive cornices, troughs, and sub-peaks rise above tremendous exposure. Following this leg of the horseshoe ever southward brought us to about ca 10,000' and a high glacial basin under the summit. Here, the first-ascent team chose to follow the northwest ridge to the summit. We chose a more ski-friendly route by crossing under the summit and traversing southwest to a rime-blasted col with dizzying views of the Gulf of Alaska. We booted the final few hundred feet to the summit, reversed our route on the descent, and arrived back in base camp 12 hours after starting (IV AI3 70°).

KEVIN DITZLER

ST. ELIAS MOUNTAINS

Peak 11,720', second ascent, new route; Celeno Peak, first ascent; Ocypete Peak, second ascent, new route. In the '60s and '70s the Twaharpies in the University Range saw a flurry of activity. Large-scale, well-funded Japanese and American teams made first ascents (sometimes together) of most of the large mountains in the area. A Polish team visited the range in 1984, and among other ascents climbed a beautiful direct line from the north to the summit of Peak 11,720'. A lost gem, Celeno Peak (13,395') remained unclimbed and forgotten to almost all—until now Celeno was possibly the highest unclimbed peak in the United States.

Meanwhile, Jay Claus was growing up nearby at his family's lodge in the heart of the St. Elias Mountains. Jay is a third-generation bush pilot and climber. I like to tell him that he has these mountains in his blood. He had been dreaming of climbing Celeno as long as he could

[This page] Skinning up the corniced ridge on Mt. Steller. The team climbed two variations to the orginal route up the northwest ridge. *Ruedi Homberger*

[This page, top] The Twaharpies, showing (A) Aello Peak, (B) Ocypete Peak, and (C) Celeno Peak. Celeno Peak may have been the highest unclimbed peak in the United States. *Ruedi Homberger* [This page, bottom left] Jay Claus leading alpine ice in the Black Couloir on Peak 11,720'. *Kevin Ditzler* [This page, bottom right] The Black Couloir on the south face of Peak 11,720', which Ditzler and Claus climbed to access Celeno Peak. *Jay Claus*

remember. On April 9 I had the pleasure of standing on the summit with him.

With six-plus days of food and fuel, skis, and a shovel, Jay Claus and I climbed the 4,500', ice-choked Black Couloir out of Canyon Creek Glacier (ca 7,000') to our first camp on the ridge west of Peak 11,720'. The next morning, April 8, we summited Peak 11,720' via a new route from the south (IV WI4 70°). From the summit, we traversed the ridge east to another unnamed point and dropped into the Balcony (ca 11,000') on the north side of the Twaharpies. A few hours before we arrived, Paul Claus, Jay's father and skilled bush pilot, had landed on the Balcony, leaving behind a gift: a stocked camp. His chosen landing spot was unlike any in the world—the commitment was staggering. His takeoff was guaranteed: He simply drove the Super Cub over the edge of a serac-encrusted 4,000' cliff.

We skied to Paul's cache, looked inside, and then kept climbing another 800' to our second camp just under the north side of Celeno Peak. The next day we summited Celeno from the col between Celeno and Ocypete, and spent an hour and a half on the summit with exceptional weather. The route was a classic, glaciated ski-mountaineering line (V AI4 70°). The only real event was chopping 10m off our rope to leave as a Tyrolean across a crevasse. We skied back to Paul's camp for the night to celebrate our success.

After a rest day and some strong winds, we left the tent at 5 a.m. to climb Ocypete (13,550'), first climbed by a Japanese team in 1977. We summited via a fairly direct line up the north face, under the notch on the twin summit. The peak was so small and exposed that we had to take turns on top. The climb took us approximately 16 hours round-trip. The face proved to be fun, moderate climbing with lots of ice and mixed climbing, and tons of exposure (V AI4 M4 70°). The ski back to camp was bathed in sunset with colors so deep they will saturate my memories forever.

The next evening Paul returned and offered us an escape from the incoming weather. After some debate, we agreed and soon found ourselves rocketing over the cliff. While the debate of our climbing style, due to the plane support, still leaves questions even as I write this, it is undeniable that this trip was truly an experience in the mastery of mediums—snow, ice, rock, and even the air.

KEVIN DITZLER

Mt. Short, Siri's Peak, Ocean Peak, and other summits, first ascents and new routes. In early June 2012, Sam Thompson (U.K.), Sara Arbos Torrent (Catalan), Arnaud Sors (France), and I traveled to a remote and relatively unexplored part of the St. Elias Mountains. We spent 31 days on the Jefferies and Fraser glaciers, which are located about 30 miles north of Mt. St. Elias near the Alaska-Yukon border. Overall, we summited 13 peaks (ca 10,000–12,000'), making first recorded ascents of nine peaks in addition to climbing three new routes on others.

Landing on the upper Jefferies Glacier (ca 8,000'), we climbed Mt. Short (10,360'), Boris Peak, and others, and then moved camp to the upper Fraser Glacier, where we climbed some of the highest summits in the area, including Siri's Peak (12,050') and Ocean Peak (11,050'). In general, the rock was of poor quality. We therefore made the decision to choose our routes based on the quality of ice and snow on a particular line. (North faces were often in good condition.) Generally we climbed peaks by the easiest routes (PD–D); hence, there is still potential for some excellent new lines, with great technical climbing, in addition to many ski descents.

BORIS KORZH, *U.K.*

COAST MOUNTAINS

Peak 7,100', Galvanized; new route potential. Most of the mountains surrounding Haines are geologically not good to climb without snow on them. However, there are quite a few exceptions to this rule, especially in the mostly unexplored wilderness of the surrounding area. The granite spires in a cirque two miles east of Klukwah Mountain (7,000') have caught the attention of a handful of local climbers. Yet, the area remains undeveloped because of its access, which requires either a plane or navigating up the Chilkat River for 12 miles, then bushwhacking over six miles into the cirque.

After many weeks of poor weather during the summer of 2012, the skies finally improved. Dave Sundnas and I quickly jumped into local pilot Drake Olson's Cessna to scout the possibilities. As Drake circled the towers, it appeared the imposing rock walls were of good rock quality; the cirque formed a six-mile perimeter of walls ranging from 400' to 1,200'. We flew back to Haines, excited by what we saw, and assembled our gear, also preparing for the possibility of a long hike out.

The following day, July 19, Drake landed us below an imposing set of granite towers. After setting up camp, we climbed up the glacier to get a closer look at the steepest tower in the center of the cirque. The obvious line appeared to involve 1,200' of climbing through cracks, chimneys, and several large roofs. We agreed it looked like too big of an undertaking, and, instead, we set our sights on the taller south tower, which had a nice-looking, and easier, south-facing buttress.

We awoke early to clear skies and climbed 1,000' to the uppermost snow ramp at the base of the skyline buttress on the south tower. From there we climbed six pitches up cracks, flakes, chimneys, and slabs (5.6-5.9). We finished our route, Galvanized (900', 5.9), on the summit around 5 p.m. We descended by climbing the northeast side of the tower via a large snowfield, then rappelling 200' off the north tower and downclimbing 600' of isothermal snow onto the main glacier.

We spent the remainder of our time exploring the cirque. Most routes would involve lots of cleaning, but one could spend years putting up new routes in the area if only the weather would allow. We've provisionally called the area Rapa Nui, after the statues of Easter Island; the central tower resembles one. 📷

WILLIAM WACKER, *AAC*

Horn Spire, various attempts; west ridge, second ascent, first free ascent. Horn Spire is located on the western edge of the Juneau Icefield and completes the highest point of the greater Icefall Spires.

[This page] Rapa Nui's unclimbed central tower, located outside Haines. *William Wacker*

Until now, the peak had seen only one recorded ascent, by the west ridge (Benedict-Buckley-Lingle-Tickell, 1973), which required aid techniques to ascend steep rock sections [*AAJ 1974*]. Since the first ascent, many of the snow slopes and surrounding glaciers have receded. Still, Horn Spire contains two unbelievably aesthetic ridges and numerous faces yet to be climbed.

Beginning in 2010, several climbers set out with Mike Miller or I to attempt new routes on the mountain. In late April 2010, Miller and Jim Thompson made an attempt on the direct west face of the mountain from the Thiel Glacier, but bailed due to objective hazards. In May 2010, Lauren Evanson and I set our sights on the unclimbed north ridge, but we bailed due to objective hazards from warm temperatures. In mid-June 2010, Miller and Steve Cashen attempted the unclimbed east ridge. They retreted only about 500' from the top due to an unprotected face. In May 2011, Miller, Cashen, and Ben Still set out to repeat the west ridge route. 700' of steep snow climbing led them to a 200' rock step on the ridge, which they climbed with a mix of free and aid. Above this point, they found unconsolidated wet snow and they retreated.

Miller waited for a weather window later in the summer when snow conditions would be more consolidated. Finally, Miller, Still, and I flew into the mountain via helicopter on August 14, 2011, hoping to repeat the west ridge. As on the May 2011 attempt, we began on the southwest aspect to gain the west ridge. Once on the ridge, we left crampons and axes to lighten the load. Ben free-climbed a 200' rock step at 5.9 and another short 5.8 step. [*The first-ascent team used aid*]. We left sleeping bags, food, and a stove on a ledge and continued up three more pitches of beautiful, solid granite. From here, the ridge angle backed off and widened, allowing us to unrope and run several hundred feet to just below the base of the now snow-free summit.

Demoralized, we gazed up at the remaining 500' maze of weathered, rotten rock. There was no clear line to the summit. The final three pitches consisted of loose, runout slabs punctuated with

[This page, top] Horn Spire's unclimbed, heavily corniced north ridge. *William Wacker* [This page, bottom] The west ridge of Horn Spire and unclimbed southwest face, *William Wacker*

precarious blocks held together by kitty litter. It was the worst rock imaginable without any snow or ice to hold it together. Only 100' below the horizon, it was still doubtful if the summit was attainable. The last pitch was the steepest, consisting of rotten blocks barely held to the mountain (5.7 R). Ben followed this by leading another dangerous pitch. We reached the summit as the sun went down.

After locating the summit register from the first-ascent party in the fading light, we began our first rappel. Seven double-rope rappels brought us midway along the west ridge to our bivy. We crawled into our bags after 18 hours and finished the 3,000' descent in the morning. 📷 📄 🔍

WILLIAM WACKER, *AAC*

Mendenhall Towers, West Tower, The Fall Line. In October, during a rare high-pressure system, Gabe Hayden and I managed an interesting new line in the Mendenhall Towers, outside Juneau. In an attempt to further promote the "hike in, hike out" approach ethic, we opted to hike from Montana Creek over Grandchild Peak. This is not a recommended approach route for this time of year.

We had no idea what to expect. October is generally not a good climbing month in southeast Alaska, because it is uncommon to see a single day without precipitation. We packed for bear—a big-wall rack, ice screws, etc. The north faces were out of condition, so we opted for a line on the west side of the West Tower, starting on the west ridge and leading onto the west face. The west ridge has been climbed several times since Scott Fischer and party made the first ascent over 20 years ago.

Gabe and I made our camp in the moraine on the south side of the towers to escape the wind. From there, we skied to the western toe of the tower and began our ascent. The first few thousand feet climbed steep snow slopes with some crevasse navigation. The meat of the climb began as we gained the saddle between the Rabbit Ears and the West Tower. From there, a fun pitch of M5 dumped us onto the west face. The rest of our line probably only makes sense in the conditions we had. A wind crust covered the rock, adding some stability to many of the difficult sections. We simul-climbed the face in three pitches before reaching the windy, knife-edge summit ridge. We called our route the Fall Line (1,110m, 65° M5).

RYAN JOHNSON, *AAC*

Stikine Icefield, Peak 7,031', new route, Deepwater Horizon. In summer 2011, Mike Miller, Ben Still, and I set our sights on a remote mountain at the end of a 35-mile-long, glaciated fjord, Endicott Arm, roughly 80 miles south of Juneau. I knew it would be a challenge to find a place to land a boat. We loaded Mike's 19' fiberglass boat, the *Nunatak,* to the gills with climbing gear, drysuits, packrafts, winches, static line, sheet metal (for docking), and 100 gallons of fuel for the 160-mile round trip.

As we approached the back end of the fjord, we spotted a break in the walls below the Dawes Glacier. We first tied the boat off to pitons but had to winch it higher to avoid the pummeling debris from the active icefall above. After a full day we established our base camp 25' above sea level.

The following morning we awoke to dense clouds and light drizzle, and began traversing through the lower part of the 4,000' granite slabs until reaching a hanging valley separating the Dawes Glacier from Peak 7,031'. Over the next several hours we climbed through old-growth forests and into a maze of rock, ice, and snow. Finally, at the toe of the upper glacier, we slogged through 40° snow and ice for about 2,000' and onto a snowfield below the summit. At ca. 5,700', we approached the base of the summit pyramid by climbing a 300' couloir of steep snow. This gained the summit ridge, where I led two pitches of straightforward 5.7. At 9 p.m., after 11 hours of climbing, we reached the summit in full alpenglow. We rappelled to the snowfield and then downclimbed the snow slope below. After reversing the involved lower approach, we arrived back at sea level, happy to find the boat still intact on the slabs below camp. [*Peter Celliers, Glen Hearns, and David Williams climbed peak 7,031' via a different route in May 2007, ascending the north ridge and west-facing glacial slopes.*]

We spent the following two days climbing a moderate route on the south side of Mt. Sumdum (6,666'), which separates Tracy Arm and Endicott Arm. With prop strikes and hull damage following the two climbs, we were just barely able to limp the *Nunatak* back into Juneau. She has not been in the water since.

WILLIAM WACKER, *AAC*

Mt. Burkett, northwest face, Can't Knock the Hustle. On October 5, John Frieh and I met in Seattle and flew to Petersburg, where we spent part of the day hanging out with Dieter Klose before being flown onto the Stikine Icecap by Wally, our Temsco Helicopters pilot. Wally landed us at the Burkett Boulder, and we followed a ridgeline John had previously used to reach a bivy site at the edge of the Burkett Glacier.

The next morning we negotiated the Burkett Glacier to the Burkett Needle–Mt. Burkett col and descended to a safe entry point for the northwest face of Mt. Burkett. We then simul-climbed the northwest face over the course of the day, encountering very enjoyable moderate ice and mixed terrain in increasingly windy conditions. Near the summit ridge, the wind was so strong that I was lifted up trying to swing my ice axe. We exited the northwest face one pitch below the summit, onto the west face, and were finally sheltered from the wind. Neither of us was willing to stand on the summit and resorted to belly-crawling so we were not blown into Canada. The descent down the Golden Gully (Bearzi-Klose, 1980; *AAJ* 1981) was fairly straightforward, with only one stuck rope on seven or eight rappels, followed by a long downclimb of the lower portion of the route.

We returned to camp after approximately 16 hours on the go and enjoyed a few hours' rest before hiking down to the Burkett Boulder on October 7. Wally picked us up around lunchtime, and by that evening we had returned to John's house in Portland, Oregon, after making the first ascent of Can't Knock the Hustle (IV 5.8 AI4) on Mt. Burkett over a long weekend away from our families.

DOUG SHEPHERD, *Los Alamos, NM*

[This page] Mt. Burkett's northwest face, climbed in a long weekend from Seattle. The climbers approached through the col below Burkett Needle, the peak to the right. *John Scurlock*

CANADA

COAST MOUNTAINS

The Blade, IncogNeato; Stiletto Peak, The Canadian Club. On August 6, 2012, Blake Herrington, Scott Bennett, and I flew into the Sunny Knob base camp on the Tiedemann Glacier of the Waddington Range. We were accompanied by our very good friend and talented photographer Forest Woodward. We spent two weeks in the range, during which we experienced generally clear and hot weather, constantly active seracs, and the breaking up of glaciers

We climbed two new routes: the southwest face of the Blade by our line IncogNeato (500m, ED1 5.10+ C1) and the southwest face of Stiletto Peak by the Canadian Club (450m, ED1 5.11-). We accessed both faces via a several-hour technical approach up the Stiletto Glacier from Sunny Knob, which sits at the confluence of the Stiletto and Tiedemann glaciers. Both routes were sustained 5.10 outings, offering outstanding and well-protected climbing, unlikely passages through blank-looking sections, and a healthy amount of shattered alpine choss. The one pitch of aid on IncogNeato involved ducking left beneath several roofs to access the more western-facing headwall. This pitch will likely go free in the 5.12 range, but, late in the day, the sideways lead didn't invite any redpoint attempts from us.

Both routes were climbed in single-day pushes without bolts or pins. We descended the Blade via a circuitous night of rappels to return to the Stiletto Glacier beneath the Blade-Dentiform col. A vastly superior descent was used from atop Stiletto Peak: We rappelled 200m down the north face from a notch just north of the summit, and then downclimbed onto the upper Tellot Glacier, circling back to Sunny Knob via Plummer Hut and the range's eastern margins.

We also attempted a new line on the central south face of Mt. Asperity, to the right of the Elson-Richardson route [*AAJ 2011*] and made a two-team ascent of the classic Skywalk Buttress on Mt. Combatant.

We were all very impressed with the Waddington Range, finding it to offer a truly big-mountain experience with good access. We would like to thank the American Alpine Club and the New Zealand Alpine Club for providing grants to help defray the cost of our trip.

Graham Zimmerman, *AAC*

[This page] (1) The Canadian Club. (2) IncogNeato. *Graham Zimmerman*

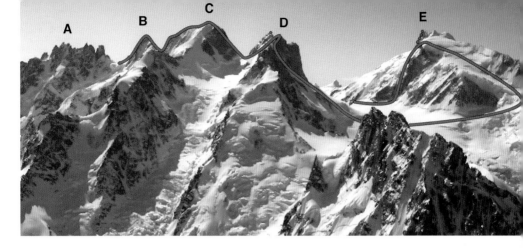

[This page] Waddington Peaks: (A) Serra 5 (B) Mt. Asperity (C) Mt. Tiedemann (D) Mt. Combatant (E) Mt. Waddington. Haley traversed the peaks from right to left. *John Scurlock*

Mt Waddington to Mt. Asperity, high peaks solo traverse; first solo ascents. In mid-August 2012, I had an opportunity for a free helicopter ride into the Waddington Range with landscape photographer Scott Pick and his wife, Marina. We flew from Bluff Lake to the Plummer Hut on the evening of August 11, and I departed at 8 a.m. the next morning for the Tiedemann Glacier. It took most of the 12th to climb up to the Waddington-Combatant col, where I bivouacked. The Tiedemann Glacier icefall was much more broken-up than it appears from below, and the objective hazard was significant.

On August 13, I soloed the north face of Mt. Waddington via the Flavelle-Lane route (TD+, 75°), and headed toward Mt. Waddington's main summit in deteriorating weather. I soloed the summit tower via the standard route (M4) in a storm of freezing rain, and then had an epic descent back to the Waddington-Combatant Col in the sleet storm. The Flavelle-Lane had been soloed once before, by German climber Frank Jourdan, but he made it only to the northwest summit. I believe my ascent was the first solo ascent of Mt. Waddington. On August 14, I soloed the northwest summit of Mt. Waddington and then the main summit of Mt. Combatant. From here I descended for a third bivouac at the Chaos Col (Combatant-Tiedemann col). On August 15, I soloed Mt. Tiedemann via the west face and Mt. Asperity via the west ridge, and made a fourth bivouac at the Asperity-Serra 5 Col. On August 16, I briefly considered attempting Serra 5, but realized I was too psychologically drained, and instead descended to the Tiedemann Glacier via Carl's Couloir.

Frank Jourdan had also done some solo climbing on both Mt. Combatant and Mt. Tiedemann in 2004, but it turns out he didn't reach either summit. So, in addition to Mt. Waddington, I believe I made the first solo ascents of Mt. Combatant, Mt. Tiedemann, and Mt. Asperity.

COLIN HALEY, *AAC, Seattle*

North Joffre Creek, new routes; Mt. Athelstan, new route; Mt. Rexford, north couloir. Bruce Kay and partners have continued to develop the North Joffre Creek rock in the Mighty Mouse area, on the east face of the Mouse's Tooth, an alpine granite cliff band located outside of Pemberton. There are now a half-dozen separate and intertwined routes with difficulties up to IV 5.11 (current info at squamishclimbing.com). Nick Matwyuk and Skyler des Roches climbed a long moderate to the right of Standing Wave on the Fantastic Wall of Mt. Athelstan (600m, III 5.7). Maxim de Jong, Shaun Neufeld, and Drew Brayshaw completed the first ascent of the north couloir on Mt. Rexford in spring 2012. The route was mostly snow climbing with some ice at the crux (60-65°). It gained 1,300m from the logging road to the summit, and had three or four pitches of roped climbing.

DREW BRAYSHAW, *Canada*

LOGAN MOUNTAINS

Mt. Proboscis, At Dawn We Ride; Women at Work, one-day free ascent. After much research and discussion in spring 2012, Ben Ditto, Mason Earle, Bronson Hovnanian, and I combined efforts for an expedition to Mt. Proboscis. Our primary goal was to establish a new free route on the southeast face and, hopefully, free the Original Route (Kor-McCarthy-McCracken-Robbins, 1963). In 2010, a team of three women also tried to free the Original Route and instead climbed a variation that ended on Costa Brava (Women at Work, VI 5.12 R, Sorkin-Illingworth-Stifler; *AAJ 2002, AAJ 2011*). The final pitches of the Original Route are untouched since 1963.

On August 19, the four of us arrived at the base via helicopter. We found the wall impressively wide and with much uncovered ground. The next day, we all attempted the Original Route in a free push. The first five pitches were wet, with the last two being "waterfall pitches." At 4 p.m., at the base of pitch nine, halfway up the route, we decided to bail. The next day, as Ben and I rested, Mason and Bronson checked out our potential project, which partially followed the Grendel (VI 5.10 A4, Righter-Epperson-Kalous-Daniels; *AAJ 1997*). From the ground, it looked like a thin crack system snaked its way to the upper headwall. The first ascent team had told us the cracks weren't free-climbable, but we had also been informed that the face next to the route was highly featured and could possibly go free. Kevin Daniels had even supplied us with more than 50 bolts for our attempt. Mason and Bronson made it up three pitches, following some of the Grendel initially, but soon diverted into new territory. They fixed a rope and rappelled to the ground.

For the next eight days we had bouts of rain and snow, but we made progress on the route during most of that time. We found incipient, closed-off seams that would take nothing larger than heads and beaks. However, the face did turn out to be highly featured with knobs and edges on perfect rock, and some gear could be placed behind flakes. We often hand-drilled bolts from stances or off hooks, sometimes with exciting 20' to 30' runouts right off the belay. Most of the pitches were climbed onsight, with only a few being done on aid at first.

On August 30, Ben and I went for the Original Route once again while Mason and Bronson returned to the new route. Ben and I climbed past our previous high point and into the headwall of the Original Route but agreed the dirty upper part would probably require a lot of work and effort to free-climb; we opted for the Women at Work variation. The rock on the upper wall was extremely loose—a lot like climbing through organ pipes. But after 13 hours of climbing, Ben and I reached the summit. After re-leading a 100' traverse, we made our way back down the wall and staggered back to camp, relieved to have made the first one-day, all-free ascent of Women at Work (VI 5.12 R). [*The first one-day, all-free ascent of Proboscis was completed by Josh Wharton and Jonathan Copp via Costa Brava in 2001; that route shares terrain with Women at Work.*]

The next day, Bronson and Mason jugged 1,000' to the high point on our project and led from there to the summit via two pitches near the upper headwall of Costa Brava. Mason then spent two more days redpointing three pitches that had been done on aid. On September 3, he redpointed the final and hardest pitch in a snowstorm. Our team had finally freed all the pitches on our new route, At Dawn We Ride (15 pitches, VI 5.12c R).

KATIE LAMBERT

ST. ELIAS MOUNTAINS

Mt. Logan, extended unsupported traverse. Joshua Foreman, Graham Kraft, Luc Mehl, Josh Mumm, and John Sykes made an unsupported traverse of Mt. Logan, traveling 370 miles from Yakutat, Alaska, to McCarthy, Alaska. They started out by crossing Disenchantment Bay in pack rafts, attempted Logan by the east ridge, got avalanched off, circled around to the other side of Logan (some 130 miles), climbed Logan to the 19,551' summit from King's Trench, then skied and pack-rafted out to McCarthy. Their trip totaled 30 days. More info and photos at thingstolucat.com/logan-traverse/.

From information supplied by STEVEN GRUHN

BUGABOO PROVINCIAL PARK

Snowpatch Spire, South Howser Tower, North Howser Tower, and other summits, new routes and first free ascents. Jonathan Schaffer and I had an incredible three-week trip to the Bugaboos this past summer. Experienced but young, our plan was simple: climb new routes on as many big walls as possible. Jonny and I hiked into the park July 17 carrying back-breaking loads, the prelude to many crack-of-noon starts, abundant slimy groveling, blisters on our palms from thousands of hand jams, and the discovery of many immaculate, unclimbed features in the range. We also experienced a few inadvertent glissades and close encounters with storms. All of these details characterize what we would describe as a successful trip. We spent a total of five days shuttling gear and enjoyed generally favorable conditions

We spent our first few days trying to complete mostly free routes on Snowpatch Spire. After a relaxed morning on our first day, we decided to try the Beach. We left camp at 10 a.m., and by the time we reached the west face of Snowpatch Spire the weather looked grim. Traversing over the immense south face provided excellent exposure and made us yearn for bigger walls. We climbed

[This page] Crossed Fish Peak, showing the new route Red Fish, Blue Fish. *Tim Gibson*

the clean offwidth and hand cracks capped by a roof for the route's first free ascent (IV 5.11-).

The following day, after another 10 a.m. start, we attempted to free Tam Tam Boom Boom Pili Pili (IV 5.11+), which follows an immaculate dihedral high on the west face of Snowpatch Spire. Lacking gear and time for continued redpoint attempts, we were able to traverse right to another corner system, a fun pitch that may have been climbed before, and into the Beckey-Rowell (IV 5.10+). Later in the trip Jean-Pierre "Peewee" Ouellet informed us that he had freed Tam Tam with many pins and sliders a dozen years prior.

After a rest day, we left camp hoping to attempt a new route on the north face of Snowpatch Spire. However, as we wandered across the Crescent Glacier, we noticed the east face basking in sunlight. We couldn't resist its allure, and so at the last second (11 a.m.) decided to explore this sunny face. We climbed the first pitch of Labyrinth (V 5.12) then branched right, following a long, ever-steepening hand and finger crack to a nice ledge. On the third pitch we climbed a bouldery, pin-protected arête leading to thin face climbing above. Due to lack of time, neither of us pulled off a clean ascent of this pitch, but it will likely go free at 5.12+. Another powerful fingercrack led us to the ledge where the Parker-Bradshaw and Sunshine Wall meet. From here, we angled up and right via steep and sometimes frightening offwidthing to the top of the Tom Egan Wall and returned to camp before dark. We don't feel we climbed enough new

[This page, top] Schaffer bringing up the rope, high on Doogie Howser, the first new route to be climbed free and onsight up North Howser Tower's west face, not to mention in a blazing fast 12 hours. *Tim Gibson* [This page, bottom] North Howser Tower, showing approximate locations of: (1) Real Mescalito (Johnston-Lavigne, 2007). (2) Doogie Howser (Gibson-Schaffer, 2012). (3) Young Men on Fire (Gore-Hollinger, 1994). *Mark Piché*

terrain to claim this as a new route, but we're providing a name and grade as incentive for others to return and enjoy the quality climbing of this link-up: Cherchez La Femme (V 5.12 A0) contains incredible, hard climbing on stunning features and in a stunning setting.

We moved our base camp to East Creek Basin on July 24 during a complete whiteout. The forecast was not inspiring for the following five days, but we awoke to blue skies on our first morning. After a casual morning in the sunshine, we started up broken terrain on the northwest face of Crossed Fish Peak, which had only seen one ascent. After 1,000' of weaving up broken lower terrain and a short traverse below a small waterfall, we reached the steep, gray wall that had looked impressive from camp. Unfortunately, this face is the result of a relatively recent rockfall event. Unlike the small flakes that characterize most of the loose granite in the Bugaboos, we found the features on this wall to be much larger and more precarious. The dihedral that perfectly splits the wall looked improbably blank upon closer inspection. We chose a right-facing dihedral to the left instead, which turned into a splitter crack, only to disappear halfway up the headwall. Unwilling to give up, Jonny traversed left around an arête and proceeded to utilize creative gear placements on thin and extremely lichened terrain for an hour-long lead. This pitch involved a short pendulum (5.11 A0) that was followed free at 5.12-. From here, we climbed through wet and mossy terrain in a black gash to the summit. Our new route, Red Fish, Blue Fish (IV+ 5.11 C2) will never become a classic, but it afforded us a grand adventure, taking all that we could muster to summit and descend.

We spent most of the following day waiting out a hailstorm, but eventually climbed a variation

[This page, left] Wide Awake Tower, showing the new route Midnight Marauders. The only other route on this steep wall is Wild Fire (Isaac-Maddaloni, 2003), which climbs mostly left of the new route, though the exact line is unknown. *Tim Gibson* [This page, right] Schaffer jamming a steep corner on Midnight Marauders. *Tim Gibson*

[This page, left] South Howser Tower. Compassion Club (left) climbs a massive chimeny system; it was climbed free and onsight in a day. The Wandering Direct (right, approximate) links features across the northwest face before joining the Beckey-Chouinard. *Mark Piché* [This page, right] Gibson follows an immaculate corner on Compassion Club. *Jonathan Schaffer*

to Crack of Noon (III 5.10) on the north summit of East Peak. After a day shuttling more food to East Creek Basin, we were stormed off a new-route attempt on Wide Awake Tower. Jonny and I soon found ourselves alone in the valley. We had no source for weather reports, but the skies appeared stable for two days, so we set our sights on the west face of North Howser Tower, the main objective of our expedition.

On July 30 we succeeded with our first alpine start of the trip, leaving camp at 3:45 a.m. At 6 a.m. we began simul-climbing the opening dihedral of the Shooting Gallery to the Seventh Rifle gully. Upon reaching the upper headwall, we climbed a series of cracks and shallow corner systems between Real Mescalito and Young Men on Fire. The climbing varied from sustained face climbing on dikes and sills to technical stemming and straight-in jamming. After one "breakthrough" pitch, which bypassed a section of blank roofs, we continued up 10 *very* long pitches to reach the summit ridge. We scrambled to the south summit by 6 p.m., completing Doogie Howser (VI 5.11+) free and onsight in a 12-hour push.

After a much-needed rest day, Jonny and I returned to the route we had started on Wide Awake Tower, a nearly 1,500' wall littered with steep and clean lines, but with only two established routes. Leaving camp at 1 p.m., we began climbing just right of Wild Fire. The first pitch climbed a strenuous stem-box to a roof followed by splitter cracks. The second pitch's "moss-width" forced Jonny to implement his entire gardening repertoire to send. We then joined Wild Fire for one pitch before trying a difficult face traverse out right from a bolted belay. Unable to free this section, we tensioned to the arête (potentially 5.12+/5.13), where we climbed a very thin, technical, and dirty dihedral (5.12 A1). The next two pitches were clean, splitter finger and hand cracks in a hanging dihedral. After a wildly exposed, moonlit summit pitch, we finished Midnight Marauders (V 5.12 A1), and returned to camp at 3:30 a.m. This route stands out as one of the best and most difficult we accomplished on our trip, and we would encourage others to return and try freeing it.

After a rest day, we headed back to the Pigeon Feathers Group to explore potential new routes on some smaller features. Loose scrambling, two splitter offwidth pitches, and a very thin finger crack define our route Two Birds, One Stone (III 5.12+ A0) on what we are calling Owl Tower. Our route could easily be turned into a short, moderate outing by avoiding the upper flare and finger crack, and instead continuing up a clean dihedral that parallels the second pitch.

With our psych and stamina waning, and no amount of tape able to prevent our hands or fingers from bleeding, we motivated for our final objective, an unclimbed chimney system splitting the northwest face of South Howser Tower, which Jonny had spotted on the cover of the guidebook before our arrival. At an impressively reasonable hour we traversed below the Beckey-Chouinard to the base of the route. We started in the main feature but were soon discouraged by a mossy squeeze chimney with loose flakes. We were able to bypass this section to the right via clean flakes and a steep finger crack from which, luckily, we were able to squeeze our way back into the main feature. The climbing ranged from clean corners to sopping chimneys full of microbial mat communities, leading directly to the summit. Our new route Compassion Club (V 5.11+) provided a perfect finale to our stint in the Bugaboos.

We placed a total of six pins, left a couple of lengths of cordelette, and used no bolts on our five new routes. Jonny and I would like to thank the AAC's Mountaineering Fellowship Award for helping fund our expedition. 📷 🔍

TIMOTHY GIBSON, *AAC*

South Howser Tower, northwest face, The Wandering Direct. In July, Jean-Pierre Ouellet and Matt McCormick climbed a new route on the northwest face of South Howser Tower. The Wandering Direct (IV 5.11 R) starts briefly in the chimney that defines Compassion Club (Gibson-Schaffer, 2012); it then breaks right across darker rock and trends up and right, following cracks, face features, and a chockstone-filled chimney, before reaching the white headwall on the Beckey-Chouinard.

From information supplied by MATT MCCORMICK *and* JEAN-PIERRE OUELLET

CANADIAN ROCKIES

Canadian Rockies, summary. Big alpine ascents in the Canadian Rockies are few and far between. A variety of reasons for this undeniable fact have been suggested: bad rock, remoteness, poor forecasts. There may even be some merit to all of them. But I believe the real reason is both simpler and more complex: There simply aren't that many people, locals or visitors, who are into hard alpine climbing in what is a demanding but unglamorous mountain range. So, when a half-dozen harder mountain routes get done, it makes for a banner season. 2012 was one such year.

Josh Wharton kicked things off with an incredible sending spree in May. In the space of a week he climbed three routes, an ascent of any of which would make most alpinists' season. Together with Chris Alstrin he made a rare (possibly the seventh) ascent of the hard classic the Wild Thing (VI WI4 M7) on the northeast face of Mt. Chephren (3,307m). After only a day's rest, taking advantage of the continuing high pressure, he followed that up with the second ascent to the summit of the much tried Infinite Patience (VI WI4 M5) on the Emperor Face of Mt. Robson (3,954m) with Jon Walsh. After just another day's rest he finished off the week with a rare winter-conditions ascent (possibly the second) of the Greenwood-Locke route (V M6) on the north face of Mt. Temple (3,543m) with Dylan Johnson and Mikey Schaefer.

Early summer is generally not conducive to alpine climbing in the Canadian Rockies,

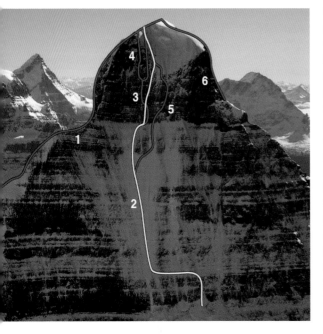

with masses of isothermal snow still smothering the peaks. But after a wet start to the summer, August and September more than made up for it, with week after week of perfect blue skies. It was prime weather for the mountains over Woolley Shoulder, one of the epicenters of hard alpine climbing in the range. The second half of the summer saw some interesting activity on the peaks there. The north face of Twins Tower (3,627m) is arguably the biggest, baddest wall in the Canadian Rockies. The north face was first brought to climbers' attention by the ascent of a neighboring feature, the northwest ridge (Abrons-Carman-Millikan, 1965). In August, Brandon Pullan and Ian Welsted made what was likely only the second ascent of the technically moderate but very remote Abrons Route (V 5.6). Around the same time, on neighboring Mt. Alberta (3,619m), Joe Mills and Raphael Slawinski put in a strong effort on the south ridge (5.10+). However, they did not summit, and descended upon joining the Japanese Route (V 5.6).

The big news from Woolley Shoulder came in early September, when Jason Kruk and Joshua Lavigne not only made the second ascent of the crux portion of the Anderson-House route (VI WI5+ M8, 2008) on the north face of Mt. Alberta, but also added a difficult direct finish to the climb. Although they climbed during the last days of calendar summer, conditions were already more conducive to mixed rather than rock climbing. Starting at the bottom of the face, they climbed snow and ice until reaching the upper headwall. On the headwall, they joined the Anderson-House and climbed multiple pitches of M7, which gained the prominent WI5 ice pillar in the center of the face. [*A point of aid was used after ripping a pin from the first ascent in a fall.*] Above, they reached an enormous cave at half-height on the headwall, which they explored deep into the mountain before bivouacking. The following day, they climbed directly out the left side of the cave. Steep, thin, and sustained drytooling continued directly up the headwall for many pitches (M7+), often through loose rock with inadequate gear. The difficulties only subsided when they reached glacier ice near the summit ridge and simul-climbed to the summit (1,000m, WI5 M7+). They descended the Japanese route.

Other parties also took advantage of the same wonderful high pressure to make noteworthy ascents. In mid-September Ian Welsted teamed up with the veteran Jim Elzinga to make the first ascent of the Elzinga-Welsted route (IV 5.6 WI3 M4) on the remote Mt. King George (3,422m) [*see*

[This page] Mt. Alberta, north face. (1) Swigert-Tenney, 1985. (2) Lowe-Glidden, 1972. (3) Anderson-House, 2008. (4) Kruk-Lavigne, 2012. (5) Brazeau-Walsh, 2006. (6) Blanchard-Elzinga, 1990 (arises from other side to gain northwest ridge). [All route lines are approximate.] *John Scurlock*

report below]. Cirrus Mtn. (3,270m) is best known for the ice climb Polar Circus on its south side, but last September Maurice Perreault and Robb Schnell added Cloud Nine (IV WI2 M5) to the north face of the peak. The route proved instantly popular, at times attracting multiple parties in a single day. On the repeat front, Mills and Slawinski made the third ascent to the summit of Infinite Patience on Mt. Robson.

The 2012-13 winter season was remarkable for what seemed like a revival of interest in "big" M-routes. After being established more than 10 years ago, multi-pitch test-pieces like the Real Big Drip (200m, WI6 M7) and Cryophobia (200m, WI5+ M8) saw only sporadic traffic. This winter, however, established them firmly as hard classics, with many successful ascents. Even the route Rocketman (350m, WI5 M7), arguably the biggest and most alpine of the M-routes, saw what was likely its first winter ascent by Alex Hollaus and Gery Unterasinger.

A number of noteworthy new M-routes also went up. Across from Cryophobia a dedicated crew, comprised of Pat Delaney, John Freeman, Will Mayo, and Will Gadd, put up Nophobia (5 pitches, M11) up a wildly overhanging wall. The route is a contender for the hardest multi-pitch M-route in the Canadian Rockies. The iconic Stanley Headwall also saw some new-route activity, with the highlight being the God Delusion (175m, WI5+ M8+) by Slawinski and partners, essentially a direct start to the previous season's Man Yoga (250m, WI5 M8).

Every winter the mile-high south face of Mt. Wilson becomes adorned with enticing daggers and smears. While the ones pouring over the lower rock bands have already been largely explored, higher up on the peak there is no shortage of unclimbed ice. Two new mixed routes were established last season nearly halfway up the face. Jon Simms and Unterasinger climbed Dancing With Chaos (2 pitches, WI5) to establish the spectacular Cythonna (2 pitches, WI5 M7) above, while Slawinski and Jerome Yerly slogged up the five-pitch Hypertension (WI5 M9) to establish Engel (85m, WI5+ M8).

RAPHAEL SLAWINSKI

Mt. King George, east face, Elzinga-Welsted. On September 15, 2012, Jim Elzinga and I went to the beautiful Height of the Rockies Provincial Park in British Columbia and completed a moderate gem on Mt. King George (3,422m), having made two previous attempts on the route.

To reach the route, we approached via the King George Glacier, staying left of the hanging glacier higher up the face. We started as for the east face route (Campbell-Nagy-Varnam, 1984) then began climbing the right-most gully, which is left of the large seracs on the right side of the face. Depending on the temperature and state of the ice, one can either climb an ice

[This page] Mt. King George. (1) Southeast ridge (Brown-Carter-Hurst, 1970). (2) East face couloir (Congdon-McNab, 1980). (3) Elzinga-Welsted, 2012. (4) East face (Campbell-Nagy-Varnam, 1984). (5) East face/north ridge (Aemmer-Fynn, 1919). *Kevin Barton*

gully or rock. When we climbed the route in mid-September, there was no ice on this lower part of the route, although there had been on previous attempts. Above, we continued up a snowy gully with occasional easy ice steps to a band of mixed climbing. We climbed a long pitch of mixed terrain with scant pro (M4 R) to an obvious overhang barring the way. In colder conditions an ice pillar formed here and could be climbed directly. Lacking the pillar, we traversed 5m left to another gully system, climbing 30m before moving up and right into a narrower gully for an additional 30m. The gully widens above, and a mix of snow and ice steps lead toward the last technical pitch, a WI3+ pitch in a large corner. We continued a few hundred meters to the summit ridge to complete the Elzinga-Welsted (IV 5.6 WI3+ M4 R). We descended via the normal route to the Queen Mary–King George col, and did a couple of rappels to the glacier. 📷

IAN WELSTED

BAFFIN ISLAND

EAST COAST

White Bay, Polar Molar, Bonfire of the Vanities. After climbing in the Upernavik region of Greenland (see report elsewhere in this Journal), our team made a four-day crossing to Pond Inlet aboard Dodo's Delight, mainly under sail. Our goal was to discover new lines in an area of fjords 40 miles southwest of Pond Inlet settlement. After some exploration we found a series of impressive, completely unclimbed white cliffs, including a miniature Half Dome, in White Bay. On August 3, three of my crew, Steve Bradshaw, Clinton Martinengo, and Andrew Porter, all from South Africa, established Bonfire of the Vanities (280m, 5.11a) on a formation dubbed Polar Molar. They had hoped to climb the main buttress on Polar Molar, but apparent cracks turned out to be blind, so they opted for a line much farther right.

There is huge potential in this area, but the climbing will be hard: Some of the rock is friable and the rest is compact, making it very difficult to protect naturally. However, the team made their ascent without recourse to pitons or bolts. It is hoped this tradition will continue here, as in northwest Greenland.

[This page] White Bay, east coast of Baffin Island. Polar Molar is on the far right. There is only one route on this entire section of coastal cliffs. *Bob Shepton Collection/South African Arctic Expedition*

We were held up by ice for five days in Pond Inlet, but then finished the expedition by traversing the 2,800-mile Northwest Passage. My boat was left to overwinter ashore, in Nome, Alaska. Our expedition received a Gore-Tex Shipton-Tilman grant and a Gino Watkins Memorial Award, for which we are most grateful.

BOB SHEPTON, *Alpine Club, U.K.*

Sam Ford Fjord, Polar Sun Spire, north face, Superbalance. In May 2012, Marcin Tomaszewski and I completed a new route on the north face of Polar Sun Spire in Sam Ford Fjord. We began climbing on April 14, and after 24 days on the wall finished our new route Superbalance (VII M7+ A4) on May 7.

There are two other routes on the north face. In 1996 the American team of Chapman, Hollinger, and Synnott spent 39 days establishing the Great and Secret Show (VII 5.11 A4 WI4). And in 2000 the Norwegian team of Bo, Hagen, Roisli, and Wiik spent 19 days

[This page, top] Following pitch 27, "We were like soldiers in the trenches. We had no choice. We had to fight arm-by-arm from the bottom to the top. Bad conditions are not a sufficient excuse. We resolved to climb every day," said Tomazsewski. [This page, bottom] Polar Sun Spire. (1) Norwegian Route. (2) Superbalance. (3) The Great and Secret Show. *Marek Raganowicz (both)*

establishing a route on the pillar on the east side of the north face (VII 5.10 A4). In comparison with these expeditions, we arrived at the fjord very early in the season and experienced low temperatures (-20°C on average) but relatively stable weather.

We chose the most natural unclimbed line on the wall, a large, red crack and corner system, which we called the Boomerang. The cold temperatures allowed us to climb loose sections up this feature, but unfortunately we still found some pitches dangerously runout because of loose rock. We tried to free climb as much as possible, and on the sixth pitch we freed the most difficult section of the route at M7+. Higher up, we crossed the Norwegian route via an offwidth crack to reach a large unclimbed corner system on the headwall, which we called the Arena. The quality of rock was much better on the headwall. Starting from our third portaledge camp, we climbed the most difficult aid pitch on our route (pitch 23, A4), which required two rivets, some hooks and heads, and many beaks in different sizes.

Climbing on the north face of Polar Sun Spire in a team of two was a big challenge for us, and we are happy that the conditions allowed us to complete such a beautiful, natural, and logical line without excessive aiding or drilling. 📷 🔍

MAREK RAGANOWICZ

Perfection Valley, Belly Tower, east face, The Door; White Wall, east face; Mt. Cook, northeast pillar, Levi is Coming. Big-wall climbing on Baffin Island was a personal dream for many, many years—a dream that was always in my mind but simultaneously far from becoming reality.

In June 2012, Riky Felderer, Ben Lepesant, Matteo Mocellin, William Peterson, Eneko Pou, Iker Pou, and I traveled to Perfection Valley on Baffin Island's east coast. We arrived in Clyde River by plane on June 3 and then traveled with our outfitter Levi Palituq by snowmobile across the frozen Inugsuin Fiord to Perfection Valley, which lies approximately 70km southwest of Clyde River.

During our 43-day expedition (June 7–July 20) we established four first free ascents. The longest and hardest of these was the the Door (630m, 16 pitches, VI 8b), which climbs the east face of Belly Tower and contains a super-hard crux pitch (8b),

[This page] Iker Pou working a crux section of the Door, protected by fixed gear. *The North Face/Riky Felderer*

freed by IkertPou and I. The 16-pitch route was established between June 20–July 7, and required 27 bolts, five pitons, and three beaks.

On July 13, Mocellin, Lepesant, and I opened Hotel Gina (320m, 6 pitches, 6b+) while Felderer, Eneko Pou, and Iker Pou opened Hotel Monica (320m, 6 pitches, 6b+), both on the east face of the White Wall. And, on July 17, the Pou brothers and I climbed one of the most beautiful routes we've ever opened, Levi is Coming (420m, 11 pitches, 6b), on the northeast pillar of Mt. Cook. 🗎 🖸 🔍

HANSJÖRG AUER

AUYUITTUQ NATIONAL PARK

Mt. Thor, southwest face. On July 19, Canadian climbers Bill Borger Jr. and John Furneaux climbed a new free variation on the far right side of Mt. Thor's southwest face. They began on July 17, trending up and left toward a large horizontal slope where they likely joined the southwest face route (Berube-Thivierge-Webster, 1994). From the lower-angle break, they traversed directly right, then straight up to gain the previously established south ridge route (5.8), which they followed to the summit. They called their variation the Great Escape (5.10+).

ERIK RIEGER, *from information supplied by* BILL BORGER JR.

Mt. Loki, south buttress, first free ascent; Mt. Asgard, south tower, north face, Sensory Overload. On the morning of July 17, Joshua Lavigne, Ines Papert, and I got off the plane in Pangnirtung. Three hours later we were cruising past icebergs in the fjord, propelled by our outfitter's fishing boat. After three days of rugged trekking, frigid creek crossings, and tantalizing vistas of Weasel Valley's huge granite walls, we arrived on the Turner Glacier, directly below the north face of Mt. Asgard. We spent another big day returning to the valley bottom to retrieve a cache of supplies and equipment that had been placed in the winter by snowmobile, which was followed by a much-needed rest day.

With great weather, we set out for the nearby south buttress of Mt. Loki, the second most beautiful peak in our vicinity. A continuous crack system led from glacier to summit, and we climbed it in 13 60m pitches (650m, 5.10+). Old rappel stations were encountered the whole way. We suspect we repeated the only route described in the guidebook, put up by Kiwi climbers some 20 years earlier. It was likely the second ascent and first free ascent, and was very similar in quality and length to the Bugaboos ultra-classic Beckey-Chouinard.

[This page, right] The Door, shown here, climbs compact granite on the east face of Belly Tower. *Hansjörg Auer*

Following another rest day, we committed to our main objective, the unclimbed, 1,200m north face of Mt. Asgard's south tower. With three days of food, fuel, and good weather forecasted, we started at the toe of the northwest prow and made good progress, leading in blocks of three to five pitches. After 12 pitches, we ditched our bags on a big ledge and began exploring options. We climbed two traversing pitches toward the west face, where we hoped to find access to a spectacular system of corners and face cracks, but to no avail. After reversing the traverse, we climbed two pitches of difficult wide cracks and fixed 75m of rope to speed things up the next day.

The next day, we ascended our lines and continued to the top, eventually wrapping around to the west face. Here, we found by far the best climbing of the trip. Although the stone quality had been excellent the whole way, it seemed to get better the higher we got. By 11 p.m., we all stood on the summit, shrouded in thick fog and precipitation. With previous knowledge of the descent route , we decided to rappell the south side of the mountain, hoping to escape before conditions worsened. After an involved descent in poor weather, we arrived back at camp 60 hours after we started.

All 29 pitches of our route Sensory Overload (1,200m, 5.11+ A1) were climbed free and onsight, except for a five-meter section of icy squeeze chimney. Had it been dry, it would have been a straightforward bit of 5.10. The other aid on the route was one wet move on the final pitch. Technically, the hardest climbing was 5.11+ (easier than we had expected) and this route would be a good candidate for a single-day, all-free attempt by a two-person team. 📖 📷

JON WALSH, *Canada*

Mt. Asgard, south tower, south face, Free Bavarian Direct (The Belgarian), first free ascent. A couple of moves, no more than one or two meters. That's not far. Not nearly as far as the 10,000km we have covered to get here and finally decode the moves needed to make it a full free climb. Ten-thousand kilometers for a couple of meters—isn't that kind of crazy?

The dream had been around for some time. Our fascination with the Bavarian Direct (Bruckbauer-Grad-Guscelli-Reichelt-Schlesener; *AAJ 1997*) began in 1996 when we saw a slideshow from a successful expedition by our friends. Sitting with beers in a darkened room and listening to the hum of the projector, we realized from the photos that the Bavarian Direct could possibly be climbed free! For years, other objectives edged their way into first priority—El Capitan, Latok, Nameless Tower, Antarctica.

Then, in the summer of 2009, the Belgian team of Nico and Olivier Favresse, Sean Villanueva, Stephane Hanssens, and the Spaniard Silvia Vidal completed an 11-day push to try and free the route. They climbed up to 5.13b in headpoint style, but in the end they didn't have enough energy to free the seventh pitch of the climb. It seemed up to us to see what we could make of it. We asked Mario Walder, with whom we had climbed in Patagonia and Pakistan, to join us for the expedition.

The 60km approach from the end of the fjord proved to be very long, and the approach couloir leading to the base of the climb looked like a battlefield. Rocks the sizes of half a car were lying around. Right at the start of the first pitch we were taken very much by surprise because Nico and his team had rated the whole business 7c. For us it felt more like 8a+. We thought, well, if that is supposed to be a 7c, then what will the crux be like? Is it possibly an 8b or harder? Would we be able to free it? The reality in the mountains, though, is that it's often not enough to be a good climber with a whole lot of experience—you also need a bit of luck. We hoped luck would be on our side.

For some time, the weather was poor. We retreated to base camp, played cards, and told jokes. Eventually our patience paid off and the weather improved. The route proved incredibly challenging.

You could easily end up falling 15m, and if you did that at the wrong point, you'd either end up dead as a doornail or severely injured. Even on the last few meters, Asgard did us no favors. What counts is that we managed to reach the top and find a way back to safety together, and at the end of the day we had a fantastic time. There was no hierarchy within our team, no envy on the mountain. We had a laugh together and we froze our butts off together. We reached the summit plateau on August 9 in moonlight, having completed a team-free ascent of the face by the Free Bavarian Direct (or Belgarian, 700m, 28 pitches, 8a+).

Overall, it was a brilliant performance by the first ascensionists in 1995 as well as by our Belgian friends in 2009. This legendary route, with its minute holds, is a real treat. It's not often that everything falls into place. 📷

ALEXANDER HUBER *and* THOMAS HUBER,
Germany

[This page, top] Thomas Huber, high on the Asgard headwall. *Adidas* [This page, bottom] The Free Bavarian Direct (The Belgarian) on the south face of Mt. Asgard's south tower. *Adidas*

GREENLAND

WEST GREENLAND

Upernavik region, Red Wall of Agparssuit, Flight of the Dodo and Don't be Gull-able; Impossible Wall, Improbability Drive. After a comparatively benign passage from Scotland to Greenland in my 10m sailing boat, Dodo's Delight, we made a long motor up the west coast. Either there was no wind, or the wind was against us. Eventually, we arrived at the Sortehul Fjord, close to Upernavik.

This year my crew was the Nerdy Bunch: Steve Bradshaw, David Glass, Clinton Martinengo, and Andrew Porter from South Africa. They were so named as they were always in front of their computers. In 2010 I'd dubbed my American-Belgian team the Wild Bunch, due to their high fives and dancing at the top of climbs.

The South Africans chose to warm up with new lines on the Red Wall, that pleasing playground for pioneering routes. [*See note later in this section regarding potential access difficulties with these cliffs.*] Landing by dinghy in rather turbulent conditions on July 9, two pairs started lines on the east face from the obvious diagonal grassy ramp (72°39 N, 55°53 W) right of Seagulls' Garden (400m, 5.11, Ditto-Favresse, *AAJ 2011*). Andy and Dave climbed Don't be Gull-able at 21 (5.10d) C1. They pulled on gear to surmount a roof at the top of the initial corner, and after ca 300m, having joined the 2011 Italian route Little Auk (450m, 7a, Argentero-Maggioni-Villa, *AAJ 2012*), were unable to find an independent route though the final wall. From this point they scrambled left up an easy ramp to the top of the cliff. Clinton and Steve followed a direct line left of Don't be Gull-able to produce Flight of the Dodo (400m, 24/5.11d). In the meantime, the skipper had moved to the other side of the promontory due to a change in wind direction, causing one pair to walk all the way around the fjord searching for it, one climber with his feet bound in tape rather than enduring tight rock shoes.

After a brief rest the team was ready for the main project, a new route on Impossible Wall. They chose a line adjacent to the 2010 American-Belgian route, and with similar climbing.

[This page] One of the crux sections of Improbability Drive. *Bob Shepton Collection/South African Arctic Expedition*

Improbability Drive (850m, 31 pitches, 26/5.12b), climbed July 12–21, was sustained, technical, and challenging. Four camps were made, with occasional nights spent on portaledges. They finished up the last two or three pitches of the American-Belgian route. We then moved to Baffin Island, as described elsewhere in this *AAJ*. The expedition received a Gore-tex Shipton/Tilman grant and a Gino Watkins Memorial Award, for which we are most grateful. 🖸

Bob Shepton, Alpine Club, U.K.

Upernavik region, Sarqarssuaq Fjord, Drowning in a Sea of Light. Lee Roberts, Dave Rudkin, and I left the U.K. on July 24. Three days and four plane rides later, we arrived in Upernavik, where we were met by our local contact, Nikolas Sorenson. Our freight was delayed, so it wasn't until July 30 that we were dropped off at the head of Sarqarssuaq Fjord on the south side of Qaersorssuaq island, ca 30km from Upernavik (see map *AAJ 2011*).

Our main objective lay on the large cliffs above the east side of the fjord. On our first real attempt, Dave led the crux pitch at E5 6b and we continued up to easier angled ground to a ledge more than 400m up. A storm then forced us into a difficult and dangerous retreat, and we eventually got back to camp at 9 a.m., having been on the go for 24 hours.

On August 9, with a forecast for a couple of days of good weather, we reascended our ropes carefully, and then led through in blocks to our high point. Above the ledge I led a loose pitch at E3, continued for a couple more pitches, and then Lee took over, leading to the top via a final headwall with great rock and protection (E2). It had been a 12-hour push, and we were rewarded by stunning views and a memorable walk down. We named our route Drowning in a Sea of Light (800m, 20 pitches, E5 6b C1). Apart from pitch four (30m), all were climbed free and onsight with no bolts or pegs.

Unseasonable rain characterized most of our trip, but we did manage to climb two six-pitch routes on a crag close to base camp (on which I had climbed in 2010): Heroes of Hotness (E3 6a, with a stunning third pitch) and Palmolive (E1 5a). We would like to thank the British Mountaineering Council, Welsh Sports Association, Alpine Club, and Gino Watkins Memorial Fund for their financial backing. 📄

Olly Sanders, U.K.

Regulations governing nesting seabirds in Greenland. Climbs on certain seacliffs in Greenland, including recent ascents in the Upernavik area of West Greenland, are off-limits at times because

[This page] Looking south down Sarqarssuaq Fjord to the 800-meter line of Drowning in a Sea of Light. *Olly Sanders*

of regulations protecting nesting seabirds. These rules prohibit entering within certain distances of breeding colonies of seabirds or sea ducks in protected areas during the official breeding season, which generally runs May 1 to August 31. It is possible to obtain more information on the laws and regulations covering nature, wildlife, and historic sites in Greenland from the following contacts:

• The Ministry of Domestic Affairs, Nature and Environment, P.O. Box 1614, DK-3900 Nuuk, Greenland. Tel.: +299-345-000; Fax: +299-325-286; nnpan@gh.gl; naalakkersuisut.gl/en/

• Greenland National Museum and Archives, P.O. Box 145, DK-3900 Nuuk, Greenland. Tel.: +299-322-611; Fax: +299-322-622; nka@natmus.gl; natmus.gl

Many countries may have similar rules protecting nesting birds on seacliffs. Exploratory climbers are encouraged to research and follow all relevant regulations.

From information supplied by NICHOLAS PER HUFFELDT, *Denmark*

EAST GREENLAND

LIVERPOOL LAND

North Liverpool Land, various ascents. In April, Natasha Sebire and I made the long journey from our homes in Australia to the northernmost part of Liverpool Land. From Constable Pynt we hired dog sleds to travel north along the frozen Hurry Fjord, through the Klitdal Valley, and across the Carlsberg Fjord. After the two-day journey, we were dropped 65km north of Constable Pynt, at the start of a glacier from which we could access far North Liverpool Land. We progressed on skis, hauling our 160kg of food and equipment in pulks, ascending the glacier and heading east across the icecap to the Neild Bugt region. We finally set up base camp at 71°21'53" N, 22°04'05" W, at an elevation of 493m and near Cone Nunatak, which was climbed in 2007 by Jim Gregson's team (*AAJ 2009*).

Our goals were to climb new peaks and paraglide from their summits. With fantastic weather and generally light

[This page, top] Mt. Mighty, with the Australian route. *Gemma Woldendorp* [This page, bottom] Natasha Sebire stands in front of Castle Peak and the route of the Australian ascent. *Gemma Woldendorp*

winds for the two weeks we were at base camp, we made first ascents of seven peaks, flying from the summits of four. The peaks ranged from easy hike-ups, to ski traverses, to mixed snow/rock routes. Highlights included a nice rock and snow ridge to the summit of Castle Peak (744m, 71°20'47" N, 22°03'19" W), which had a broad, domed, snow summit, allowing us an exciting fly down, and the biggest peak at the edge of the icecap, dubbed Mt. Mighty (1,001m, 71°21'20" N, 21°58'39" W). The final 55° hard-packed snow slope of the summit ridge was a little disheartening, as we knew we couldn't launch from it. However, we were delighted to find that the far side of the

summit was rounded, and we had a most exhilarating flight, looking down on the route we had just climbed.

We returned to Constable Pynt on ski via the Klitdal, reaching it after seven days of travel and two sitting out bad weather. In all we had exceptional weather in our five weeks in Greenland, losing only five days to bad weather. 📄 📷

Gemma Woldendorp, *Australia*

Bjerring Pedersens Glacier, various ascents. On June 25, 2011, my wife, Betsy Winston, and I arrived in Constable Pynt to celebrate our honeymoon by climbing and exploring in Liverpool Land. Because Hurry Fjord was still full of pack ice, and could not be crossed by boat, we were forced to hire a helicopter. Luckily, we managed to strike a good deal with a pilot, who flew us the same day. We were dropped off at 500m on the Bjerring Pedersens Glacier and established our first base camp (70°45' N, 22°03'W). Over the next four days we climbed three summits south and southeast of camp: a ca 930m peak we named Snow Blade; a ca 1,400m peak we called Hoodoo Peak; and another summit, accessed by four pitches of rock climbing (5.7) that we called Pixity Peak. [*The Bjerring Pedersens Glacier flows east to the sea immediately north of Sandbach Halvo, and is situated directly on the far side of Hurry Fjord from Constable Pynt. People have ski-toured and traveled through this area of South Liverpool Land for years, but climbing records are sketchy, so it is uncertain how many of the peaks noted here have been previously ascended.*]

On the 30th we moved camp to a pass (650m, 70°42' N, 21°58' W) between the Bjerring Pedersens and Age Nielsens glaciers, and spent the next eight days exploring the Age Nielsens and Hans glaciers south of the Bjerring Pedersens.

On August 2 we hiked five and a half kilometers south-southeast from camp to the base of a 300m couloir, which we climbed (65° max) to a small saddle at ca 700m. To the west of the saddle

[This page] Viking Peak is the highest summit and was climbed via the main snow couloir to a small saddle, and then up the rocky ridge to the summit. Elf Peak is the prominent rocky top just right of the small saddle, while Dwarf Peak is hidden behind it. *Michel Raab*

we followed a 250m ridge of snow and 4th class rock to the top of what we named Viking Peak (ca 850m). Returning to the saddle, we moved south and climbed a 100m ridge of 3rd class rock to Elf Peak (780m), and then to the east of the saddle made an exposed 90m traverse along a snow ridge to Dwarf Peak (ca 700m).

Our next objective was the Korsbjerg group, which offered granite spires and steep couloirs, though high temperatures, rockfall, and slough avalanches were major hazards at this time. On the 4th we attempted a spire located two and a half kilometers west-northwest from camp. We climbed 200m up the west side of the south face until blocked by a section of loose rock. Two days later we climbed a steep snow gully across from this spire, then a further two pitches of mixed snow, ice, and rock. Above, one rock pitch through a short tricky roof, followed by a pillar and chimney, led to a summit, which we named Blue Dragon's Thumb (200m, 5.8+ 55°).

On the 7th we climbed a ca 750m peak located three and a half kilometers southeast across the glacier from camp. We followed the northwest ridge up chimneys and faces separated by ledges. We named the summit Inuit Peak (300m, 5.5).

On the 9th we began our ca 60km exodus to Constable Pynt, along the Sodal Valley and around Hurry Fjord. This involved multiple shuttles down the valley. Once at the north end of the fjord, we crossed the Ryders Elv River, with its muddy bottom and silty waters up to chest deep. We arrived just in time to catch the July 13 midday flight to Iceland. The weather remained stable throughout our stay, and fortunately we never ran into polar bears. We would like to thank Paul Walker, through his company Tangent Expeditions, for logistical support and wise advice.

MICHEL RAAB, *Switzerland*

RENLAND

First ascents of Mirror Wall, Cockpit, and El Güpfi. From mid-July to mid-August, Basil Jacksch, Christian Ledergerber, Vera Reist, and I from Switzerland visited southeast Renland, establishing four long, hard trad routes. Renland is remote and still relatively unexplored, offering an ideal venue for first ascents on granite walls up to 1,000m high.

We flew to Constable Pynt. Scoresby Sund still has much ice in July, and we had to charter a helicopter to take us to a base camp on the Edward Bailey Glacier, close to the entrance to an area known as the Alpine Bowl. The Edward Bailey has carved a huge valley through Renland, which is surrounded by sheer, tall rock faces and towers. The rock in the lower half of the valley is excellent clean granite.

From July 11–21 we made the first ascent of a formation known as Mirror Wall (ca 2,050m summit

[This page] On the first ascent of Atropa Belladonna.
Silvan Schüpbach

elevation) via a route we named Ledgeway to Heaven. We fixed the first 10 pitches and climbed the rest capsule style. The route follows an obvious crack line and gave 1,200m of climbing at 7b+ A1 45°. We rappelled the route leaving nuts, pegs, slings, and 23 bolts.

On the 23rd we summited the Needle (ca 2,100m) from its east side at D (5+). Although no trace of a previous ascent was found, we felt this summit may have been climbed before.

We returned to Mirror Wall on the 28th and set off on a pure alpine-style ascent of the ridge bounding the left edge of the face. Midnight Solarium gave 1,100m of climbing up to 7b 45°. We reached the summit on the July 30, having left nothing on the route, and then descended Ledgeway to Heaven.

From August 3–5 we made the first ascent of the Cockpit (ca 1,400m) in the Alpine Bowl, climbing alpine-style with a portaledge. Our 550m route, Atropa Belladonna, was climbed on natural gear at 7a+. We rappelled the route leaving nuts, pegs, slings, and three bolts.

Finally, on August 8, we made the first ascent of El Güpfi (ca 1,500m), north of the Needle. Our 500m route was again a trad climb; some nuts and slings were left behind on the descent. We named the route Die Ideallinie (7a). We filmed all our activity in the area, and as Vera is a florist (as well as a climbing instructor), we made a photographic record of all flowers seen on the island.

With the fjord now ice-free, and wanting to reduce our impact, we decided to walk out to the coast and travel back to Constable Point by boat. The 35km to the sea at Skillebugt had to be covered three times as we ferried all our heavy gear. 📷

SILVAN SCHÜPBACH, *Switzerland*

Editor's note: Mirror Wall faces more or less west and rises from the glacier dubbed the Labyrinth by the

[**This page, top**] Mirror Wall. Midnight Solarium on the left and Ledgeway to Heaven right. *Silvan Schüpbach* [**This page, bottom**] The Cockpit and line of Atropa Belladonna. *Silvan Schüpbach*

2007 Lancashire Scouts expedition (AAJ 2008). El Güpfi (named after a forested peak in Switzerland) was attempted in 2008 by an Irish expedition, which dubbed the formation the Gherkin. They tried a more broken line (UIAA V) up the right side of the north-northwest face. The Swiss climbed a prominent pillar on the far left side of this face, accessed by a couloir. In 2008 the Irish climbed this same couloir and continued to the small summit immediately northeast of El Güpfi, naming it the Northern Forepeak (PD, AAJ 2009). It doesn't appear that the Needle was climbed by the Scouts, the Irish, or a second British team that visited the Alpine Bowl in 2008 (AAJ 2009), so was likely unclimbed prior to the Swiss visit.

Renland, various ascents. Inspired by our three-week honeymoon in Liverpool Land one year earlier *[see report elsewhere in this section]*, my wife, Betsy Winston, and I decided to return to Greenland's east coast. Looking at Google Earth and pictures of the region, we chose a valley in the east-southeast corner of Renland, just south of the Edward Bailey Glacier. The remote aspect and big granite peaks interested us, and through his company Tangent Expeditions, Paul Walker provided us with logistical support.

We landed at Constable Pynt on August 1 and set off for Renland early on the 2nd in Zodiacs. A combination of wind and shallow shoreline proved to be a challenge, but after 46 hours, where we circumnavigated Jameson Land and moved up along Scoresby Sund, the boats dropped us at a beach near the toe of the glacier.

For the next four days we shuttled gear and food up the glacier and looked for climbing opportunities. Snowline was at ca 1,000m, and massive rockfall and steep broken icefalls narrowed our ability to access the heart of the range. On August 7 we set up base camp at 1,068m (71°11.196' N, 25°48.928' W). From there we found a west-facing, 300m snow/ice gully (50° maximum) that led to a small saddle at 1,423m (71°11.753' N, 25°42.397' W). We then climbed northwest along an exposed 4th and low 5th class ridge that led to easier ground, and to the summit we named Mitsy Peak (1,834m, 71°11.891' N, 25°48.247' W).

On the 9th we climbed back up Mitsy Peak and bivouacked. The next day we scouted along glaciated slopes and rocky ridges (snow and ice up to 60°), reaching a selection of tops due west of Mitsy Peak. We had amazing 360° views and spotted beautiful peaks in all directions, especially west from us, and south of the Edward Bailey Glacier.

On the 13th, after climbing a three-pitch rock route (5.9) on a small tower on the north edge of the gully that we used to access Mitsy Peak, we moved camp down glacier to 558m (71°10.683' N,

[This page] During the first day on Renland, while shuttling loads up the main glacier. Unclimbed rock walls behind. *Michel Raab Collection*

25°44.166' W) at the mouth of an adjacent glacier that we named Marmot Valley.

The next day we attempted a major peak in this valley. We headed north-northeast up the glacier for two kilometers, then along the glacier due east to a bergschrund at the head of the cirque. Once above the bergschrund, we continued east, climbing a couloir to a small saddle (400m, snow and ice to 65°). From there we headed north, climbing the south ridge of the peak, reaching a high point of 1,563m. At this point we turned around due to fatigue and limited materials to build rappels. We estimated that we were about 200m shy of our initial objective, which we named Cerro Castillito (71°11.785' N, 25°42.594' W). On the 15th we headed down to the beach and were picked up by Zodiacs at midnight.

This is a great destination for alpine climbing, with much potential for adventurous first ascents; we found no evidence of previous expeditions. We'd recommend coming earlier in the season in order to achieve further access into the range with fewer difficulties.

MICHEL RAAB, *Switzerland*

MILNE LAND

Recent access developments; Milne Land, exploration and several non-technical ascents. Ever conscious of escalating air charter costs in accessing the mountains of East Greenland, the experienced operator Tangent Expeditions has in the last couple of years set up a snowmobile service. The goal is to allow expeditions to reach various inviting mountain regions at a more attractive cost than ski-plane usage. The company now has an established forward base at Constable Pynt/Nerlerit Inaat airstrip, the jumping-off point for many groups entering East Greenland. This operation should be of great use to future parties.

In a move to expand and diversify, in 2012 Tangent acquired several rib-type inflatable boats, in order to offer a water-borne service to groups wishing to visit the Scoresby Sund district during the summer open-water season, which is better for those with rock-climbing intentions. These two modes of transport will continue to facilitate access to areas including Liverpool Land, Milne Land, Volquart Boons Kyst, Syd Kap, and Renland. There is also the potential for reaching the southern sector of the Stauning Alps. Large areas of the southern Stauning Alps remain to be fully explored, and Milne Land and Renland, in particular, hold enormous scope for alpine rock climbing and virgin big-wall objectives.

In the first three weeks of August, I led a party comprising Ingrid Baber, Alan Crichton, Sandy Gregson, David Owen, and John Robinson (all U.K.) to the northeast corner of Milne Land. Our purpose was to explore and trek in a largely unvisited area of the island, noting future potential,

[This page] The Bear Islands off the northeast coast of Milne Land. *Jim Gregson*

and to test the capability of small-boat access to this and similar locations. Our journey of more than 200km from Constable Pynt took 13 hours; we traveled through the night when calmer seas seemed to prevail. We landed at "Iceberg Bay" (70°56.9' N, 25°29.2' W) and set up camp on a raised beach. Here we had extensive views of the alpine-looking peaks of northeast Milne Land (lots of potential), the huge rock walls of Renland's southern coast, and the attractive archipelago of the Bear Islands (where boat usage would give access to what looks like exciting crags and several potential longitudinal traverses).

Rock and big-wall climbers would be advised to visit in July and August, alpinists and ski mountaineers in the colder months of late March, April, and early May. In the heat-wave conditions of August 2012 my group frequently rounded off hot days on the mountains with a swim in the iceberg-dotted sea. Tangent boats evacuated us without problem at the end of our trip. We were transported south to Korridoren Bay on Milne Land's east coast, from where a Twin Otter, which landed on the tundra, took us back to Constable Pynt. 📷

JIM GREGSON, *Alpine Club, U.K.*

Milne Land, probable first and second ascents. During 14 days in August, Line Veenstra and I climbed a number of peaks in northeast Milne Land. We accessed the island by boat from Constable Pynt, and followed the Korridoren Glacier west, moving camp often and making many side trips. We rented a rifle but saw no sign of polar bears during our travels—for the same weight, an aluminum ladder, for bridging crevasses, would have proved more useful.

We attempted to access the icefield to our north via glaciated tongues falling into the basin at 70°53' N, 25°59' W. However, and possibly due to our presence late in the season, we couldn't find a route through the crevasses that would be suitable for heavy load carrying. We eventually succeeded via a mellow couloir (less than 35°) that started from 70°52' N, 25°53' W. This allowed hassle-free access to the upper icefield. Gaining the icefield to the south of the Korridoren was straightforward via the glacier at 70°49' N, 25°55' W. Peak 1,247m was climbed as a side trip directly up talus slopes from the Korridoren. From these icefields, we climbed more than a dozen peaks, mostly easy. 📄 📷 🔍

CHRISTIAN VEENSTRA, *Canada*

[This page] Looking southwest from ca 70°50' N, 25°54' W in the Korridoren. (A) Bird Ridge (main summit not visible). (B) Rino's Horn (summit not visible). *Christian Veenstra*

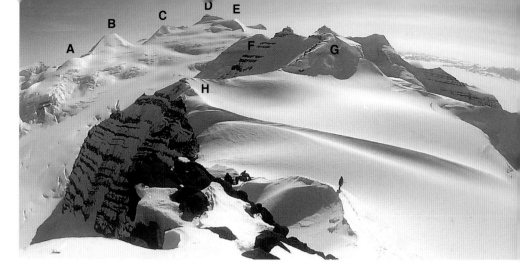

[This page] Approaching the summit of Peak 2,950m. (A) Peak 3,001m. (B) U-Turn. (C) Peak 3,400m. (D) Gunnbjornsfjeld. (E) Peak 3,480m. (F) Peak 3,047m. (G) Peak 3,003m (higher summit left is most likely unclimbed). (H) Peak 2,873m. *Marcus Tobia*

WATKINS MOUNTAINS

Five first ascents. After climbing the standard route from the east on Greenland's highest mountain, Gunnbjornsfjeld (3,693m), Carlos Calderas, Carlos Castillo, Marco Cayuso, Martin Echeverria, and I climbed several peaks to the north of Gunnbjornsfjeld that Paul Walker of Tangent Expeditions told us were previously virgin. He had advocated the northwestern flanks, as the glaciers on this side are higher, leaving a relatively short ascent to the summits. However, it would have taken two or three days to travel around the northern side of the group to a suitable campsite, so we opted to try from the east, establishing our new camp at 2,400m on the glacier that flows northeast from Gunnbjornsfjeld.

On May 6 we climbed Peak 3,047m (68°57.502' N, 29°53.026' W). From camp we headed west-southwest into the cwm below the peak. We reached the corniced north ridge and followed it to the summit.

On the 8th we set off for summits on the ridge trending north, then northeast, from Peak 3,047m. We climbed into a huge bowl west of camp and then up a 450m snow slope, which steepened to 55°, eventually moving right to hug the rocks and minimize avalanche risk. Once on the crest we headed southwest to our first summit, Peak 3,003m (68°58.278' N, 29°52.511' W). Retracing our steps, we followed the ridge easily northeast to a second summit: Peak 2,873m (68°58.418' N, 29°51.439'). North along the ridge lay Peak 2,950m (as marked on the 1:100,000 Hvitserk East Greenland map). Carlos Castillo and I climbed this beautiful pyramid, using ice screws for protection. The summit ridge was deep snow and we sank up to our hips, literally swimming to the rocky top.

On the 10th, with the weather still stable, Castillo, Echeverria, and I climbed our fifth previously virgin peak, this time on the opposite side of the glacier, on the long ridge running northeast from Gunnbjornsfjeld. We reached the col north of U-Turn (3,307m), then continued up the corniced ridge to the neighboring summit, placing screws in the ice 100cm below the snow surface. Our GPS recorded 3,001m and 68°56.681 N, 29°49.660' W.

MARCUS TOBIA, *Venezuela*

KANGERTITIVATSIAQ FJORD

Mythics Cirque, various ascents. In August AAC members Steve Beckwith (U.K.), Matthew Bunn (Australia), Matthew Traver (U.K.), and I traveled to East Greenland, intent on exploring unclimbed peaks. After congregating in Tasiilaq, we spent several days trying to locate packages containing food and gear (they arrived two months late!), and salvage plans to head south along the coast. Ultimately, the journey to our planned location proved too perilous for any of the available captains, due to unusually rough seas brought on by a warm summer and lack of sea ice.

Eventually, Salomon Gadegaard took us ca 150km north to Kangertitivatsiaq (ca 66°18'15" N, 35°42'40" W), a prospective climbing area located via Google Earth and vetted by the venerable Tasiilaq resident Hans Christian Florian. We established base camp at an extraordinary site in a cwm below a prominent collection of towers. We dubbed this the Mythics Cirque. This cirque lies at the convergence of two forks in the fjord system, the Kangertitivatsiaq and Sangmilik, and had no known previous visits by climbers. Buffered from the larger inland glaciers, the Mythics peaks hold steep walls exceeding 1,000m, though rock quality is variable.

After a few days of unsettled weather, our team divided and spent the next three weeks attempting new routes, both in the cirque proper and the surrounding areas, which were reached by foot and/or inflatable canoe. First, Bunn and I set off for the valleys to the southwest of the cirque. After exploring two small glaciers on foot, we climbed Father Tower via a new route on the southeast face and east ridge, Coronis (5.9, ca 14 pitches). This was the second ascent of this ca 1,350m tower, the first ascent via the south ridge being made the day before by Mike Libecki. Descent was via the south ridge, where we bivouacked and enjoyed the northern lights. In the meantime, Beckwith and Traver attempted the steep and imposing north face of Siren Tower, but were thwarted by heavy rockfall in the approach couloir.

After regrouping at base camp, Bunn and I chose to attempt a fast and light ascent of the highest peak at the back of the cirque, approaching via a steeper than expected and treacherously loose couloir. After a bivouac at a col, we began to ascend the steep, technical ridge toward the summit. We retreated after a couple of moderate pitches, knowing there was no safe way to descend the couloir we'd climbed. Instead, we would have to traverse four peaks to get back to base camp. Over the next 30 hours, Bunn and I completed the Tortures Traverse (5.4), making the first ascents of all four peaks, with proposed names Prometheus (ca 1,100m), Tantalus (ca 1,250m), Sisyphus (ca 1,200m), and Damocles (ca 1,250m). The ridge was generally unstable, with third- and fourth-class terrain intermixed with brief sections of low fifth class, and is not recommended.

[This page] Assembling the Tupilak on the south face of Hidden Tower. *Mike Royer*

[This page, top] Looking west into the Mythics Cirque from base camp. (A) The Squid. (B) Father Tower (ca 1,350m). (C) Hidden Tower (ca 1,350m), summit not visible. (D) Siren Tower (ca 1,350m). (E) Unnamed tower (ca 1,450m). (F) Tartarus couloir. (G) Prometheus (ca 1,100m). (H) Tantalus (ca 1,250m). (I) Sisyphus (ca 1,200m). (J) Damocles (ca 1,250m). *Mike Royer* [This page, bottom] North faces of the towers of the southern branch of the Mythics Cirque. (A) Father Tower, center of the north face, first climbed by Libecki and Pringle, 2012. See page 80 for route lines on this peak. (B) Hidden Tower, climbed via the south face (not visible). (C) Siren Tower, unclimbed. The other two peaks are also unclimbed. *Mike Royer*

For final objectives, Beckwith and Traver focused on a small, steep feature on the east ridge of Father Tower (dubbed the Squid), but retreated due to poor rock quality. Simultaneously, Bunn and I found tremendous rock quality on the south face of Hidden Tower, which was approached via canoe and foot. Our nine-pitch route, Assembling the Tupilak (5.10), might be a classic in almost any climbing destination. Our trip was generously supported by the American Alpine Club (McNeill-Nott Grant), the Arctic Club and the Gino Watkins Memorial Fund, the Alpine Club, the Mount Everest Foundation, and the British Mountaineering Council. ▤ ▣

MIKE ROYER, *AAC*

Mythics Cirque, Ataatap Tower and other ascents. Keith Ladzinski, Mike Libecki, Angie Payne, and Ethan Pringle visited the Mythics Cirque at roughly the same time as the team that named it (*see report above*) and completed numerous difficult boulder problems and two new routes on Ataatap Tower (a.k.a., Father or Daddy's Tower, ca 1,350m). Libecki made the first ascent via a three-hour solo of the south ridge (5.8), then with Pringle climbed the north-facing Built Fjord Tough pillar (1,060m, V 5.12 A2) in a 54-hour push from a bivouac 200m up the route (62 hours including descent). The route was climbed free except for one five-meter wet/rotten section. A full account appears in this *AAJ*.

SOUTH GREENLAND

CAPE FAREWELL REGION

Tasermiut Fjord, Ketil (2,010m), south face, Turbo; Ulamertorssuaq North (1,830m), northwest face, Keep Panic, Please. From June 20 to July 23, Tomas Brt (Czech), Jan Smolen, and I (both Slovak) visited Tasermiut Fjord and enjoyed largely excellent weather, so different from my first visit in 1998, when I experienced only a few days of sunshine.

Our first aim was to climb a new line on the 1,200m high south face of Ketil. Starting early on June 23 we followed an obvious rightward slanting chimney system (UIAA II-III), finding two belays that were most likely on the 1974 Austrian Route (the original route to the summit of Ketil). The chimney leads toward the right edge of the face, but near its top we broke left and climbed direct, crossing the Austrian Route where it slants back left up the south face. In 19 hours we climbed 13 pitches, the hardest, pitch 11, was a finger crack of UIAA VIII+.

After a pleasant bivouac on a good ledge we continued up corners and offwidths to an overhanging wet chimney. Here, we almost certainly followed the 2004 French route, Clémence de l'Ogre, for several pitches. We decided to climb left of the chimney, aiding a 15m wet finger crack at A2. We then continued up easier, less vertical ground until, at 9:30 p.m., after having climbed eight pitches that day, we reached a ledge below the headwall. We made our second bivouac here and reached the summit at noon the following day. We named the route Turbo (1,450m of climbing, 25 pitches, VIII+ A2) and placed only one bolt. The same day we rappelled the line of the French route, using their in situ anchors.

After four days of rest we concentrated on our main goal, the virgin 1,100m northwest face of Ulamertorssuaq's north summit. On July 1 we moved gear to the base of the wall and fixed four pitches, the last being the hardest with runout climbing at VIII. Next day we reached the end of the ropes with five days of food and then climbed until 10:30 p.m., sleeping on a portaledge at the top of pitch nine. On the following day we climbed six pitches to a large overhang, where the weather deteriorated and we spent the next three days in the ledge, waiting for better conditions. The fourth night proved critical: The rain was so strong that even the large overhang failed to shield us from the water.

On July 7 a strong wind dispersed the weather and we set out in sun, finding the moss- and lichen-covered wall above very wet. The crux proved to be an offwidth (VIII) on pitch 20. After this the climbing got easier and we reached the summit, probably only the second team to do so, at 8:50 p.m. [*Editor's note: Agier, Amy, Lemoine, Lemoine, and Walter made the first ascent in 1975 via the east couloir and east ridge, 900m, D. In 1998 Ian Parsons and Tony Penning climbed the prominent 700m pillar at the base of the east ridge—James Hopkins Pillar—but did not continue to the summit*]. At 2 a.m. we regained the portaledge, and the same day made a free ascent of pitch 17, where Smolen had fallen before. As the rain returned we descended to base camp. We named the route Keep Panic, Please (1,270m, 26 pitches, VIII redpoint). We used no protection bolts but placed some for belays.

VLADO LINEK, *JAMES, Slovakia*

Maujit Qoqarsassia, Golden Lunacy, repeat; Marluissat Peak, Three Hobbits from the Moon and Snake from Appilatoq. The Polish Mountaineering Association sent a three-man team to Greenland specifically to repeat the 2007 Kaszlikowski-Kubarska route, Golden Lunacy, on the huge sea cliff of Maujit Qoqarsassia (*AAJ 2008*). Although the team did not follow the original line exactly, they did climb the crux pitch, and in their opinion suggest a revised grade of 6c rather than the original 7a+ with one rest point. Aleksander Barszczewski, Marcin Księzak, and Jan Kuczera completed the route with one bivouac.

On July 31 the three put up Snake from Appilatoq on Marluissat Peak, above the village of Appilatoq. The 700m (21 pitches) route was climbed onsight in 16 hours at 7a+. Prior to this, on July 26, the same three repeated Two Hobbits from the Moon (also 700m) on the wall to the left, adding a new direct finish (Three Hobbits from the Moon) at 6b. Again, in their opinion the crux pitch of the original route was more like 6a+/6b, rather than the 6c quoted by first ascensionists Kaszlikowski and Kubarska in 2009.

LINDSAY GRIFFIN, *Mountain INFO*

[This page] Ulamertorssuaq North, northwest face, Keep Panic, Please (2012). Original route to summit lies behind left skyline. *Vlado Linek*

MEXICO

BAJA CALIFORNIA

El Gran Trono Blanco, Pan-American Route, free ascent and new variation; Giraffe, first free ascent.
In January 2012, Will Stanhope, Paul McSorley, Andrew Burr, and I went down to the Gran Trono Blanco, a 1,000' wall of Mexican granite, to free-climb the wall's hardest route and hopefully add our own free line. Will and Paul had previously attempted the Pan-American Route, a stellar 5.12d that takes a nice line up the middle of the face, and they were keen to go back. We also wanted to check out a classic John Long line, the Giraffe, for free-climbing potential. In typical Burr fashion, the whole trip, including travel, would be less than 10 days, the limit of time he can escape family obligations. We blasted across the border and got right to it.

The first day, Will and I hiked around to the base of the Pan-American while Paul and Andy rapped down the wall to get in position for photos. We each freed the route over a long day of effort. Paul Piana, who had done the first free ascent, recommended that we pioneer a new finish up cool cracks to the left, rather than following the chimney system for the last few pitches. Will and I were too tired and hungry to try the variation on the first day, but I came back later in the week with Paul to reclimb the route and add two pitches of good crack climbing to the left. I would strongly recommend the variation: a good 5.10 crack leading to a thin 5.11+ corner. Overall, it's much more pleasant than groveling up a chimney for two pitches.

Our team then turned our attention to the Giraffe, a great route that connects a series of proud corner systems. Generally, we followed the existing line and added some bolts to face climbing variations in a few places, avoiding some of the original bolt ladders on the aid line by climbing to the right. It took us three days of work to add the bolts and suss out the climbing. We finally freed the route in the 5.13b range—right on the edge of what we could manage in our fatigued and sunburned state. There are two

[This page] The east face of El Gran Trono Blanco. (1) Giraffe (free variation). (2) Pan-American Route. (2a) Honnold-McSorley variation. *Andrew Burr*

pitches that may be 5.13b and several 5.12s, while the rest comes in at fun 5.10 to 5.11.

The rock on El Gran Trono Blanco is as good as any granite in Yosemite, and the climbing is a pleasant mix of face and cracks. I was very impressed by the overall experience. We saw no other people for the full 10 days, and the desert was shockingly quiet. It's well worth a visit, only an hour from the border—like a southern Yosemite, but hotter and with more cacti. 🔍

ALEX HONNOLD

EL POTRERO CHICO

Land of the Free Wall, El Prisionero del Cielo. In December 2012, Stefan Krug, Sam Magro, and I opened a big new route on the Land of the Free Wall, the first to top out this part of the wall. The route climbs to the right of Land of the Free and left of the Shining Path.

I have never spent as much effort on a new route as I did on this one. Because the omnipresent cactus roots reached deep into even the smallest cracks, huge blocks of rock came off with the lightest touch—a challenge for a ground-up ascent. After five days of working our way up to the summit, Stefan had to fly home, and it took me six more full days to clean the route so that it suits the philosophy of the area. After cleaning, I redpointed the route with Sam Magro. Now it's fully bolted but demanding—a great route up good rock, with long and sustained pitches. We called the route El Prisionero del Cielo, which means Prisoner of Heaven (8 pitches, 5.12b). From the top of our route, the door is open to some untouched 400m walls above the lower Land of the Free Wall. A simple traverse with one fixed rope would grant access to these features. There is a good bivy spot on top, and it might be a good idea to start fresh before tackling what lies above. 📷

JENS RICHTER

Outrage Wall, Mi Regalo Favorito. In February 2013, Alex Honnold and Josh McCoy made the first free ascent of Mi Regalo Favorito (19 pitches, 5.13c/d). The 19-pitch line was bolted by Kurt Smith and Jeb Vetters over 21 days in the 1990s but never free-climbed. The route ascends the left side of the Outrage Wall via a plumb line leading to the summit of Cerro San Miguel. Honnold and McCoy spent four days cleaning the route and removing old fixed ropes before redpointing the line on their second attempt. The route contains at least ten 5.11 or 5.12 pitches in addition to the crux pitch (5.13c/d). ▶

From information at CLIMBING.COM

[This page] Land of the Free Wall showing El Prisionero del Cielo. *Jens Richter*

COLOMBIA

CORDILLERA DEL COCUY

Ritacuba Blanco, east face, Ocho Amaneceres. In January 2013, Marco Jubes, Dani Moreno, and I managed to put up a new line on Ritacuba (5,350m). We choose an unclimbed line on the central wall: a huge, vaulted ceiling, with many roofs. We climbed the first 100m of Tierra de Condores to reach a large horizontal break below the face, which we traversed directly left for 150m to the start of our route.

We camped on a shelf below the face and cooked with water dripping from the icicles on the wall. Our routine was to lead a pitch, fix ropes, and haul all the gear for the next day. Some leads took up to eight hours, and the climbing was made difficult by the cold, difficulty of protection, and the altitude. Due to the cold, the last pitches were the hardest. My feet almost froze—they turned purple and swelled a lot. Without any good cracks through the steep upper roofs, I used a mix of free and aid climbing, placing pitons and nuts to keep moving. After climbing seven independent pitches in the center of the wall, we traversed right and joined Tierra de Condores [*AAJ 2010*] to reach the top of the wall, thus completing Ocho Amaneceres ("Eight Sunrises," 500m, 8b A3). With sustained difficulties of 7a to 7c to overcome, we couldn't free the hardest pitch. However, eight days away from civilization and any type of technology afforded us a great adventure. 🔍

EDU MARIN, *edumarin.blogspot.com*

[This page] Ritacuba Blanco, east face. (1) Viviendo Entre Tinieblas (Gonzalez Rubio-Mazzieri-Wilke). (2) Ocho Amaneceres (Jubes-Marin-Moreno, 2013). (3) Tierra de Condores (Calderon-Gargitter-Gonzalez Rubio-Kehrer, 2010). (4) Buscando la de Anker (Caceres-Gonzalez Rubio, 2008). (5) El Lano en Llamas (Anker, 1996). *Helmut Gargitter*

VENEZUELA

Acopan Tepui, In Gold Blood. Pat Goodman, José Miranda, and I first attempted this line in February 2012 with a Jonny Copp Foundation Grant, completing four pitches, but Pat and José both got injured. We felt some serious voodoo from the wall, and so decided to come back in a year and see if the tepui gods would forgive us.

February 2013 wasn't a whole ton better—the Pemon people rose up against illegal mining going on in the jungle and kidnapped 40 miners as well as the soldiers who attempted to free them. We cheered them on from our swanky (skanky) hotel room in Ciudad Bolivar, but the uprising shut down all flights to the region for some time. Eventually a pilot agreed to drop us, along with photographer James Q Martin, in Yunek. The chieftain, Leonardo, gave big hugs and laughter as we exited the Cessna on their bush-covered landing strip. They had seen only one tourist party since our visit a year prior—a group of two trekkers. This is rough on the community, as visitors equal dollars and bartering. We had delivered a solar-power system to them in 2012 and brought a new system this time to stop them from relying on the gas generator that powers their small village.

We returned to our route, attempting to find the most beautiful and sensible free climbing, and all summited after a five-day push. After summiting, we attempted to free the two crux pitches. The first of these was pitch two, Pat's lead. He'd worked tirelessly to find a free path through this steep, blank section of immaculate Precambrian sandstone. With three distinct crux sections of V6/7 and runouts of 5.12+ between each, it was totally doable for "The Good-One"—a master of hair-raising headpoints and finicky gear. However, it also had a distinct problem: a pulsing, amber nest of healthy-looking wasps at the crux. None of us was willing to attempt cutting it loose. Pat fired through this section anyway, breathing quiet words of respect: good wasp, pretty wasp, omniscient

[This page, left] Collins on the steep fourth pitch (5.12b), preparing to transition from the sharp "double arête" to a delicate 50' traverse right. *James Q Martin* **[This page, right]** Pat Goodman bearing down on the crux second pitch after passing a large hornets' nest. *James Q Martin*

wasp. He fell higher after breaking a key hold. The voodoo continued. Pat's shoulder was tweaked, and the wasps prevailed. Pitch two awaits a full free ascent (proposed 5.13a).

The second crux, pitch four, was my lead, with 5.12+ wandering through some exciting sections of sparse but solid protection, including a bomber Lost Arrow I had placed a year prior. However, when I reached the pin placement this year, I thought, "What the... Hey, where's the pin!?" Apparently it had come out in Pat's hands the day before. Voodoo, certainly. I kept at it, now 20' out from a flared No. 00 C3 on techy 5.11+ face climbing. I begged the Tepui Voodoo Council for safe passage, and finally entered the well-protected crux: three boulder problems with a series of wild deadpoints. Eventually, all the steep jungle hiking and 400' of free-hanging jumaring caught up with me. I fell just beneath the anchors, above the crux, on our last day, last hour, and last route of my four-year mission to put up first free ascents in the four cardinal directions from my home—north, west, east, and, now, south. I was bummed, but ready to go home to my wife and kids. Someone else can send it. It didn't go free, but I certainly felt free—free to move on, free to enjoy the journey, and free to go home.

Our route In Gold Blood (V 5.12c R A0) climbs 11 pitches (11+, 13a, 12b, 12c, 11a, 11a, 11+, 10b, 10 X, 11+, easy 5th). It is truly an amazing line, with numerous, distinct sections. A big thanks to the AAC and the Jonny Copp Foundation. 📷

JEREMY COLLINS, *AAC*

Acopan Tepui, Miss Acopan. In December 2011, Matic Obid and I hired a single-engine plane to reach the village of Yunek, situated under Acopan Tepui. After mastering sign-language communication with the locals, we established our base camp close to the wall and started focusing on climbing. After repeating a few routes on the left side of the wall and overcoming the fear we'd accumulated from others' jungle stories, we scoped the wall for a new line.

Our first attempt ended on unclimbable muddy rock. Two days later, we started a bit to the left and found good rock with free climbing potential. Luckily the wall was steep enough that occasional rain showers didn't bother us too much. Four pitches later, we fixed two ropes and headed back to camp for dinner. After a rest day we jugged up and climbed the remaining four pitches, which offered steep climbing on good rock. We both had one fall on the crux pitch, but managed to climb all the others onsight. Two days later we climbed the whole route free, exchanging leads. We left minimal natural gear and pitons for the rappels, and all the pitches allowed the use of natural protection, with occasional runouts above good gear.

Following our climb, we spent New Year's Eve socializing with the locals in Yunek. It was nice to see the pristine smiles of people who are still not occupied with the problems of modern world. Before leaving, we decided to try one more climb, Purgatory (VI 5.12+, Albert-Calderón-Glowacz-Heuber, 2007), on the right side of Acopan Tepui. We repeated the route free and onsight in two days.

LUKA KRAJNC

BRAZIL

Paredão Enamorados, new routes. Karina Filgueiras and Bito Meyer opened three new routes on the Paredão Enamorados wall, near Agulhas Negras in the Parque Nacional de Itatiaia, located outside of Rio de Janeiro. In August, Filgueiras and Meyer established No Amaryllis (220m, 6° VIIb D4 E3), and in October they returned to establish two independent routes: Tragico e Sublime (180m D4 7°a A2 E4), and So Para Loucos (200m, D5 E3 7b/c A3). All three routes require a mix of free and aid climbing.

From information by KARINA FILGUEIRAS

[This page] Paredão Enamorados, showing (1) Tragico e Sublime, (2) No Amaryllis, and (3) So Para Loucos. *Karina Filgueiras*

PERU

CORDILLERA BLANCA

Pisco, south face, new route. Florian Burger (Austria) and I left Huaraz on August 18 with a plan to climb the west face of Yerupaja in the Cordillera Huayhuash, but due to unpredictable conditions were forced to choose a different objective at the last moment, opting first for the Huandoys, and then Pisco.

We decided to attempt a 400m mixed wall on the far left end of the south face of Pisco (5,752m), believing it would provide an interesting challenge. We left camp at 4 a.m. The first pitch consisted of loose snow with a hard section involving a three-meter traverse on a vertical wall to reach a snowy channel. After a pitch of 60° snow, the third lead climbed hard 70-90° ice with a final section of loose snow, which took us up to a beautiful corridor between a series of snow mushrooms. The fourth pitch continued up this channel, first through deep, loose snow, then to a rock section (5c+) that was made difficult by the lack of available anchors. I managed to traverse to a small fissure where I could fix two nuts and belay my partner. The fifth pitch began with a 40m traverse over three crevasses with very loose snow—not particularly technical, but psychologically exhausting.

I belayed at a vertical wall of loose rock and ice. As Florian approached the belay, he told me that he had been hit on the head by a block of falling ice. I believed him to have a mild concussion. Only two pitches from the summit, we kept climbing, as the descent was more dangerous than upward escape. The sixth pitch was one of the most challenging, involving 40m of climbing on brittle ice that was as thin as 7cm in places. The lack of protection led us to rely on nuts of limited psychological value. The seventh and final pitch took us up a gully of loose snow to a series of overhanging, unprotectable snow mushrooms. Using our radios, we asked a porter on the west ridge to lower us a rope to help us ascend the final five meters (A1), which were excessively dangerous because of high temperatures. We reached the summit at 4:15 p.m., completing our route El Camino Secreto de Hermann Kirchner (340m, 5c+ 50-90° A1), and descended via the west ridge.

While there have been many ascents of Pisco's south face, none have been documented well [*AAJ 1984, 2003, 2005*], so it's unknown if our route is completely new. Some years ago a Mexican team completed an unreported route farther left.

BETO PINTO, *UIAGM*

[This page] El Camino Secreto de Hermann Kirchner on Pisco's south face. The route climbs to the ridge, and the team used assistance to ascend the final five meters. *Beto Pinto*

Huandoy Este, northwest face. While climbing La Esfinge in the Paron Valley in 2011, the Ecuadorian climber Joshua Larrín (IFMGA) took interest in the northwest face of Huandoy Este (6,070m). In August 2012, he decided to try the route with aspirant guide Juliana García.

On August 15, Larrín and García departed for the Parón Valley. Their approach was relatively simple; they started from Laguna Parón and hiked up the east side of a huge moraine below the Huandoys, setting up camp on the glacier close to the wall (ca. 4,600m). After a day acclimatizing, they climbed to the bergschrund (ca. 5,000m) to stash some gear. On August 17 they left camp at 3 a.m. to start the climb. After several pitches on snow and ice above the bergschrund, they reached the first crux, a steep rock band (75°). Above this, they traversed a snow ramp to the left (north) in order to reach a second rock band, the crux of the climb, where the pair climbed four pitches on vertical mixed terrain (UIAA V+ M3/4). At the end of this section they realized they had climbed only half of the route. The rest of the day proved challenging: The climb was not very technical, but gullies filled with powder snow made it precarious. At 7 p.m. they dug a hole and bivouacked.

The following day, they climbed ice and snow gullies up to the north ridge (ca. 5,900m). They did not continue to the summit due to unsafe snow conditions and descended the same route, which they called HK (1,300m, TD+ UIAA V+ M3/4). 📷

SERGIO RAMÍREZ CARRASCAL

Palcaraju Oeste, south face, new route and tragedy. In June 2012, Asa Firestone and Gil Weiss traveled to the Cordillera Blanca. During a day trip to scope out conditions on the south face of Ranrapalca, they were enamored by the brilliant flutings on the west face of a sub-peak, Palcaraju Oeste (6,110m), above Laguna Palcacocca. After a warm-up climb on nearby Huamashraju, they returned to attempt a new line on the

[This page, top] The northwest face of Huandoy Este. *Joshua Larrín* [This page, bottom] The Horne-Weiss Memorial Route on the south face of Palcaraju (route line is approximate). *Asa Firestone*

massive 800m south face of Palcaraju Oeste. During their attempt, they awoke to find a foot of new snow and high winds. An epic post-holing session brought them back to their high point to retrieve gear and bail.

Firestone returned to the States in early July, and Weiss met up with another close friend, talented alpinist and endurance athlete Ben Horne. After a couple of acclimatization peaks, Weiss and Horne made their way back to Palcaraju Oeste for another attempt on the big south face—this time with success. However, tragedy struck when a cornice collapsed on the west ridge descent and Weiss and Horne fell nearly 1,000'. (*Editor's note: The route line drawn was suggested by Asa Firestone based on his first attempt with Weiss. The only other reported route on the south face of Palcaraju Oeste is Tempete de Joie (600m, 12 pitches, TD/TD+ 60-75° ice and mixed; Brehedon-Peyronnard, 1999), which is believed to climb farther right on the face and did not reach the summit [AAJ 2001]*).

A memorial service for Ben Horne was held in both Virginia and San Diego, and for Gil Weiss in Boulder, Colorado. They left behind hundreds of close friends and a legacy of living life under the philosophy of glorious failure over mediocre success [*see In Memoriam*]. 📄 📷

PULLHARDER ALPINE CLUB

Urus Este, south ridge; Huamashraju, west face; Pisco, Miss You Baby; various ascents. In June 2012, Michael Wejchert and Erik Eisle (U.S.) made an ascent of the rocky south ridge of Urus Este (5,420m), believing the line to be unclimbed. [*This expedition was backed by an AAC Mountaineering Fellowship.*] Previously unrecorded, the route was climbed by Smith Curry and Jason Foote (U.S.) in 2004, and it's possible it may have been climbed prior (70° M4).

On July 18, Katty Guzmán and Maria Ramírez (Colombia), along with Jared Vagy and Cory Harelson (U.S.), climbed a possible new route on the west face of Huamashraju (5,434m) in the vicinity of the Sims-Jackson route [*AAJ 2005*]. Six pitches of rock climbing (up to 5.8) led to a snowfield and the summit.

Additionally, in August 2012, Darfur Hefti and Gian Marco climbed a possible first ascent, Miss You Baby (300m, 6c+), on a rocky spur on Pisco (5,752m), starting from the Paron Valley. Further information is lacking about this climb. 📄 📷 🔍

From information by SERGIO RAMÍREZ CARRASCAL *and various sources*

[**This page**] Michael Wejchert on the south ridge of Urus Este. Wejchert and Eisle noted they were surprised by the potential for long new mixed climbs in the Ishinca Valley. *Erik Eisle*

CORDILLERA HUAYHUASH

Puscanturpa Este, Poco Loco. Inspired by Pavle Kozjek's climb Stonehenge on the northeast buttress in 2007 [*AAJ 2008*], we were eager to climb a new line on this stunning 5,410m peak. On July 13, Saskia van der Smeede, Elly van der Plas, Vincent van Beek, Bas Visscher, and I flew into Lima. From here, we decided not to go to Huaraz, but instead to Cajatambo, a small mountain village located south of the Cordillera Huayhuash. This saved us several days of hiking, and with only a two-day trek we reached our base camp, just beneath the south face of the mountain.

After climbing a few easy 5,000m peaks near our camp, we completed our last acclimatization climb, Cuyoc (5,550m), also called Puscanturpa Sur. We found a nice line through the east face that wasn't hard (UIAA IV+), with good rock. Because of the many possibilities on this face, it could be a first ascent.

We originally planned to climb the east face of Puscanturpa Este, but on the first try we were stopped by terrible snow conditions. Steep sugar snow prevented us from reaching the bottom of the face. Walking around the mountain, we saw the imposing north face. We hadn't seen this face before in pictures, so we were happily surprised and decided to give it a try. A few days later, we started climbing. The first 100m were overhanging columns without any cracks, so we climbed the first pitch of the Slovenian route on the northeast spur and traversed into the north face on the second pitch. Halfway up the face, the wind began to blow so hard that, combined with heavy snow, we decided to bail.

On July 30, we returned for a second try. We found the same brutal wind, and Saskia and Elly were so cold that they turned back. Visscher, Beek, and I kept going and climbed the steep columns with our cold hands. After an easy traverse, we found a way through the second overhanging section and entered more easy terrain. Above some loose and broken rock, we tried to climb a direct line to the summit. However, after two steep pitches (UIAA VI+) we were stopped by a blank wall and were forced to traverse left to the ridge. This ridge was so broken that we were scared to ascend it, but after a few minutes of consideration we decided to go on and soon arrived on the summit.

Because of the many sections of loose rock, we called the route Poco Loco (TD, UIAA VI+). It is likely the third ascent of the mountain and the first route on the north face. Three days later, the weather improved and Elly and Saskia also climbed the face in 16 hours round-trip. 📷

BAS VAN DER SMEEDE, *Holland*

[This page] The north face of Puscanturpa Este, showing the new route Poco Loco. The Slovenian route (Kresal-Kozjek, 2007) ascends a line near the shady skyline to the left. *Bas van der Smeede*

Jirishanca, east face to east buttress, attempt. On May 27, 2012, German climbers Michi Wohlleben, Johannes Arne, Bergau Jahn, and photographer Hans Hornberger traveled to Lima to attempt Jirishanca (6,094m). From Huaraz they headed to Chiquian, and a few days later set up a base camp above Carhuacocha (ca 4,500m) and an advanced base camp above Laguna Chaclan (ca 4,950m). Their ascent began on the east face's limestone wall via the 2003 De Luca-Piccini-Stoppini route called Suerte, which was not completed to the summit. [*See AAJ 2004 for Jirishanca's climbing history.*] The team linked Suerte to the Egger-Jungmair route [*AAJ 1958*] on the east buttress/ northeast spur, and after 10 days of climbing they descended from 100m below the summit due to soft snow. 🗐 🖸 🔍

Sevi Bohorquez

CORDILLERA CENTRAL

Nevado Carhuachuco, new route. On November 10, during a guide course by the Mountain Guides Association of Peru (AGMP), aspirant guide Xavier Ossola and Micher Quito (IFMGA) climbed a new route, Listos Para Hacer Barras (300m, MD M5/6 55-80°), to the south summit of Nevado Carhuachuco (5,507m).

They began climbing the east side of the peak at 2 a.m. from a base camp at ca 4,200m, and by 5 a.m. reached the northeast end of the glacier (ca 5,200m) that separates the peak's northern and southern summits. From there, they climbed a couloir (30m, 75-80°) toward the south peak. Because of poor ice, they exited the couloir at a rock cave with exposed climbing on poor footholds (M5/6). After an additional pitch (35m, M3) they rejoined the couloir to gain the summit ridge (150m, 55-80°), finishing on easy snow to the top (45-50°). They descended the same route. 🖸 🔍

Sergio Ramirez Carrascal

CORDILLERA URUBAMBA

Pumahuacanca, northeast face. I left Huaraz on October 14 with aspirant guide Yonny Rosales to teach a guiding course. Our itinerary included Shacsha, Huruashraju, Rurec, and Cashan, in

[This page] Listos Para Hacer Barras climbs the east side of Nevado Carhuachuco up a deep cleft in the rock before gaining the ridge to the south peak. The complete ridge to the right was climbed by Beto Pinto and aspirant guides at a more moderate grade. *Xavier Ossola*

addition to some rescue training. After a couple of days in the mountains we decided to attempt a new route on the northeast face of Pumahuacanca (5,563m). I had made my own investigation of Pumahuacanca prior to leaving for the course. According to the *AAJ*, the most recent recorded ascent was completed via the northwest face in 1969 [*AAJ 1970*].

Our plan was to start on the east ridge before traversing onto the northeast face, so we took equipment for snow travel. We left camp at 6 a.m. on October 16, crossing along the right side of Tararhua Lake, and after one hour Yonni and I arrived at the base of the wall with six additional aspirant guides. We split into pairs, hoping to climb four different routes on the face.

Yonni and I choose a direct route, and after three hours of intermittent simul-climbing we reached the summit via our new route, El Sexto Teletubbies (300m, 5c+ 50-70°). On the summit we waited for the other teams and created a large cairn while enjoying the sun. Unfortunately, one of the rope-teams had suffered an accident when a large stone fell onto the leader's fingers. We quickly descended to mid-height on the mountain to administer first aid, and after 11 hours of work we arrived back at our base camp. 📷 🔍

BETO PINTO, *UIAGM*

Nevado Chicón, northeast summit (5,495m); unnamed summit (5,024m); new route potential. On March 24, Peruvian climber Jorge "Coqui" Gálvez, who had made two previous attempts on the southeast face of Nevado Chicon (5,530m), began climbing alone toward the mountain's slightly lower northeast summit. Gálvez started his approach at 8 p.m. from the village of Huaran in the Inca´s sacred valley. On March 25, after a short bivouac on the glacier below the southeast face he started climbing at 5 a.m. The route involved 55-65° ice and nevé, with occasional loose rock sections. Gálvez self-belayed several sections and descended via the same route: Gol de Borja (300m, D 55-65°).

On July 21, Gálvez climbed the south face of an unnamed peak (5,024m) located northeast of the village of Patacancha (ca. 3,915m). After a brief bivouac, Galvez climbed solo on alternating sections of soft snow and ice, which he protected with snow pickets, pitons, and some cams in rock outcrops. The last two pitches contained waist-level snow. He reached the summit midday and descended via the same route.

Gálvez also made attempts on Pumahuacanca and Halamcoma, also located in the Cordillera Urubamba. The Urubamba contains many possibilities for new routes, with excellent weather for most of the year and close access from Cusco. 📷

SERGIO RAMIREZ CARRASCAL

[This page] Pumahuacanca's northeast face. The rock is featured yet somewhat loose. The Urubamba contains stable weather and many possibilities for new-routing. *Beto Pinto*

CORDILLERA VOLCANICA

Nocarane Volcano, southwest face, new routes. Nocarane Volcano (5,787m) is located on Reserva Nacional Salinas y Aguada Blanca, close to Arequipa. Beginning in May 2012, Xavier Ossola and various partners established three new routes on a rocky aspect of the southwest face, which does not see any sunlight.

On May 13, Xavier Ossola (France), Patricia Bolanos, Guido Mollepaza (Peru), Krista Dawn Mackenzie (Canada), and Martin Hourigan (Australia) climbed 400m up a couloir and mixed ridge (45-60°) to the ridge line at ca 5,650m. They rappelled the new route: Matrato del Viento (400m, AD French 3 60°).

On May 23, Ossola, Martin Hourigan, Miguel Zea Bellido, and Juan Carlos Velarde (Peru) climbed a new route Ah, Uh, Ah (500m, D WI3+), which shares its first pitch with Maltrato del Viento. The six-pitch route contains ice up to WI3+ and moderate rock climbing.

On June 28, Ossola, Mollepaza, Patricia Bolanos, and Alonso Medina (Peru) climbed the hardest of the three routes, Gritos de Guerra (500m, D+/MD- UIAA IV W3/4

[This page, top left] Typical terrain on the three new routes on Nocarane Volcano: Xavier Ossola leading on Maltrato del Viento. *Juan Carlos Velarde* [This page, bottom left] The southwest face of Nocarane Volcano. All three new routes ascend the rocky buttress in the vicinity of the line drawn. *Xavier Ossola* [This page, bottom right] Lagrimas De Agua, one of the new ice routes located outside of Callani. *Xavier Ossola*

M3/4). The four-pitch route begins on thin ice before climbing moderate mixed terrain to the rocky summit ridge.

Ossola, Bolanos, and Mollepaza also discovered an area with waterfall ice routes only four hours by car from Arequipa, near the town of Callani (ca. 3,850m). Water ice is an unusual formation at lower elevations in the Peruvian Andes. The trio climbed eight routes up to 25m in length. The best season is June through August. 📷 🔍

SERGIO RAMIREZ CARRASCAL

Coropuna Central II (6,161m), first ascent; Corupuna, history. In June, a group of Spanish mountaineers, Jorge Perez, Eduardo Ruiz, and Jose Martinez, climbed a new route up one of the central summits of the Coropuna massif from the south. This great snow-capped mountain, approximately 150km northwest of Arequipa, has six summits higher than 6,000m and colossal dimensions—the massif covers 83 square kilometers.

Coropuna was sacred to the Incas, but its modern history began much later, in 1910, when archaeologist Adolph Bandelier announced that Coropuna was higher than Aconcagua. In 1911, Annie S. Peck and archaeologist Hiram Bingham traveled to Coropuna to see if this curious affirmation was true. Peck reached the two eastern summits, ca 6,305m and ca 6,234m, while Hiram Bingham climbed to the highest summit, at 6,425m. The north summit, Coropuna Casulla (6,377m), was reached by Piero Ghiglione, Manuel Montañez, Victor Motta, and Mathias Rebitsch in 1952; the west summit, Nevado Pallacocha (6,171m), was climbed in 1974, by Hans Raum and Heinz Thater. Until now, the central summits, ca 6,150m and ca 6,161m, were believed unclimbed.

We started our approach from Viraco, a village on the southeast side of the volcano (ca 3,200m). On the first day we reached Aguas Calientes (ca 4,700m), establishing our base camp near thermal baths. We installed a higher camp at ca 5,025m by climbing up the center of Quebrada Buena Vista and then via rocky steps on the northwest side onto the glacier. To avoid crevasses, we climbed a long ridge to a wide col (ca 5,900m) between the eastern summits and our objective, Coropuna Central II (6,161m). From here, Perez continued alone, crossing a vast plateau before ascending the peak's east ridge to the summit.

After the climb, we verified that the central summits may have been reached in 2003 by a team of glaciologists (Thompson, et al) doing a study of the massif before erecting a meteorological station on the main summit. In September 2003, Carlos Zarate and partner climbed Coropuna Central I (6,150m). In August 2004, an additional glaciological study was done on the massif, coordinated by Walter Silverio; their team climbed five of the six main summits. However, it's believed that the route up Corpuna Central II from the south is new. 📷 🔍

JOSE MARTINEZ HERNANDEZ

[This page] The rocky point on the left of the photo is Coropuna Central II (6,161m). Coropuna's highest summit (6,425m) lies climber's right from this aspect. *Jose Martinez Hernandez*

BOLIVIA

Overview. In 2012 there were heavy snowfalls in both the rainy and dry seasons, which sometimes made for difficult conditions on the Andean faces. Conversely, the good snow cover made at least one new route possible, on Huayna Potosi's south peak. The guru of Bolivian climbing, Alain Mesili, is producing a third guidebook, which has fewer routes than his former editions but more details. It is being translated into English by Robert Rauch with the help of Chris Clarke, both La Paz residents.

A new guide to the sport climbing at Peñas has been published. This venue, set at 4,000m on the altiplano, one hour's drive from La Paz, provides fun climbing and perfect acclimatization for the visiting alpinist. Among the 30 or so established routes are five four-pitch lines, from 5 to 6a+/6b. There is also rock climbing on the granite crags above the Refugio Casa Blanca, close to Zongo Lake.

Most Bolivian rock climbers are sport climbers, without trad gear. There are naturally protected climbs at Peñas, but they are mostly ignored. However, in the mountains (for example, on the granite walls of the Quimsa Cruz), nearly all cracks are trad, though this area also has worthwhile partially bolted routes. There is good bouldering at Peñas and at Challkupuncu, a huge collection of boulders in a half-desert area at ca 4,000m near Sajama National Park, four hours' drive from La Paz.

There continue to be access difficulties in Bolivia. El Penon, the local climbing ground in La Paz, was closed, though at the time of writing some problems appear to have been resolved. And Rumi Campana, the crags above Oruro, three hours' drive from La Paz, will probably be off-limits.

ROBERT RAUCH, *Bolivia Tours*

CORDILLERA APOLOBAMBA

Palomani and Matchu Sochi Cuchi groups, various ascents. Our Slovenian expedition comprised Marta Krejan, Stanko Mihev, Vinko Mocilnik, Domen Petek, Franc Pusnik, Primoz Steharnik, Sebastjan Zapusek, and I, all from the Ravne Alpine Club. On July 8 we left La Paz in two vans for Apacheta Pampa, and on the 9th traveled 20km with horses to our base camp below and southwest of Lago Chucuyo at 4,700m. On the 11th and 12th, Mihev, Pusnik, and Mocilnik climbed a new route to the rocky Pt. 5,595m on the ridge connecting Palomani Sur with Palomani Central. They climbed the southwest face at 50-60°, calling the summit Slovenski Turn. [*This top was first crossed in 2003 during an Anglo-Bolivian traverse from Sur to Central*]. At the same time Zapusek and I climbed Peak 5,600m in the Machu Sochi Cuchi Group via the southeast ridge, naming the line Koroska Smer (50-60°).

On the July 13, Sterharnik climbed the southwest face of Palomani Tranca Central (5,633m) and then skied back down. [*This was possibly only the third ascent of the peak and first ski descent.*] Meanwhile, over July 13-14, Krejan and Petek put up a new route up the southeast face of Palomani Sur (5,626m). They climbed   through a rock band, making a 70° exit onto the upper snow/ice slopes, then continued to the final rocky pyramid, which they climbed from the right at M4. The route was named Krikosa.

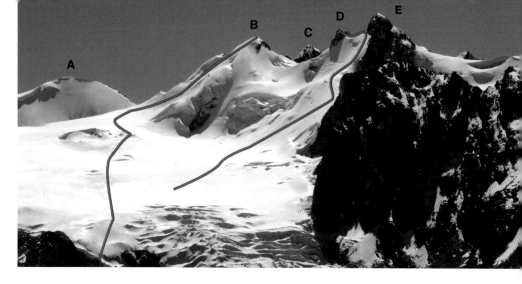

[This page, top] Palomani Group from the south: (A) Palomani Grande (5,723m). (B) Palomani Tranca Central (5,633m). (C) Palomani Tranca Main (5,638m), climbed in 1985 and possibly not since. (D) Slovenski Tower (5,595m). (E) Palomani Sur (5,626m). Left line: southwest face, climbed/skied by Steharnik. Right line: southwest face, Slovenian Route. In 2003 Charlie Netherton (U.K.) and Pedro Quispe (Bolivia) followed the skyline from the right as far as Palomani Central, in an attempt to traverse the entire Palomani Group. In doing so they made the first ascent of (E), (D), and the second of (B). They reached a foresummit of Palomani Tranca Main before descending southeast (overall grade D). *Boris Santner* [This page, bottom] The probable new route Koroska Smer on the southeast ridge of Peak 5,600m. *Boris Santner*

On July 14-15, Zapusek and I climbed two peaks, Palomani Luka (5,570m) and its west summit, that lie on the ridge east of Palomani Sur. We climbed via the southern slopes. At the same time Mihev, Mocilnik, Pusnik, and Steharnik climbed the southernmost peak in the Montserrat Group, south of Lago Chucuyo. They named the ca 5,200m peak Koroska. [*In 1997 Kevin Dougherty and Andy MacNae traversed most of the Montserrat Range, but their summits were higher, making it possible that Pt. ca 5,200m remained unclimbed.*]

Over the 16th and 17th, Krejan, Petek, and Steharnik climbed the south face of Chucuyo Grande (5,523m), with Sterharnik making a first ski descent; the maximum angle was 60-65°. On the 18th we cleaned up base camp and left. 🔍

BORIS SANTNER, *Ravne Alpine Club, Slovenia*

CORDILLERA REAL

Huayna Potosi, south peak, east face, La Ventanita de la Paz. On the lower south summit (ca 5,960m) of Huayna Potosi, the Peruvian guide Victor Hugo Rimac climbed a new line to the right of the classic Via de los Franceses (300m, AD+ 55°, Cardon-Mesili, 1974). On December 8 and 9, when the weather was unfavorable, he reconnoitered possible new routes, and on the 11th he started from Campamento Argentino in mist, with the temperature down to -7°C. He followed the French route to the bottom of the face, crossing the bergschrund at 3 a.m. in improving weather. He then moved to the right-hand side of the face, where there are mixed rock bands, and slanted up left over soft snow slopes and mixed ground to an exit on the right-hand ridge, where he joined the "Bordas-Muñoz route" (300m, AD+ 75°, Gonzalez-Hevia-Rey-Vazquez, 1990) for the last short section to the summit. The safest exit onto the right-hand ridge involved a 20m rock wall with moves of 5 and 6a. Rimac climbed his route in four hours and named it La Ventanita de la Paz (D+, 6a 50-70°). Local climbers consider it would only be feasible with good snow cover, as was the case during 2012.

SERGIO RAMÍREZ CARRASCAL, *Peru*

Charquini (5,392m), south face; Pico Milluni (5,500m), east face; Pico Italia (ca 5,750m), east face. The imposing east face of Pico Italia is unmissable to anyone climbing Huayna Potosi; the steep, 500m granite face forms a fortress-like barrier along the western edge of the Huayna Potosi Glacier, and casts an alluring orange-obsidian glow in the early morning. Given its prominence in such a popular climbing area, it is surprising that the face had not previously been climbed.

In May I returned to Bolivia to climb with New Zealand ex-pat Gregg Beisley, who lives in El Alto. With limited time available, and with the uncertainty of ongoing political demonstrations, strikes, and roadblocks in the chaotic city, we opted to minimize time traveling to remote regions by focusing on the Huayna Potosi region, located in the nearby southern Cordillera Real.

On May 15, to assist with my acclimatization, we climbed a new route on the south face of Charquini. [*The mountain lies behind 5,300m Chacaltaya, the world's highest ski piste, which in the age of global warming now seldom has enough snow to ski. The Charquini group has many different routes of ill-defined location, mostly by the late Stanley Shepherd*]. We left Gregg's house at 4 a.m. and drove to within one hour's walk of the glacier below the south face. We climbed a five-pitch, sustained mixed line that led to the west-southwest ridge, which we followed to the summit. The crux first

[This page] East face of Huayna Potosi's south summit. (1) Southwest ridge (AD, 1963). (2) Via de los Franceses. (3) La Ventanita de la Paz. (4) Bordas-Muñoz route (1990). *Sergio Ramirez Carrascal*

pitch was slightly overhanging and precarious (M5), and this eventually led to thin vertical ice (AI4), which eased off near the ridge.

To further extend my hypoxic exposure, and to determine whether I could sustain a high-intensity climb at altitude, on the 18th we climbed a new route on the northeast face of Pico Milluni (250m, two pitches, F5c/6a and 6b, then simul-climbing to the summit). We descended the obvious gully immediately north.

Next day we walked three hours from the Casa Blanca Hut to the base of Pico Italia and fixed two pitches (70m) in a sustained crack and chimney system, the first being the crux at around 6c (adequate natural gear, including two pitons). The following morning we left the hut at 4 a.m. and jumared the fixed lines in the warming rays of the sun. Carrying a full rock and ice rack, stove, and bivouac equipment made the jugging difficult, and in the end I had to haul while Gregg somehow managed to jumar up the chimney without flipping upside-down. We pulled up our fixed lines, tied into a single rope, and began long sections of simul-climbing between occasional harder steps.

The tightly packed granodiorite face doesn't have clearly defined cracks or corner systems, making the way not obvious, but we followed the most aesthetic path up the wall. The climbing was engaging and well protected as we linked disconnected corner systems, chimneys, runout slabs, and occasional overhangs. After eight pitches, we pulled over the final steep buttress and onto the summit ridge.

It was 2 p.m. and a steady stream of clouds blew from the verdant jungle to the east. Yet even as lightning forks pierced the blanket of Amazonian clouds, the weather in the mountains remained cold and stable. We changed

[This page, top] Erik Monasterio on the west ridge of Charquini. *Gregg Beisley* [This page, bottom] East face of Pico Italia showing the "normal" south to north traverse, and the 2012 rock route on the east face buttress. *Erik Monasterio*

into our ice climbing equipment, and Gregg led out on the last two pitches across the mixed ridge and onto the summit slopes. The final easy steps to the top felt like a formality after the demanding climb on the buttress. We had initially intended to follow the ridge all the way to the summit of Huayna Potosi, but after downclimbing mixed ground to the col between the two peaks, we opted to abseil to the glacier and cut across to the normal descent route on Huayna.

Overall, the length and variety of climbing made it a very demanding route, which took 16 hours to complete. Gregg and I have climbed a lot in Bolivia, and we feel this is the hardest climb in the Huayna Potosi region, and one of the hardest in Bolivia (600m, TD+). 📷

ERIK MONASTERIO, *New Zealand/Bolivia*

Hampaturi Group, Serkhe Khollu (5,546m), Los Alcaldes de Serkhe Khollu; Huayna Potosi Group, Charquini (5,400m), Beisley-Monasterio Route, second ascent. On July 20 Robert Rauch and I made what we believe is the first ascent of a route on the right side of the southwest face of Serkhe Khollu (the next major break to the right of La Venganza del Don Gringo). Our route, Los Alcaldes de Serkhe Khollu, follows an obvious moderate ice couloir on the right side of a prominent rock buttress to gain open snow slopes. Above these slopes, we climbed enjoyable mixed terrain for a few pitches to exit around the left edge of a serac band onto the main ridge, which we followed to the summit. We climbed 14 roped pitches plus a fair amount of unroped ridge climbing, and rated the climb IV WI4 M4. We descended west via the non-technical normal route. The ascent took us 14 hours car to car, and 18 hours from door to door in La Paz. Other than some irritating rockfall before the upper snowfields, we found the route relatively free from objective hazards, and quite enjoyable.

Previously, on May 31, we repeated the five-pitch mixed route on the south face of Charquini that Gregg Beisley and Erik Monasterio had established earlier in the year. [*See report above.*] A sturdy 4WD is required to attain the parking area near the foot of the Charquini Glacier, but this avoids a tedious hour or so marching up the moraine. Though it is not clear if this route will form every year, we would recommend it as a technical acclimatization climb. We walked west off the ridge in the direction of Milluni, then descended to the main glacier on the southwest side of Charquini.

CHRIS CLARKE, *Bolivia*

[This page] Right side of the southwest face of Serkhe Khollu showing (1) La Venganza del Don Gringo (Rauch, 2011) and (2) Los Alcaldes de Serkhe Khollu (2012). The photo is taken during the rainy season (while skiing) and the face has much less snow in the normal climbing season. *Chris Clarke*

Hampaturi Group, Jati Khollu (5,421m), southeast ridge. Jati Khollu, situated in the southern part of the Real, is little known but makes a great acclimatization climb for 6,000m peaks. Glacial retreat prompted Robert Rauch and I to find a new way up the southeast ridge. From Laguna Jachcha Khasiri, it used to be possible to climb onto a glacier and head directly to the summit (400m, AD, Yossi Brain–Jason Davis, 1995, see also *AAJ 2012*). We had to continue around the left side of a higher lake, newly created by glacial recession, to reach the snow. We then climbed the glacier and the southeast ridge to the summit (PD/AD).

JANETTE HEUNG, *AAC*

Illimani (6,439m), south face, possible new route. Argentinian mountain guide Gustavo Lisi and Robert Rauch from Bolivia climbed Illimani's rarely visited south face by a possible new route (ca 1,200m, WI4 R 65-75°), very near the 1978 Jacquier-Mesili route, the first line up the south face. The two started left of the 1978 route but likely followed much of the same ground higher on the face. This was Rauch's third route on Illimani's south side since 2009.

ROBERT RAUCH, *Bolivia Tours*

[This page] South face of Illimani (6,439m). (1) Southwest ridge (1,450m, III 70°, Dowbenka-Ziegenhardt, 1983, but most probably descended in 1972 by Mesili and Sanchez during the third north-to-south traverse of the three main summits). (2) Nada es Seguro (1,450m, V WI3+, Hendricks-Hendricks-McNeill, 2001). (3) A line claimed to have been climbed in 1972 by Alain Mesili with Nicolas Jaeger (1,200m, TD, WI4 5.5). (4) Puerta del Sol (1,200m, ED1, WI5 R M5, Ichimura-Yokoyama, 2006). (5) Inti Face (600m, TD+, WI5, Satoh-Yamada, 2006). (6) Phajsi Face (1,200m, TD+, WI4+, Satoh-Yamada, 2006). (7) South Face Original (1,200m, D+, 60-75°, Jacquier-Mesili, 1978). In 1988 Patrick Gabarrou soloed Hubert Ducroz on the south face, but the location of this line remains unclear. *Robert Rauch*

CHILE

CENTRAL ANDES

Cajon del Estero Aucayes, Cinco Mil; new route potential. In December I traveled to the Cajon del Estero Aucayes, using horse support to reach a base camp at ca 2,500m. The next day I left for a group of mountains that run from north to south and close this valley from the east. Cinco Mil (3,658m) lies along this chain. From base camp it took five hours to reach the base of the mountain. I ascended the southwest face on slopes never steeper than 40° to a final section of steeper rock. The ascent was not technical—the focus of the climb was to explore an area very little visited by mountaineers. This area has high potential for first and second ascents and new routes.

ELVIS ACEVADO, *Chile*

Colmillo Este, Colmillo del Diablo. The first weekend of November, Ulises Espinosa and I, members of the Perros Alpinos Mountain Group, went to Cajon de lo Valdés, a valley containing many classic peaks. Our objective was the unclimbed Colmillos del Diablo: three rocky towers that run from west to east between the hills of Diente del Diablo and Retumbadero Alto.

On the first day we reached Valle de lo Valdés and installed a camp at ca 3,000m. The next day we advanced to the end of the valley, where we climbed snow slopes (30-40°) to the base of the towers, an area highly exposed to rockfall. We decided to try Colmillo Este (3,751m), ascending snow slopes (60°) to a pass between Colmillo Este and Colmillo Central. From here, a narrow snow ridge led to the base of a rocky tower about 40m tall. The climbing never exceeded 5.7, but had few options for protection and the rock crumbled easily: Colmillo del Diablo (750m, 5.7).

ELVIS ACEVADO, *Chile*

Cerro Panamericano. In April, the Perros Alpinos mountain group traveled to the Nieves Negras, located near the border of Chile and Argentina on the south side of San José Volcano. Our objective was Cerro Panamericano (4,501m), which we had tried in 2005 and 2007 unsuccessfully, and which has had few ascents with very little information.

Jaime Wastavino, Juan Carlos Caro, and I approached via the beautiful Valle del Río Volcán to install a base camp at ca 3,000m. We began our ascent at 4 a.m. by a full moon, and progressed rapidly to the base of a hanging glacier. With less snow on the mountain than expected, we quickly gained the summit ridge, which contained the greatest difficulties. The ridge required climbing up to UIAA IV, with very high exposure. A tower about 6m tall with good rock crowns the summit. The route was climbed free, without technical equipment (1,500m, UIAA IV).

ELVIS ACEVADO, *Chile*

Punton Amarillo. In November, Chilean climbers Alvaro Vivanco, Juanita Guerra, and I, along with the German climber Max Beckmann, traveled to the Cajón de Navarro, in the V region of

Chile, an area north of the Cordillera Central. Our objective was the unclimbed Punton Amarillo (4,157m), located near Paso Fronterizo Los Libertadores along the border of Chile and Argentina. We bivouacked along the Estero Navarro and then ascended slopes of loose rock to reach the base of the mountain, followed by snow slopes (45-55°) with many *penitentes* that hindered our progress. After four hours our group reached the summit (1,100m, 55°). 📷

ELVIS ACEVADO, *Chile*

NORTHERN PATAGONIA

COCHAMÓ

Summary, various routes. It's likely that more meters of new routes were opened in the 2012–13 climbing season than any other in Cochamó's history. In addition to the reports that follow, three other difficult routes were established. Chance Traub and partner established Positive Affect (1,000m, 5.12b) on Arco Iris Wall. Italian climbers Lorenzo Lanfranchi, Mirko Mase, Simone Pedeferri, Mattia Tisi, and Andrea Zaffaroni established Perdidos en el Mundo (870m, 23 pitches, 7b+) up the north face of Cerro Walwalun over four days. Lastly, Cristian Gallardo and Daniel Seeliger established Doña Deborah Dedos (420m, 5.12b) on Atardecer Wall.

DANIEL SEELIGER, *Chile*

El Monstruo, La Presencia de mi Padre. I felt an instant attraction to El Monstruo when I saw one of the few existing pictures of the biggest, most remote wall in the Cochamó region. The details merely confirmed the aptitude of the name: There were no trails to its base, nor to the valley, nor even to the adjacent valley, Valle Trinidad. A switch was flipped in my brain, as if by Dr. Frankenstein; I was programmed to see this project through, not in spite of the challenges it posed but because of them.

After 30-plus days over four years of concentrated route-finding and trail-breaking, mostly solo (a slow death by bamboo), I forged a trail that takes the truly committed from Cerro Trinidad to a high saddle (provisionally named El Paso Querido del Caso Perdido), across a sweeping rocky traverse to a serene high-altitude lake, down a vertical Valdivian forest to the valley floor, and then across some marshy terrain to the base of the wall.

I finally began opening a free route on El Monstruo in March 2012 with my dad, Michael Conroy. After several weeks confined by heavy precipitation to trail work and quality tent-time, my father and I decided we hadn't come so far to be turned back by a little moisture. So we racked up and began climbing, cleaning and equipping the first three pitches and an alternate first pitch in the persistent Patagonian rain. With only one day before we absolutely had to pack out to make a plane home, we opened pitches four through nine amid hummingbirds under a bluebird sky.

I opened the rest of the route in February 2013 with various partners, including Brian Stuenkel, Sean Willis, Jaimie Rault, and Nick Foster, over the course of 16 days. Highlights include toe-tingling hand-drilling on exposed, unprotected terrain, pulling a roof 800m up, amazing bivouacs, the summit snowfield, and, of course, numerous condor flybys. I called the route La Presencia de mi Padre (1600m, 28 pitches, 5.10+).

Shortly after the successful ascent, friends Chris Moore and Cooper Varney made an incredible second ascent of the route in a whirling seven hours, confirming the grades and the

[This page] La Presencia de mi Padre ascends the left side of the remote El Monstruo in 28 pitches. With a trail finally built and only two established routes on the massive formation, there's much more to do. *Nathan Conroy*

overall adventure of getting to the wall and then up it. Time to the base varies with the hiker and load—anything from a record 2:46 to over 12 hours, with six to eight hours being about average.

One older route ascends El Monstruo. The obvious corner/chimney that begins on the north side was opened in 2006 by two Polish climbers, Boguslaw Kowalski and Jerzy Stefanski, and named La Gran Raja (The Great Crack, 1,300m, 7a). However, I have been informed there was aid on the route (A1), which would make mine the first free ascent on the face. Jerzy and Boguslaw are the only other climbers to reach El Monstruo, and they did so in alpine style. They went light and fast, pushing through dense forest and bamboo, streams, and then leaving their cooking and sleeping comforts behind to do the route in only two days. This is how I first explored the approach; hence, I have gained much respect for the fast and committing style of the two Poles.

NATHAN CONROY

Pared La Paz, A Poto Pelao Po. The initial project for Cyril Mokobodzki, Polo Barneoud, Nicolas Rotureau, and I (all from France) was to open a new 1,000m route in Cochamó, on the Central Cerro Trinidad. But after 10 days of nonstop rain, we downsized our goals. After days of talks with Dani Seeliger, the area expert, we chose a 500m wall, Pared La Paz, in the Paloma Valley. We left for the wall as soon as the sun came out.

After getting lost during the approach, Polo, Moko, and I started working on the route while Nicolas prepared the base camp below. The first three pitches were quite demanding and required a lot of aid climbing in dirty cracks. We fixed 200m of ropes to help us avoid using the portaledge.

After three days of climbing and bolting, we eventually reached easier face climbing and then slab that made it possible to reach the summit before another period of rain.

After a great bath in the river on our return, we called the route A Poto Pelao Po, which means "naked butt." We did not free the ca 430m route, but believe the first three pitches are 7a, 7c, and 7a, and the rest is around 6a/b (eight pitches total). Despite missing our original goal, four days of climbing great granite in a magical valley, with pipe and harmonica music from a Chilean team climbing adjacent to us, made it an unforgettable experience. 📷 🔍

NICOLAS GEOFFROY, *France*

Anfiteatro, new routes. In February 2013, after six sunny weeks of climbing in Cochamó, May Martin, Tyler Gagne, and I finished our trip by opening two new routes on Cerro Espejo in the Anfiteatro. The first, Antes de la Lluvia (475m, 5.8), wanders up a natural weakness through ramps and corners for 275m before reaching a large, left-trending staircase. From here 200m of easier climbing gains the summit shoulder. The second, Through the Looking Glass (440m, 5.11b), takes a steeper, more direct line just to the left of Antes de la Lluvia. It follows good cracks in a prominent right-facing corner system for three pitches before exiting the corner and climbing the clean outside face for two bolted pitches. It is possible to rappel via fixed anchors or traverse across a ledge to the 200m great staircase shared with Antes de la Lluvia. 📷 🔍

SETH PUTNAM

Pared del Tiempo, The Doppler Effect. In mid-January 2013, I arrived in Cochamó without sleep (lost on a bus), a partner (summiting Fitz Roy), or a plan (*plan?*). All I had was an awesome weather forecast. On the bus ride in, I met a large group of climbers and posed, somewhat maniacally, the question, "Hey, do any of you want to open a route?"

[This page, left] A Poto Pelao Po on Pared La Paz. *Nathan Conroy* [This page, right] Anfiteatro. (1) Excelente mi Teniente. (2) Through the Looking Glass. (3) Antes de la Lluvia. *Nathan Conroy*

[This page, left] Cooper Varney sending the crux 5.12b tips crack of the Doppler Effect. *Chris Kalman* [This page, right] Pared del Tiempo and the Doppler Effect. Soon afterward, a major variation, the Coriolis Effect, was established. *Chris Kalman*

To my surprise, four days later, after scoping out a stunning arête in El Anfiteatro, two of those climbers from the bus were working on a new route with me. Looking down, I saw Chris Moore with a face full of dirt, working like a madman to clean a nice finger crack. Further down I heard Cooper "Payaso" Varney swearing like a pirate as he finished clearing our approach trail, which would later be dubbed the Pan-American Super Highway, a.k.a. Trail of Tabano Tears. Looking up, I saw a beautiful, stunning headwall, and two table-sized mini-summits before the true top of the route. We were halfway there.

The three of us climbed the Doppler Effect in what seems to have become typical Cochamó style. We were able to access the middle of the route via a fourth-class trail to the base of a knife-edge arête. From the midpoint, we worked simultaneously up and down: cleaning, establishing new pitches, and bolting both on lead and rappel, by hand and by power drill. Twice, the route went up one way only to be abandoned for an option to the left or right. The route climbs 16 pitches, mostly following a sharp arête, with a fantastic mixture of crack and face climbing to the final summit of Cerro Laguna.

The Doppler Effect (600m, 5.12b) includes several stellar pitches: the third-pitch dihedral, the seventh pitch's bolted knife-edge arête, pitch 10's V-slot, and pitch 13's crux finger crack. We climbed the route all free in a push on January 23, with Cooper Varney onsighting the crux 5.12b pitch. This is the first route on the wall, which we named Pared del Tiempo, in honor of all the time and good weather we enjoyed while opening the route.

CHRIS KALMAN

Pared del Tiempo, The Coriolis Effect. The sensation of being a climber and walking into Cochamó Valley for the first time—especially after six months of planning and working, 8,000 miles of travel, and not one day of climbing for a month and a half, is tremendous. Right away, I found myself in a group of climbers dedicated to the development of these monster walls, and to the preservation of the valley.

Just two weeks before my arrival, on the east side of the amphitheater above La Junta, Chris Kalman, Cooper Varney, and Chris Moore had established the Doppler Effect, thus opening a new 650m wall they named Pared del Tiempo. After hauling up supplies to a bivy cave in El Anfiteatro and climbing one of the soon-to-be ultra-classic routes, Al Centro y Adentro, I joined Tate Shepherd, Shawn Wright, and Rhain Phifer to work on an elaborate variation to the Doppler Effect. Our inspiration was to create a long, sustained, moderate route, of which there are very few in the valley. After five days of searching, cleaning, and bolting where appropriate, we established the Coriolis Effect (5.11b/c). As much as we would have loved to rate the route 5.10, it seems that Cochamó continues to be a wonderland for the 5.11 climber.

Our line crisscrosses the Doppler Effect, borrowing six of the 17 (or so) pitches and goes at mostly 5.10+, with one beautiful pitch of 5.11a (a long overhanging finger and hand crack) and a crux 5.11b/c pitch that climbs through some horribly thin face moves to a sharp hand crack through a roof. Both routes offer clean rock, incredible exposure, and fun climbing in an alpine setting. From the summit, one can see from the Reloncaví Estuary in Chile to the spires of Frey in Argentina. Descending with double ropes is fairly straightforward to the top of the sixth pitch, where one can follow fourth-class terrain with a fixed hand-line to the south and then down a long scree gully. ▣

EVAN A. BELKNAP

AYSÉN REGION

Cerro Meliquina, southwest face. I had been eyeing a line on the southwest face of Cerro Meliquina (2,602m) since my 2011 trip to the peak and successful ascent of the northeast face [*AAJ 2012*]. In 2012, I was fortunate enough to revisit the mountain, which is located in the Cordon La Torre, between Rio Leones Valley and Rio El Canal Valley (the closest town is Puerto Rio Tranquilo, which lies north).

On November 26, Erik Bonnett and I, both NOLS instructors, got to take advantage of our students' rest day and left our camp (ca 1,800m) at 6 a.m. to try the route. We ascended to a pass (ca 2,000m) below the southwest face, then simul-climbed about 450m before beginning a traverse

[This page] The southwest face of Cerro Meliquina, showing the route Los Azules Brillosos. It was the second time the author climbed the peak by a new route. *Max Fisher*

along the ridge to the summit. The traverse was mainly on loose, snow-covered rock. About 200m from the summit we did a short rappel to reach easier ground and summited around 1 p.m. We descended the north ridge and arrived at the rappel station from my previous climb. We continued down to the glacier to camp, arriving at 4 p.m., able to share a fun story with the students.

This was the first ascent of the Cerro Meliquina's southwest face: Los Azules Brillosos (600m, AI2+ 5.4) A few days after our climb, three students and I climbed Cerro La Torre (2,300m) (45° Class 3). Overall, this area has great mountaineering objectives, many climbed by NOLS groups, and some impressive alpine climbing potential too.

MAX FISHER

CORDILLERA CASTILLO

Cerro Castillo, Torreón Chala (north tower). Cerro Castillo is a rocky massif located outside of Aysén, Chile. It contains a central tower surrounded by various other needles and black rock, which is where it derives its name. When viewed from the Carretera Austral, the interesting topography makes it hard to forget the towers.

On November 28 Manuel Medina and I, born and bred in Chilean Patagonia, traveled to Cerro Castillo, 100km south of Coyhaique, to attempt the unclimbed north tower, Torreón Chala. We began the climb on the 29th. The climbing was difficult and delicate because of the rock quality. We had to negotiate the labyrinth that the mountain presented us, as is common in the Cordillera Castillo, and summited at 12:45 p.m: Si Mato Truco y Si Mata Quiero (370m, D+ III 5.10).

The nearby towers in this astonishing setting are waiting for climbers to reach their summits. [*Editor's note: In October 2012, Franco Cayupi, Pablo Miranda, and Daniel Zapata made an additional ascent of a large tower northwest of Cerro Castillo: Cerro Facon (5.8 80°). Further details are currently lacking.*]

PABLO MIRANDA, *Chile, translated by Marcelo Scanu*

TORRES DEL PAINE

Cerro Catedral, east face, first free ascent; Cerro Cota 2000, east face, first free ascent. Stephane Hanssens, Merlin Didier, and I spent January 14 to February 12, 2013, in the French Valley, living in a cave and climbing big walls. We did not see anybody except for the one day we went to the ranger station to ask for a weather forecast; the rest of the time it was just the three of us in the upper valley. Without a consistent weather forecast, we did get shut down hard by the weather a few times.

We free-climbed two routes of exceptional quality. The first was the first free ascent of the east face of Cerro Catedral (1,000m, 7c+), finishing off a project called Los Fabulosos Dos, a variation of La Escoba de Dios, which was attempted by our friends Mason Earle (U.S.), Peter Rhodes, and George Ullrich (both U.K.). Unfortunately they had to bail due to bad weather, but all credit goes to them for envisioning this line. We fixed ropes for two days before spending a week on the wall capsule-style. The weather was exceptional, with only two days of bad conditions during our ascent. There were even days we had to wait for the shade because it was too warm for technical climbing! I never thought that would be necessary in Patagonia. Our summit day, however, was cold and icy, and required some suffer-fest battles.

[This page] Cerro Cota 2000 (left) and Cerro Catedral (right). Both routes were climbed free (difficulties to 7c+) and ascend high-quality cracks and dream dihedrals, like the one below, high on Cerro Catedral. *Supplied by Sean Villanueva*

Our second climb was the first free ascent of the east face of Cerro Cota 2000 (500m, 7c+), the big rock face left of Cerro Catedral. At first we thought we were doing a new line, but we found bolts and pitons from the 1993 Italian route (Canzan-Moreolo-Panciera-Raccanello-Valmassoi). Without any pre-fixing, we spent a week on the wall. The weather was really bad this time—we only had two decent days. Many days were spent just hanging in our portaledge, being levitated and beaten against the wall by the strong winds. With almost no food left, and mentally prepared to bail, we got our good day, climbed to the summit, and then walked out of the valley with no extra food. Both lines had impeccable rock with perfect cracks and dream dihedrals. 📷 🔍

SEAN VILLANUEVA, *Belgium*

North Tower, east face, Plate Tectonics. Amy Ness and I began climbing the east face of the North Tower on January 9, 2013. We planned for 12 days on the wall for an all-free, capsule-style ascent. During 15 days on the wall, we had 10 days of fantastic weather. However, with good weather comes rock fall, ice fall, avalanches, and things that want to be pushed out of memory: the chopping of ropes, meteor showers of rocks, and the slow destruction of our portaledge.

We began climbing at the toe of the buttress on a seahorse-shaped flake 30m above the glacier, just right of a giant left-facing corner capped by a dark roof. From here, the wandering began. We ascended dikes, slammer splitters, and crystal pods. The quality of rock transformed the entire way—from great, to terrible, to unreal, to bulletproof and sharp. En route we discovered travels from the past—an aborted Chilean route named Hasta Chonchi by Francisco Parada and Felipe Gonzales Donoso, who attempted the line twice. We know our route crossed theirs twice and joined it for a pitch and a half.

From pitch 13 onward, the climbing got wild, as we cut hard right out of an always-dripping alcove toward the headwall. We worked the Gateway Pitch (pitch 13) for a day and a half, placing three bolts and fixing three pitons. We set our high camp here for the rest of the journey and battled this 45m pitch of sustained 5.11 and 5.12 climbing. Once it was completed, we stretched our heads back and gazed at the headwall's coarse, slammer, overhanging cracks.

Day 12 had us in the middle of the headwall (pitch 14). Supplies were low and rationing had begun far below. We talked about how much time the Gateway Pitch had cost us, but we knew we had to be close to the *cumbre*. Pitch 14 went at 5.11 C1—the two meters of horizontal C1 will go free on a rail below the roof. The summit at this point had become more important than freeing the pitch, so we decided to press on. Above, we fixed 70m up a fantastic 5.11 offwidth.

An early rise the following day had us jugging 160m of fixed line above our camp for the final summit push. Of our six remaining pitches to the summit, the first two were 65m rope-stretchers (sustained 5.10). The next four pitches climbed through a sea of blocks, meandering around to the south side of the prow on the final summit cube. By pitch 18 we had dumped all nonessential gear and begun simul-climbing. We toped out our route, Plate Tectonics (3,000', 21 pitches, VI 5.12 C1-) on January 23 in a full whiteout.

[This page] East face of the North Tower. (1) Plate Tectonics, 2013. (2) Kaweskars, 1993. (3) Born Under a Wandering Star, 1995. Plate Tectonics was nearly the first all-free route on the tower. It shares some terrain with the aborted, nearby route Hasta Chonchi. *Myles Moser*

The camera flashed red, took one photo, and then died.

We spent two days descending the route, facing intense rock fall and little to eat. We later found out that a record heat wave had swept over Patagonia. We were fortunate to be part of this weather window in Valle Ascensio—we just happened to feel the tower shift and move the entire time.

[*Editor's note: Following the climb, Moser and Ness made an attempt on the east face of the Central Tower, hoping to establish its second free route. They climbed 13 pitches free (up to 5.11) before a massive storm forced them to bail. They tentatively called the unfinished route Going for a Wander.*]

MYLES MOSER, *AAC*

North Tower of Paine, Zuko Traverse. In December 2012, I flew to Patagonia with Andrej Grmovsek, another Slovenian. We arrived in El Calafate, but one of our bags wasn´t that lucky, and we spent four days there, hearing exotic new stories about our missing bag every day. We managed to carry all of our food and equipment to base camp in two heavy loads. At the time, it was snowing and there were no climbers to be seen. A few days later the weather improved; however, I now had a fever. I knew the days of good weather were rare, so I started packing.

We decided to try Riders on the Storm on the east face of Central Tower. On the first day we climbed 13 pitches with the second jumaring, and then bivied on an obvious ledge. The next morning, while fighting an icy offwidth on pitch 17 for more than an hour, we knew we were moving too slow to escape the incoming weather, so we rappelled and reached our tent in the afternoon.

A week later the weather cleared again, and this time we hiked to the west faces. New Year's Eve was spent on a nice flat bivy site below the walls, eating pasta and drinking Zuko. The next morning we started climbing an obvious non-icy line up the north summit of the North Tower, which we thought was an existing line called Armas y Rosas. After reaching the north summit, we made two rappels into the notch and climbed a few more pitches to the main summit. Our initial plan was to traverse the towers, but there was too much snow, so we rappelled the Monzino Route.

After talking with Steve Schneider, it was clear that we climbed a new line, which was a consolation prize for our failed attempt on the traverse. We named it Zuko Traverse (650m, V 5.10+), after the fizzy beverage we drank so much. It climbs a large corner immediately to left of Los Esclavos del Barometro and to the right of Armas y Rosas, joining both of these lines two pitches below the north summit of the North Tower.

LUKA KRAJNC, *Slovenia*

[This page] Myles Moser leading up featured granite below the steep upper headwall on Plate Tectonics, North Tower of Paine. *Amy Ness*

Summary, other ascents. In January 2013, Steve Schneider climbed the South Tower with Ivo Kusanovic and Schneider's wife, Heather Baer. Kusanovic was the first regional climber (Punta Arenas) to climb all three Torres del Paine, and Baer was the first woman to summit all three towers.

In Februrary, Pedro Cifuentes (Spain) completed the second solo traverse of the three main Torres del Paine after a 29-day endeavor with a portaledge (enduring storms up to eight consecutive days). He began on Espiritu Libre (500m, 5.11 A1), which climbs the north ridge of the North Tower to a subsidary northern summit. He then descended 100m to the gap below the main summit, which he climbed via Cuenca es Unica (250m, 5.11 A1). He then rappelled the standard Monzino Route on the south ridge to reach the gap below the Central Tower. On the Central Tower he climbed the Bonington-Whillans Route (800m, 5.11d A2). From the summit of the Central Tower, he descended the Kearney-Knight Route to reach the gap below the South Tower. On the South Tower he climbed the Aste Route (900m, 5.11 A1) and descended the southeast buttress via Hoth (1,100m, 27 pitches, 5.10+ A4 WI2/3).

In 2002 American Steve Schneider climbed all three towers in a single crossing. In a 51-hour round trip from the Campamento Japanese, he climbed the Monzino Route, up and down, to the south summit of North Tower, the Bonington-Whillans to the Central Tower, and then the Aste Route, up and down, to the South Tower. However, no one prior to Cifuentes appears to have followed the complete skyline of all three towers.

From information supplied by STEVE SCHNEIDER *and* LINDSAY GRIFFIN, *Mountain INFO*

TIERRA DEL FUEGO

Monte Giordano, west ridge, Shark's Fin Ridge. In April 2012, Jorg Heller, Robert Jasper, and I climbed the west ridge of Monte Giordano in Tierra del Fuego's Cordillera Darwin. The peak lies east-southeast of Monte Buckland (1,746m) in the western Cordillera Darwin, southeast of Isla Dawson. We reached the region by charter boat, having sat out a violent storm on a lonely island partway through the journey. Upon arriving, the bay we had hoped to anchor in proved too dangerous, and eventually the boat was tied securely to a cliff to prevent it from being damaged by storms.

Our approach was typical of the Tierra del Fuego: bushwhacking through dense rain forest and open swampland. Foul weather, for which is area is renowned, prevented us from establishing

[This page] Robert Jasper rappelling in the dark after a short weather window allowed the team to make a rapid ascent of Monte Giordano's west ridge. *Ralf Gantzhorn*

[This page] Approaching Monte Giordano's west ridge (the Shark's Fin Ridge), the obvious sweeping ridge line to the left. *Ralf Gantzhorn*

a base camp at the foot of the peak, and we were forced to operate from the boat. However, we knew what to expect: In 2010 we climbed a new route on Monte Sarmiento, at the western end of the Cordillera Darwin, perhaps the most famous peak in this little visited range.

Our first attempt on Giordano failed—Heller cracked a rib. However, three days before our scheduled departure, a weather window appeared and allowed for a rapid ascent. We reached the previously unclimbed summit shortly after midnight in bright moonlight, returning to the boat in a 27-hour round-trip. The spectacular shape of the ice-encrusted west ridge led us to name it the Shark's Fin Ridge. Maximum difficulties were M7. On our maps Monte Giordano showed an altitude of 2,042m, but a GPS reading on the summit recorded the altitude at 1,517m. 🖸

RALF GANTZHORN, *Germany*

Editor's note: Giordano lies east-southeast of Monte Buckland (1,746m) in the western Cordillera Darwin, southeast of Isla Dawson. Until this year Buckland had only one ascent, in 1966 by the strong Italian alpinists and Patagonian activists Alippi, Ferrari, Guidici, Machetto, Mauri, and Pirovano, from an expedition led by Carlo Mauri. These Italians approached via the southern Agostini Fjord and made the first ascent via the southwest ridge.

In 2012, Daniel Gross, Markus Kautz, and Robert Koschitzki from Germany made the long-awaited second ascent, this time approaching from Fitton Bay to the north and climbing the northeast ridge and northeast face (D), with a crux pitch of WI4 90°. This team managed to set up a high camp at 1,100m, and later in the expedition were able to make the first ascent of nearby Monte Niebla (1,430m) via the northeast face.

ARGENTINA

NORTHERN ANDES

Volcán Tres Picos, first ascent. Volcán Tres Picos (6,037m) lies northwest of the Pissis massif, outside Catamarca, and until recently was one of the last virgin 6,000m peaks in the Andes. In 2010, Pablo Lukach and party attempted it without success. Lukach returned in January 2013 with Esteban Pacheco. From base camp, they walked a short distance before establishing a camp near the Pissis-Pillán col (ca 4,850m). They established a second camp near Pissis' west glacier, then crossed the heavily crevassed glacier and walked along the volcano's enormous crater to both summits, calling their route Wallya Buena.

Marcelo Scanu, Argentina

Basque Traverse, Ojos del Salado to Volcán San Francisco. In February 2012, Jabi Txikon, Juan Nogueras, and Arkaitz Ibarra set out to for a 200km traverse of some the highest volcanoes on Earth. They acclimatized on Las Grutas (ca 4,000m) from February 1–5, and then they were taken by car to Puertas de Aguas Calientes on the way to Ojos del Salado (6,893m), where they would begin the traverse.

On February 8, they arrived in Agua de las Vicuñas to worsening storms, and on the 10th they reached El Arenal (Camp 1, ca 5,750m) on Ojos del Salado. They left for the summit early the next day, and at 9 a.m. they reached the summit plateau (ca 6,280m) and found much soft snow. Nogueras retreated, but Txikon and Ibarra continued, reaching the summit at 2 p.m. in bad conditions.

On February 12 they walked toward Volcán El Muerto (6,488m), and on the 13th they began to climb the south face. The climbing consisted of deep snow and ice runnels, so they ascended the face roped, and all three climbers reached the summit. Very tired, they descended the normal route and were forced to traverse around the volcano to reach their base camp.

The next day they walked toward El Fraile (6,062m), a volcano on the Chilean border. On February 15, Txikon and Ibarra reached the summit via a new route on a very steep, snowy face from 5,400m to 5,800m, calling it Maddi (AD+ 55°). They descended by scree.

On the 16th they approached the south face of Volcán Incahuasi (6,638m), which required a long descent to reach a camp at ca 5,500m on a very steep slope below the face. The next day they summited Incahuasi by the steep and snowy south ridge.

On the 18th, they approached Volcán San Francisco (6,016m) by the Valle del Fraile, and the next day they left camp at 2 a.m. and reached San Francisco's south face in three hours. The mountain had seen only one prior ascent, by Marcelo Scanu, 10 years prior. They climbed a steep ridge of rock and nevé, and reached the summit at 10 a.m., concluding their astonishing eight-day, 200km traverse. 📷

Marcelo Scanu, Argentina

[This page, top] Resting below an ice wall on the Ojos Del Salado–Pissis traverse. *Arkaitz Ibarra*
[This page, bottom] Ojos Del Salado (6,893m), the highest volcano in the world, covered in fresh snow during the Basques' massive traverse. The climbing was primarily nontechnical, but the team covered over 200km in eight days and tagged five summits over 6,000m, including a new route on El Fraile. *Arkaitz Ibarra*

Ojos del Salado to Pissis traverse. Ojos del Salado (6,893m) is the highest volcano on Earth and the second highest summit in South America. Pissis (6,800m, unofficially) is the second highest volcano on Earth, and the third highest summit on the continent. Basques Jabi Txikon and Arkaitz Ibarra linked both summits in an astonishing 240km traverse, between January 22 and January 31, 2013. Unfortunately, both received some frostbite. 🗎 📷

Marcelo Scanu, *Argentina*

Puna region, various ascents. During the second half of January 2012, Argentineans Sandra Odriozola, Christián Chávez, Matías Barberis, Pablo Barberis, Federico Barberis, and I explored the high-mountain desert Puna, in the northern province of Catamarca. Some early ascents were made by the Incas, and by Walther Pench in 1912-1913, but many summits are still unclimbed. We ascended a number of peaks, including San Franscisco (6,016m), Cerro Camila (4,932m), Bertrand (5,188m) by a new route on the north face, Pabellón (5,331m), and others. 🗎

Marcelo Scanu, *Argentina*

Nevado Tres Cruces, east face and first winter ascent; other winter ascents. Nevado Tres Cruces (6,749m) was the last peak over 6,500m on the continent without a winter ascent. Basques Jabi

Txikon and Arkaitz Ibarra climbed the peak by a new route, a very steep glacier on the east face. On August 30 they began to acclimatize in Las Grutas. On September 5 they made camp at ca 5,000m in high winds, and the next day they were pinned in camp by the wind. On September 7 they moved camp to ca 5,400m.

On September 8, they ascended Cerro Solo (6,240m), making its first winter ascent in windy conditions. From there, they studied the Tres Cruces glacier, now known as Glaciar de los Vascos. On September 10, after another day pinned in camp because of high winds, they started up at 4 a.m. In two hours they began climbing the glacier in very low temperatures. They entered the glacier through a gash and started with 10m of vertical climbing on bad ice. Above another short section of bad, wind-sculpted ice, the ice improved, and, moving right, they found a nice, direct route to the summit. High on the route they encountered rockfall and more bad ice (70°), with crevasses and strange, wave-like formations formed due to high pressure in the ice. Near the summit, the terrain improved again. They reached the top at 4 p.m., finishing Ruta Etxerat, which means "to home." They returned to camp at 9:30 p.m.

With some additional days remaining, the two Basques ascended Vicuñas (6,067m) and Barrancas Blancas (6,119m), both in Chilean territory, and also first winter ascents. 📄 📷

Marcelo Scanu, *Argentina*

Cerro Huayco (6,450m), northwest face. Argentines Glauco Muratti and Guillermo Bianchi made the first ascent of this volcanic summit on December 10. A subsidiary summit 2km southwest of Cazadero (6,658m), Cerro Huayco is one of the tallest volcanoes on Earth. Muratti and Bianchi began in Catamarca and approached the mountain via the Río Salado. They then walked for a few days, establishing their last camp at over ca 6,000m in an ancient crater filled with sulphur odor, undrinkable water, and nice turquoise lagoons. They climbed to the summit by the northwest face.

Marcelo Scanu, *Argentina*

Cerro Bonete, first winter ascent; south summit, new route. The volcano Cerro Bonete (6,759m), located outside of La Rioja, is the continent's fourth highest summit, the world's third highest volcano, and until now was the highest summit in South America lacking a winter ascent. On June 9, Basques Javi Txikon and Arkaitz Ibarra traveled to the Veladero hut (ca 4,375m) to acclimatize and wait out bad weather. On June 21, the beginning of the South American winter, they walked 28km in very bad weather before pitching camp below the mountain (ca 4,960m). On June 22 they

[This page] Nevado Tres Cruces with the Basque route up the steep glacier. *Arkaitz Ibarra*

erroneously climbed the south summit (6,668m) by the southwest face, calling their new route Ruta Mendizale. They rested the following day, and, on June 24, they reached the main summit via the southwest face after 12 hours of climbing. They returned to the hut the following day.

Marcelo Scanu, *Argentina*

CENTRAL ANDES

Vallé Colorado, Boris Avdeev Route, new routes.
Over a period of three weeks in December 2012 and January 2013, Anton Karnoup (Michigan, AAC) and I climbed a number of routes in Vallé Colorado, beneath the slopes of Mercedario (6,720m) in the Cordillera de la Ramada, approximately 100km north of Aconcagua. It was clear, sunny, and empty for the duration, and all snow slopes below 5,000m had turned to penitentes from the sun. We focused our attention on the cirque below the Negro Couloir (southwest of Cerro Negro), an area that contained multiple unclimbed, daylong ice routes with good rock on the west side, especially in chimneys. All routes lead either to the summit of Cerro Negro (5,600m) or to the smaller peak Negro Chico (5,200m), west of Cerro Negro.

The longest route we climbed took us two days round-trip. The route consisted of three large icefalls, separated by fields of penitentes and some rock. The first four pitches were all 55-60m (WI3–WI4 M3), and located in a chimney. The left side of the chimney ran with a waterfall most of the day, but to the right of it was a narrow runnel of ice, resembling Colorado's famous Ames Ice Hose. The runnel stays in the shade all day, making for solid climbing, though it is generally hard to keep the belayer protected from falling ice. After four pitches, we spent the night on a flat scree platform (ca 4,600m).

The next day, we climbed 100m of fourth-class rock to reach the second icefall (55m, WI4), which ends on smooth rock with a thin crust of ice. Eventually, after several hundred meters of fighting penitentes, we reached a broad icefall at ca 4,900m (40m, WI5). The easier part of it was still overhanging. After this, several hours of snow and alpine ice led us to the distinct col along the ridge between Cerro Negro and Mercedario. From the col it was only a 30-minute scramble to the top of Negro Chico. We spent the night at the col and then descended to the west, first along

[This page] The first part (240m) of the Boris Adeev Route climbs a runnel of ice just right (in the shade) of the main, sun-baked icefall. Above, the route tackles a penitente traverse and a steep final pitch (WI5). All told, 1,000m of climbing. *Dmitry Shapovalov*

[This page, left] Cascada del Aguilas (left, previously climbed) and Pecho Frio (right, new). Both routes are five pitches long (240m). *Dmitry Shapovalov* **[This page, right]** Climbing thick ice on a steep portion of Cascada del Aguilas. *Dmitry Shapovalov*

the main ridge, then south down penitente slopes to a broad scree shoulder. At the far end of it, a couloir led us left (east), the top of which we marked with a cairn. This descent route did not require a single rappel and can be used for other routes leading to Negro Chico. We named the route after Boris Avdeev, a great rock climber and friend who died skiing the Dana Couloir in Yosemite: Boris Avdeev Route (1,000m, WI5 M3).

We also climbed several other routes nearby: Chapaev de Los Andes (3 pitches, WI4 M3), an alternative to the start of Negro Couloir; Pecho Frio (5 pitches, WI3+), and the magnificent Cascada del Aguilas (5 pitches, WI5). Anibal Maturano, author of the local guidebook, believes that all routes were first ascents except for Cascada del Aguilas, which was climbed by Argentineans Javier Giuliani and Fabrizio Oieni in 2011. All routes require 60m ropes, a handful of ice screws, and small rock protection. 📷 🔍

Dmitry Shapovalov, *Canada, AAC*

Aconcagua, summary. In the 2012 season, 6,989 people traveled to Aconcagua—3,688 planned to reach the summit, and 3,301 visited the area for trekking. (The preceding season's figures were 3,497 and 2,630.) The climbers were 18 percent Argentinian and 82 percent from abroad. One climber died, and 203 were evacuated due to diseases and accidents, with 114 evacuated from Plaza de Mulas alone. There was an important helicopter rescue on the south wall. The park has accumulated more personal to account for these increases, including 50 rangers, 18 rescuers, and 22 doctors specialized in high-mountain medicine. In one year, 50 tons of garbage were extracted from the park.

Marcelo Scanu, *Argentina*

CHALTÉN MASSIF

Summary, various routes. According to various estimates, more than 150 people climbed the Ragni Route (600m, 90° M4) on the west face of Cerro Torre during the 2012-2013 summer season. This is more than twice as many people as climbed it in the previous 40 years, since its first ascent in 1974. The conditions resulting from extremely dry weather were partly responsible, with the climb involving mostly well-protected ice climbing rather the usual unprotected rime. It also appears that the removal of the bolts along the southeast ridge resulted in a rediscovery of the Ragni Route's obvious natural line to the summit. It turns out that the physical presence of the bolts was not nearly as important as their psychological impact, and their tendency to focus attention on the manufactured path, rather than on the mountain's natural features.

Austrian Markus Pucher blasted the second solo ascent of the Ragni Route, free soloing it in a mere 3 hours 15 minutes from a plateau 150m below the Col de la Esperanza. Immediately right of the Ragni Route, Argentines Gabriel Fava, Wenny Sánchez, and Roberto Treu climbed an impressive 350m variation, from the top of the Elmo to the base of the last pitch. The Directa Huarpe offers

difficulties similar to those found on the Ragni Route, with one slightly harder section involving 15m of rime-covered ice (95°). Later in the season Fava, Sánchez, and Treu climbed Guasos on the Rock, a 450m variation (5.11 A1) to Mate, Porro y Todo lo Demás on the west face of Fitz Roy's Goretta Pillar, as well as a five-pitch variation on the north face of Aguja Rafael Juárez: Los Sanjuaniños (5.11).

The most creative ascent of the season came from the hands of Americans Josh Huckaby and Mikey Schaefer, who climbed Aguja CAT, then traversed south onto Aguja Cuatro Dedos and climbed all four fingers before descending to the col with Aguja Inti, and then climbed over Agujas Atchachila and Pachamama before descending. In all they climbed about 25 pitches (around eight of them new) and made close to 40 rappels. They took three days to complete this beautiful traverse, which they christened Manos y Mas Manos, referring to all the hand jamming involved as well as a play on the name Cuatro Dedos.

On the west side of the Cerro Pollone massif, German Carsten von Birckhahn and Argentine Martin Kroussottsi climbed No Entiendo, a new route on the southeast ridge of the Gran Gendarme.

[This page] The Directa Huarpe (right), a new 350m variation to the Ragni Route (left). More than 150 people climbed the Ragni Route on Cerro Torre's west face during the 2012-2013 season, affirming its place as the standard line to the summit, once the bolts on the Compressor Route were chopped [*AAJ 2012*]. *Dani Ascaso*

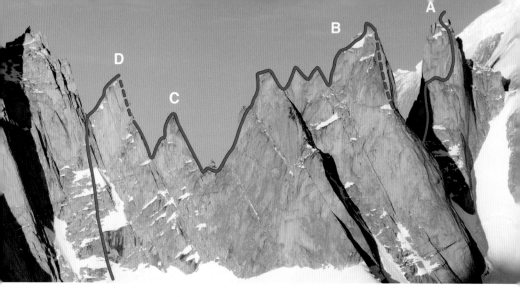

[**This page**] Manos y Mas Manos traverse. This creative enchainment was climbed by Mikey Schaefer and Josh Huckaby over three days from right to left: (A) Aguja CAT, (B) the four fingers of Aguja Cuatro Dedos, (C) Aguja Atchachila, and (D) Aguja Pachamama. *Rolando Garibotti*

Later, Von Birckhahn and Lukas Pflug climbed a new route on the northwest ridge of the same tower, the Perfekt Day (400m 7a). Von Birckhahn and Pflug, with Sebastian Straub, also climbed Zigzag, a line that climbs seven new pitches on the west face of Aguja Tito Carrasco, to join the north face route (Kauffman-Toman, 2010).

On the east side of the Pollone massif, Japanese Katsutaka "Jumbo" Yokoyama and Ryo Masumoto established a 300m "sit start" to the east ridge of Aguja Pollone, climbing also a beautiful three-pitch direct start to La Granja. From the summit they rappelled west to climb past Aguja Stefan, traversing the ridge to join Re Puesto! on the ridge to Cerro Pollone's east summit. In all they climbed 29 pitches, all free (to 5.11+). Later, Yokoyama and Masumoto completed the first free ascent of Judgment Day on the south face of Aguja Poincenot, finding difficulties to 5.12.

A number of variations went up on Aguja Guillaumet. Americans Pete Fasoldt and Eli Simon climbed Dirigo (300m, 5.10 C1 50°) on the east face: seven new pitches between the Slovene route and the Anker-Piola. Just to the left, Argentines Charly Cabezas and Diego Simari climbed a three-pitch variation to the right of the Gambler.

The most important ascent on Cerro Fitz Roy, and probably in the entire range, was the first ascent of Un Mar de Sueños, a massive new route on the southeast face. [*See feature article earlier in this* AAJ.] Also on Fitz Roy, Argentines Iñaki Coussirat and Carlos Molina did the second ascent of El Corazón, a striking line on the east face. Americans Kate Rutherford and Madeline Sorkin completed the first team female ascent of Mate, Porro y Todo los Demás, for the fourth team female ascent of the peak. Previously unreported, the third team female ascent of Fitz Roy was carried out in late February 2012 by Argentines Cintia Percivati and Luciana Tessio, via the Afanassieff. (The first team female ascent of Fitz Roy was by Slovenes Tina Di Batista and Monika Kambic, via the Franco-Argentine, in 2004; the second by Milena Gomez and Dörte Pietron in 2012, via the Afanassieff.)

On the south face of Aguja de la Silla, Hungarians Tomas Kovacs, Bence Lam, and Aron Urbanics climbed Carril Rapido, a five-pitch new line (5.10).

Much has changed in this massif in the last few years. Climate change has affected the weather patterns to the point where long good-weather windows have been a common occurrence; the nearby town of El Chaltén provides an ever-expanding myriad of services and comfort; accurate weather forecasts allow parties to climb with little apprehension, while collective knowledge and plentiful route information have left few unknowns. The mythical "great range" where the likes of Jose Luis Fonrouge, Casimiro Ferrari, Jim Donini, Silvo Karo, Ermanno Salvaterra, and many others made history is no more. Today, instead, this massif is a phenomenal playground where hundreds of climbers are having deeply fulfilling experiences. We may shed a few tears for what has been lost, but it is hard not to have a big smile on one's face for what is happening. [*Go to www.pataclimb.com for up-to-date information and topos for climbs on the Chaltén massif.*]

ROLANDO GARIBOTTI, *Argentina*

Cerro Torre, southeast ridge, fair-means ascent. After three days of rest following a new route on Fitz Roy, Tadej Kriselj and I made a fair-means ascent of the southeast ridge of Cerro Torre, following the Kennedy-Kruk line with the Lama-Ortner variation (900m, 5.12b A2 75°). We used an A1 variation on pitch 12, but we mostly free-climbed and only used aid on a few occasions to save time; we also didn´t use jumars. In the end, it was much less adventurous than the experience we'd had a few days before on Fitz Roy. The climbing proved to be less demanding than our imaginations made us think it would be, but it was still challenging and aesthetic. ◨

LUKA KRAJNC, *Slovenia*

Cerro Torre, bolt-less ascent of Corkscrew. From January 24–26, 2013, Chad Kellogg and I made the second ascent of Cerro Torre's Corkscrew route: a link-up that climbs the first two-thirds of the southeast ridge, traverses across the hanging icefield on the upper south face, and then finishes on

[This page, left] Colin Haley leading Cerro Torre's final pitch. Haley and Chad Kellogg climbed a portion of the southeast ridge sans bolts during their ascent of the Corkscrew, a route that links the southeast ridge with the Ragni Route via a traverse across the upper south face's hanging icefield. *Colin Haley* **[This page, right]** Only a year after the controversial bolt-removal on Cerro Torre's Compressor Route [*see AAJ 2012*], Luka Krajnc and Tadej Kriselj repeated the southeast ridge, mostly free-climbing the Kennedy-Kruk line with the Lama-Ortner variation. *Tadej Kriselj*

the 1974 Ragni di Lecco route. The first ascent of the Corkscrew was made in November 2008, by Ole Lied and Trym Atle Saeland.

On January 24, we leisurely climbed to a bivouac at the Col de la Paciencia. On the 25th we climbed the Corkscrew route in under 24-hours round-trip from the col, descending via the southeast ridge.

While Ole and Trym had been forced onto the Compressor Route's then-existing bolt ladders by bad conditions, Chad and I were able to climb the southeast ridge directly, without using the bolts, thanks to excellent rock climbing conditions. I highly recommend this route. It is among Cerro Torre's moderates (speaking relatively, of course), and allows one to climb most of the classic terrain on both the southeast ridge and the Ragni route. For us, the difficulties of the Corkscrew were 5.10 A1 AI4+.

COLIN HALEY, *Seattle, AAC*

Torre Egger, west face, Notti Magiche. Three years ago, at a round table in Lecco, Italy, Mario Conti and Carlo Aldè showed Matteo "Berna" Bernasconi and me a few photos of the west face of Torre Egger. This little information was enough for Berna and I to tackle the challenge of opening the first route on this immaculate wall. With no experience in Patagonia, I had no idea of what to expect.

During the winters of 2011 and 2012, Berna and I tried our best. We learned a lot about Patagonia—its mountains and its unpredictable weather—and we also learned a lot about opening a new route on a big wall in such a remote place. In 2012, Berna and I arrived at a highpoint just 30m below the col that divides Punta Herron from Torre Egger (Col Lux), only to retreat due to a massive fall that left us hanging from one cam [*AAJ 2012*]. Little was missing to complete our route, but we had to go back in 2013 to properly finish the job. We decided to add a third person, in order to be lighter and safer on the wall. Luca Schiera, a talented youngster from Lecco ready for his first experience outside Europe, was the first to come to mind.

[This page] The west face of Torre Egger, showing Notti Magiche with the Hotel Egger bivy marked. The line starts on the 1996 Cavallaro-Salvaterra attempt and then climbs new terrain to the col. The author notes potential for an independent line from the Hotel Egger bivy to the summit. *Matteo Della Bordella*

[This page, top] Luca Schiera leading steep rime ice on Torre Egger after joining the Huber-Schnarf route at the col that seperates Punta Herron and Torre Egger. *Matteo Della Bordella*

The 2013 trip started under the best omen. Arriving in Chaltén, the three of us immediately climbed Cerro Standhardt by the route Festerville. After that, though, the *suerte* flew away and we got more than three weeks of mostly bad weather. Thirty-five days after the start of our trip, Berna had to go to back to Italy. Luca and I decided to give it a last try. On February 20, we headed to Circo de Los Altares and then to Filo Rosso, where we pitched our tent. We waited for seven days in bad weather. Finally, on February 28, we received a forecast for four days of good weather.

The first day we climbed three easy pitches (UIAA V) and overcame the snowfield at the base of the wall (60°). We then reclimbed terrain from the previous Cavallaro-Salvaterra attempt (1996) for 300m (mainly slabs up to 6c), sometimes jugging fixed ropes left from our 2012 attempt. Above, the wall became steeper and we continued straight up on the right side of the obvious big dihedral. After two pitches on the right (6c and A1, maybe-free climbable at around 7b/7b+ if not icy or wet) we climbed the dihedral itself for five pitches through some icy sections (6c A1), until a tricky tension traverse (one bolt) led to a scary, long pitch on chossy, black rock (A2). After this, we climbed two brilliant crack pitches, mainly free-climbed but with few rests (potentially free at 7a/b). Eventually, we reached a belay under a small roof, two pitches below the 2012 highpoint, where we spent the night at the "Hotel Egger," hanging in our harnesses with our feet in the haul bags.

Above, our 2012 attempt, which we called Die Another Day, goes straight up for two pitches, climbs a face (6c), and then goes directly up an impressive overhang, overcome with aid climbing on a tiny seam (A2); it stops 10m below an overhanging corner. The 2013 line, Notti Magiche, briefly follows Die Another Day from the Hotel Egger bivy, and then trends left, following a logical system of cracks. Unlike the year prior, the wall was free of ice and snow under the col.

On the morning of March 1, we climbed from below the roof (A1) and then straight up for 10m. We then climbed left up two steep but easy pitches (6c) to the last, thrilling pitch (7a A1), which leads directly to the col. We arrived at the col at 4 p.m., melted some snow, prepared the bivy, and finally took a little rest. We thought of opening an independent line to the top, but it seemed forced, so we followed the existing Huber-Schnarf route for the final 200m, and on March 2 at 11:20 p.m., Luca and I stood on the summit of Torre Egger. It was the moment I desired and dreamt of for three long years.

After many rappels down the route, we reached our tent at the Filo Rosso on March 3,

[This page, top] Luka Krajnc leading solid cracks on Dulce de Leche, a 400m new route on El Mocho. The Torres in the background. *Tadej Kriselj*

bringing down all the fixed ropes we used. We called the route Notti Magiche ("Magical Nights," 1,000m, 7a A2 WI4), a name that ironically recalls the uncomfortable bivys and also those truly magical Patagonian nights. In total, we placed six bolts on the route (three belay bolts and three protection bolts), but Salvaterra and Cavallaro had previously placed another eight belay bolts in the first part. Some fixed gear remains as rappel anchors. The face is mostly free climbing on rock with some aid sections, but ice gear is essential for climbing the final snow mushroom. The 2012 attempt, Die Another Day, which stops 30m below the col, is waiting to be finished. ▤ ▣ ◌

Matteo Della Bordella, *Ragni di Lecco, Italy*

El Mocho, new route, Dulce de Leche. At the end of our visit to Patagonia, Tadej Kriselj and I used a short window of good weather to climb a new route on El Mocho. At first, we followed the approximate line of the Elorza-Moises attempt, then followed splitter cracks of all sizes to the top. We named our route Dulce de Leche (400m, 5.11+). We set a personal record of eating 9kg each of this creamy heaven in the six weeks that we were in El Chaltén.

Luka Krajnc, *Slovenia*

Fitz Roy, east face, The Real Kekec. After climbing the North Tower of Paine [*see Chile section of Climbs and Expeditions*], I was joined by Tadej Kriselj from Kamnik, Slovenia. When the morning bus dropped us in El Chaltén, the weather was perfect. We repacked our bags and headed to Paso Superior an hour later. It was our first time in Patagonia, so everything was new and interesting to us. Our plan was to climb Linea di Eleganza on the east face of Fitz Roy; however, when standing under the wall early next morning, we could see long streaks of water melting from snowy ledges. It was clear that free-climbing the route would be very difficult. But we had to climb something.

We started climbing toward an old Slovenian route called Hudiceva Zajeda (Jeglic-Karo-Knez, 1983). After sharing a pitch, we moved right to another crack system to avoid falling rocks and ice. We repeated the mantra of "let's climb one more pitch and see if it goes," and after 400m we reached our first bivouac. The next morning we woke to a cloudless day, and after the initial routine of shivering to get the blood running again, we warmed up and continued climbing. Good cracks and corners led us higher and higher into undiscovered terrain. In late afternoon we were in the middle of steep terrain with no ledges in sight. Just before night, an icy chimney with limited protection led us to a flat ledge for our second bivy. It seemed so surreal; we couldn't believe this was really happening. We had one light sleeping bag between us and spent those few hours shivering and waiting for the alarm to ring. The steep wall loomed above, and neither of us wanted to show our doubts.

On the third day the weather was less than perfect. The climbing was steep, and on some pitches our haul bag never touched the rock. As we were now 800m up, with no fixed anchors and a light rack, backing off didn´t sound appealing. With the rain and wind, we really had to try hard, and after some intense pitches we could see the angle ease up a bit. Two pitches before the top of Goretta Pillar we joined the Casarotto route. Our third bivy was spend on the top of the Goretta, where we finished our last food.

On the fourth day, we followed the Casarotto to the top, summiting in the afternoon, only six days after Tadej left home. After a short break, we descended the French route. At three in the morning we reached the Brecha de los Italianos, where we crashed on the first flat spot we saw. On the fifth day we made the remaining rappels to the glacier. Our route, the Real Kekec (1,200m, VI 5.11+ A2), conains 800m of new terrain, and was climbed without bolts or jumars. We named the route after a legendary Slovenian movie and song that started playing on our music player during the descent. 📷

LUKA KRAJNC, *Slovenia*

[This page, left] The Goretta Pillar on Fitz Roy, showing (1) The Real Kekec, which climbs the first pitch of (2) Diedro del Diablo before moving right up 800m of new terrain and joining the (3) Casarotto route to the summit. *Rolando Garibotti* **[This page, right]** Tadej Kriselj heads up steep cracks high on the Real Kekec. *Luka Krajnc*

Fitz Roy, north face, Persiguiendo el Avión. After doing two first free ascents in the Torres del Paine [*see Chile section*] Stephane Hanssens and I headed back to El Chaltén. (We had already been there in December and climbed the Ragni route on Cerro Torre.) On our last three days in South America (early March), a very good weather window appeared, so we headed up the hill for a last time. We went for the northwest face of Fitz Roy and climbed nonstop, even through the night.

Our route climbed new ground to the Grand Hotel and finished up El Flaco con Domingo. We onsighted every pitch but one, on which we lowered back down for the redpoint. All said: 1,800m of climbing, 900m of new ground, with difficulties to 7b+. The route took us 31 hours base camp to summit and 46 hours round-trip. We took a one-hour nap on the glacier, and then we had to run down to El Chaltén and Rio Gallegos to catch our plane! We called the climb Persiguiendo el Avión (Chasing the Plane, 1,800m, 7b+). 📷 🔍

Sean Villanueva, *Belgium*

Fitz Roy, north face, Samba do Leao. This route is certainly one of the best first ascents I have ever done, especially given the enormity of the wall. While I was unsure how difficult some sections would be, the route looked fairly obvious and of good quality. In 2012 I attempted the potential line a few different times, but with bad weather I was not successful, and so had to put it off until this year. Thus, in January of 2013, I set off again with Sergio Tartari, a great friend and partner.

We failed on our first attempt due to bad weather, and managed instead to repeat one of the best routes on the north pillar of Fitz Roy, Mate Porro y Todo lo Demás. After that, we rested and relaxed in El Chaltén and looked for a third partner for the new route. Finally, Serginho called his friend Flavio Daflon in Rio de Janeiro, and with luck, Flavio appeared in El Chaltén the afternoon before our next attempt, totally ready to go.

We left El Chaltén in poor weather, headed for Piedras Negras, on the afternoon of February 22. The next day we started early, and at about 8:30 a.m. we arrived at the base. We waited for the sun to hit the wall before we began climbing. Sergio led off first by climbing a dihedral on a pillar that protruded from the middle of this smooth wall. We had spent so much time going over photos and videos beforehand that we had already divided the climb into sections: Primero Muro, the lower section ending on Gran Hotel; the imposing ridge of the north wall, Segundo Muro; and the final section up to the summit, the Headwall.

The crux of the Primero Muro was a traverse that connected a pillar with an obvious dihedral that dominates the middle of the wall. Sergio arrived just where we had planned after three long pitches of 6b/6b+, which was slightly easier than we had anticipated. Next, it was my turn. I put in a bolt to protect a blank section and connected to the big dihedral. From then on it was great climbing in the shade. When we arrived at the Gran Hotel we had a welcome rest.

The beginning of the next day was tough, but once the sun heated up the wall, the quality of the Segundo Muro was obvious. The line we chose was split with cracks. By the middle of the second day, our line appeared to stop, and it became apparent that we would have to get to the wider crack system next to us. Luckily, the photos revealed a crack that began just where the dihedral we were climbing ended. Without being able to see it from below, but with faith in our photos, we connected the climb by a perfect line. Once we arrived on the northwest arête, we settled in for the night, and were rewarded with a beautiful sunset awash in colors and clouds.

The third day was fairly windy but sunny, and the climb was sheltered and somewhat warm. On pitch 12 we joined the second and third pitches of the Hoser Chimney, then we crossed

Afanassieff, and then on the "Headwall" we went to the left of a variation of Gabriel Rocamora y Susy Tarditti. Without knowing about this variation, we shared about 30m through the middle of this third wall, and after that, our route headed right.

Many times I wondered why nobody had tried to climb this obvious route. It seemed the only answer was a big roof with a wide crack on the third headwall. However, we climbed around the roof via the face to the right, making the climb relatively easy, even though it took a few tries. The top had perfect cracks in orange granite; one could choose whichever size looked the most appealing! We reached the summit at about 4:30 p.m. and descended the Franco-Argentine route. At last light we arrived at the Brecha de los Italianos, bivied, and continued the rappels at first light. I named the route Samba do Leao to honor my two Brazilian friends on the first ascent, and for the challenge this climb meant to us, with each section representing a distinct lion hunt (1,300m, 6b+).

LUCIANO FIORENZA, *translated from Spanish by Pam Roberts*

De l'S, south face, Besos to Pesos; Aguja Bifida, north face, Gunnison Direct. In late January, David Allfrey and I established a new route up the center of the south face of De l'S. We left town in the morning and then climbed the first 1,500' to the large terrace where most of the south face routes begin. The climbing was excellent, and we did this portion in approach shoes, with some soloing and simul-climbing, in a few hours. We had a romantic dinner at our bivy below the upper wall, then proceeded to spoon all night long. We began our intended line a little after 10 a.m. the next morning.

The climb takes an aesthetic plumb line to the summit. The rock quality was excellent, as was the climbing. From the terrace, we climbed 11 pitches, almost all of them being difficult and overhanging. After several sections of 5.12 we reached the final pitch, a 12' roof with a finger and hand sized crack, which we gladly aided. The roof will likely go free at 5.13 and make for an incredible day of crack climbing. Besos to Pesos (3,000'; 1,200' of new terrain, 5.12 A0) was

[This page] The north face of Fitz Roy, showing (1) Samba do Leao, (2) El Flaco Con Domingo, (3) Persiguiendo el Avión, and (4) Afanassieff. [*All route lines are approximate*.] A number of other established routes, not shown here, ascend the north face of Fitz Roy. *Doerte Pietron*

[This page, top] Jonathan Schaffer hand-traversing on De L'S after climbing 1,200' of new terrain on the south face. *David Allfrey*

[This page, bottom] David Allfrey following a steep dihedral on Besos to Pesos on De L'S. The route contains several sections of 5.12 crack climbing. *Jonathan Schaffer*

completed with leader and follower climbing free and swapping leads with a small pack.

In late February, Adam Ferro and I established a new route up the center of the north face of Aguja Bifida. We hiked to within a short distance of the base of the wall, which required hours of glacial shenanigans. (It may be wise to do this approach earlier in the season.) After a leisurely morning we began climbing unstable snow and mixed terrain right of the Lüthi-Bresba start for several hundred feet to the base of the rock wall.

While belaying the first pitch, a large piece of ice fell from above, striking my leg. Fortunately, the climbing wasn't terribly difficult and was of extremely high quality. After 1,000' of climbing we joined the Lüthi-Bresba to the summit. We found no evidence of rappel anchors off the summit and were forced to build our own. Gunnison Direct (2,500'; 1,000 of new terrain, 5.11 C1) is an exceptional free route aside from a small tension traverse on the upper Lüthi-Bresba. It was completed in a day with both leader and follower free-climbing and swapping leads. 📷

JONATHAN SCHAFFER, *AAC*

Mojon Rojo, west face, El Zorro. On February 21, Sarah Hart and I made the first ascent of the west face of Mojon Rojo, calling our route El Zorro (700m, 5.10 A1). The west face of Mojon Rojo, while of modest altitude, is quite striking from the Niponino bivouac, and I had wondered about climbing it for a long time. From afar its metamorphic rock does not look very solid, but to our surprise, the rock on Mojon Rojo was not merely tolerable but in fact quite solid and very enjoyable.

The first half of our route climbed a subtle buttress, and was mostly simul-climbing up to mid-fifth-class, with one harder section (5.10 A0). At the top of the buttress we followed an easy gully, which took us to the crest of the west ridge, at a notch with a tower. The route from here climbed spectacular crack systems on the face just left of the west ridge, with features always connecting just enough for enjoyable 5.10 climbing. As we neared the top of the face we almost entered a giant squeeze chimney, which is clearly visible from down on the Torre Glacier. However, I opted to continue connecting face cracks. The climbing remained 5.10 until the last few meters of the face, where I aided on knifeblades (A1). Once on the west ridge, one more pitch reached the lower, northwest summit of Mojon Rojo. From here, a spectacular section of simul-climbing on a true knife-edge ridge, and one short rappel, took us to the base of the main summit tower. Two rope-lengths of mid-fifth-class allowed us to join the scrambling terrain on the east face, and soon we surmounted the exposed V0 boulder problem that is the true summit of Mojon Rojo. Although we had planned to return to Niponino, it was clear on Mojon Rojo's summit that the easiest descent was to the east, down to Laguna Sucia. We descended this way, and it is definitely the best plan for future ascents. 📄 📷

COLIN HALEY, *Seattle, AAC*

[This page] The new route El Zorro is the only route on Mojon Rojo's spectacular-looking west face. The unconfirmed rumors of bad rock quality proved false; the route links high-quality crack systems up the face at a relatively moderate grade. *Colin Haley*

LOS GLACIARES NATIONAL PARK

CENTRAL SECTION

Cerro Moyano, east buttress; Cerro Norte, east buttress. In November 2012, Oriol Baró and I climbed two new routes, one on Cerro Moyano, the other on Cerro Norte. These two mountains lie between Lago Argentino, Lago Viedma, and the Upsala Glacier in Argentine Patagonia, Los Glaciares National Park. You need a week of stable weather to climb in this very little visited zone, which often has bad weather.

It took us two days from the Estancia Helsingfors to reach our base camp between the two mountains (ca 740m). The next day we climbed the Ruta del Espolón Este (1,900m, MD+) on the east buttress of Cerro Moyano (2,640m). It took us 20 hours round-trip, descending by the same route. After two days of unstable and windy weather, we explored the valley looking for new routes and climbed to the northeast summit of Cerro Norte (2,580m) by its east buttress (1,800m, MD) in 14 hours, descending by the same route. The next day we reached Estancia Helsingfors in one day.

We would like to thank Victor, the ranger in Puesto Moyano, who provided us with information to reach the mountains, gave a jacket to Oriol, and invited us to eat after our climbs.

JORDI COROMINAS, *translated by Marcelo Scanu*

[This page] Cerro Norte: (1) East buttress, Baró-Corominas, 2012. (2) North face, Kautz-Koschitzki-Sass-Wagner route, 2009. Cerro Moyana: (3) East buttress, Baró-Corominas, 2012. (4) North face, Kautz-Koschitzki-Sass-Wagner route, 2009 (approximate, most of the route is out of view in a gully behind the northeast ridge). *Jordi Corominas*

Editor's note: The most recent recorded activity on Cerro Moyano and Cerro Norte was in 2009, when German climbers Kautz, Koschitzki, Sass, and Wagner ascended both peaks via new routes [AAJ 2009, 2011]. On Cerro Moyano they climbed an independent route on the north face (D+ WI5) near the first ascent route, the Argentinian Route (Cuinas-Serrano-Vieiro, 1976). On Cerro Norte they climbed the first route on the north face, a long ice ramp (TD WI4+ M5). Other known routes on Cerro Norte include the first ascent route (Skvar-Skvar, 1970) and the icy east face (Ferrari, 1986), among one or two other routes rumored on the east and west aspects. It's likely that both routes climbed by Baró and Corominas are new.

Cerro Murallón, El Pilar del Sol Naciente and history of climbs and attempts. Cerro Murallón (2,656m) rises above the Southern Patagonia Ice Cap, along the Argentina-Chile frontier. Although it has received several new routes in the past decade, including the first ascent of the southeast pillar in 2012, the peak hasn't been summited since 2003.

In January 1961, Jack Ewer and Eric Shipton (Great Britain), along with Eduardo Garcia and Cedomir Marangunic from Chile, climbed from the northwest to the long summit crest, reaching what they believed to be the highest point in the middle of a storm. The geography of the summit ridge is such that, coming from the west, Shipton and partners likely reached a sub-summit before a wide gap, to the east of which is the highest summit.

In 1974, José Luis Fonrouge and Rafael Juarez (Argentina) made an attempt from the southeast. It is unclear if they attempted the southeast ridge or the east face.

Ten years later, in February 1984, Carlo Aldé, Casimiro Ferrari, and Paolo Vitali (Italy) completed the first ascent of the northeast ridge (1,300m, 5+ A3), and also the first confirmed ascent of the peak. They fixed three ropes in the crux section but otherwise climbed alpine style.

In November 1999, Bruno Sourzac and Laurence Monnoyeur (France) made an alpine-style attempt on the east face. They climbed to within 350 meters of the top of the wall (A2 M5 90° ice). They were caught in a fierce storm and had difficulty descending, leaving most of their equipment on the face as anchors.

In October 2003, Rolando Garibotti (Argentina) and Silvo Karo (Slovenia) climbed the peak from the southwest, following a series of easy glacial tongues. This was likely only the peak's second ascent.

One month later, Stefan Glowacz, Robert Jasper, and Klaus Fengler (Germany) climbed the Lost World, a line up an obvious pillar on the far west side of the north face (1,100m, 6b M8). They climbed the route in a day and retreated upon reaching the summit ridge.

Two years later, in November 2005, Glowacz and Jasper returned to climb Gone with the Wind (1,000m, 7c+ A2), a steep line in the center of the north face. They spent several weeks working on the route, fixing 500 meters of rope, which were left in place. Their new route ended at the summit plateau.

Finally, in late 2012, Lise Billon, François Poncet, Jeremy Stagnetto, and Jerome Sullivan (France), along with Pedro Angel Galan Diaz (Spain), completed the southeast pillar (El Pilar del Sol Naciente, 1,000m, 7b A1 WI6 M6). They descended from the top of the pillar. [*See Sullivan's feature article about the climb earlier in this AAJ.*]

Rolando Garibotti, *Argentina*

ANTARCTICA

ELLSWORTH MOUNTAINS

Overview. Mt. Vinson (4,892m) continues to attract large numbers. One hundred and seventy individual climbers reached the summit during the 2012-13 season (a total of 184 successful ascents). Fourteen guides made two or more ascents. Only four clients failed to top out. Neighboring Mt. Shinn (4,660m) received five ascents.

American guide Robert Anderson and his clients did the probable first ascent of a 2,880m peak five kilometers south of Vinson base camp. This attractive ice peak forms a pyramidal end to the ridge dividing the Cairns and Tulaczyk glaciers, the unclimbed southern arm of the western ridge of the Vinson Massif.

In late December, Antarctic Logistics & Expeditions (ALE) guides Maria Paz "Pachi" Ibarra and Todd Passey led the returning German client Ralf Laier on the first ascents of three peaks: Mt. Allen (3,430m) and Mt. Liptak (3,052m) in the southern Sentinel Range, and Robinson Peak (2,038m) further south in the Heritage Range. Allen was climbed from the south, ending in a difficult corniced ridge, and took two attempts. Liptak had a mixed summit ridge of loose rock, after steep snow and ice on the northern slope. Robinson Peak, a rocky summit in the Pioneer Heights Range, was approached from the west, across the Rennell Glacier, and then climbed by the south ridge, with some technical rock pitches and exposed scrambling. The trio traversed the summit to the northern side, and traveled back around the east to reach their skis on the southern col.

Further south, in the Independence Hills, Scott Webster and friends made the first ascent of an elegangt unnamed ice peak north of Beitzel Peak and just south of the famous Minaret Peak, a distinctive rock tower visible to all who flew out of the old ANI base at Patriot Hills. With their American friend Andy Hein, they also made rare repeats of Mt. Simmons and Mt. Fordell. 📷

DAMIEN GILDEA, *Australia*

[This page, left] The south face of Allen. The first ascent route finished up the corniced southeast ridge. *Todd Passey, Antarctic Logistics & Expeditions LLC 2013* [This page, right] Looking south from Craddock. (A) Strybing. (B) Allen. (C) Liptak. (D) Southwick (3,087m). (E) Severinghaus Glacier. (F) Nimitz Glacier. *Damien Gildea*

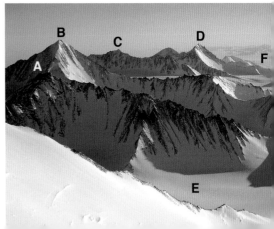

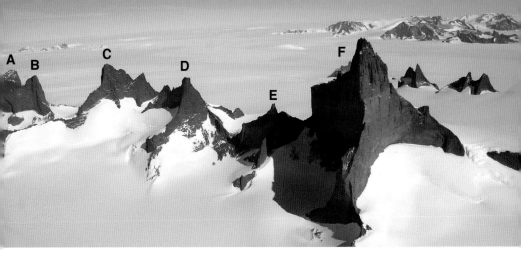

QUEEN MAUD LAND

Fenriskjeften Mountains, Ulvetanna (2,931m), northeast ridge. On January 20, 2013, Leo Houlding, Alastair Lee, Jason Pickles, Chris Rabone (all U.K.) and Sean Leary (USA) completed the first ascent of the huge northeast ridge of Ulvetanna, and fourth ascent of the mountain.

The nature of the ridge, the anticipated climatic conditions, and the commitment to film the entire ascent dictated that fixed ropes be used. Starting from the steep toe of the ridge, the route was hard from the start: course granite cracks, sometimes ice-filled and with hollow flakes and sections of crumbly rock. After around 17 pitches, fixed with 1,100m of rope, the lead climbers reached a col at the start of the Dinosaur's Back: the long, narrow arête that turned out to be the "world's scariest British VS." Any wind when trying to cross this section could have been disastrous. Eventually,

[This page, top] The spectacular Ulvetanna group from the northeast. (A) Holtanna (2,650m). (B) Holsttind (2,577m). (C) Kinntanna (2,724m). (D) Stetind (2,558m). (E) Hel (2,335m). (F) Ulvetanna (2,931m). The northeast ridge divides the sunlit north face from the east face. The north face is around the same height as El Capitan, while the unclimbed east face is 300m higher. Peaks of the Filchnerfjella are visible in the distance. *Stein-Ivar Gravdal*
[This page, bottom] Leo Houlding free-climbing at ca –30˚C. *Alastair Lee*

a two-portaledge camp was established on a good ledge (the Plateau of Great Expectations) below the 400m headwall.

On the final push, the five started from base camp, regained the portaledges, and started fixing the headwall. The first pitch, a steep compact slab, required two hand-drilled bolts, after which a spectacular series of cracks and corners took them 200m higher to a giant roof. Offwidths and chimneys led on to the Snow Petrel Pillar, at which point they were hit by a three-day storm. Summit day provided the worst conditions of the expedition, with wind chill bringing the effective temperature down to –35°C. Houlding and Leary had planned a BASE jump from the summit, an idea that was soon abandoned. It took five grueling days to descend to base camp, stripping the mountain of all ropes.

The ca 1,100m-high ridge had more than 1,700m of climbing (35 pitches), making it the longest rock climb on the continent. Technical difficulties were remarkably high, given the harsh Antarctic climate: British E6 6b and A2/C2. The initial pillar was said to be reminiscent of Half Dome's Regular Northwest Face, with the headwall more like the right side of El Capitan's southeast buttress. [o]

LINDSAY GRIFFIN, *Mountain INFO*

Wohlthat Mountains, Bertha's Tower, Gammie Hannah's Tower. If there was one thing that defined and controlled this trip—like a psychotic maestro conducting a death-metal-rock-and-roll orchestra—it was the unrelenting wind: fierce, biting, destroying, hypothermic-hammering, schedule-delaying, katabatic wind.

Our trip took place from November 1–December 24. Antarctic winds delayed our flight from Cape Town with the Russian company Antarctic Logistics Center International, leaving us stuck in South Africa for a week. Then, on arrival at Novolazarevskaya, the Russian base in Queen Maud Land, we were told we could be delayed up to 10 days more. Fortunately, a pilot was willing to fly in risky conditions, with the caveat that wind or lack of visibility might make it impossible to land near the mountains. This flight on a Basler 76 was the most expensive part of our expedition. If it did not succeed, we could not afford to take another. Fortunately, after around two hours in the air, Keith Ladzinski, Cory Richards, Freddie Wilkinson, and I landed safely at 71.890409° S, 13.555481°.

Our first goal was to circumnavigate our chosen island of granite towers in a previously unclimbed eastern part of the Wohlthat Mountains. We spent five days on this ski tour, looking for routes to climb. When we returned to base camp, we found our circular-walled shelter half filled with snow from the spindrift, and two tents destroyed. We moved camp closer to the rock

[This page] The "ship's prow" of ca 600m Grammie Hannah's Tower. The first-ascent party ascended the right skyline. *Mike Libecki*

towers for additional protection.

For the next two weeks we endured relentless, numbing wind. While trying to avoid frostbite, we shuttled loads and climbed and fixed ropes to a high camp 350m up a massive, ominous rock tower. We then ascended to our high point with enough food and supplies for at least seven days. After spending the next five days working from a portaledge camp, we reached the summit.

We had climbed through sculptured mazes of stone flames and waves. It sometimes seemed we were on a skyscraper of petrified Swiss cheese. At one point I found myself climbing over an expanse of orange and white quartz crystals, using the jewels and gemstones for hand and foot holds. We named the summit Bertha's Tower, and graded the ca 600m route VI 5.11 R A3+. Bertha was my grandmother, and she always told me, "The time is now!" She thoroughly supported my choice to pursue a life of climbing and adventure.

We had enough time to climb one more stunning tower. It was a classic ridge up the back of a ship's prow, and took only 12 hours camp-to-camp. We named it Grammie Hannah's Tower, this time after Freddie's grandmother. The ca 600m route was 5.6.

My previous two trips to Queen Maud Land, in 2003 and 2005, were simply stepping stones to this incredible challenge of wind, cold, and some of the wildest rock formations I could imagine. Huge thanks goes to National Geographic, the Copp-Dash Inspire Award, and the Polartec Challenge Grant for helping make this trip possible. However, we would not have stepped out the door without the time and energy from countless other people. 📷 🔍

Mike Libecki, *AAC*

ANTARCTIC PENINSULA

Beascochea Bay, various ascents. Three expeditions all targeted the same area of unclimbed mountains on the peninsula this season. Just south of the Waddington Bay–Argentine Islands region, Beascochea Bay is surrounded by peaks on three sides, those on the northern side being over 2,000m high. Personnel from the British Antarctic Survey were active in the area in the 1960s, but no major ascents were made. British climber Phil Wickens returned for his third season in four

[This page] The first-ascent route (600m, VI 5.11 R A3+) up Bertha's Tower. *Mike Libecki*

[This page, left] Hannah Baker climbs a steep ice arête just above the major crevasse on Peak 1,475m. *Phil Wickens* [This page, right] Second camp on the Belgica Glacier with Peak 1,475m behind. *Phil Wickens*

years, aboard *Spirit of Sydney*, leading a British team that made six ascents (*see full report below*). There were also ascents of Cape Perez, a steep-faced promontory on the southern side of Collins Bay, including one by a Brazilian team led by Joao Paulo Barbosa, traveling aboard *Sauvage*. This group had also planned to attempt Mt. Rio Branco but found it too difficult in the time they had left. Soon after, however, Rio Branco received its first ascent by a group aboard *Podorange*. This team, led by French alpinist and guide Antoine Cayrol, climbed the mountain from the north.

DAMIEN GILDEA, *Australia*

Beaschochea Bay, six first ascents. Hannah Baker, Derek Buckle, Jamie Goodhart, Mike Pinney, and I (all U.K.), Stefan Jachmich (Germany), and Bjorn Riis-Johannessen (Norway) traveled on the *Spirit of Sydney* to an unclimbed range north of Beaschochea Bay. Favorable ice conditions allowed us to disembark from the yacht at an audacious landing, allowing us to move up the broken Trooz Glacier, and after four hours establish base camp on the Belgica Glacier, below the peaks. On the first day, January 11, the whole team was able to make the first ascent of Alancer Peak (1,592m) by the northeast ridge, an easy snow ascent (PD+) with fine views.

The following day we all climbed unnamed Peak 1,333m via the northeast face (AD), again a largely straightforward ascent, except for a large crevasse crossed by a steep and elegant ice fin.

The dominating peak of the area is Valiente (2,270m), further south. Utilizing a day of thick cloud to move camp up glacier, the whole team set off to climb it over a 2,032m snow dome (north-northeast flank, F). Baker, Goodhart, Jachmich, and I then continued onward to make the first ascent of Valiente via the east ridge (F). A ski descent, followed by a recrossing of 2,032m, made this a long, tiring day.

Two days later came our first totally cloudless day, and the whole group elected to try an attractive mountain above camp, first skinning to a shoulder where we deposited skis. Two successive ice slopes and a short ridge on the north flank brought us to the summit (1,475m, AD).

On the 17th we descended to the yacht, and the weather deteriorated, making further climbs too dangerous. Thanks to the Mt. Everest Foundation, the Alpine Club, and a 2013 Julie Tullis Memorial Award for financial support.

PHIL WICKENS, *Alpine Club, U.K.*

SOUTH SHETLAND ISLANDS

Livingston Island, Sharp Peak (474m). In the northeastern section of Livingston Island, a Chilean team of Gabriel Becker, Nicolas Danyau, and Gonzalo Lllul, traveling aboard the *Ocean Nova*, made the first known ascent of Sharp Peak via its east face. The team reached the summit in 10 hours from the coast near Edinburgh Hill.

> DAMIEN GILDEA, *Australia, who thanks Robert Anderson, Gabriel Becker, Todd Passey, Nick Lewis, and Rachel Shepherd (ALE), and Scott Webster for help with this entire report*

EUROPE

*The following climbs appeared on the "Super Big List" of 2012 ascents prepared for the 2013 Piolets d'Or jury (www.pioletsdor.com). This list was compiled by Claude Gardien (*Vertical *magazine), Manu Rivaud (*Montagnes *magazine), and Lindsay Griffin (*American Alpine Journal*). The online version of this report has links to complete information on each ascent.*

ECRINS RANGE

Pic Gaspard (3,883m). First ascent of Gérons la Canicule on the north face. In August, Max Bonniot and Arnaud Guillaume (France) climbed a vague spur on the left side of the face, finishing up the summit ridge (600m, TD+ 6b+ M4).

Meije (3,982m)–Ailefroide (3,953m). In a remarkable four-day winter link-up, Nicolas Draperi and Julien Loste (France) climbed Salsa Pour Trois Etoiles (750m, 6b) on the north face of the Meije, then Pilier des Temps Maudits (1,100m, 6a+ A1) on the northwest face of the Ailefroide.

Barre des Ecrins (4,101m). First ascent of Coup de Barre, j'Ecrins le Pire on the south face. The 1,250m route was climbed in one day in August by Max Bonniot, Mat Détrie, and Pierre Labbre (France) with difficulties rated ED+ VI/6 M6 6b A1+.

MONT BLANC RANGE

Mont Blanc (4,810m). Ciao Walter is a new 850m route on the Frêney face by Simon Deniel and Patrick Gabarrou (France). In late July, the pair followed an obvious couloir and icefall right of the 1961 Bonatti-Zappelli, then crossed the latter route, keeping left of it to the summit slopes. A week earlier, the pair climbed Super Abominette, which takes the obvious couloir right of the Innominata Ridge to join Gabarrou's 1984 route Abominette.

Petit Dru (3,733m). Jeff Mercier and Korra Pesce (France) did the first winter and second overall ascent of the little-known 1979 Czechoslovak Direct on the north face of the Petit Dru. The two made their three-day ascent at 6a M5.

[This page, top] Julien Desecures leads pitch seven of Full Love on the north-northeast face of Aiguille de Peigne. *Jon Griffith* [This page, bottom] The line of Eyes Wide Shut on the northeast face of Mont Rouge de Greuvettaz, on the Italian side of the Mont Blanc Massif. *Bracey-Helliker Collection*

Aiguille des Pèlerins (3,318m). In exceptional early October conditions, Jeff Mercier and Korra Pesce (France) turned the sustained 1967 Dard-Repellin route on the north face (600m, VI and A2) into a modern mixed route. After climbing the first three pitches and leaving ropes in place the previous afternoon, the pair climbed the 16-pitch route in 13 hours at V/5+ M7 90°.

Aiguille de Peigne (3,192m). Jeff Mercier and Korra Pesce, together with Julien Desecures (France) and Jon Griffith (U.K.) climbed the north-northeast face direct, using a diagonal ramp to access the upper half of the possibly unrepeated Fullalove-Robertson route (550m, VI A3). Hard mixed climbing and poorly protected thin smears provided difficulties of V/5+ M6 85° on the route they called Full Love.

Mont Rouge de Greuvettaz (3,480m). First ascent of the 900m northeast face via Eyes Wide Shut (ED1 M6 UIAA IV+ A0). Climbed in one day in mid-November by Jon Bracey and Matt Helliker (U.K.) with a rappel descent of the route during the night.

BREGAGLIA RANGE

Piz Badile (3,308m). First solo and third overall ascent of Memento Mori by Rossana Libera (Italy), who made a two-day ascent of this objectively threatened 800m route, originally graded VI+ A3.

DOLOMITES

Cima Margherita (2,845m. Over three days in January, Luca Giupponi, Rolando Larcher, and Fabio Leoni (Italy) did the first free and first winter ascent of Via Cembridge (550m, 7b+ 6c obl.) on the steep north face.

Sassolungo (3,181m). Over the first two days in March, Wolfgang Hell (Italy) and Pavol Rajcan (Slovakia) made the first ascent of Cold Fusion (950m, 22 pitches, VII- M8 WI5+) on the east face.

Marmolada di Penia (3,343m). On the south face, in August, Hansjörg Auer and Much Mayr (Austria) made the first free ascent of the previously unrepeated L'ultimo dei Paracadutisti (A4, Frizzera-Leoni-Maffei, 1988). The 750m route contains no bolts and was redpointed at 8b+.

Scotoni (2,874m). First ascent of Agoge (400m, VIII/VIII+) on the southwest face, to the right of the 1952 Lacedelli route. Manuel and Simon Gietl (Italy) climbed the route after several previous attempts, using only trad gear and a few in-situ pitons, with 14 pitches, some of them bold.

Tre Cime di Lavaredo (2,999m). Simon Gietl (Italy) and Roger Schäli (Switzerland) completed a two-day winter traverse of the Tre Cime in mid-March. The pair climbed the Via degli Scoiattoli on Cima Ovest, descended the south face, and climbed the Dulfer on Cima Grande to a bivouac below the summit. They descended the south face and climbed the Cima Piccola via the southwest face.

JULIAN ALPS

Loska Stena, Jalovec Group. David Lama and Peter Ortner (Austria) climbed a new route over three days in late February on the Briceljk section of the broad, ca 1,000m north face of Loska Stena. The two completed 1,300m of climbing, with poor protection and difficulties of VII M6.

NORWAY

Troll Wall, Romsdal. The father-and-son team of Ole Johan Saether and Sindre Saether made the second overall and first free ascent of the ca 1,200m Krasnoyarsk Route. The 25-pitch line went at Norwegian 8– (5.12-), with many pitches of 5.11.

Editor's note: Two highly notable European ascents were not included on the Piolets d'Or list. In September, the Catalan alpinist and runner Kilian Jornet traversed Mont Blanc via the Innominata Ridge in 8 hours 43 minutes, running from the church in Courmayeur, Italy, to the church in Chamonix, France. Also in September, Alessandro Baù, Alessandro Beber, and Nicola Tondini made the first free ascent of Colonne d'Ercole (1,200m, IX VIII+ obl.) up Punta Tissi on the northwest face of Civetta. The same trio established this route between 2009 and 2012, with some aid but no bolts.

MIDDLE EAST

TURKEY

Geyikbayiri, Geyik Sivrisi, Crazy Eye. The Geyikbayiri area is popular for sport climbing, but when Michael Pearson and I traveled there in July we had trad in mind. Our goal was the possibly unclimbed 600m northwest face of Geyik Sivrisi (Sivridag). This limestone face is about three hours' walk south from the sport area. The mountain has two tiers separated by a large terrace. Our plan was to approach the terrace via a gully through the first tier and then cherry-pick a good line on the upper tier.

We set off at 2:30 a.m. on July 8 with five liters of water each and a streamlined rack. The gully leading to the terrace soon became technical, and we had to pitch the final part. We found a lone bolt before this technical section, evidence that another party had belayed or bailed at this point. The 55m pitch above was tricky and had very little gear (E1 5b). After this it took an hour to get to the base of the main face.

The upper wall was mostly solid limestone. The crux second pitch afforded some nice climbing (5b), but gear was not great. We reached the summit at 5:30 p.m. after nine pitches (500m of climbing) plus the pitch in the gully, and called our new route Crazy Eye. 📄 📷

IAN FAULKNER, *Oxford University Mountaineering Club*

IRAN

ZAGROS RANGE

Bisotoon, overview, and 2012 International Meet. The second International Rock Climbing Festival, organized by the Iranian Mountain Federation and Iranian Alpine Club, took place in mid-October on the magnificent ca 2,700m Bisotoon. This mountain in western Iran, near the city of Kermanshah, has a vast, complex 1,200m limestone wall on the southeast face, variously reported as up to eight kilometers wide. There are approximately 60 routes, leaving plenty of space for additions. The rock is outstanding: generally sound, well featured, and almost uncomfortably abrasive. Several huts are situated on terraces a little above half-height on the face, suitable for two-day summit routes, though many established lines descend from partway up the wall.

The first route on the southeast face was Abarmard, put up in March 1969 by Ebrahim Babai, Kiumars Babazadah, Gholamhossein Vahabzabeh, and Bijan Sadeghi. There is no guidebook, so foreign climbers will be largely reliant on locals—a good source of information is the "climbers' café" below the cliff.

The first international festival at Bisotoon took place in 2010. In October 2012, around 100 Iranian climbers hosted 52 foreign visitors, the vast majority French. (There is a long tradition of climbing here by the Groupe de Haute Montagne.) Australians, Danes, Germans, Italians, Slovenians, Swedes, and Swiss were also represented. Current economic sanctions, part of an effort to discourage Iran's nuclear program, make obtaining a visa more or less impossible

[This page] The southeast face of Bisotoon rises behind a caravanserai where participants in the second International Rock Climbing Festival were housed. *Golriz Farmani*

for those holding only U.K. or U.S. passports.

Several new lines were completed during the meet. Nineteen-year-old Sébastien Bouin from France and 25-year-old Hassan Javadian (a former Iranian climbing champion) established but did not redpoint a five-pitch bolted line with a crux of 5.14b. They hope to finish it at a future date. Hassan Gerami and Hamid Safaghi, assisted by Amer Ezoji, Hossain Hizomker, and French guide Leslie Fucsko, completed the second part of Festival Route, which now has 12 bolted pitches up to 5.12c. The first part was climbed during the 2010 international festival—maybe they will complete it to the summit during the third? Slovenians Luka Lindic and Marko Prezelj, French Sam Beaugey and Emmanuel Pellisser, and Iranian mountain guide Hesam Karaji climbed Golden Spatula over two days. The 1,100m route to the top of the mountain was completed with trad gear only (6b). Several shorter new routes also were climbed.

Apart from the lack of beer, politics and religion had no impact on the event, and the response from participants was highly enthusiastic. There will likely be a third festival in October 2014. 📷

From information provided by Gus Morton, *U.K., and* Ebrahim Nowtash, *France*

Bisotoon, various routes. In January 2013, Miquel Sanchez, Alfons Valls, and I climbed a possible new route on Bisotoon. Along with Joan Solé and Edu Sanchez, we first repeated a classic line, Gharagash (1,200m, MD), to get a feel for the rock. This took us two days, with a night in a bivouac hut on the wall, but is doable in one. We found snow and ice in the top half—we obviously got there a little early in the season, but an unexpected cold wave didn't help.

After this we decided to open a new line while Joan and Edu repeated the French route Merci M. Shirzadi (700m, ED 7a, Dauger-Guillaume-Thivel; *AAJ 2001*). This route has been superseded in many places by a bolted line put up by an unknown party. Our route, Different Problems (650m, MD 6b+), follows an obvious pillar up the far western side of Bisotoon. We climbed 16 pitches in 10.5 hours, leaving a sling, a piton, and two bolts. 📷

Araceli Segarra, *Spain*

OMAN

Musandam Peninsula, various ascents. The Musandam Peninsula is a 700-square-mile enclave of Oman at the tip of the Arabian Peninsula, separated from the rest of the country by a 45-mile-

wide swath of the United Arab Emirates. The mountainous core of the Musandam is called the Ru'us al Jibal (the mountain tops) and is often referred to as the "Norway of the Middle East." This range, the northern terminus of the Al Hajar al Gharbi (Western Hajar Mountains), is slowly being subducted beneath the surface of the Persian Gulf. What's left above sea level is an intricate maze of rock and water attached to the mainland by a slender, 10-mile-long isthmus. In some places the land is nothing more than a knife-edged limestone fin rising straight from the ocean.

The goal of our expedition, from October 27 to November 17, was to explore the Ru'us al Jibal's climbing potential from a 44-foot catamaran, our floating base camp. We focused most of our attention on the section of the peninsula between Khawr Shimm and Khawr Habalayn, two of the biggest fjords in the Ru'us al Jibal. Our team included Jimmy Chin, Hazel Findlay, Alex Honnold, Renan Ozturk, and Mikey Schaefer, plus two Omanis, Abdullah Said Albusaidi and Faisal Alwahaibi.

At the back of the nine-mile-long Khawr Shimm (a.k.a. Elphinstone Inlet) we established several first ascents on the limestone walls rising above the village of Sibi. Alex, Hazel, and I soloed the north face of a 665m, unnamed mountain just south of the village. The route was mainly fourth class with several sections of mid–fifth class.

Two days later, we split into three teams and established three first ascents, sharing some sections, on the 900m west face of Jebel Letub. The rock quality was variable, from choss to solid limestone. Much of the stone was extremely sharp; Jimmy and Mikey's lead line was severed by a falling stone while Mikey was leading. (Mikey didn't realize it until he was belaying Jimmy up and suddenly reeled in the severed end of the rope.) Climbing on the three routes was in the 5.9 to 5.11 range, and no bolts or pins were placed. Honnold soloed a couple of other new routes in this area, including the 600m Captain Synnbad's Buttress (5.10a), which he called perhaps his best outing of the trip.

Other highlights included: the first known deep-water solos on the uninhabited island of Jazirat Salamah, which lies in the Strait of Hormuz; a two-pitch route by Hazel and Alex in Fakk al Asad (the Lion's Mouth), a gap where the Gulf of Oman meets the Persian Gulf; and several new deep-water solos and the first ascent of a 150m tower in a zone we dubbed Sand Castle Bay, which lies in the Ghubbat ash Shabus bay, near Ra's Dillah.

Due to its strategic military location on the southern shore of the Strait of Hormuz, the Musandam was closed to tourism until 1997. Perhaps the first climber to explore the area after it opened to outsiders was Read Macadam, a Briton living in Muscat. Swiss, British, and other teams

[This page] The 900m west face of Jebel Letub, above the village of Sibi. (1) General line followed by three separate pairs of climbers for the wall's first ascent; each team did variations low on the face. (2) Captain Synnbad's Buttress (Honnold, 5.10a). (3) Honnold solo (5.6). *Mark Synnott*

of climbers also have done both deep-water solos and longer routes. For more information on the Musandam's climbing history and established routes, visit the website of Toby Foord-Kelsey, author of UAE Rock Climbs: www.redarmadapublishing.com.

The most rewarding part of a visit to this fascinating part of the world is the opportunity to meet and interact with the local inhabitants, who live in isolated fishing villages that can only be reached by boat. In a region fraught with political uncertainty and violence, Oman—and the Musandam Peninsula, in particular—is an oasis of peace and stability. We would like to thank the National Geographic Society, the Omani Coast Guard, and the Omani Royal Police for their generous support and assistance. 📄 📷

Mark Synnott, *AAC*

Western Hajar, Jabal Kawr, Jabal Murri, Jabal Nakhus, various routes. During December 2012 and January 2013, I made my fifth climbing visit to Oman's Western Hajar mountains, this time with Dave Wynne-Jones. To make the most of the waning moon, on arrival we threw ourselves at the committing north face of Jabal Kawr. This is farther west than earlier lines opposite Jabal Asait, and has previously been neglected, as it is hard to observe in good light and lacks any convenient descent.

We left the Mazub road end early on December 30 with only light clothing, a few bars, and four liters of water. We followed a pillar with smooth slabs on either side, which produced a 17-pitch route, the Dark Side (680m, TD- VI-). This led to a large terrace from which there was no exit except by scrambling to the main Kawr plateau at 2,400m. From here we faced a long, complex descent, and the events that unfolded highlight the fragility of ultra-light climbing in this terrain. After failed attempts to navigate around drop-offs in darkness, we sat out the frigid night in a stone shepherd's hut on the plateau. As we searched for a descent in the morning, somehow we became separated. Dave faced a survival scenario with no food or water, only the ropes, a headlamp, and a lighter. Next day I returned with Rob Gardner and his search team from Muscat, and we found Dave severely dehydrated but otherwise in good shape.

After some recovery days, we took advantage of the precarious Nadan road to make the first climb in the impressive cirque that surrounds this remote settlement on the south side of Jabal Kawr. Triassic Superbowl (430m, TD- VI-) takes the north side of the Nadan Pillar. We descended via the sustained AD+ slabs of my own 2007 route on the south face [*AAJ 2008*], finding a dropped rock shoe from the first ascent. During the rest of our visit we completed several 200m to 300m routes above Sidaq village, on Jabal Murri, and on Jabal Nakhus. 📄 📷

Paul Knott, *New Zealand*

[This page] The Dark Side (17 pitches), the first route up the north face of Jabal Kawr. *Paul Knott*

AFRICA

ETHIOPIA

Gheralta Massif and Adwa Mountains, new routes. Inspired by previous trips to Ethiopia by climbers such as Pat Littlejohn and Majka Burhardt, Dan Rothberg and I spent two weeks in the country's northern Tigray region in search of serious rock adventures. We first visited the Gheralta Massif, an imposing group of soft-rock buttresses near the small town of Hawzen. Our most prominent Gheralta route was a three-pitch climb ascending one of the middle pillars of the main buttress, by way of a moderately strenuous offwidth and chimney system. We named our route the Great Cornholio (5.10-) as a tribute to both the quality of the rock and our highly sophisticated senses of humor.

Our second destination was the Adwa Mountains. These striking domes are composed mostly of trachyandesite; the rock is generally excellent and well featured, but protection is sparse. We first did a warm-up climb on the central ramp on the north face of Debre Gundo, with two pitches of easy but runout roped climbing and 500' of fifth-class brushy scrambling and fun, easy soloing: Burrs in My Shu-Ho (800', 5.8 R/X).

From this first summit, we gained a clear view of the lower southeast buttress of Samayata, the range's highest peak. After a daylong reconnaissance hike, we picked a line up the right side. We hiked back the next day with our gear and made sleeping arrangements in the house of a

[This page] Local gear-testing; a rope shredded by jugging in the Gheralta Massif. *John Collis*

[This page] The southeast buttress of Samayata in the Adwa Mountains. (1) Approximate line of Costa Brava. (2) 11 Pitches to Nowhere. *John Collis*

friendly Tigrinya man, unaware that a wedding celebration would occur the next morning in his house. Our climb was delayed by a breakfast of injera and the blood and intestines from a freshly slaughtered goat, which provided some excellent sending energy.

Our line followed 11 pitches of discontinuous face features and ledges, with long runouts. Extended gardening sessions on lead and our late start left us climbing the last two pitches by moonlight. We stopped upon reaching a ridge one to two pitches beneath the lower buttress' summit, where the climbing became steeper and more runout than we were prepared to handle. We made eight long rappels down the chossy gully on the other side of the ridge and named our partial new route 11 Pitches to Nowhere (5.10 R/X).

JOHN COLLIS, *AAC*

Gheralta Massif and Samayata, new routes. In January 2012, the Spanish team of Marco Jubes, Edu Marín, and Toti Valés established two long, difficult free climbs in Ethiopia's mountains. The first, Arenas Movedizas (350m, 7b+/c), ascends a wall above the village of Hawzen in the Tigray area. Corners and poorly protected chimney climbing were highlights, along with meeting a 76-year-old "monk" sitting on top with his feet over the edge.

They then moved to the Adwa Mountains, where Jubes and Marín found a long, difficult line on Samayata. Costa Brava (850m, 8a) climbs nine pitches up a steep lower tower, followed by two rappels and traverses to reach the upper wall. This brought five more pitches and scrambling, with the crux on the 60m 12th pitch, which Marín led at 8a with only three or four pieces of protection. They spent a cold night without food or water after this pitch, and then summited the following morning.

DOUGALD MACDONALD, *from information at Desnivel.com and Edumarin.blogspot.com*

RUSSIA

Murmansk, Khibini Mountains, Vudyavr mixed routes. Sergey Nefedov, Alexey Romanov, and Max Sotnik explored the winter climbing potential of Khibini in the Murmansk region, just east of northern Finland. These mountains rise to 1,200m, and the area has been developed for skiing. In February the climbers found deep snow and high avalanche danger, so they focused on the most easily accessible peak, Vudyavr, with walls from 120m to 170m. They climbed three separate four- to five-pitch routes (M4–M6), dry-tooling on rock and frozen turf.

From a report on PLANETMOUNTAIN.COM

Franz Josef Land, exploration. After eight years of research, I obtained permission to go to Franz Josef Land, a 192-island Arctic archipelago, on my never-ending search for unclimbed walls and towers. In July I got a ride there on a Russian sailboat. I found what I'd dreamed of: the northernmost walls on the planet, unclimbed of course. Unfortunately, I also encountered some major obstacles, including rockfall and the local polar bear population. (The previous year, two Russian scientists had been killed by bears.) I was able to free-solo one climb, definitely the northernmost technical rock route, and reconnoiter the area in depth. There are at least nine world-class formations, with walls 400m to 500m tall, between 81°N and 82°N latitude. I plan to return as soon as possible.

MIKE LIBECKI, *AAC*

[This page] Rock formations (ca 300m) about 5km south of the route that Mike Libecki soloed for the first technical climb in Franz Josef Land. *Mike Libecki*

Caucasus, Kara-kaya Main (3,646m), new route in winter. Alexander Lavrinenko and Taras Tsushko (Ukraine) added a route to the ca 750m limestone wall north of Bezengi, climbing as a two-man team in the dead of winter. The new line ascends the western bastion, starting right of Land of Mist, a route that Lavrinenko climbed in 2009 with Eugene Poltavets and Maxim Polyakov. The two men started February 15 and completed 22 pitches, with 480m of aid out of 1,100m of climbing. They joined the 2009 route for five pitches on the upper wall before finishing independently on the morning of the 11th day. 🖻

Provided by ANNA PIUNOVA, *Mountain.ru*

Crimea, Morcheka, free routes and controversy. Russian climber Sergey Nefedov, who in 2010 had freed the 335m route Machombo at 7c+, revisited Morcheka in May and free-climbed four other routes or variations on Crimea's traditional limestone wall. This included a free ascent of Center (10 pitches, 7b+) with a variation start. Nefedov and partners spent two days replacing old bolts and pitons on the popular aid route. In September, Nefedov became embroiled in controversy when he returned to Morcheka and joined a team of sponsored American climbers. He and American Cedar Wright rap-bolted (with a power drill) a line linking variations of other climbs, and the resulting route, dubbed *Cold War*, angered local climbers, who said Nefedov, from St. Petersburg, and Wright had not conformed to the local ethics of ground-up ascents. The bolts eventually were chopped. More info at www.thebmc.co.uk/cold-war-in-the-crimea.

LINDSAY GRIFFIN, *Mountain INFO, and PlanetMountain.com*

TAJIKISTAN

ZERAVSHAN RANGE

FANSKY GORY

Parandas, north face, new route. Mt. Parandas (4,250m) has an 800m north wall with lots of overhangs but also decent ledges, so one can climb without using a portaledge. The sun hits the north wall for only 1 to 1.5 hours a day. I had studied a line on the right side in 2010, but during that trip we climbed a different route on the left [*AAJ 2011*].

Sergey Maksimenko, Taras Tsushko, and I began climbing our new route on August 3. A slab that looked problematic from below was found to be difficult but not hopeless. We spent two nights in a tent on a good ledge, fixing pitches above. We then pulled up the ropes and followed beautiful corners, spending the third night sitting on top of a flake. We transferred to the left by pendulum, found ourselves in a corner again, and climbed past an overhang. Above this was a blank wall that forced us to join the Mogila Route for one long pitch. Where the Mogila Route turns sharply left, we continued up, crossing an overhang to reach a huge roof, which we bypassed to the right.

After another night in the tent, it seemed the route was about to get easier, but this was an illusion. An overhanging wall with poor features led to corners and a less steep but broken wall.

There was ice in the corners and on the ledges. We did not make it to the ridge before dark, and had another sitting bivouac. On the morning of the sixth day, after 40m of difficult climbing, we reached the ridge. By 11 a.m. we were on top of Parandas, and then rushed down. I think is the most difficult line climbed on Mt. Parandas. We did 23 pitches on the wall and placed 17 bolts (seven for belays). 🖼

ALEXANDER LAVRINENKO, *from a report at Mountain.ru provided by Anna Piunova and translated by Ekaterina Vorotnikova*

PAMIR

Peak Korzhenevskaya (7,105m), traverse via new route up west ridge. Today there are at least 17 unique routes to the summit of Korzhenevskaya. Fourteen of them start from the Moskvin Glacier, two from the Mushketov Glacier, and only one from the Fortambek Glacier. The latter, the northwest ridge, is the route of the mountain's first ascent (Ugarov, 1953), but it has never become popular. This route approaches through a rocky gorge, up three steps of the glacier, and then up the steep northern buttress. The approach is dangerous because of rockfall, and the upper ridge continues for 2.5km above 6,500m. The route may only have been repeated three times since 1953. Our goal was to reach the 1953 route via the west ridge, avoiding dangerous sections of the entrance gorge and the northern buttress of the northwest ridge.

We approached the Fortambek Glacier on foot from Devsiar settlement, planning to have most of our gear transported by helicopter. However, unrest in Tajikistan delayed helicopter flights and disrupted many expeditions, and we were the first climbers at the Moskvina Glade base camp. With no flights, we were forced to acclimatize without our high-altitude boots and down parkas, and did not dare to go higher than 5,600m. After five days we descended to the Moskvina Glade and found it back to normal, with the dining room and bathhouse open for business. Our food and equipment arrived, and after two days of complete rest, on August 5 we started our ascent by trekking to the Fortambek advanced base camp, carrying 30kg packs.

From the Fortambek Glacier the route followed a narrow and interesting gorge to the upper cirque of the pass dividing the Fortambek and Korzhenevskaya glaciers. Remnants of a large glacier hung over the cirque from the west ridge of the massif. We climbed a line of rocks in the gap between hanging icefalls. We managed to cover this distance twice, during exploring and our final push, without being hit by avalanches. Above the level of the icefalls the kingdom of snow began, and here a shovel became our main tool. We used it not only to prepare our bivouacs, but also to clear a path through deep snow all the way up to the ridge. During the exhausting ascent of a 40° slope, we fought with the shovel for every step, before reaching the crest at around 6,100m on August 12.

Now the way was easier, following the winding ridge, narrow in places, with compact snow. Splendid views of the Pamir opened around us. After two days of snow climbing we reached the northwest ridge. We were back on an established route, and psychologically it was easier. However, during the next five days we experienced all the difficulties that befell the first-ascent party on the northwest ridge.

After traversing steep snow around a huge rocky gendarme hanging over our camp at 6,465m, another good section of ridge climbing allowed us to accelerate our pace to a high top of 6,782m. But then the ridge line dropped to a tremendous snow plateau, where we encountered a blizzard and

[This page, top] Peak Korzhenevskaya (7,105m) from the west. (1) Northwest ridge, the first ascent route (Ugarov team, 1953). (2) West ridge variation (Ivanov-Petlitskiy, 2012). (3) Southern crest normal route (Tsetlin team, 1966). *G. Selnikov, provided by Anna Piunova* [This page, bottom] (A) Soming West (4,290m). The route lay beyond the sunlit ridge dropping into the valley. *Michal Kleslo*

barely avoided treacherous crevasses. Wind, snow, and poor visibility plagued us all the way to the top, and we were back to the same step-shovel-step-shovel routine. Our last camp was at 7,060m, just below the top. Early on the morning of August 19 we reached the summit. The sky overhead was clear, while dense clouds lay below. Over the next three days, with improving weather, we descended the normal route (Tsetlin, 1966), before reaching Moskvina Glade 18 days after leaving. [*An extensive report on this arduous traverse, with many photos, is available in Russian at Mountain.ru.*]

ALEXEY IVANOV *and* VLADIMIR PETLITSKIY, *from a report provided by Anna Piunova and translated by Ekaterina Vorotnikova*

Gissar Range, Soming Valley, various ascents. In September we made a four-day trip to Soming Valley in the central Gissar Range, just south of Iskanderkul Lake. According to the Tajik Federation of

Mountaineering (FAT), all peaks west of the Belaya Pyramida–Hodzhalakan area are still virgin, owing to their remoteness from former Soviet alpine camps. Prior to 1990, climbers had plenty of closer peaks to try, and afterward this area's 4,000m peaks were no longer of interest to climbers.

From a tourist camp at Iskanderkul Lake, we hiked one day to reach our base camp near Lake Soming. On day two, Jan Dolezal (Slovak) and I climbed an unnamed peak in western Soming Valley via its southern ridge. A glacier traverse and steep scree slopes brought us to Tomsk Pass (4,100m), from which the south ridge gained the top in five 30m pitches (III-IV) on slabs and in chimneys, with surprisingly solid rock. Descent was via a 200m scramble along the northeast ridge, followed by a scree traverse back to Tomsk Pass. We called the peak Soming West (4,290m).

On day three, we tried to climb the highest peak in this valley but were forced back from the pass by snow and fog. On the last day we managed to climb an easy peak above camp via the eastern couloir. Due to its position directly above Soming Lake, we suggest naming the peak Soming Ozernyj ("Lake Soming," 4,240m).

If anyone wants to climb some easy, virgin peaks, the western Gissar Range is your playground. From Dushanbe airport you can drive to the trailhead in two and a half hours. 🔲 🔍

MICHAL KLESLO, *Czech Republic*

KYRGYZSTAN

PAMIR ALAI

KARAVSHIN

Traverse of Peak 4,810m, 1,000 Years of Russian Christianity, and Kotina; new route on Kotina; various other ascents. In mid-July I traveled to the Karavshin region with Peter Fasoldt. Our goal was the first alpine-style enchainment of the three major peaks dividing the Ak-su and Kara-su river valleys: Peak 4,810m, Peak 1,000 Years of Russian Christianity (4,507m), and Kotina (4,520m). Viewed from the east, these mountains form an elegant ridge of golden granite rising 6,000 feet above the valley floor. The ridge runs two miles in linear distance, all of it steep and technical.

A hot but flat 30-mile hike brought us to base camp in the Kara-su. We had planned to camp in the Ak-su, many miles closer to the peaks we wanted to climb, but the Kyrgyz Army chopper pilots we'd paid to shuttle our equipment dropped it in the wrong valley. We discovered this at the road head, and there wasn't much we could do but hike in.

We arrived under stormy skies and stricken with dysentery after drinking water from the Karavshin River. Our friendly camp cook, Victor, offered a folk remedy: a shot of vodka mixed with a heaping teaspoon of salt. It didn't work. Stewing in the cook tent, the resident climbers complained about the scuddy weather pattern. But a few days after we arrived on July 26, a windy storm blew through the area. For the next month we had mostly clear skies with occasional afternoon squalls.

We chose a new line on the relatively unexplored west face of Kotina for our first attempt. Other than the 2006 Polish line Czarna Wolga (*AAJ 2007*), we knew of no other routes to the summit on this 5,000-foot face. From base camp, we hiked southeast toward the col between Kotina and Peak 4,810, then cut back north on a ledge system that took us past a rockfall zone and up some slabs to a large orange block. From here we trended generally up and left over 5.9 terrain for about 500 meters. On a ledge below a prominent orange buttress, we stepped right into a low-angle system for about 150 meters, followed by another 150 meters of steeper rock to gain the large ledge on top of the buttress. We scrambled left up a ridge for another 200 meters, then improvised our way up a steep snowfield and on to the summit. It was 4 p.m. We had some bivy gear, but we hoped that we wouldn't have to use it.

The Poles had reported a difficult descent to the east and into the Ak-su, which we hoped to avoid by descending to the north then back west into the Kara-su. Just below the summit I set off a talus explosion that ended with my left ankle trapped Aron Ralston–style under a huge block. Pete built a haul system to hoist it off of me, and by some miracle I escaped with only minor lacerations. Nice to have a solid partner. Clouds engulfed the mountain and night fell quickly. Like the Poles, we got sucked down the massive east face of Kotina. We rappelled many times with our single rope. Around midnight we bivied on the only ledge in sight. The next morning we landed safely in the Ak-su. We called our route An Inconvenient Truth (1,200m, VI 5.9+).

We decided to repeat some established lines next. We climbed the incredible Perestroika Crack (900m, VI 5.12a) on Russian Tower (Peak Slesova) in about 20 hours camp-to-camp. Then we climbed the Big Yellow Moon variation (700m, VI 5.12a) on the southwest arête of the Central Pyramid. Carrying Petzl 8.8mm aluminum bolts and hangers is essential, along with a keen eye to spot the in situ sleeves they screw into. Later in the trip we would also repeat the Alperien route (V 5.10+) on Asan, an excellent wide crack route offering incredible views of the west face of 4,810 on the descent.

After a few days of rest we were geared up for an attempt at the big traverse. On August 14,

[This page] Pete Fasoldt rappels toward the stunning, knife-edged south ridge (600m, 5.10+) of Peak 1,000 Years of Russian Christianity. *Josh Finkelstein*

[This page, top] Josh Finkelstein traverses toward Kotina (4,520m) early on day three of the Clear Water Traverse. *Peter Fasoldt* [This page, bottom] The Clear Water Traverse (VI 5.11) ran from left to right (south to north) over Peak 4,180m, Peak 1,000 Years of Christianity, and Kotina, covering about two miles of technical terrain over three days of climbing. Fasoldt and Finkelstein approached the traverse from the Ak-su valley (near side in this photo) and descended the far side of Kotina to the Kara-su valley. *John Dickey*

we hiked south up the Ak-su valley, scrambled 1,000 meters up to the col between Asan and Russian Christianity, and then bivied below the finger crack marking the start of the regular south face route on 4,810 (700m, V+ 5.10+). The south face is mostly 5.7–5.9 on good rock, with five or six sections of harder climbing up to 5.10+. We were able to short-fix almost all of it, and by 2 p.m. we were on the summit, just in time for the daily storm, which arrived like clockwork.

The storm intensified into one of the strongest we saw on our trip as we descended the north face of 4,810. The face ran with water, and snow sloughed down around us. About 500m lower we found a protected bivy site just east of the small rock spire between 4,810 and Russian Christianity. We spent a cold, wet night dreaming of morning sun. When it finally arrived, we climbed 100 feet of verglassed 5.9 up the west face of the rock spire to gain some elevation, then embarked on a series of traversing rappels that landed us in a gully somewhere above the col between 4,810 and Russian Christianity. A rising traverse followed by two more rappels and some downclimbing brought us to the col proper.

We started climbing the south ridge of Russian Christianity (600m, V 5.10+) around 2 p.m. and topped out around 8 p.m., after short-fixing and simul-climbing most of the route, a splitter line that we thoroughly enjoyed in the warm afternoon sun. On top of Russian Christianity we found an established bivy site just southeast of the summit block, where we spent a plush night.

The next morning we traversed the amazing ridge between Russian Christianity and Kotina. We climbed unroped for about a quarter mile, then tied in when things got more technical and exposed. A couple of hundred meters later we started rappelling, traversing north once more toward Kotina. We landed on more ridge terrain and traversed along an intrusive band for another quarter mile to the base of the south face of Kotina, which may not have been climbed previously. Climbing through a steep crack down low, we aimed for a prominent corner system on the south ridge, which offered an athletic pitch of 5.11. After about 1,000 feet, we reached lower angle terrain and unroped. In another 500 feet of scrambling, we passed some tat left by the Poles in 2006 and started to recognize features we had seen on our first trip up Kotina.

Around 3 p.m. on August 17 we reached the summit, where Pete came up with the bright idea to descend An Inconvenient Truth rather than try to contour north and west, an endeavor at which we had failed the last time we attempted it. We sped down familiar terrain, stretching the ropes and downclimbing where possible to save what little bail gear we had left after 50 rappels. We even managed to retrieve a No. 2 Camalot I had forgotten at a belay while climbing An Inconvenient Truth. By 8 p.m. we were back on the ground. There was about one foot of cord and one brass nut left on the rack.

Running the ridge between the Ak-su ("white water") and Kara-su ("black water") river valleys, the Clear Water Traverse (VI 5.11) was an unforgettable adventure with my good friend Pete. 🔲

JOSHUA FINKELSTEIN, *AAC*

Editor's note: During the summer of 2012, German climbers Joe Häbel and Laurin Wissmeier climbed a long variation to An Inconvenient Truth (Fasoldt-Finkelstein, 2012) on Kotina, which they called Awesome Fucking Dihedral. The two climbed 10 or 11 new pitches up a prominent corner system, all free at French 6c, leaving only one piton. They report that the route has "outstanding quality at a moderate grade and length," and that the fourth pitch, in particular, deserves five stars.

Kara-su valley, Kotina, northwest arête, Dreaming Spires. In August and September 2012, Tom Codrington, Ian Cooper, and I, from the Oxford University Mountaineering Club, took on the big walls of the Karavshin. After patching our way across the country, mollifying men with guns and sharing vodka with local headmen, we arrived in the heartland of Central Asian big walling. On one of our many rest days after a 10-day ascent of Peak 4,810, we spied a new line on Kotina from the Kara-su Valley. [*Editor's note: On Peak 4,180m, the team climbed the Mirror Route (Rusyaev, 1988) all free. This was possibly only the second free ascent since Lynn Hill and Alex Lowe did it in 1995s.*]

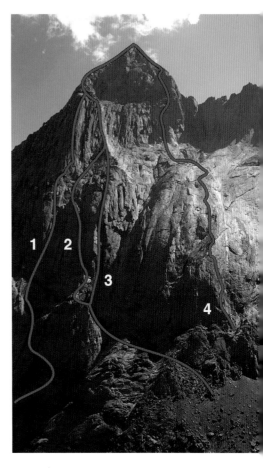

Over three days we fixed a few hundred meters of rope up the soaring, unclimbed northwest-facing arête of Kotina, taking the cleanest line through some of the wildest and steepest features on the mountain. We tackled the rest of the line alpine-style in another three days. Fantastic three-star climbing on splitter granite cracks, corners, and detached roofs led us through consistently steep territory, sustained at F6b/6b+, to the very top of the buttress, without a single pitch of easy ground. The rock was solid and clean all of the way, and we free-climbed all 26 pitches (up to F7a), placing one bolt at a belay anchor. There were two large ledges on the route, splitting the cliff into three roughly equal lengths. These made ideal bivy spots.

Within minutes of getting to the top of the buttress, a snowstorm broke out and we quickly started the grim abseils without scrambling to the summit of Kotina. These abseils began a few meters to the right of the end of the route, and used a mixture of threads and expansion bolts for anchors. We bivvied again on the upper ledge in a small cave before finishing the descent the next day. We named our line Dreaming Spires after its terminal feature, a hugely exposed pillar of golden granite with a knife-edge ridge connecting it to the main massif.

We give our heartfelt thanks to the Irvine Fund, without which we could never have dreamed of such an adventure.

Ian Faulkner, *Oxford University Mountaineering Club, U.K.*

[This page] The west (Kara-su) side of Kotina (4,520m). (1) Dreaming Spires (Codrington-Cooper-Faulkner, 2012), to top of buttress. (2) An Inconvenient Truth (Fasoldt-Finkelstein, 2012). (3) Awesome Fucking Dihedral (Häbel-Wissmeier, 2012). (4) Czarna Wolga (Kuczera-Magiera-Stefaski, 2006). *Jan Kuczera*

Ak-su valley, Slesova (Russian Tower), La Fiamma d'Oriente, first free ascent. After a long and eventful hike to base camp in August and a week of recovering from illness, Madaleine Sorkin and I set off for a warm-up on Perestroika Crack that ended in us coming down after the crux due to bad weather.

A few days later we started up what would be the highlight of the trip. Eric Decaria had told us about a free possibility to the right of Perestroika Crack called La Fiamma d'Oriente (7 A3+, Groaz-Pancheri-Zanetti, 1999). This climb followed Perestroika Crack for two pitches and then took a crack line up and right. This pitch was one of the gems of the route, with technical seam climbing and finicky gear (5.12a). The next pitches were in the 5.10 range and led up to the crux, which was on bullet rock but had minimal gear. The first "good" piece was 20 feet off the belay and required 5.11 moves. The remainder was difficult slab climbing with quarter-inchers as protection. This pitch was in the 5.12c R range. This led us to a lower-angle slab that went into a corner system. A few more 5.11+ to 5.12 pitches on steeper terrain brought us to back into Perestroika Crack after an incredible 200-foot, 5.10 hand crack. In all, we climbed 19 pitches on La Fiamma.

On the summit Madaleine and I could not believe we had completed a two-day ground-up onsight of the route. We placed no bolts and never brushed a single hold. This climb was a gift from the climbing gods.

NIK BERRY, *USA*

Ak-su valley, various routes. During three weeks in August, Anna Backlund and I visited the Ak-su area. Our main goal was the 800m Perestroika Crack. Before this we climbed a new line on the lower section of Peak Slesova or Russian Tower. To the left of the established Magic Mountain, we put up Lazy Lizard (14 pitches, 6b). No bolts were placed. We topped out by the fifth pitch of Perestroika Crack, giving us a good preview of that route. After climbing Perestroika Crack, we turned to Peak 3,850m, where we climbed a new route called Magic Line: 12 pitches, including what we called Black Magic Corner (7b+). For the descent we fixed single anchor points. The route starts 20m right of an Italian route (1998). On the central pillar of Peak 3,850 we also put up a shorter route (5 pitches, 7b), which we named Leaning Flower Tower. 📄 📷 🔍

KRISTER JONSSON, *Sweden*

ZAALAISKY RANGE

Lenin Peak, southwest rib of west ridge. In August the Russian and Latvian team of Mikhail Babich, Vladimir Lavrinenko, Andrei Lebedev (leader), Yuri Maksimovich, Valdis Purins, Oleg Silin, and Ivan Zhdanov completed 36 days of trekking and climbing along the Zaalaisky Range, of which Lenin Peak (7,134m) is the highest point. During this trip they went through nine mountain passes and reached several summits of the Zaalaisky, including Lenin Peak via a new route: the southwest rib of the west ridge.

On the 30th day of their trek, the group climbed up from the south to Razdelnaya Pass (6,100m), the traditional location of Camp 3 for the popular route up Lenin's western ridge. On the morning of August 30, while two climbers summited Lenin via this route, the other five participants (Babich, Lavrinenko, Lebedev, Maksimovich, and Zhdanov) climbed up the west shoulder (6,400m) of Lenin and then descended to the south on the Malaya Saukdara Glacier at the altitude of 5,910m.

From here they would climb a steep rib to the Parachutists' Plateau at 6,915m near the top of the west ridge.

On August 31 the team ascended the rib to 6,500m, with mostly snow and ice climbing and short rock walls between 6,200m and 6,400m. The next day they climbed the snowy upper part of the rib and set up the camp on Parachutists' Plateau. In the morning of September 2 the weather deteriorated into a whiteout. Relying on GPS, the group tried to summit but were forced back to high camp. Two hours later it cleared but became much windier. Nonetheless, they reached the top and then, in a snowstorm with visibility of only 5m to 20m, descended the western ridge to 6,585m, where they had a sleepless night in high winds and heavy snow. The next morning they descended the normal route to the Lenin Glacier.

Supplied by ANNA PIUNOVA, *Mountain.ru, and translated by Ekaterina Vorotnikova*

KYRGYZ ALA-TOO

Ala-Archa Range, Teke-Tor (4,441m), northeast face, Korean Light Way. The Corean Alpine Club sponsored a four-man team to climb the northeast face of Teke-Tor in the Aksai Range. Ahn Chi-young, Kim Kyoung-rae, and Lee Ki-geun completed their new route, Korean Light Way, on July 9.

The first seven pitches consisted of easy snow and ice (45-60°) to the main headwall. Rockfall was a constant concern. From the eighth pitch onward, the real climbing began. By afternoon, the climbing became vertical, and as the leader dry-tooled up steep rock he had to take care to avoid pitching rock onto the climbers below. The rock was so poor and cracks so flaring that solid protection placements often could not be found. At 4 p.m. lightning and hail showers began, and fog inundated them completely. The climbers waited out the storm for 30 minutes and then climbed with haste for fear conditions would worsen. After 16 pitches they reached the left shoulder of Teke-Tor and climbed easier terrain to reach the top just past 9 p.m.

The team descended via the north ridge until they were halted by darkness and rested until 4 a.m. They continued down a snow and scree gully and reached base camp 36 hours after leaving. 🔍

Supplied and translated by PETER JENSEN-CHOI

[This page] Lenin Peak (7,134m) from the south. (1) West ridge (Kovalev, 1954). (2) Southwest rib of west ridge (2012). (3) Southwest rib (Yushin, 1967). *Courtesy of Anna Piunova*

Editor's note: Teke-Tor's climbing history is not well documented, but at least two other ascents of this face appear to have been completed. Florian Hill (Germany) and Mariew Vasily (Russia) climbed the "east face" by a route they called Djamila (880m, V+ M4+). And in 2009 a Latvian team climbed the buttress on the left side of the northeast face (Russian 3B/4A UIAA IV+), left of the Korean route, descending by the north ridge and gully. It's likely that many ascents from the Soviet era also were completed on this peak.

Shamsi Tuyuk Valley, various ascents. The Shamsi Tuyuk area lies approximately five main valleys, and 50km east, of the well-developed Ala Archa Range. Before the visit of a British expedition in July-August there were no recorded climbs. In the course of 14 days the team ascended six prominent peaks up to 4,383m, via nine routes at grades of AD and below.

LINDSAY GRIFFIN, *Mountain INFO*

WESTERN KOKSHAAL-TOO

Kokgart region, various ascents; At Bashi range, various ascents. Our International School of Mountaineering expedition (nine members and three guides) initially set out to explore the Kokgart region of the West Kokshaal-Too, starting in late August. This lies to the west of the established climbing in the range, opposite the military base of Orto Kaskasu. Sights were set on the impressive main peak, which the locals call Peak Kokgart (4,541m), but this proved too tough an objective, as did most of the other large peaks. However, several lower peaks were climbed by routes up to grade AD. The area would seem to offer countless technical challenges in the TD to ED grades, with imposing mixed faces up to 800m and fine ridges of compact, marbled limestone.

The team then moved to the central At Bashi range and had a more fruitful time, establishing a base camp at ca. 3,892m and doing seven first ascents of peaks, including the big snow mountain (4,751m) marked on all detailed maps of the range. We gave this

[This page, top] The limestone peaks of the Kokgart region, with Peak Kokgart (4,541m) in center-right. *Pat Littlejohn* [This page, bottom] Peak Ortosu (left) and Idyn Tolgon Kezi (a.k.a. Full Moon Peak) in the central At Bashi range. *Pat Littlejohn*

mountain the Kyrgyz name Idyn Tolgon Kezi, meaning "full moon." The more pointed peak to the west of this, Peak Ortosu (4,626m), provided a good mixed outing (AD) up the west flank and onto the north ridge.

Moving around to the north side of the At Bashi range, we stopped at Tash Rabat, famous for its ancient *caravanserai*, which happens to be located in a valley full of towering limestone cliffs. ISM teams established the first routes here in 2010 and added three more on this trip, including the 400m Spine Line Ridge, a fine alpine outing at AD+.

The final destination of the trip was the Son Kul region, Kyrgyzstan's limestone canyonlands, where a new canyon to the south of the established climbing areas was explored and found to provide excellent climbing. Eleven routes were established, up to 350m in length and E2 grade (5.10b), making about 30 routes in the canyons in total. We left eager as ever for our next trip to Kyrgyzstan. 📷

Pat Littlejohn, *International School of Mountaineering*

Dzhirnagaktu Glacier, various ascents. Continuing the work of the 2010 Krakow expedition, Conor Gilmore, Azwan Isa, Ronan Kernan, Bradley Morrell, and Alek and Vladimir Zholobenko visited the Dzhirnagaktu Glacier basin, just west of Kyzyl Asker, where in 16 days they made first ascents of two prominent summits, two summits of dubious prominence, and six new routes on previously climbed peaks.

The team established base camp on August 16 at 4,200m in the middle of the glacier, seven days after being dropped north of the valley by truck. Highlights of the trip are reported below; see the online version of this story for details of all ascents.

On the 20th, Isa, Morrell, and the Zholobenkos made the first ascent of Ledenaya Strečoza (Ice Dragonfly, 4,892m) by the west ridge (Butterflies and Hurricanes, D-). This is a prominent peak at the head of the western branch of the glacier and, climbed from a col at 4,665m, had a section of Scottish 3/4.

Nochnoi Motyl (Night Butterfly, 5,056m), which lies close to the head of the main glacier, where it splits into west and east branches, was first climbed in 2010 from the south. On the 28th Morrell and Alex Zholobenko climbed the North Face Corridor at TD-/TD (ice to 70-80°).

On the 26th Gilmore and Kernan made a traverse (Eagle Traverse) of the previously virgin border peak Uighur (4,979m). They climbed the north face to west ridge, then descended the east

[This page] Rock Horse, showing the 2012 route (TD) on the northwest face. The peak had been climbed twice before. *Bradley Morrell*

[This page] North face of Nochnoi Motyl, showing the North Face Corridor (2012). Peak to the left is Uighur. *Tomasz Owerko*

ridge (D). On the 30th the same pair made the first ascent of the northwest face of Skalni Kon (Rock Horse, 5,189m), a peak on the Dzhirnagaktu–Kyzyl Asker divide that was first climbed in 1985 by Kazakhs, and then again in 2010 by Poles. The 800m route was graded TD (Scottish IV, 5 in the upper section). They descended the west ridge, and then southwest to the main glacier (AD).

The expedition was grant-aided by the Mt. Everest Foundation, Mountaineering Ireland, and Queens University Belfast.

LINDSAY GRIFFIN, *Mountain INFO, with information from Bradley Morrell, Northern Ireland*

Ochre Wall, new variation; Kyzyl Asker (5,842m), attempt on southeast face. In late September, Ryan Johnson and Samuel Johnson (unrelated) attempted a huge ice and mixed route on the ca 1,400m southeast face of Kyzyl Asker, reaching 5,300m on the first day. The pair hoped to tackle the mixed headwall the following morning, but a snowstorm that began during the night pinned them under a tarp at their bivouac, and after 24 hours they began rappelling, narrowly escaping injury from avalanches during the descent. [*This is the same route attempted by several parties, including three attempts by Ines Papert and various partners.*] On the 600m Ochre Walls, they climbed Mr. Casual (IV AI5), a new thin-ice finish to the left of the route Beefcake (Decapio-Isaac, 2001).

DOUGALD MACDONALD, *from information supplied by Samuel Johnson*

TENGRI TAG

Khan Tengri (6,995m), north face direct, rare repeat. Kazakh climbers Ildar Gabassov, Vaso Pivtsov, and Alex Sofrygin completed a rare ascent of the ca 3,000m direct north face of Khan Tengri over nine days in August. The last ascent, by Russian climbers Pavel Shabalin and Ilias Tukhvatullin, was in 2005 and was featured in *AAJ 2006*.

DOUGALD MACDONALD, *compiled from online reports*

AFGHANISTAN

CENTRAL HINDU KUSH – KOH-E-BABA MOUNTAINS

Bamyan skiing and ice climbing. In late February and March, John Trousdale, Elliott Woods, and I traveled to Bamyan to check out the potential for backcountry skiing, snowboarding, and ice climbing. I was also hoping to kite-ski on some frozen lakes in the region. I had been in the area on two previous expeditions [*AAJ 2010 and 2011*], but those trips were in the summer. In late winter, the lakes were frozen, as suspected, and there were several inches of old, creamy snow on top the ice. Great 20 to 30 mph gusts provided enjoyable kite-skiing. Frozen waterfalls formed from the overflow of the lakes, and though I sampled a couple different route possibilities, it was too warm to climb safely. Ice climbing and kite-skiing in this area are probably fantastic in January or early February.

We then went to Bamyan village and into the Koh-e-Baba, finding first ski descents in the Dukani Valley, near the villages of Yeti Mak, Jawkar, and Kushkak. Approaches were easy and our maximum altitudes came close to 4,000m. These mountains are beautiful, and the potential for quality skiing enormous, but we experienced mostly less than ideal conditions. I would expect much better conditions in a normal year. 🔘

MIKE LIBECKI, *AAC*

HINDU KUSH

Overview 2012 and Noshaq 2011. Few climbing expeditions visited the Wakhan Corridor during the summer, and all were affected by hostilities. Surprisingly, the hostilities in question were not those in Afghanistan, but in Tajikistan, through which most climbers must enter and exit the mountains. Fighting broke out in Khorog while the teams were climbing, and the resultant closure of the Afghan-Tajik border led to difficulties for several expeditions in leaving the country, as recounted in the online versions of these reports.

No parties went to Noshaq (7,492m) in 2012, but there was a successful and previously unreported ascent in late summer 2011 by Russian climbers, who were the first mountaineers from

[This page] Mike Libecki climbing on the outflow from a lake at Band-e-Amir. *Elliot D. Woods*

any of the CIS nations to summit Afghanistan's highest peak. The team wanted to climb alpine-style, so first acclimatized by climbing Pik Mayakovsky (Qullai Mayakovskiy, 6,096m) in the southwest corner of the Tajikistan Pamir, following the normal route up the south face (AAJ 2012). Denis Apraksin, Yuri Bakhmurov, and Dmitry Siskin then attempted Noshaq's west ridge in alpine-style. Bakhmurov stopped at 7,200m, but the other two continued to the main summit. Acclimatizing on the Tajikistan peaks, close to Khorog, before attempting some of the high peaks further south, may be a useful consideration for those wishing to minimize their stay in Afghanistan's Wakhan Corridor. ▶

LINDSAY GRIFFIN, *Mountain INFO, and Malgorzata Skowronska, Poland/U.K.*

Mir Samir (5,809m), attempted first winter ascent. James and Edward Bingham, Quentin Brooksbank, and Mark Wynne (U.K.) attempted the first winter ascent of Mir Samir, a mountain in the remote upper section of the Panjshir Valley, made famous by Eric Newby in his best seller A Short Walk in the Hindu Kush. Their objective was the unclimbed north face, although if conditions prevented this they planned to try the northeast ridge, the same route attempted by Newby and Hugh Carless in the summer of 1956, and the line more or less climbed on the first ascent of the mountain in 1959 by Germans. From the date of the first ascent to 1978, Mir Samir was climbed frequently, and up to the time of the Soviet invasion had nine or 10 different routes, but it has not been climbed since. Unfortunately, a number of factors led to the expedition being cut short after five days' hard travel in deep snow in the approach valley. ▤ ▣

Compiled from information supplied by JAMES BINGHAM, *UK*

Keshni Khan Valley, White Pyramid (5,612m GPS) and other ascents. Alexandre Darrioulat, Franck Mazas, and Arnaud Pasquer (France) visited the Wakhan in July and August. Their original goal was an ascent of Noshaq, but due to the unrest in Tajikistan, the authorities at Ishkashim would not allow them to enter the Qazi Deh Valley leading up to the mountain. Fortunately, in Qazi Deh village they found a copy of Carlo Pinelli and Gianni Predan's guidebook, *Peaks of Silver and Jade,* in which they read about the Keshni Khan Valley, two drainages east of Qazi Deh. They were granted permission to enter this, as it has no border with Pakistan. Several

expeditions climbed here during the 1960s and '70s, and it was visited again during the first six years of the new millennium by Pinelli, Predan, and others.

[This page, top] Koh-e-Qalat from the northeast. The 2012 ascent of the north top climbed the broad snow/ice couloir to the small col, and then left up the skyline ridge. *Alexandre Darrioulat*

The French established base camp at 4,300m and first climbed the north top of Koh-e-Qalat (5,505m, altimeter). This involved a long and boring walk (reconnaissance recommended) along moraine to climb a broad, northeast-facing snow/ice slope of ca 40° to a 5,360m (GPS) col on the northwest ridge. Here, they left their packs and then climbed the icy ridge, reached a beautiful granite pinnacle marking the north top. To reach the south summit, no more than 10-20m higher, would have involved traversing the top of a steep, icy "toboggan run" ending 1,500m below. As there was no easy possibility of belaying across this, they returned. The route was thought to be AD-. Although there are conflicting altitudes in past reports and on various maps, this is most likely the peak first climbed by Austrian Karl Graztel in 1970, repeated by Poles in 1976, and quoted as 5,508m.

Two days later they established a high camp on the glacier at 4,924m. The back wall of the valley is formed by a high ridge running from Koh-e-Keshni Khan (6,755m) to Koh-e-Wark (6,136m). The cirque below is divided in two by a small but attractive summit, Koh-e-Tokan (ca 5,200m), climbed in 2006, most likely for the first time, by Italian instructors and Afghan students from Carlo Pinelli's Mountain Wilderness training program. The three French first reconnoitered the southwestern sector of the cirque to find a route to the high ridge. They found only one safe line, and on the way climbed a small, unnamed summit of ca 5,200m, well to the west of Koh-e-Token. Although steep and impressive from the north, it had easy snow slopes on the south flank, which they followed to the summit at F.

Their next excursion saw them follow a glaciated route onto the high Keshni Khan–Koh-e-Wark ridge, at a point approximately one-quarter of the way along from Koh-e-Wark. Here they

[This page, top] Arnaud Pasquer on the summit of White Pyramid. In the distance, to the southwest, is the broad north face of the Noshaq massif (7,492m). To its right the flat-topped dome-like peak is Gumbaz-e-Safad (6,800m). Unknown peaks of the northern Mandaras Valley in the foreground. *Alexandre Darrioulat* [This page, bottom] The steep, mixed east-northeast face of Koh-e-Wark. This peak has only been climbed twice, in 1963 (Austrians) and in 1976 (Poles). In the foreground is the small but elegant unnamed peak climbed in 2012 by snow slopes on the far side. Koh-e-Tokan is just off picture to the left. *Franck Mazas* turned west (toward Koh-e-Wark) and climbed to a fine, snowy summit, ca one kilometer from Koh-e-Wark, which they named White Pyramid. The view was breathtaking, and while there are no previously recorded ascents, the climb was straightforward (PD) and the French are dubious about claiming a first.

Future parties should keep in mind that a lot of time is needed to conclude negotiations and hire porters before entering any valley in this region. Local people who have worked on previous expeditions are kind, full of advice, and glad to help visiting alpinists.

LINDSAY GRIFFIN, *Mountain INFO (from information provided by Alex Darrioulat and Franck Mazas, France)*

Koh-e-Rank (5,930m), second and third ascents, west-east traverse. With Mary-Rose Fowlie (who hadn't climbed for 20 years) and my brother Bill (who'd never climbed) both coming along as base camp support, two of us planned to visit the upper Qala Panja Glacier and attempt Rohazon Zom (6,535m) from the northwest. [This peak has only been climbed once, in 1968 by Austrians from the southwest (Pakistan). In 1976 Poles climbed the northeast ridge from the next valley east of the Qala Panja, but only reached the north top.] When my climbing partner pulled out, we decided to go anyway, and after a number of delays arrived in the Wakhan. As happened last year, all the organization (guide, transport, etc.) I'd put in place evaporated, but fortunately Malang, whom I had met last year, helped us procure our travelling permit and a translator to help with porters. We reached Qala Panja after a six-hour drive from Ishkashim in a battered Land Cruiser. Here, the police commander insisted we pay for two porters to guard base camp during our stay.

We were forced to establish base camp relatively low at 3,200m, and consequently spent the next eight days ferrying gear to a high camp on a rocky knoll at 5,000m, the final section involving several belayed pitches on granite. After a day of rest and acclimatization we walked four hours across the upper névé to reach the frontier ridge, where we could see Rohazon Zom and a closer,

smaller, and attractive peak called Koh-e-Rank. Mary-Rose and I decided this would make a suitable acclimatization ascent prior to an attempt on Rohazon Zom, and after a day back in high camp set off at 3 a.m. for an ascent of the east ridge. Accessing the crest involved a nasty snow bridge, followed by steep, unconsolidated snow, but the ridge itself proved straightforward. On the descent we made a huge rappel over the bergschrund and reached camp 12 hours after leaving.

[This page] Koh-e-Rank showing (1) east ridge and (2) northwest ridge. In 2012 the east ridge was first climbed up and down for the second ascent of the route and mountain, then a new traverse was made via an ascent of (2) and descent of (1). *Pat Deavoll*

Mary-Rose and I decided it would probably take five to seven days round-trip to summit Rohazon Zom, and wondered as a team if we'd be strong enough. We turned again to Koh-e-Rank. The east ridge had been climbed in 1968 by Isobel and Henri Agresti, but the northwest ridge remained untouched, so we made a west-east traverse in 14 hours after trying unsuccessfully to get onto the east face (a bergschrund precluded this.) The ascent involved another troublesome bergshrund crossing, followed by a nasty pitched traverse across the bottom of the north face under a series of large ice cliffs. This gave access to the northwest ridge about 200 meters above the base of the mountain. We belayed several pitches of moderately steep ice up a beautiful knife-edge ridge to gain access to the summit snow slopes, up which we slogged to the top. We descended the east ridge and used our previous abseil anchor to get back to the glacier.

PAT DEAVOLL, *New Zealand*

BIG PAMIR

Koh-e-Wakhan Range, various attempts. Ben Mitchell, Cecelia Mortenson, Danny Uhlmann, and I traveled to the Big Pamir in May to explore the potential for ski mountaineering and alpinism, and make first ski descents of unclimbed or rarely climbed peaks. We chose the Koh-e-Wakhan because of the relative lack of interest it has received since climbers began visiting Afghanistan again in 2003 after 25 years of absence. We chose May because we wanted a thick snowpack yet tolerable temperatures and spring conditions.

The Wakhan has heaps of potential for alpinism and trekking, and visiting tourists in the poverty-stricken Badakshan province are providing a significant infusion of badly needed revenue. Security is resonantly good in most of Badakshan, though there are naturally some exceptions. In common with previous parties we entered Afghanistan through southern Tajikistan; this country is not without its own set of serious security problems and political instability. For assistance in planning a visit to the Wakhan, we recommend

[This page] Ben Mitchell at the turnaround point on the north face of Peak 5,538m. (A) Koh-e-Zemestan (6,092m, both maps), thought to be unclimbed. (B) Koh-e-Zemestan East (6,080m, climbed in 1971 by Poles via the east ridge). (C) Kotal-e-Zemestan (5,650m pass). (D) Koh-e-Moshkel (6,063m Austrian; 6,103m, Polish), thought to be unclimbed. (E) Zemestan Glacier (Austrian map; Barabar Glacier, Polish map). *Dylan Taylor* [Next page] Koh-e-Pamir (6,320m Austrian map; 6,288m Polish map) from the southwest, showing the line of the 2012 attempt. The Italian Carlo Pinelli made the first ascent of this peak in 1971. It was climbed again by Austrians in 1975. The skyline ridge on the right leads toward unclimbed Peak 6,009m (Austrian; 5,950m Polish). *Dylan Taylor*

contacting Adab Shah in Ishkashim. He knows the area intimately, but expect to pay hefty fees for vehicle transport, fuel, guesthouses, and Mr. Shah's assistance.

We traveled two days in a Toyota Hilux up the Corridor to the village of Ptukh, where we hired porters for an easy two-day hike northwest to base camp on the lower Issik Glacier, a little above 4,000m. We then developed plans for three 6,000m peaks: Koh-e-Seh Aspe Safed (6,101m); Koh-e-Zemestan (6,092m), and the highest in the range, Koh-e-

Pamir (6,320m, Austrian Map; 6,288m Polish Map; 37°08'07" N, 73°15'42" E Google Earth). [There are two useful maps to this area: a Polish sketch map produced after a 1971 expedition, and an Austrian contour map published in 1978. Where heights differ, both are recorded.] However, we were plagued by stormy weather and a tricky snowpack. We turned back no more than 100m from the summit of Koh-e-Seh Aspe Safed East (6,040m) in whiteout and heavy snow, but the ski descent was fun. We climbed a striking 1,000m couloir toward the left side of the southwest face of Koh-e-Pamir, but searched futilely for a reasonably safe line up the continuing summit (northeast) ridge, which was 50° ice covered with a thin slab of rotten snow. Our aluminum crampons and short ski-racing axes did not inspire enough confidence to commit to such terrain, so we bailed and skied the couloir instead.

Our final attempt went little better. We didn't like the look of the teetering seracs threatening Zemestan's north face, so we turned our attention to a more aesthetic, unnamed 5,538m peak (Austrian; 5,568m Polish map) on the ridge to its east. We attempted the north face, but conditions toward the top forced us down and around onto the northeast face. Here, the 50° couloir exit was guarded by slabby rotten snow, so once again we were obliged to wave the white flag, this time a painfully close 50m below the summit. I believe my GPS had us near 5,700m at this point, but my confidence is low both in the map and data we recorded. The topography around Zemestan and on the upper reaches of Koh-e-Pamir was quite different from the (Austrian) map.

We probably found worse weather in May than most Wakhan visitors experience during summer. (One may not want to visit in the month of August, during which Ramadan is observed by much of the local population.) Feel free to contact me at taylorfoto@gmail.com with questions about logistics and visiting Afghanistan as an "American tourist." For more images of the region visit www.tayloralpine.com. 📷

DYLAN TAYLOR, *AAC*

Koh-e-Ak Su range, Koh-e-Elgha Eli IV (ca 5,725m), northwest face and southwest ridge. In July our international team of five climbers started from Dushanbe (Tajikistan) on a nine-day approach to unexplored valleys in the eastern end of the Wakhan Corridor, southeast of Lake Chaqmaqtin. The team comprised Sarah Sheridan (Australia), Malgorzata Skowronska (Poland), Mariusz Hoffmann,

Andreas Schnall, and me (all from Germany). From the roadhead at Sarhad-e-Boroghil we trekked for five days with yak and horse caravans, past Kyrgyz nomad settlements and Lake Chaqmaqtin (Firestone Lake) into the valley of Elgha Eli, which is named after a kind of willow bush that grows in the lower part of the valley. Our goal was to explore this valley and the Terghen Qorum. We were helped during our preparation by a record of local valley names recorded by Remy Dor and Clas Naumann in their 1978 book Die Kirghisen des Afghanischen Pamir.

On July 26 we established base camp at 4,500m, whereupon a storm moved in and put down 30cm of snow. Next day things improved, and by the 29th we had placed a high camp in a glacier basin we named Yach Bandaan-e Bozorg (Great Icefield). In contrast to the moderate approach to base camp, the way to high camp was over the worst moraines imaginable, making progress

extremely hard. At the far end of Yach Bandaan-e Bozorg we discovered a névé slope that led to the summit ridge of a peak, like a white staircase to heaven. This was our route. And what name could be more suitable than Roh-e-Asmaan—staircase to heaven?

We left camp at 4 a.m. in two teams, traveling to the head of the glacier on snowshoes. We changed into crampons for the névé slope and climbed this west-southwest for ca 250m to the ridge, where we were met by the rays of the rising sun. The temperature rose quickly under a clear, deep blue sky. We cached our snowshoes and continued southwest close to the crest, which steepened to more than 45°. The ascent to the summit, which we reached at 9 a.m., was PD+ but strenuous. Our two GPS units measured 5,732m and 5,719m; summit coordinates are 37°09'38" N, 74°16'18" E. To equal the spread we chose the average of 5,725m as the official summit height.

There was a fine view deep into Pakistan and China, and immediately to the east we could see the neighboring valley of Terghen Qorum, which according to our Google Earth research is home to the highest peaks of the Koh-e-Ak Su. However, from our viewpoint, we were not completely convinced.

We now realized that we were not on the highest summit. There were three more summits, all a little higher, to the northeast, so we have dubbed our peak Koh-e-Elgha Eli IV. The simple ridge implied by Google Earth and old military maps was actually a sawtooth involving steep climbs and descents, and we were too late to continue to higher tops; the shark-fin summit of II would have involved climbing a 55° snow face. There are great challenges here for future expeditions, including the ca 1,000m north faces from the Terghen Qorum Valley. 📑 📷

CHRIS NETTEKOVEN, *Germany, www.wakhanexpedition2012.jimdo.com*

[This page] Unclimbed peak on west side of Elgha Eli Valley. *Chris Nettekoven*

PAKISTAN

Peak Fees. In 2013 the Pakistan Government continued its policy of discounting peak royalties. In short, there is no peak fee for mountains below 6,500m, and substantial discounts remain in place on royalties for higher mountains. See the online version of this report for full details.

INFORMATION PROVIDED BY ASGHAR ALI PORIK, *Jasmine Tours, Islamabad, Pakistan.*

HINDU RAJ

Shayaz Massif, clarification. During climbs of Koh-e-Rank in the Wakhan Corridor of Afghanistan, Pat Deavoll from New Zealand photographed the little-known Shayaz Massif, across the border in Pakistan. (This massif should not be confused with the much higher Shayoz Zom, sometimes quoted as "Shayaz," which lies just east of Koh-e-Urgent.) From her photos, it's clear the peak the Japanese called Shayaz (6,050m) after climbing it in 1993 was not the highest peak of the massif, as thought, and there are several higher peaks in the range that have never been attempted. See photo caption for details.

LINDSAY GRIFFIN, *Mountain INFO*

[This page] Looking southeast at the remote peaks of the Shayaz Massif from the Afghan border close to Koh-e-Rank (5,930m). In 1993 Japanese made the only ascent of (B), a peak they called Shayaz, by the route marked (AAJ 1994), and quoted a height of 6,050m. This was designated Shayaz I. The Russian map of this area gives this point as 5,969m, and gives (A), the highest summit of the massif, an elevation of 6,026m. While the topography of Russian maps is usually very good, their altitudes are often a little low, making the Japanese assessment more realistic. However, it is clear from this photograph and the Russian map that "Shayaz" is not the highest peak in the group. (C) is distant Shahan Dok (6,320m). *Pat Deavoll*

WESTERN HIMALAYA

Nanga Parbat (8,125m), Mazeno Ridge history. The complete Mazeno Ridge of Nanga Parbat was undoubtedly one of the most famous unclimbed lines on the great peaks of the Karakoram/Himalaya, having been attempted many times, and by some of the world's greatest mountaineers. It is arguably the longest ridge on any of the 8,000m peaks, variously quoted as 10 to 13km. Sandy Allan and Rick Allen, accompanied for much of the way by Cathy O'Dowd (South Africa), Lhakpa Rangdu Sherpa, Lhakpa Zarok Sherpa, and Lhakpa Nuru Sherpa (Nepal), completed the first full traverse of the ridge with a successful summit of Nanga Parbat, followed by a trying descent of the normal route on the north face. A full account appears earlier in this *AAJ.*

The Mazeno Ridge had previously been attempted by nine different parties, starting in 1979 with a large French expedition that began the route from Mazeno Pass, fixed a lot of rope, and climbed a minor summit. In 1992 Doug Scott's international team, starting from the Rupal Valley, climbed important new ground, summiting three Mazeno peaks. No one improved on this performance until 2004, when Doug Chabot and Steve Swenson traversed the ridge to Mazeno Gap, but due to illness and exhaustion were forced to descend the Schell Route to the Rupal Valley (*AAJ 2005*).

Previously unreported in the *AAJ* was the 2008 traverse to Mazeno Gap by Germans Joseph Lunger and Luis Stitzinger. This pair made a long approach from Diamir base camp toward Mazeno Pass, but a little before reaching it cut up left, climbing a spur onto the main ridge well before the point reached by previous parties from the Rupal side. After seven days they reached the final (and highest) Mazeno peak for its second ascent. At this point they ran out of steam and provisions, so they descended toward the gap, then escaped north via the 1978 Messner Route, which they down-climbed and rappelled in nine hours.

LINDSAY GRIFFIN, *Mountain INFO*

Winter 2012–2013 overview. Although difficult weather conditions shut down all but one expedition attempting 8,000m peaks in Pakistan, a Spanish pair succeeded on the lower Laila Peak above the Gondokhoro Glacier. Laila (6,096m), well seen on the standard trek from the Baltoro Glacier over the Gondokhoro La to Hushe, is one of the most spectacular snow/ice peaks in the Karakoram. After one attempt that came close to the top, José Fernandez and Alex Txikon reached the summit on February 18, 2013, having made a grueling push up the west face from their top camp. Earlier, the pair had plowed a trench through deep snow to reach Camp 1 at 5,200m, then in improving weather arrived at Camp 2 (5,600m) the following day. They then took 10 hours, battling through snow reported to be sometimes chest deep, a temperature of –35°C, and winds estimated to gust 60 km/hour, before reaching the summit.

Laila had several ascents before the "first official" in 1997 by an Italian team via the northwest ridge. The original ascent had been made 10 years earlier by Andy Cave, Tom Curtis, Sean Smith, and Simon Yates (U.K.), during a productive trip to the Hushe region, which also saw the first ascent of Namika (6,400m). They climbed Laila by the great snow and ice slope of the west face.

Elsewhere four teams were attempting the first winter ascent of Nanga Parbat. Daniele Nardi and Elizabeth Revol made an alpine-style bid on the Mummery Rib, first attempted in 1895. In three days they reached ca 6,400m, en route to their planned Camp 3, before retreating in the face of constant spindrift and severe weather (winds of 100kph and temperatures of –48°C were reported).

[This page, top] Looking south down the Gondokhoro Glacier from Gondokhoro La, a memorable view for those making the Askole–Baltoro Glacier–Hushe trek. The prominent ice spear left of center is Laila. The winter ascent was made via the right skyline, the west face as seen in profile. *Tomas Fernandez-Montesinos, supplied by Carlos Penalva* [This page, bottom] Diamir Face of Nanga Parbat in winter. (1) Normal (Kinshofer) Route. (2) Mummery Rib attempted in 2013 to 6,400m. Mummery and his Gurkha companion Rajobir reached 6,100m in 1895. (3) 1978 Messner Route. (4) Line used by Sandy Allan and Rick Allen on July 14-15, 2012, to reach the summit. (5) Line attempted by Sandy Allan, Rick Allen, Lhakpa Rangdu, and Lhakpa Zarok on July 12. Other routes and variants on this face are not shown. *Daniele Nardi*

They spent two more nights at Camp 2, hoping for better conditions, but then gave up. Their full report can be found at the *AAJ* website.

An American-Hungarian team attempted the northeast face (well left of the existing Diamir Face routes) via the line tried in 2000 by Hanspeter Eisendle, Hubert and Reinhold Messner, and Wolfgang Tomaseth, which stopped upon joining the 1978 Czechoslovak Route at around 7,500m. Poles Marek Klonowski and Tomek Mackiewicz, on their third Nanga Parbat winter expedition, attempted the Schell Route on the Rupal side. From a bivouac above the Mazeno Gap, Mackiewicz made a bold solo attempt on the summit but turned back at around 7,400m.

The fourth team was actually one man, the little-known Joel Wischnewski from France, attempting a highly ambitious solo climb of the southeast pillar. When nothing was heard nor seen of him for some time, his agent in Pakistan launched a search. Three experienced Pakistan mountaineers climbed up the lower part of his proposed route, but never found any trace of the Frenchman.

The historic first winter ascent of Broad Peak, and subsequent tragedy, is reported later in these pages.

LINDSAY GRIFFIN, *Mountain INFO*

KARAKORAM

BATURA MUZTAGH

Darwo Chhok (5,860m), southwest face, attempt; Kako Peak (ca 4,900m), east face. Approaching from Chalt through Bar and Baltar, Italians Florian and Martin Riegler, accompanied by photographer Monika Mehlmauer and Christoph Mohl (Austria), attempted the ca 1,000m rock wall that forms the southwest face of Darwo Chhok on the east side of the Toltar

[This page, top] Daniele Nardi during a 2013 winter attempt on the Mummery Rib of Nanga Parbat. *Elizabeth Revol* [This page, bottom] Belayed by his brother, Martin Riegler starts the headwall on Kako Peak. This image was taken after the first ascent. *Monika Mehlmauer*

Glacier. They had previously tried this in 2008, climbing around 14 pitches before retreating due to bad weather and illness.

In 2012 conditions on the face again proved too dangerous, so after 15 pitches they descended. Instead the Riegler brothers made a four-day, alpine-style first ascent of a lower rock spire, dubbed Kako Peak (Big Brother). They climbed the east face by a 1,100m route named Ramadan (6c/7a and two wet pitches of A2). The summit was reached on August 1. Bolts were placed on some belays.

Kako Peak lies immediately above the moraines of the Baltar Glacier at 36°28'06.11" N, 74°23'27.21" E, at the end of the southwest ridge of Pt. 5,275m, a summit on the south-southeast ridge of the unclimbed Dadayo Chhok (5,940m). The first part of the east face, which rises out of grassy slopes, is slabby, but the upper headwall gave very steep granite climbing.

LINDSAY GRIFFIN, *Mountain INFO, from information supplied by Martin Riegler, Italy*

SPANTIK-SOSBUN RANGE

Sosbun Group, Solu Glacier, various ascents. Searching for a part of the Karakoram that might offer solid rock and had rarely been visited, I decided on the Solu Glacier. Only a few expeditions had ever gone there, most peaks were still untouched, and parts of the valley featured some of that legendary Karakoram granite. The Solu is immediately south of the Hispar and Biafo glaciers, so we could reach it in a few hours' Jeep travel from Skardu, following the Shigar and Basha rivers to the village of Bisil. We were fascinated by the hospitality and culture of the local villagers, and as they'd hardly ever had close contact with non-Pakistanis, we all had a happy, moving, and interesting time.

Narrow paths led to the Solu Glacier, and we spent a lot of time exploring the glacier and its side valleys. Next to the pastures of Pakora, towering above our camp at a little lake with a sandy beach, we discovered the huge rock face of Pakora Brakk. The dimensions of this face exceeded anything we could climb with our available gear, but at the foot of the main section, Gaby Lappe,

[This page] Peaks of the Pakora Glacier, with the route to Braunschweig Brakk (5,301m GPS). Most of the first-ascent route lies behind the prominent rock rib. *Kai Maluck*

Clemens Pischel, and I climbed a rock pillar to give the route Zhunzhe (170m, UIAA IV+/V-).

Immediately west of Pakora Brakk, and dividing the pastures of Pakora into two parts, a distinctive stream came down from a side valley. The upper section of this valley contained the Pakora Glacier, surrounded by a number of impressive rock faces and sharp peaks, all unclimbed. I chose the middle peak at the back of the glacier, and soloed up its southeast gully. This steepened to 50° and led to the summit ridge, which I followed southwest to the highest point (mainly II and III with a step of IV+, and a short section of 55° ice). I named the peak Braunschweig Brakk (35°58'44" N, 75°23'40" E, 5,301m GPS).

Now sufficiently acclimatized, we headed toward the highest mountain in the area, Sugulu (6,102m, named by the 2000 British expedition). We spent two full days at a 4,600m advanced base camp, and climbed Gang Shole (4,860m), a rocky top on the ridge coming down from a point east of Sugulu. Then, Clemens Pischel and I moved up to a high camp north of Gang Shole at 5,200m. Shortly after pitching the tent and beginning the inevitable snow-melting marathon, snowfall set in and did not stop. Next morning, knowing that we were running out of time and supplies, we decided to climb as far as we could. In poor visibility we navigated through an icefall between 5,200m and 5,500m, until arriving on the watershed ridge. Here we continued west along a corniced crest, and then past Ice Cream Peak, the highest point reached by the 2001 British expedition (see below), until ca 250m below the summit of Sugulu we were turned back by an ice cliff. 📷 🔍 ▶

KAI MALUCK, *Germany*

Editor's note: Although Auden and Tilman (in 1937), and Mott and Russell (in 1939), penetrated the lower part of the valley, there is no known report of mountaineering activities in the Solu Glacier before the visit of a British expedition in 2000. Ken Findlay, Paul Hudson, Dave Wilkinson, and Karl Zientek established base camp above the place on the glacier known as Sugulu. During the approach they'd been informed by locals that around 1995 an expedition climbed three peaks from the glacier basin west of Sugulu. Unfortunately, information on who they were and exactly where they went was extremely sketchy. The 2000 expedition climbed one peak, Sekha Brakk (Dragonfly Peak, ca 5,450m), on the Hispar watershed. Wilkinson returned the following year with Bill Church, Steve Kennedy, and Stuart Muir, climbing over what has now been named Gang Shole, and making the first ascent of Ice Cream Peak (ca 5,800m, AD) as part of an attempt on Sugulu.

PANMAH MUZTAGH

Baintha Brakk (Ogre, 7,285m), north face reconnaissance; Hispar Muztagh, Muki (6,330m), traverse; Peak 5,966m; Sosbun Group, Solu Hidden Tower (ca 5,850m), northeast and northwest faces. In five expeditions to different areas of the Karakoram, I've climbed virgin peaks and new routes up to 7,000m, but never seen a place like Snow Lake, its particular features making it so aptly named. In July and August we had to approach the foot of the mountains on skis, towing our gear on sleds, as in Alaska. And the weather there during the summer was not unlike that of Patagonia, making even the easiest ascent a treacherous proposition.

Daniele Bernasconi and I reached base camp (4,700m), at the entrance to the Sim Gang Glacier, and without wasting time skied the 20km up glacier to the foot of the north face of the Ogre. This is an impressive face, embroidered with many seracs. There are "weak points," if you accept

[This page, top] The Solu Towers from the entrance to Sim Gang Glacier. (A) Solu Peak (5,901m). (B) Solu Tower II (5,959m). (C) Solu Tower I (5,979m). (D) Unnamed. (E) Solu Hidden (ca 5,850m). (1) Tunstall-Venables, 1987. (2) Venables, solo, 1987. (3) Barmasse-Bernasconi, 2012. *Hervé Barmasse* [This page, bottom] Northwest along the Tahu Rutum Glacier. (A) Muki, with traverse marked. (B) Tarci Peak. *Hervé Barmasse*

the constant exposure to avalanches and icefall. We identified a feasible line, the northeast ridge (leading toward the unclimbed east summit), that is not too difficult but undoubtedly dangerous.

We returned to base camp and set out from there on July 7 to continue acclimatizing by making an ascent of the well-summited Workman Peak (5,885m), north of the Hispar La. Then we set off north across Snow Lake and onto the Tahu Rutum Glacier, from where, on the 11th, we made the probable first ascent of a 6,330m (GPS) primarily snow/ice peak (Peak ca 6,400m on Miyamori and Swiss maps) via a traverse. This peak lies on the long ridge running east from Tahu Rutum, and is northwest of Tarci Peak (ca 5,800m), climbed in 1999 by Italians (*AAJ 2000*). We had waist-deep snow on the ridge, and no adequate equipment to protected the mixed sections. We named it Muki.

After nine days at or above base camp, we felt ready for the Ogre, confident that our remaining 22 days in the area would be more than enough for an attempt. However, from the 12th to the 28th, winter descended on base camp. There were only two days of fine weather, useful for drying sleeping bags and attempting two lower mountains. On the 22nd we climbed an easy, possibly virgin

5,966m (GPS) that lies on the continuation ridge northwest of Peak 5,925m (Miyamori and Swiss maps; see Dom Brakk in *AAJ 2012*). We made a ski descent from the summit.

Later, we did the likely first ascent of Solu Hidden, the most northerly rock tower in the Solu Group. The ascent, via a rock buttress, a long snow/ice slope, and more difficult climbing, proved exciting.

The weather cleared on July 28, allowing us to return to the Ogre to assess conditions: Even the vertical rock walls were covered in a thick blanket of snow.

Afterward, I looked at the same old glass—was it half empty or half full? The end of a dream is only the beginning of a new adventure, but our four ascents did not replace the joy we would have felt if we'd been able to attempt the Ogre. I have to accept that the glass is half empty. 🄾

HERVÉ BARMASSE, *Italy*

Baintha Brakk (a.k.a The Ogre, 7,285m), southeast ridge, southeast face, and south face, first ascent. After returning to Skardu for a rest after a new route on K7, Kyle Dempster and Hayden Kennedy joined Josh Wharton (USA) on the Choktoi Glacier. There have been many attempts to climb the Ogre from the southeast, nearly all via the elegant southeast pillar. However, in 2009 three French alpinists climbed a cunning, complex line to outflank the pillar and reach the upper south face, which they climbed to 6,800m before retreating (*AAJ 2010*). The three Americans chose to attempt the same line. A full account of this ascent, only the third overall of the Ogre, appears in this *AAJ*.

LINDSAY GRIFFIN, *Mountain INFO*

Latok II Southeast top (ca 7,020m), southwest face, Théorème de la Peine. In June the four-man French team of Antoine Bletton, Pierre Labbre, Matthieu Maynadier, and Sébastien Ratel connected lines of weakness up the previously untouched right side of the southwest face of Latok II (7,108m), just failing to reach the mountain's highest point.

The four established base camp at 4,800m, but were faced with consistently unsettled weather and were unable to make any meaningful acclimatization. They spent only one night at ca 5,800m, on the approach to the col below Latok II's northwest ridge, and climbed lower peaks close to camp. Then they received a text saying there would be a three-day weather window followed by 10 days of snowfall. Ready or not, it was now or never. After a bivouac at the foot of the face on the night of June 2, they climbed the initial 500m snow slope, and then followed a series of rising snow ramps cutting left through vertical granite walls. The weather deteriorated, and spindrift-swept runnels, giving "Ben Nevis ambience," led to a very poor bivouac site.

The next day was vastly better, so they continued up steep mixed terrain to make an early bivouac on a large snow terrace at 6,200m, where they could dry gear in the evening sun. They left at 2 a.m. on the June 4, traveling light and hoping to find an easy passage through the final rock wall to the summit ridge, where they would link with the original route at ca 6,700m. Unfortunately, they found hard climbing up powder-covered slabs and deep, scary snow on the summit ridge. At 6 p.m. they reached a small but distinct "bump," less than 100m below the main summit, and decided to call it a day. The forecast storm was due early next morning, and they wanted to escape the bottom of the face—a huge funnel for falling snow—before it was too late.

Regaining their bivouac site at 1 a.m. on the 5th, they hastily packed gear and then rappelled through the night. Despite falling asleep at anchors, and taking care constantly to check each other's

[This page, top] The 2,000m southwest face of Latok II. (1) Northwest ridge integral (Spanish, 2009). (2) 1993 Austrian attempt. (3) Southwest face and northwest ridge: Nomadu (Germans, 1997). (4) Tsering Mosong (American-German, 1997). (5) Théorème de la Peine, to southeast top (2012). *Matthieu Maynadier* [This page, bottom] (A) Latok II (7,108m). (B) Latok I (7,145m). (C) Latok III (6,949m). (1) Northwest ridge (Spanish, 2009). (2) Upper part of Théorème de la Peine and high point (S) on the southeast top (ca 7,020m). (3) 2006 American variant. (4) Southeast ridge (Italians, 1977). (5) South-southeast pillar (Japanese, 1979). (6) West face (Russians, 2011). (7) Southwest ridge (Japanese, 1979). *Matthieu Maynadier*

actions, they made it safely to the rimaye at 10 a.m., picked up skis, and were back at base camp by 1 p.m.

Greg Child's well-known book *Mixed Emotions* was translated into French as *Théorème de la Peur*. As a salute the French have named their new line Théorème de la Peine (*peine* being "suffering"; 2,000m, ED1, M5). 📷

From information supplied by MATTHIEU
MAYNADIER, *France*

Editors note: Latok II has been summited five times, more than any of the other peaks in this famous group. On the first ascent, by the southeast ridge, three Italians reached what appeared to be the top (the same point reached by the French) and, highly disappointed to find it wasn't, took a further three hours to reach the summit. On the second ascent of this route, in alpine style, three Americans also thought they'd reached the summit until, fortunately, clouds parted and revealed their mistake. They took 30 minutes to reach the main summit. The southwest face was climbed for the first time in 1997—twice. An American-German expedition climbed the high-altitude big wall Tsering Mosong, and a week later two other members of the same expedition climbed the left branch of the central couloir to the northwest ridge, which they followed to the summit. Prior to this there had been an attempt on the left side of the face by Christian Stangl and Austrian friends, which was only briefly noted in AAJ *1994. This party drove in a 1961 Land Rover from Austria and spent 68 days at base camp. They attempted the big wall left of the central couloir, but bad weather prevented them from getting above 6,100m.*

BALTORO MUZTAGH

Sarpo Laggo Peak (6,208m), southeast ridge; Trango I (6,363m), south-southwest face to foresummit. Before Aymeric Clouet, Christian Trommsdorff, and Patrick Wagnon ventured further up the Baltoro Glacier to make an attempt on Gasherbrum V (see report elsewhere in this section), I accompanied them to the Trango Group. After an approach to Shipton base camp, a warm-up ascent on good granite close to camp, and a few days of snow, all four of us skied up the Trango Glacier to the Sarpo Laggo Pass (5,704m), crossed in 1937 by Eric Shipton and Bill Tilman to reach the Sarpo Laggo Glacier and thence the north side of K2. We spent a night here, and then Christian and I

[This page] Steep mixed ground on day two of Théorème de la Peine. *Matthieu Maynadier*

went back to base camp while the other two scouted a possible route up Sarpo Laggo Peak, northwest of the pass. We all left base camp again on May 28 and skied to the pass, where we spent the night again before following the southeast ridge, in deep snow, to the summit. We reached the top after an exhausting 12-hour climb and camped for the night just below the summit cornice. After spending a few hours next morning enjoying fine Karakoram scenery, we descended to the pass, camped again and returned to base camp on the 31st. [*There is no record of Sarpo Laggo Peak having been climbed before this ascent.*]

With the forecast offering only one and half days of good weather, and avalanches falling from the Uli Biaho side, we decided to attempt Trango I (a.k.a. Trango Ri), the highest of the Trango peaks, in lightweight style, taking sleeping bags but no tent. On June 4 we climbed a complex route up the south-southwest face, starting from the base of the large southwest-facing couloir between Trangos I and II. In 14 hours from base camp (ca 1,800m of ascent) we reached a southern foresummit, about 150m below the top. Three of the climbers continued for one hour but then retreated. After a bivouac in strong wind and temperatures down to –21°C, we descended the following morning. [*Editor's note: It is not known by whom, or even if, Trango I was climbed previously, but the line of the Austro-French attempt is most likely new.*]

LISI STEURER, *Austria*

[This page, top] The first-ascent route up the southeast ridge of Sarpo Laggo Peak. *Lisi Steurer*
[This page, bottom] Looking almost north over the Trango Glacier. (A) Kruksum (6,572m). (B) Trango I (6,362m). (C) Austro-French bivouac. (S) Small southerly foresummit. (1) Austro-French Route (ca 1,800m, 2012). (2) West couloir to Trango II (ca 1,700m, 55° M5, first known ascent Auer-Dung, 2006, but likely climbed before). The green area at the base of these routes is the normal Shipton base camp. *Dodo Kopold*

Uli Biaho Gallery, Nilam Najang; La Reina Roja, Sadu Masu; Trango II (6,327m), southwest ridge, Is Enough. While at Trango base camp Jakob Schweighofer and I climbed three possible new routes. On August 9, and with the Slovakian Martin Krasnansky, we put up Nilam Najang (the Inside Dream) on the southeast pillar of a formation across the glacier we have named Uli Biaho Gallery. [*This lies directly below Uli Biaho Great Spire (5,594m), and right of Uli Byapjun (ca 4,800m), with its Warming up Ridge, climbed by Grmovsek and Karo in 2006*]. The ca 450m route had 14 pitches up to 7a+ C2. The three hardest pitches were only climbed free by the followers. The climb was relatively sustained, with the fourth pitch (55m, 7a+) a beautiful double crack, while the sixth (40m, 7a) was runout. There is a nice bivouac site at the top of the route.

On the 13th, Jakob and I climbed Sadu Maso to the top of the summit above Sadu Peak. In 2003 Antoine and Sandrine de Choudens climbed seven pitches to 6c on the left arête of the southwest face of a prominent ca 4,400m rock tower 10 minutes' walk above Trango base camp. They named the point from which they descended Sadu Peak. Over four days in June 2007, Luis Carlos Garcia Ayala and Ali Mohammad continued this line to a second, more prominent summit, climbing a total of 17 pitches at 5.10b A1. They named the summit La Reina Roja, and their route Morning Star. At the time we were unaware of this ascent, and for much of the upper

[This page, top] Southwest ridge of Trango II. (1) Austrian descent. (2) Severance Ridge. (3) Is Enough. To the right stand Trango Monk and Trango Tower. *Jakob Schweighofer* **[This page, bottom]** Martin Krasnansky on a fine crack on Nilam Najang. *Jakob Schweighofer*

section climbed different ground to the left of the ridge, moving back right at the top of our 16th pitch, where we found an in-situ anchor. We continued to the top, higher than the finish to Morning Star, and descended the Trango Tower gully.

We climbed a total of 1,200m in 22 pitches up to 6c, though there was much easy terrain. This is a perfect acclimatization-day ascent, with a short approach and descent. The climbing is good, with a wide variety of cracks, corners, and slabs.

From August 17–19 we climbed a variation to Severance Ridge, the southwest ridge of Trango II, first climbed by Clearwater, Frimer, and Johnson in 2005 (1,600m, VI 5.11 A2 AI3 M5, no summit, *AAJ 2006*). Our route to the summit has a vertical interval of 2,100m from the glacier (1,000m rock climbing; 1,100m snow/mixed). We named it Is Enough and rated the difficulties 6c+ M4 80° snow. [*In the upper section the pair avoided the Shield, climbed in 2005, by traversing right across slabs, then ascending up and right over snow/mixed to gain the southeast ridge, which they climbed to the summit. This is likely the third ascent of Trango II*]. We descended to the northwest and then into the south-southwest couloir, which in its lower section separates the southwest ridge from Garden and Garda peaks. 📷

FLORIAN DERTNIG, *Austria*

[This page] A wonderful panorama southeast from the summit of Trango II. (A) K7 (6,934m). (B) Yermanendu Kangri (7,163m). (C) Masherbrum (7,821m). (D) Mandu East (7,127m). (E) Mandu West (7,081m). (F) Urdukas (6,320m). (G) Seemingly unnamed. (H) Liligo Glacier. (I) Great Trango northeast (6,231m). (J) Great Trango Main (6,286m). (K) Great Trango southwest (ca 6,250m). (1) Great Trango normal route. (2) Top section of Krasnoyarsk Route. Lower left foreground is summit of Trango Tower. *Jakob Schweighofer*

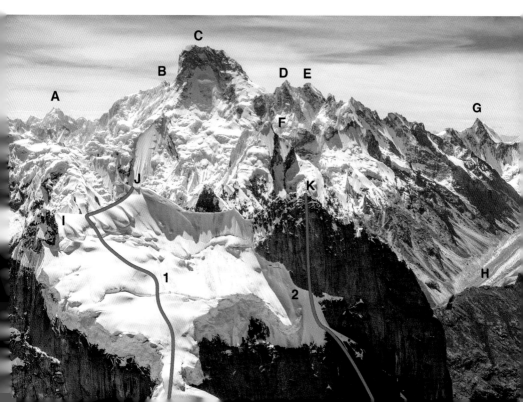

Great Trango Tower, northwest face, Out of Reality, not to summit; various other ascents. Looking for somewhere to spend a nice summer holiday, I didn't think I would once again be going to the Trango Glacier. But if you ask me now, "Why again?" my answer would be simply that I love this place.

Martin Krasnansky and Michal Sabovnik had never been to the Karakoram and were hungry for rock, as was I. While Martin discovered the effects of altitude in base camp, Michal and I explored new ground on the south face of Great Trango. To the right of my 2005 route, Assalam Alaikum, we climbed ca 500m up to UIAA VII+ on super-runout slabs, until we got lost somewhere on this huge face and retreated.

We then decided to climb the northwest face in alpine style, without bolts and a portaledge. The northwest face has two parts: entry slabs and the steep headwall. We wanted to try the deep, icy slot on the right side of the pillar climbed originally by Ukrainians, the obvious steep couloir between Parallelniy Mir and Lost Butterfly. [*Editor's note: This great pillar was climbed by a team from the Ukraine in 2003, but above, on the final wall leading to the southwest summit, they retreated. The line was completed in 2007 by a team from Krasnoyarsk, and in 2011 another line on the pillar, Paralleniy Mir, to the right of the 2003/2007 line, was climbed by an all-female Russian-Ukraine team, which finished up the Krasnoyarsk route from the top of the pillar*].

On our first day Michal and I climbed a series of amazing slabs and corners, sharing a few

[This page, left] Michal Sabovnik settles down for a comfortable bivouac in the haulbag on the third night of Out of Reality. *Dodo Kopold* [This page, right] Northwest face of Great Trango seen from the Uli Biaho Gallery. (1) Krasnoyarsk Route (2007). (2) Out of Reality (2012). (3) Parallel Worlds (1999). (4) Azeem Ridge (2004). Assalam Alaikum climbs the face right of (4). For other routes on the northwest face see *AAJ 2012*. *Dodo Kopold*.

bolt belays with the Ukraine/Krasnoyarsk route. We stopped below a V-shaped crack streaming with water, making our bivouacs separately, five meters apart. Next morning the crack was dry. We climbed it and continued up a long section of offwidths. In a long day we reached the headwall.

Our third day started with another steep offwidth, followed by a technical traverse to reach the snowfield where I was nearly killed in 2005. By midday we had reached the start of an overhanging mixed section with free-hanging ice. We dubbed this "the Illuminati," after a well-known mixed route (M11+ WI6+) in an Italian Dolomite valley. Climbing this at 5,200m, on loose rock with no bolts, was incredible. We didn't get to bed until 2 a.m., Michal in the haulbag, me on a tiny ledge only fit for sparrows.

After an awful night and a terrible day climbing icy chimneys in falling snow, we reached the top of the pillar and a junction with the Ukraine/Krasnoyarsk route. At this point, 400m from the main summit (6,286m) in poor weather, we settled down to bivouac, thirsty like never before. Then our stove was gone, dropped. Without water we'd be fucked. Sitting on a small ledge I contemplated my existence, and next day chose life. We retreated without the summit but with a beautiful line, which we have named Out of Reality (ca 1,500m, 7a WI6 M7 A3). A big disappointment was the discovery of abandoned trash at various places on the northwest face. By the contents it was very obvious which party had dumped it. Leaving rubbish on the walls is something I just don't understand.

Later, Martin, Michal, and I climbed a line to the left of Nilam Najang on Uli Biaho Gallery, joining this route at the top of pitch nine. We did this in one day at 7b and C2, naming it Paradise Circus. Michal and I also climbed the standard route up Great Trango in a 14-hour round trip from base camp. 📷 🔍

DODO KOPOLD, *Slovakia*

Muztagh Tower (7,284m), northeast spur, Think Twice. The pioneering photographer Vittorio Sella took his famous picture of the Muztagh Tower in 1909. Since then only five expeditions have climbed one or both of the twin summits [the east is the main top, the west several meters lower]: British and French climbers in 1956; British in 1984; Swedish in 1990, and our Russian team in 2012.

To research our route, I talked with Vadim Geshkenbein, who was there in 1994. He gave me much interesting information regarding the southern side of the peak and advised me to contact Bruce Normand, who had visited the northern flanks in 2005. Bruce too gave us invaluable information. It was he who consulted with Pavle Kozjek before his ill-fated expedition to the mountain's northeast face in 2008. [*Editor's note: From the summit of 6,001m Tsetse, above the Moni La, Normand saw that an active band of seracs threatened both the true north face and north ridge, and that the unrepeated southeast ridge sported gargantuan cornices. This left two viable lines: the poorly defined northeast spur, which falls directly from the main summit and has a very steep rock barrier between 6,600m and 6,900m, and an easier, predominantly snow/ice line on the far left of the northeast face, leading toward a col on the southeast ridge between the main summit and a distinctive sharp top named the Black Tooth (6,702m). It was the latter line that Slovenians attempted in 2008 before Kozjek fell to his death].*

After a five-day walk from Askole, Sergey Kotachkov, Alexander Lange, Sergey Nilov, and I arrived at base camp (4,600m) below Muztagh Tower. Once established we reconnoitered the approach to the ca 2,000m northeast face. This was easy at first, but later proved more difficult due to a maze of crevasses on the Younghusband Glacier. For a better view of the face, we climbed

[This page, left] The 2,000m northeast spur of Muztagh Tower showing the Russian line Think Twice. [This page, right] On the headwall. *Supplied by Anna Piunova (both photos)*

to 5,500m on the flanks of the Skilbrum massif opposite the peak. We had a pleasant surprise: no avalanche or icefall visible for the 20 hours we were there. The northeast spur, which Bruce had recommended, looked beautiful and safe. We dubbed it "the saw" due to its appearance.

Next we reached the Moni La (5,566m) at the head of the glacier and inspected the north ridge, which rises from it. We also looked at the British route on the northwest ridge, hoping to see a feasible descent. The north ridge appeared more difficult than it had looked in photos we had seen. It was also considerably more dangerous than the northeast spur. The British route looked long and not at all easy. We spent a night on Moni pass and then descended to base camp, where we were stuck for almost a week, amusing ourselves with slacklining, playing dominos, and washing.

On August 9, Alex, Sergey Nilov, and I crossed the bergschrund below the spur at 5,250m, carrying two rucksacks and a 70L haulbag filled with food and gas. We anticipated spending 14 days on the mountain. At first we ascended 50-60° snow slopes right of the spur. Alex and I led, saving Sergey for the headwall. On our first day the sun was strong, the snow was wet, the packs were heavy, and we were thirsty. From time to time we prayed for clouds. Our shy requests were fulfilled. Next day it started to snow and continued for a week. During this period we ascended slowly to ca 6,200m, and then sat in our tent for a couple of days.

The weather finally cleared on the 17th. After drying gear we set out to reach the headwall. There we found amazing snow formations, where warm southerly winds had blown snow and ice over the north side of the mountain, plastering it to vertical rock walls. It looked horrendous, so we decided to make a long, rising, rightward traverse to the north-northeast ridge. This proved challenging and time consuming, and was led entirely by Nilov: 600m of free climbing up to 6a/6b with one pitch of A2.

On the 23rd, one day before reaching the ridge, we ran out of food save for a few sweets, and once on the crest someone turned off the good weather. On the morning of August 24 we finished the remaining gas, and by evening had climbed to within 300m distance of the summit. Strong wind pinned us down for the night in a crevasse, but we struggled to the east top, the highest summit of Muztagh Tower, at seven the following morning—the 25th—17 days after beginning the route.

Our plan now was to retrace our steps a little, and then turn left and traverse snow slopes below the crest to reach the northwest ridge, then cross it to northwest face, descending the British Route. However, the weather was bad, visibility poor, and by midday we found ourselves blocked by an icefall. We either had to reascend and find another way, or rappel directly downward. Opting for the latter, we continued down the objectively dangerous north ridge/face, battered by spindrift and narrowly missed by large avalanches. We carried on through the night, even after our headlamps gave out, and 23 hours after leaving the summit we were safely standing on the Younghusband Glacier.

We took only two climbing ropes plus two static ropes that we used occasionally for moving gear. We took a hand drill and placed eight to ten bolts, nearly all at bivouac sites. Apart from these, and inadvertently dropped ice gear, nothing was left on the mountain. We named our route Think Twice (3,400m of climbing, ED 6a A2 M6). [o]

DMITRY GOLOVCHENKO, *Russia, supplied by Anna Piunova, mountain.ru*

Broad Peak (8,047m), first winter ascent and tragedy. Led by veteran Himalayan winter mountaineer Krzysztof Wielicki, a small Polish expedition arrived at Broad Peak base camp on January 23 and began establishing camps on the normal route.

At 5:15 a.m. (dawn) on March 5, Maciej Berbeka, Adam Bielecki (who one year previously made the first winter ascent of Gasherbrum I, see *AAJ 2012*), Tomasz Kowalski, and Artur Małek left Camp 4 at 7,400m for a summit attempt. This departure time was based on three things: good conditions and a good weather forecast for the coming days; the traditional "rule" of not setting out at night on high mountains in winter; and the fact that the climbers had reached camp quite late, having climbed directly from Camp 2 (6,300m), and therefore needed adequate rest. Above 7,700m there were three crevasses, and the most difficult was secured with a fixed rope.

Berbeka and Bielecki swapped leads to the ca 7,900m pass between Broad Peak Central and Broad Peak Foresummit (Rocky Summit, 8,028m), arriving at around 12:30 p.m. From here they roped as two teams, Bielecki and Malek in front, followed by the highly experienced Berbeka, 58, an IFMGA guide, with the much younger (27) Kowalski. In summer it is normally only a few hours from the pass to the summit. However, the climbers found unexpected technical difficulties, not present in summer, on route to the Foresummit, which they reached at around 4 p.m.

All decided to continue, moving separately. Bielecki reached the main summit at 5:20 p.m., Malek at 5:50 p.m., and the remaining two at 6 p.m. Each member started to descend immediately. At this altitude in winter, waiting for others

[This page] Adam Bielecki on the main summit of Broad Peak, with K2 visible behind. *Adam Bielecki*

simply brings on rapid general physical deterioration and hypothermia, making it more risky for the entire team.

None of the climbers had reported any signs of weakness or difficulty during the ascent. They could have upheld the "let's stick together rule" and abandoned their attempt, but conditions and the forecast were exceptionally favorable: nighttime temperatures between –29° and –35°C, almost no wind, no clouds and therefore perfect visibility. Under these circumstances chances of success were deemed very high.

Unfortunately, once they left the summit Kowalski suddenly deteriorated and had difficulty descending. It took him 12 hours to reach the pass (normally around an hour in summer), where it is surmised he remained. Berbeka did not descend with Kowalski, who made radio contact on a couple of occasions and reported seeing Berbeka once or twice lower down the mountain. Bielecki returned to Camp 4 at 10:10 p.m.; Malek arrived at 2 a.m. on the 6th. In the early hours of that day Berbecki was spotted at 7,700m, though during the descent he never made radio contact.

Bielecki and Malek had technical problems with their radios and were unable to use them, but on separate occasions both tried to reascend to look for their team members (Bielecki during the night, and Malek the following morning). After just a few steps they realized they were too exhausted.

On the 6th, the experienced Pakistani mountaineer Karim Hayat set out from Camp 2. He reached the crevasses at 7,700m, but despite good visibility saw no sign of Berbeka and Kowalski. With still no sign on the 7th, Wielicki reluctantly had to accept that, having now spent two nights out with no bivouac equipment, the two climbers had no further chance of survival.

This was the seventh attempt to climb the mountain in winter. The first of these stands out as one of the most remarkable in the history of winter Himalayan climbing. In 1987–88, the great Polish expedition leader Andrezj Zawada took a team to Pakistan to attempt K2. Zawada's concept was well ahead of its time; the first 8,000m peak in Pakistan was not summited in winter until 2011.

By the end of February 1988 the Poles had failed to get higher than 7,000m on K2 but were well acclimatized. Maciej Berbeka and Aleksander Lwow, two of the strongest mountaineers of their day, were given permission to make a light and fast attempt on neighboring Broad Peak. Lwow gave up high on the mountain, leaving Berbeka to continue alone. He reached the "summit" in strong winds and gathering gloom, and during the descent bivouacked in a snow hole in the vicinity of the 7,900m pass, before reaching the top camp at 7,300m next day. Later, Berbeka realized he had made a mistake, having stopped on the Foresummit, only ca 400m distant from the main top.

Berbeka came to global prominence in 1981, when he made a new route on the south face of Annapurna, climbing direct to the Central Summit. In January 1984 he made the first winter ascent

[This page] Maciej Berbeka below Camp 2. *Adam Bielecki*

of Manaslu, only the second 8,000m peak to be climbed during the calendar winter season. One year later, on another major Zawada expedition, he made the first winter ascent of Cho Oyu via a new route on the southeast pillar. Berbeka's ascent of Broad Peak made him only the fourth person to achieve first winter ascents of three 8,000m peaks, and out of the world's 14 8,000ers, only K2 and Nanga Parbat have not now received a winter ascent.

LINDSAY GRIFFIN, *Mountain INFO, from information provided through Artur Hajzer, Adam Bielecki, Artur Malek, and Krzysztof Wielicki*

Gasherbrum V (7,147m), south ridge, attempt. Aymeric Clouet, Christian Trommsdorf, and Patrick Wagnon hoped to attempt the west face of Gasherbrum IV (7,925m), but once established at base camp it was obvious that the big faces, particularly the west face—the so-called Shining Wall— were far too heavily laden with new snow. Instead the three opted for Gasherbrum V, which has no recorded ascent.

A small weather window allowed Clouet, Trommsdorff, and Wagnon to make an attempt on the south ridge of the main summit, approaching up the Gasherbrum South Glacier to the east. The three reached a bivouac at ca 6,500m, below the steep rocky upper section of the south ridge. Here, they decided snow conditions and an approaching unstable air mass made it too dangerous to continue. During the descent, which they began in the evening to minimize risk, an avalanche struck the team and Wagnon was injured. They managed to rappel to the glacier, cross to the east side, and descend to a safe campsite at 5,300m. It took another two days to regain base camp, with Wagnon at first crawling on all fours using kneepads made by cutting up sleeping mats. Eventually he was evacuated by mule to Askole. 🗎 🖾

LINDSAY GRIFFIN, *Mountain INFO, from information supplied by Christian Trommsdorff and Patrick Wagnon, France*

MASHERBRUM RANGE

Note on Ihakora identity. Many maps show Ihakora (6,172m) as a peak north of the Gondokhoro La, above the West Vigne Glacier. However, the real Ihakora is likely a peak at the northeast apex of the Gondokhoro Glacier north branch (north of Vigne Pass), climbed in 1955 by the Harvard Karakoram Expedition. On modern maps this mountain would appear to be unnamed Peak 6,170m, at the apex of the North Gondokhoro and West Vigne Glaciers. 🗎 🖾

LINDSAY GRIFFIN, *Mountain INFO, from information provided by Carlos Penalva*

CHARAKUSA VALLEY

Link Sar (7,041m), northwest face attempt. Will Sim and I (U.K.) chose the Charakusa Valley for our first expedition to the Greater Ranges because the objectives suited our climbing style—technical alpine—and base camp would be reasonably dry and warm, to keep the psyche high. There are plenty of accessible ca 6,000m peaks, all manageable in a day. If we didn't get a crack at anything big, we'd still get quite a lot done.

We warmed up with the British Route on Naisa Brakk, the northwest ridge of Sulu Peak

(camping on the summit to aid acclimatization and then downclimbing the large central couloir on the west-northwest face), and finally the Diaper Couloir on Beatrice. Toward the end of our stay we climbed Fathi Brakk from the south.

Link Sar, southeast of K7, has not been climbed. The northwestern side is heavily guarded by threatened approaches (seracs) and complex glaciers. Narrow approach valleys result in it being difficult to scope the routes, adding to the adventure. We attempted it by the northwest face, but found unconsolidated snow in dangerous amounts. There is a stunning rock line to the top from the south, but it is threatened by a serac part way up. There are two prominent summits: After plenty of research, I am still unsure which is the higher. [*Editor's note: Griffith has written a fine summary of climbing in the Charakusa Valley's three main areas, which can be read in full in the online version of this report.*] 📄 📷 🔍

JON GRIFFITH, France

K7 (6,934m), east face. Kyle Dempster, Hayden Kennedy (both USA), and Urban Novak (Slovenia) climbed the east face in a ca 50-hour round trip from the top of the approach couloir. They had attempted the line in 2011. They climbed through the night, passing their previous high point, and the following night bivouacked on a small ledge. Next day difficult mixed terrain and waist-deep unconsolidated snow led to the summit. There were six pitches of WI5, and a number of M6 on perfect granite. They took no tent, knowing they were unlikely to be able to pitch it, and shared two sleeping bags and one foam pad. The three rappelled the route. A full account of this ascent, which was only the fourth overall of the mountain, appears earlier in the *AAJ*.

LINDSAY GRIFFIN, MountainINFO

Charakusa Valley, various ascents. Shingo Ohkawa and I arrived in the Charakusa Valley in early July. Our main goal was to establish new rock routes, and by Shingo's direct quote, "pick the low hanging fruit." We were successful in establishing a few new routes and accidentally freeing an old aid line.

We began with the almost obligatory ascent of the British route on Naisa Brakk (5,200m), perfect acclimatization for other climbs in the area. While standing on top, we noticed a spire with an obvious dihedral splitting the face below the summit. On August 9, after three hours of ascending heinous talus fields, Shingo, fellow American Erin Wilson, and I started up the spire. The

[This page] The Second Pillar of K7 West with the line Pilastro dei Bimbi, climbed free in 2012 by Americans. To the right is the giant southwest pillar of K7 West, the scene of many unsuccessful attempts. *Jesse Mease*

[This page] Shingo Ohkawa reaching the summit of Naisa Brakk. Behind and in right center is the new route Right On Dude!, following the very obvious corner on the sunlit face of the unnamed spire. *Jesse Mease*

climbing was delicate, and the rock somewhat loose, but fun and exciting. On the ca 5,600m top we found two bolts, so were unable to name the peak after Ali, our awesome cook, as we'd hoped. However, we called the new route Right On Dude! (355m, seven pitches, 5.10+ R). We rappelled the backside of the pillar, adding two bolt anchors.

The next few weeks were littered with rain and short weather windows. On two occasions we made the one-hour walk from base camp to the relatively small Iqbal Wall, where we climbed two lines, possibly new.

Our last effort was the striking Second Pillar (4,950m) at the base of K7 West. We had only one day of good weather to make the attempt. We climbed unroped for ca 450m and bivouacked in the rain on a monster ledge. When we awoke next morning it was clear. We racked up and began climbing as soon as the sun kissed the stone, moving upward on what we hoped was unclimbed terrain. However, we soon passed old Italian iron, which spoiled our plans of a first ascent. We reached the summit at dusk.

Months later we discovered an Italian team had climbed the route in 1998, naming it Pilastro dei Bimbi (600m, 17 pitches, UIAA VII+ A3). We managed to climb the entire route free and onsight, proposing a grade of 5.11 (though much of the climbing was fun 5.10).

JESSE MEASE, *AAC*

NANGMA VALLEY

Zang Brakk (ca 4,800m), southwest face, variant. In July Raul Gonzalez and Mikel Urabain Saez spent 22 days in the Nangma Valley climbing a route on Zang Brakk. Unclear about the location of existing routes on the left side of the south face, they started just to the left of Ali Baba. On their first attempt, they climbed 13 pitches, and on the second they reached the summit. They called their variant Altenative emo Insugente (700m, 7a A1), but it is unclear how much of this was new. 🗎

LINDSAY GRIFFIN, *Mountain INFO, from information supplied by Mikel Urabain Saez, Spain*

TAGAS GROUP

Khane Valley, Levski (5,733m, GPS), west face; Grey Tower (5,435m), east ridge. In September 2011, Doychin Boyanov, Mihail Mihaylov, and I explored the Khane Valley immediately south of Nangma Valley [*AAJ 2012*]. In August 2012 we three, together with Tervel Kerelov, returned. We reached base camp (Boulder Camp) on the First Terrace at 4,080m on the 7th. From here Kerelov decided to attempt Peak 23, solo, while the remaining members of the expedition chose Levski Peak. This summit, difficult on all sides, is situated on the main ridge dividing the Khane and Nangma valleys, and is immediately southeast of the well-known Shingu Charpa (5,910m). In two days, August 13-14, we climbed the 650m west face at 6a M6 AI4, completing the route in 14 50m pitches with a bivouac high on wall. We reached the summit via mixed terrain, then snow, at 10 a.m., and then made 10 rappels to the base, returning to our high camp at 5,050m in late afternoon.

On the 17th we explored access to the Grey Tower, which lies on the south side of the valley, above a col (Bulgarian Saddle, 5,107m) south of Meligo Peak. Access to the col, a 300m couloir that is seriously exposed to stonefall, had to be completed before 8 a.m. On the 19th Boyanov and I climbed for five hours to reach the Saddle. We pitched a tent and rested there until 2:30 p.m., after which we inspected the first 300m of Grey Tower's east face. Next day, in perfect weather, we started climbing at 6 a.m., and reached the summit after 13 pitches between 5 and 6b (predominately 5b/c). While only nuts and cams were used for protection, each belay was equipped with two pitons, which provided anchors for the rappel descent (11 rappels and 80m of downclimbing). We stayed in the camp overnight, so that we could descend the dangerous couloir very early next morning. During this descent we abandoned 200m of rope.

There are altitude corrections to the photographs that appear in the *AAJ 2012* report. Meligo is ca 5,750m, and we felt this peak would be better attempted from the next valley south via easier slopes. Grey Tower is 5,435m GPS. In the picture on page 277, the route of ascent is the left skyline. The col between Grey Tower and Meligo is the Bulgarian Saddle. Sofia is ca 5,720m, Rila ca 5,800m, Tangra Tower ca 5,820m, Agil ca 5,880m, and Hidden Tower ca 6,030m. 📷

NIKOLAY PETKOV, *Bulgaria*

Khane Valley, Peak 25, attempt. Anna Pfaff and Camilo Lopez attempted the west face of Peak 25 from a high camp at the so-called Bulgarian base camp (4,650m). The two climbed a 60-65°snow/ice couloir and mixed terrain to a headwall, followed by ca 500m of runout slabs (5.8 to 5.11). They turned back in the face of blank, poorly protected rock, estimating they were ca 200m below the top. They also attempted Peak 46, north of the entrance to the valley, but retreated in rain. 🗎

From information in the blog of ANNA PFAFF, *USA*

INDIA

EAST KARAKORAM

Rimo III (7,233m), southwest face, attempt; Dunglung Kangri (6,365m). Our Indo-British expedition comprised Satyabrata Dam (Indian leader) and me (British leader), Paul Figg, Simon Yearsley (both U.K.), Dan Singh Harkotiya, Tashi Phunchok, and Konchuk Thinless (India), the British artist Rachel Antill, and liaison officer Raj Kumar.

Satya Dam is a renowned explorer, mountaineer, influential ex-military commander, past leader of an Indian Everest expedition, and was liaison officer on our Vasuki Parbat expedition in 2010. His prestige, and the large number of trouble-free trips to India made by the British members over the last 20 years, were no doubt instrumental in our gaining permission to visit the Rimo peaks. The army at Siachen Glacier base proved very helpful, and two soldiers accompanied us throughout (at army expense), in addition to our military LO.

We approached from the west via the North Terong Glacier. Crossing the Terong River was made possible by a Tyrolean fixed by the joint Indian Army–IMF expedition attempting

Rimo I (7,385m), which was ahead of us. Unfortunately, we had snowfall on 15 of the 26 days spent at or above base camp (4,950m), and never experienced temperatures less than -7°C.

After exploring a route up the horribly boulder-strewn glacier and icefall to reach the basin beneath the southwest face of Rimo III, we acclimatized by climbing to 6,400m in the couloir between Rimo III and II. Then, from a high camp at 5,775m below the southwest face, we climbed through the night up a couloir left of the elegant central buttress of Rimo III, reaching a high point of ca 6,200m before descending the following morning in a snowstorm that turned to rain below 6,000m. After more days of snowfall, and realizing the face would not clear, we decided to attempt an attractive unclimbed peak at the end of a ridge southwest of the Rimo group, west of previously climbed peaks Sondhi and Sundbrar.

On September 13 we scrambled 500m to a bivouac on a rocky spur at 5,600m. It snowed overnight, but we left at 6:30 the

[This page] Southwest face of Rimo III. *Watercolor by Rachel Antill*

following morning, climbing a south-to-north rising line across two icefields (hard, brittle ice) and two, loose snow covered rock spurs to a final icefield, which we climbed direct to a gendarmed ridge at the top of the southwest face (ca 6,000m). We followed the attractive crest east to reach a ca 6,180m col between the forepeak and summit pyramid, then moved together with intermediate ice screw protection before climbing three harder pitches to the summit. Winds were gusting 40-50mph, and in a whiteout it all felt very Scottish. The ascent was 700m from the bivouac, 1,200m from the glacier, AI3. Our altimeter recorded 6,365m, and we named the peak Dunglung Kangri, which in local Ladakhi means "sharp, windy mountain." The expedition was grant-aided by the Mt. Everest Foundation, British Mountaineering Council, Alpine Club, and Polartec.

Using traditional siege tactics, the Indian Army–IMF expedition climbed high on the original 1988 Japanese route up Rimo I, but missed the summit due to bad weather. 📷

MALCOLM BASS, *Alpine Club, U.K.*

Rongdo (Rongdu) Valley, first ascents. We were a modest group of four climbers: Dr. Jeff Dolinsky, his wife, Joan, and me, all from Canada, along with Andy Selters (USA). We were accompanied by climbers Kunzang Sherpa (sirdar) and Arvind Raman (LO), two climbing staff, Nangang Bhote and Danuru Sherpa (Dawa), and three cooks/support staff. Our objectives were at the head of a beautiful and remote valley called Rongdo in the Nubra area of Ladakh. It is situated between the east and west arms of the Shyok River, and north of the Indus. In 1909 Tom Longstaff traveled close to what is today Rongdo village (3,000m) while exploring the Siachen Glacier and Saltoro areas. It gave me quite a thrill to look west across the lovely, wide, meandering Shyok, and imagine Longstaff moving slowly up the opposite bank on his way north—to be so close to his footsteps!

Rongdo valley has seen virtually no tourism, save one Indo-American mountaineering expedition in 2005. This team descended the valley in two days from the Satti area to the north

[This page] Rimo Group from the North Terong Glacier. (A) Saigat (6,130m). (B) Rimo III (7,233m). (C) Rimo II (7,373m). (D) Rimo I (7,385m). (E) Dunglung Kangri (6,365m). The first-ascent route up Dunglung Kangri's southwest side is shown. *Simon Yearsley*

[*AAJ 2006*]. I initially called the four main peaks at the head of the valley Rongdo I to IV (all just over 6,000m), but we have since applied local names consistent with Tibetan culture, which forms the foundation of Ladakhi society. These names have been registered with the Indian Mountaineering Foundation.

On August 5 we headed northeast up Rongdo Valley from the village, following the south side of the river. We finally established base camp on the 10th at 4,802m, and advanced base at 5,181m on the 14th. This latter camp lay just below our main climbing objective, Ngapo Kangri ("blue sheep" in Ladakhi) or Rongdo I (6,350m). This was a glorious, grass-covered camp, suitable for casual football and Frisbee.

On the 18th, after several reconnaissance trips, eight members of the team climbed the west sub-summit (6,000m) of Balden Lhamo (named after a female goddess) or Rongdo III. They reached the col between Rongdo III and IV, then continued up the southwest ridge, returning to camp in a 10-hour round-trip. On the 22nd, six climbers ascended Chamba (the future Buddha, 6,170m) or Rongdo II via the southeast glacier (10 hours round-trip). On the 23rd, Nangang and I climbed the upper west rock ridge of Ngapo Kangri to about 60m below the corniced summit (12 hours round-trip). At the same time Andy and Arvind were ascending the same peak via its south-facing slopes, first on talus and rock ledges, then up the avalanche-prone southeast aspect to easier-angled slopes, from which they finally gained the summit (14 hours round-trip).

On the 27th, Arvind, Dawa, Kunzang, and I headed up the main glacier to attempt the true summit of Balden Lhamo (6,120m). We placed a high camp at 5,690m. After an early departure next morning, we got to the col at 6,060m above the icy headwall but retreated in the face of poor weather and more technical ice than we were prepared to climb.

On the 29th, Andy and Nangang left a high camp at 5,181m, several kilometers northeast of our advanced base, to climb Gazgazri (Ladakhi for the lammergeyer vulture, 6,160m). They ascended the southwest ridge, then traversed onto the icy south face. Several short pitches, the last being 70° hard ice, led to the summit dome, and thence the highest point. They returned to base camp after a 14-hour day.

After a memorable last night at base camp, singing freely together around a huge dung fire, our well-harmonized group began the descent of the enchanting Rongdo Valley, taking two days to reach the village. During this time we were once again astounded by solid-looking rock walls several hundred meters high on both sides of the valley—a rock climbers' paradise. 📷

JOIE SEAGRAM, *Canada*

[This page] Looking east-southeast into the cirque at the head of the Rongdo Valley. The snow-covered mountain in center is Rongdo III; the rocky summit on the right of the picture is Rongdo IV. Rongdos I and II are off picture left. *Joie Seagram*

HIMACHAL PRADESH

Pangi Region, Shiva (6,142m), northeast ridge, The Prow of Shiva. Andrey Muryshev, who attempted the difficult northwest ridge of Shiva in 2010, was one of very few people to have seen in detail the new route Paul Ramsden and I hoped to try, and had been extremely helpful with information and photographs. In his e-mail, which arrived the month before we were due to leave, he didn't rate our chances too highly. "Frankly, I cannot imagine how you will do it. Do you mean the northeast buttress? It is ca 700m of climbing above the col and it is October—all the rock will be frozen. On the other hand, the ice will be scarce, as the buttress is very steep. So it will be very hard dry tooling and very hard protection. I saw your route on Siguniang. It is much easier. Still, your idea inspires me."

Paul and I took the view that being inspired was good. It looked a great line, and we had to give it a go. And maybe it would turn out more amenable than it looked in Andrey's photos.

And so by early October we had flown to Delhi, driven for two days to the road head at Saichu, walked for one day with horses, and then, with the help of a few hastily mustered porters, ferried our equipment up to a base camp at 3,900m in the Tarundi Valley. Above and to the west, the Prow of Shiva, as we christened it, looked challenging. But it also looked safe from objective danger, and through binoculars it appeared that the area's predominately loose, shaley rock gave way to granite as the Prow started to steepen.

Acclimatization consisted of four nights out from base camp, checking out the approach to the Prow and sucking in as much thin air as possible. A peak at ca 5,500m on the ridge stretching north from the Prow gave a fine climb and a wonderful point for viewing our intended route.

We began our attempt by taking two days to get through the complex glacier terrain leading to the foot of the east flank of the ridge. The next section, gaining the crest of the ridge at the start

[This page] Shiva from the peaks of the Miyar Valley to the east. The Prow of Shiva is marked. Point ca 5,500m, climbed during acclimatization, is the small, pointed top just right of the prow. Fowler and Ramsden descended the left skyline ridge to the snowy saddle, then worked back right through the icefalls and rock bands to reach a col at the base of the prominent spur more or less in the center of the picture. *Andrey Muryshev*

of the meat of the route, caught the morning sun. We climbed it during the night, reaching a great "chop the top off the ridge" bivouac spot at 9 a.m. the following morning. Challenging snow and ridge climbing led to what looked to be an impasse. The crest of the buttress was indeed granite, but the hoped-for ice on the smooth slabs of the north side was, at this point, too thin and intermittent for us to climb. The crest was very sharp, and dismissing the northerly slabs left only one other possibility: aiding an overhanging crack on the east side and hoping that the fault line, which eventually crossed to the north side, would continue in a climbable fashion. Fortunately it did.

After a fine bivouac on an undercut rock balcony, with several hundred meters of space beneath our feet, the climbing continued up off-vertical, ice-choked cracks, fortunately with good protection every now and then. Paul enjoyed a memorable ice axe belay, and I recall a particularly memorable lead, struggling up a blank overhanging groove to gain a steep, wide, snow-choked crack. The climbing ranged from numerous pitches up icy cracks in Chamonix-style granite to long, protectionless leads on thinly iced slabs reminiscent of winter climbing on Ben Nevis.

On our sixth day out from base, mixed climbing up steep grooves and exciting detached flakes led us to below the final area of vertical rock. A ledge system leading right, around the crest, gave us hope of sidestepping this obstacle and reaching the summit that night, but an unexpected impassable gap and afternoon bad weather saw us bivouacking again. The only way out was an ice-choked chimney splitting the headwall. My lead was not the most elegant, but by 10 a.m. on day seven we reached a final snow ridge and broke through a cornice to reach the summit. The panoramic view south was glorious. It had been a brilliant climb, and a short hug was felt to be appropriate.

After a bivouac not far below the top, we descended the upper part of the south ridge. Our plan had been to go down an unclimbed spur marking the south end of the east face. The other two members of our team, Steve Burns and Ian Cartwright, had attempted to climb this, but were turned back in the face of poor snow conditions. From its top we too felt conditions didn't look good

[This page] About halfway up the Prow, Mick Fowler heads up the first pitch on day six above base camp. *Paul Ramsden*

and so (with much peering at images of the east flank stored on our digital cameras) we continued further down the south ridge to a snowy saddle more or less marking its lowest point. From there we descended hard left, though icefalls and rock steps on the southeast flank, to reach the lowest snowy saddle on the east spur that we had originally planned to descend. We crossed this, picked up Steve and Ian's tracks, and followed them down to base camp, arriving at lunchtime on day nine. 🔲

MICK FOWLER, *Alpine Club, U.K.*

Editor's note: Although the first ascent of Shiva has been widely reported as taking place in 1988, correspondence with Tsunemichi Ikeda of the Japanese Alpine News *reveals that the mountain was first climbed in 1973 by an expedition from Rikkyo University Alpine Club, led by Shigeru Suzuki. This team climbed the south ridge. The second ascent took place in 1975, when a Toyohashi Alpine Club expedition, led by Hiroaki Kaneda, climbed the southwest face and south ridge. Two other parties, Japanese and Indian, have repeated this line.*

Pangi Region, Shakkar Peak (5,500m), northwest face and east ridge. Ian Cartwright and I made a one-day approach from Shiva basecamp at 3,850m in the Tarundi Valley into the high subsidiary valley to the east. Our goal, the pyramidal peak at the head of this valley, while not particularly high, is the highest in the group east of the Tarundi. The peak had a big feel to it and offered great views.

Leaving the tent around 5:30 a.m., we made an easy climb onto the glacier and followed it up to the northwest face. There was no problem crossing the bergschrund, and the first half of the face was reasonable snow-ice at 45°. Above, it steepened and we used rocks on the left to belay two pitches. The upper section was 50-55°. Here, the snow deteriorated to deep powder, and we moved together as there were no worthwhile belays, plowing a precarious path to the east ridge 100m short of the summit.

On the crest above, we managed to bypass a 60° step of completely unconsolidated snow by following a sort of trough on the south flank, which featured some rock and ice. The final 50m to

[This page] Shakkar Peak (5,500m) from the east ridge of Shiva, showing (1) the route of ascent, and (2) descent. *Steve Burns*

the summit were reasonable, and we reached the highest point at around 10 a.m. Our climb had been ca 500m and AD under the conditions. Our altimeter read 5,500m on top. We named the mountain Shakkar Peak, as a tribute to all the sugary snow. 📷

STEVE BURNS, *Alpine Club, U.K.*

HIMACHAL PRADESH

MIYAR VALLEY

Forgotten Peak (5,889m), southeast face, Never Ending Story. In mid-August, Phil Varley (U.K.), Marek Zoladek, and I (both Polish) arrived in the Miyar Valley, and after a period of bad weather established an advanced base at 4,850m on the Chhudong Glacier. This was the site of the high camp that Marek and I used during our 2006 expedition, in which we made the first ascent of Masala Peak (5,650m, *AAJ 2007*). On August 20 we left early and made the 10km hike toward the glacier head. Our goal was the first ascent of a peak Marek and I had tried in 2006. At first the glacier was dry ice, but in the last three kilometers it turned to soft snow, knee-deep in places.

Starting at 6 a.m., we crossed an icefield and reached the bottom of a couloir, which we simul-climbed, finding an old peg from our previous attempt. After 200m, with interesting icefall sections more than 70° at their steepest, we moved left onto the slabby, granite southeast face. Low down we negotiated the crux pitch, which had couple of runout moves of British VS (5.7). Eight full-length pitches took us to a rocky couloir, which we followed to the summit.

We started a rappel descent at around 4:30 p.m., and a little later were hit by strong winds and heavy snowfall. We headed left (facing out) toward the couloir. Unfortunately, this involved

[This page] Upper Chhudong Glacier from slopes of Forgotten Peak. (A) Veneto Peak. (B) Thunder Peak. (C) Three Peaks Mountain (a.k.a. Mahindra). (D) Tawa I. (E) Tawa II. (F) Citta di Frascati Peak. (G) Tawa V. *Michal Apollo*

negotiating sections of loose rock, and while pulling the wet ropes Marek was hit on the temple by a fist-sized rock. Although this at first looked serious, he continued to lead all the rappels. Once in the couloir we came across the old pegs Marek and I had used to bail six years previously, when we were hit by bad weather. By 6:30 a.m. we had dragged ourselves back to camp. We named our summit Forgotten Peak and our ca 500m route Never Ending Story (UIAA V+ WI4). ▣

MICHAL APOLLO, *Pedagogical University in Krakow, Poland*

Toro Peak, south face, Get Up in the Morning; David's 62 Nose (ca 4,850m), southwest face, D'yer Mak'er. In 2009, Pawel Fidryk and I visited the Miyar, where we made three ascents. We first climbed an obvious crack system on the left side of Toro peak's south face. Completed on August 21, this gave 300m of amenable UIAA V, followed by 300m of walking/scrambling to the summit. We named the route Get Up in the Morning.

In continuing good weather we climbed another new line, this time on the west side of David's 62 Nose. We found rappel anchors (nuts and slings) on the initial cracks, but nothing above. We called our 350m climb (nine pitches) D'yer Mak'er, and found difficulties of UIAA VII in the upper section. *[Editor's note: This route takes a parallel line right of Lufoo Lam (350m, UIAA VII+, Grmovsek-Grmovsek, 2007), cuts through Shim Nak (13 pitches, 6b, Arpin-Delege-Iannilli-Perri, 2004), and finishes up an excellent crack system right of the latter.]* We rappelled the face south of our route, and then back down the initial cracks.

On the 27th we repeated Long Life Ridge (1,000m, 5.9) on Tamadonog (ca 5,300m). After this the weather turned bad, with 30cm of snow at our 4,800m advanced base.

KRZYSZTOF BANASIK, *Poland*

[This page] The view from Get Up in the Morning on Toro Peak's south face. Below is the lower Chhudong Valley, and to the right a part of the steep northwest face of Castle Peak. In the background lies the unclimbed Chhudong Matterhorn. *Adam Rys*

Chhudong Valley, new routes and second ascents. Iza Czaplicka, Ilona Gaweda, Bartlomiej Klimas, Joanna Klimas, my husband Adam Rys, and I, all from Poland, spent from August 15–September 1 in the Miyar. There were few days without rain, which meant that while short routes were manageable, longer adventures were not.

Some of us acclimatized with the second ascent of the 2009 Polish route Get Up in the Morning on Toro Peak, while others repeated Clandestine (250m, Cacioppo-Giuliani-Iannilli, 2008) on the lower slabs of the southwest face of David's 62 Nose. We then moved to the Chhudong Valley. Here, on August 20, my husband and I climbed a new route on Gou Gou Peak (ca 5,100m), on the east-facing slabs left of Gou Gou Ridge. This was mostly slab climbing at UIAA V, but with a VI+ dihedral at the top. The rock was very good, and we named it Happy Couple on Holidays (750m). On the same day our four friends put up two adjacent routes on the northeast face of Nazomi Peak (ca 5,150m), well to the right of the 2008 Australian route. These were Scary River Dream (300m of climbing, V+) and Stradomska 27 (300m of climbing, V+, further right but with the same finish).

In 2011, Peschel and Schaar climbed a southerly foresummit to Chhudong Matterhorn, which they named Gutzele Peak (ca 5,250m, *AAJ 2012*). My husband and I repeated their route, with variants, up the south rib (500m, 5.9R), recording an altimeter height of 5,400m at the foresummit. However, we were disappointed by the rock quality, and it didn't look any better on the continuation to the Matterhorn. When it started to hail, we retreated.

Various members of our team also climbed new ground on the ca 800m southeast face of Dome Peak (5,650m) and on the northwest face of David's 62 Nose.

[**This page**] The current state of the south face of Toro Peak. (1) West flank (2004, scramble). (2) Get Up in the morning (Polish, 2009). (3) Lopez-Pfaff (2008). (4) Indian (2012). (5) American (2008). (6) Russian (2008). (7) Indian (2012). (8) East Ridge (300m, UIAA V+, Slovenian, 2007). Not marked is the 2011 Peschel-Schaar route, which climbs the prominent black streaks right of 3, then continues left of and then right of the 2008 American route (5). JAMES peak to right. *Samiran Kolhe*

There is still much potential for new routes and virgin peaks in the Miyar, though in parts the rock is bad. We concluded that east and south faces in the Chhudong Valley were best. ▤ ▣

MAGDA DROZD-RYS, *Poland*

Toro Peak (4,970m, 2008 GPS reading), partial new routes on south face and southeast ridge; retrobolting. Three Indian climbers completed a partial new route up the south face of Toro in July, unwittingly following the 2008 Lopez-Pfaff route (5.9) to the large basin about halfway up, and then continuing more or less straight up, to the left of the 2008 American Route (Fredell-Lampley, 5.9). Unfortunately, they placed bolts on almost every belay, using a power drill. The difficulties were estimated at 6a+.

Samiran Kolhe and Richard Khear then climbed a nine-pitch line near the southeast ridge, with maximum difficulties of 6b+ (no bolts placed). Their route begins to the right of the Russian Route (350m, 5.9, Kozlov-Savelyev, 2008), joins it at around half-height, and then follows it, with variants, to the summit. ▤

LINDSAY GRIFFIN, *Mountain INFO, from information provided by Samiran Kolhe, India*

ZANSKAR

Lenak Valley, Nga Tsoey Kangri (L13, 6,080m), first official ascent. After reading a report by Kimikazu Sakamoto on the exploration of Lenak and Giabul valleys (*AAJ 2012*), Karin Kosaka, Yusuke Morimoto, Yuki Sawada, and I as leader, all from Kyoto University Alpine Club, planned to attempt virgin peak L15 (6,070m) in the left branch of the Lenak Nala. On September 9 we established base camp at ca 4,800m, and the same day walked to the foot of L15 at ca 5,050m. From this viewpoint an ascent seemed both difficult and dangerous due to steep, unstable scree and avalanche potential. Instead, we decided to attempt L13.

After establishing two higher camps, on the 14th Morimoto and I climbed scree slopes and 30° snow to the col between the east and west summits of L13. Fifteen minutes along a broad ridge led to the east top. Back at the col we roped up and climbed three pitches to the west summit (6,080m), a rocky top on which we were disappointed to find a cairn. Back in Delhi, we were recognized as the first official ascensionists and named the peak Nga Tsoey Kangri. ▤ ▣ 🔍

HIROAKI OGIHARA, *Kyoto University AC, Japan*

Lenak Valley, L10 (6,165m), north face and east ridge, first official ascent; L11 (6,045m), attempt. Young students Yuchiro Iida, Shimpei Kubota, Kensei Mitsui, Tomoyuki Takayama, and I as leader arrived in Darcha on August 18 and then took the road that is being constructed over the Shingo La to Padam. We walked to aid acclimatization, and after eventually turning west into the Lenak Valley, took the right branch and established base camp at 5,100m. We fixed five ropes up the icy north flank of the east ridge of L10, rested on September 1, and on the 2nd left camp at 1:30 a.m. and from the top of the ropes climbed another 150m to the ridge. Broken rock and hard snow led to the summit. To our surprise this "virgin" summit sported remains of old and ragged prayer flags.

On the 4th we established a new advanced base at 5,400m below L11, which lies to the east of L10 [photo in *AAJ 2012*]. We climbed the north face to the east ridge, finding that once the sun hit the face, conditions deteriorated badly and rockfall was frequent. Once on the crest we saw that two large crevasses, which would force a long detour, barred direct access to the summit. 📄 📷

TAISUKE OHORI, *Japanese Alpine Club, supplied and translated by Tamotsu Nakamura, AAC Honorary Member*

Giabul and Namka Tokpo valleys, various ascents and G22 (6,050m) attempt. In August, with five other members of the Scottish Mountaineering Club, I visited the Namka Tokpo valley of Zanskar, not that far from the frontier with Pakistan. The attraction wasn't the potential for border conflicts, for which Scots are developing a reputation, nor was it the availability of whisky, because we'd brought our own. The draw was a report written by Kimikazu Sakamoto (*AAJ 2012*), who alerted the expeditioning world to a group of jagged mountains and not-impossible access. And the fact that a group of 70-year-olds got to the foot of these mountains gave us hope we'd have a decent chance. It was only later we realized that the average age of our group wasn't too much below that of the Japanese. But it was enough.

We reached base camp in the Namka Tokpo (4,400m, 33°02'43" N, 77°07'26" E) eight days after landing in Delhi. Sakamoto's G22 was our primary objective. We established advanced base at ca 4,900m, southwest from base camp and above Purgatory Moraine. The group then split into two teams. Geoff Cohen and Des Rubens would travel northwest and attempt Peak 6,150m (as marked on the Olizane map; between G18 and G22); Bob Hamilton, Steve Kennedy, Andy Nisbet, and I would head south to G22.

From the col south of G18, four pitches along exposed snow slopes on the south flank took Cohen and Rubens to the northwest ridge of Peak 6,150m. The rocky arête was followed to a prominent level section, after which an easier-angled snow ridge led to the top. The climb was about AD, and the peak named Mama Ri (Old Man's Peak).

[This page] Looking southwest from G26 up the Namka Tokpo. (A) Shan Ri and route of ascent on southeast ridge. (B) Unclimbed G22. (C) Mama Ri and route of ascent up northwest ridge. *Andy Nisbet*

Hamilton, Kennedy, Nisbet, and I established Camp 1 (5,400m) just below the col separating G22 and G23. On the 17th we reached the southeast ridge of G22, which was at first rocky then snowy. Arriving on a subsidiary summit (Shan Ri, or Snow Leopard Peak, 5,750m), we saw that the continuation was considerably less surmountable than anticipated. We moved back to the col, decided it was too early to return to Camp 1, and so carried on southeast along a snowy ridge, then loose rock, to the tottering summit tower of G23. Gaining its top required UIAA III rock climbing, and we didn't dare sneeze when on it. We dubbed this 5,850m peak Scottish Ri. 📋 📷

SUSAN JENSEN, *U.K.*

Temasa, Gompe, and Haptal valleys, exploration. South Zanskar is an exciting mountain area with many virgin peaks. In 2012 we did our third expedition to explore valleys in these mountains and identify unclimbed peaks.

Temasa Nala is the next valley north of the Raru, and has been used by locals to reach Udaipur via the Kang La (5,468m) and Miyar Valley, and also to go to Kilar via the Poat La (5,490m). The route over the Kang La is also used infrequently by trekkers, but it involves glacier travel and is nowhere near as popular as the route from Padam to Darcha over the Shingo La (5,045m). In 2007 my friend Satyabrata Dam trekked up the Miyar and crossed the Kang La and then the Poat La via the Tidu Glacier, publishing exciting photos of Peaks 6,294m and 5,995m [*AAJ 2008*]. These still appear to have no recorded ascent.

Gompe Tokpo is the second valley north of the Temasa and runs southwest from Padam. Though a fine panorama of the Gompe Tokpo peaks can be seen from the villages of Thonde and Karsha, I could find no evidence of them having been visited by climbing expeditions.

I planned to explore these valleys from late June to early August. The team comprised Toshihiro Katsumata (64), Mitsuhiko Okabe (71), Masaki Shibata (66), and me (72). We were accompanied by three kitchen staff, two horsemen, and 10 horses. As there are no official names for any of the peaks in Southern Zanskar, to aid identification I have labeled summits T1, T2, T3, etc., for peaks in Temasa Nala and Gompe Tokpo; H1, H2, etc., in the Haptal Tokpo; and M1, M2, etc.; in Mulung Tokpo.

We followed the Temasa Nala to the Tidu Glacier, and originally planned to penetrate the Tsewang Tokpo to see T9 (6,107m) and T7. [*Editor's note: T7, map height 6,022m, GPS 6,117m, was*

[**This page**] Unclimbed H26 (5,840m) above the Yurachku Glacier in the Haptal Tokpo valley. *Kimikazu Sakamoto*

[This page, left] Unclimbed T16 (6,431m) in Gompe Tokpo. *Kimikazu Sakamoto* [This page, right] Unclimbed T4 (6,294m, center). Behind and to the right is T6 (5,995m). *Kimikazu Sakamoto*

climbed by a British party in 2011 and named Evas's Peak.] However, the entrance was too steep and unstable for our horses, so we had to abandon the idea.

After visiting Gompe we had a little time to spare, so decided to look at the next major valley north, the Haptal Tokpo, which rises southwest from Sani Gompa on the Doda River. In the lower Haptal a canal was being built to supply water to the hydroelectric plant, and a small refuge stood on a large flat area. Our guide thought this might have been built for trekkers, to popularize the now seldom-used trekking route up the Haptal and over the Umasi La (5,342m) to Kishtwar. We were unable to visit the Chhogo Tokpo, the major southern side branch of the Haptal, as the river was too difficult to cross, even by horse.

During our travels we identified 21 significant unclimbed peaks, most of which are open to mountaineers. We hope our exploration will help climbers attempt these in the future. 🗎 📷 🔍

KIMIKAZU SAKAMOTO, *Japan*

Raru Valley, Katkar Kangri (R35, 6,148m), Muktik Skal (R26, 6,243m GPS), Lama Soo (5,947m, altimeter); Skilma Kangri (5,979m), east ridge. In August, Panos Athanasiadis, Nikos Lazanas, George Voutiropoulos, and I made a number of first ascents in the Raru Valley. In the past this has been erroneously referred to as Reru. However, everywhere the name of the village is written as Raru, and all local people confirm that Reru is incorrect. We reached the village of Raru (3,789m) by vehicle, and from then on were charged 120 rupees per night, per tent, for all days spent in the mountains. On the 17th we started walking up the Raru Valley, taking the left fork into Katkar Nala. Next day we made base camp (4,460m) at 33°10' 44.2" N, 76°59'40.9" E. *[Peaks of the Raru were photographed and identified in 2009 by the Japanese explorer Kimikazu Sakamoto. The same year a small British party also visited the Katkar and climbed two peaks from an unnamed subsidiary glacier basin to the east: Skilma Kangri, 5,979m, via the north face and west ridge, and Mt. Jules, 5,800m, via the south face. See AAJ 2010.]*

After reconnoitering R35 from the northeast, we attempted the south-southeast face on August 24 but were defeated by a steep, rotten tower above a shoulder at 6,080m. Next morning Athanasiadis and Voutiropoulos tried the east ridge. They reached a 5,700m col on the ridge via a snow gully (60° at the top), then continued up the crest (generally 50-60° but with one step of 80°) to the summit. As this is the most prominent peak in the Katkar Valley, we named it Katkar Kangri. The 700m route up the east ridge was graded D+ (UIAA III/IV 50-80°).

On August 28, Athanasiadis and I set off for R26, located on the watershed ridge between the Katkar and Nateo valleys. It took eight hours to reach a secondary glacier tongue east of the mountain, where we camped at 5,520m. Next day we climbed a couloir (45°) directly to the northeast ridge. Just before a rock barrier forming the steepest section, we found a loop of thick static rope. Unable to discover any references to this peak, we later concluded it must have been left during an unsuccessful attempt. Above, the ridge was sharp,

exposed, and the rock poor. We kept to the left flank, only regaining the crest at ca 6,150m. From there 200m of rotten rock (II/III) led to the summit (6,243m GPS, 33°10'37.5" N, 76°56'47.2" E). We have named it Mutik Skal, which means "lost pearl" in local dialect, and graded the 500m route D+ II/III 45-50°.

Meanwhile, Voutiropoulos and Lazanas had ventured up the moraine of the Skilma Kangri Glacier and camped next to a small lake (5,190m) at the foot of Mt. Jules. On the 29th they climbed the unnamed peak northeast of Skilma Kangri, naming it Lama Soo, "the monk's tooth" in local language (5,947m altimeter). The pair climbed the 500m north flank at AD (average angle 30°; 50° maximum). They descended the east ridge toward Mt. Jules, crossing two subsidiary peaks of 5,820m and 5,795m before returning to camp.

Leaving early next morning, they reached the col between Lama Soo and Skilma Kangri, and from there continued up the east ridge of Skilma Kangri (500m, D- 70° maximum), recording

[This page, top] Katkar Kangri showing line of first ascent up north flank and east ridge. (C) High camp (5,100m). (L) Katkar Lake. *Nikolaos Kroupis* [This page, bottom] Skilma Kangri showing (1) north face to west ridge (first ascent, 2009), and (2) east ridge. Lama Soo is just off picture left. *Nikolaos Kroupis*

an altimeter reading of 6,020m. They descended the route in seven rappels. This was the second ascent of the peak. 📄 📷

NIKOLAOS KROUPIS, *Greece*

Ang Tung Range, Petze Kangri (6,130m) and Lugzl Pombo (6,414m). In August, Aditi and Rajesh Gadjil, Vineeta Muni, Lt. Col. Shamsher Singh, and I visited the Ang Tung Range, northwest of Pangong Lake. The Ang Tung is a small group of peaks west of the Koh Lungpa Valley. This valley had never been visited by any mountaineering expedition.

We trekked two days up the Koh Lungpa from the village of Yurgo and established base camp at Vimgul (5,210m) on August 4. We first chose to attempt a peak of 6,130m (34°06.794'N, 78°18.665'E), and set up an advanced base at 5,675m on its southern slopes. Leaving at 7 a.m. on the 9th, we climbed the east face together with Sherpas Pemba Norbu and Nima Thondup; all the party except for Aditi reached the top at 11 a.m. We named the summit Petze Kangri, Petze meaning "baby yak" in Ladakhi dialect.

We now set up another camp at 5,850m, on ice and to the northeast of Lugzl Pombo (34°06.578'N, 78°17.897'E). On the 17th we climbed a steep ice slope to the 6,000m col between Lugzl Pombo and Petze Kangri, fixing 100m of rope. After ferrying more equipment from base camp, on the 19th we explored the northeast ridge of Lugzl Pombo, passing the first big gendarme on the left, and climbing the second (ca 6,250m). On this section we fixed 250m of rope. On the 20th we left camp at 6 a.m., fixed a further 300m, and a little before midday Rajesh, our two Sherpas, and I reached the top after climbing through a cornice onto the final north-south summit ridge. We returned to camp at 3 p.m., having recovered most of the fixed rope and gear. 📄 📷

DIVYESH MUNI, *Himalayan Club, India*

WESTERN GARHWAL

GANGOTRI

Unnamed Peak 6,565m, attempt. A joint expedition comprising members of the British and Indian armies attempted unclimbed Peak 6,565m, situated on the eastern rim of the Shyamvarn Bamak. This glacier basin flows south into the Raktavarn Bamak and has at its head the big peaks of Yogeshwar (6,678m) and 6,803m. A reconnaissance showed the most feasible route to be the north ridge, rising from a col on the rim. Above Camp 2, a route was found through the icefall as far as

[This page] Lugzl Pombo and route of ascent up northeast ridge. *Divyesh Muni*

6,050m, but then bad weather set in and further attempts were called off. 📑

LINDSAY GRIFFIN, *Mountain INFO*

CENTRAL GARHWAL

Arwa Spire (6,193m), north face, Fior di Vite, first free ascent. On September 28 Simon Gietl and I stood on the summit of the Arwa Spire. Only 10 days previously I had been walking the long exhausting path from the last villages to the foot of this mountain. It was my third time.

In 2002, as a young alpine guide, I made the first ascent of the north face of the spire with the older and more experienced Stephan Harvey and Bruno Hasler (Switzerland). Back then, as a 23-year-old, a lot of this stuff was completely new to me and everything was exciting. We fixed some rope up the prominent north couloir of the then virgin central summit, and set off with a portaledge. From the top of the couloir, we found the rock too cold and snowy to free climb in rock shoes, so aided four pitches to reach easier ground and the summit, which we felt was possibly the highest of the three. We celebrated with the Italian Grappa, Fior di Vite, which became the name of the route. The line was 800m in length and the difficulties UIAA VI+ A2 80°

In 2011 Simon and I wanted to transfer our vision of alpine-style climbing at lower altitudes to the massive rock faces of the Himalaya. Our goal was a free ascent of Fior di Vite and after training, both mentally and physically, we felt ready. We reached the area with cameraman Daniel Ahnen, but in the early stages of the expedition, Daniel and a companion were walking toward the face in order to capture pictures, when at ca 5,400m Daniel fell 50m into a crevasse. For five days, with the help of the Indian military, we tried to rescue him but were unable to make any voice

[This page] The north face of Arwa Spire. (1) East ridge (Benson-Benson, 2000). (2) Fior di Vite (Gietl-Schäli, 2012). (3) British attempt (Cool-Parnell, 2000). (4) British attempt, Powell-Wills, 2000. (5) Capisco (Harvey-Hasler-Schäli, 2002). *Frank Kretschmann (funst.de)*

or visual contact. The expedition was abandoned.

Ten years after the first ascent I was back again. The climbing proved challenging, route-finding extremely difficult, and placing solid nuts and cams often impossible. It was a cruel struggle with cold fingers and toes. We were thirsty and felt the altitude, so staying focused was a demanding task. I carried a medallion in memory of Daniel, and fixed it with a sling on the summit. Those weeks after his tragic accident were among the most difficult in my entire life. Simon and I climbed the entire route free at 7a M6 90°. None of the rock pitches on the headwall was less than 6c.

The success of this expedition took a lot of patience and the right team of friends. Apart from the ever-reliable Simon, I was accompanied by experienced climber and cameraman Frank Kretschmann, guide Andrea di Donato, and my girlfriend Yuri Kato, who gave great mental support. Q

Adapted from information supplied by ROGER SCHÄLI, *Switzerland*

Semartoli Valley, various ascents. In September, Joanna Campbell, Michael Cocker, John Kentish, Paul Padman, Michael Pinney, Stuart Worsfold, and I, all members of the Alpine Club, traveled by way of Joshimath to the Semartoli Valley. A joint Indo-British expedition had visited the area in June 2007 to celebrate the 150th Anniversary of the Alpine Club (*AAJ 2008*), and Harish Kapadia, a member of this expedition and authority on the Indian Himalaya, had suggested that it more than justified further exploration. The 2007 expedition referred to it as Kagbhusandi Valley, but locals call it Semartoli, and closer inspection of the 1:200,000 Indian Himalaya map shows quite clearly that the river in the valley that both we and the 2007 group visited is the Semartoli Nala. Kagbhusandi is the adjacent valley south of the 4,630m pass named Kankul Khal.

The Semartoli is easily reached from Govind Ghat, the starting point for trekkers to the popular Valley of Flowers and for pilgrims visiting the holy lake of Hem Kund. Within three days we had established base camp alongside the river at Raj Kharak (3,815m). We were later in the season than the 2007 expedition, and conditions differed markedly: Glaciers were dry, heavily crevassed, and littered with complex boulder-fields in their lower reaches. We eventually abandoned our primary objective, the unclimbed northwest face of Barmal (5,879m), largely because of its poor condition.

[This page] Roger Schäli high on Fior di Vite. The final snow slope on the north face of the east summit is visible left. *Archive Roger Schäli, supplied by Frank Kretschmann (funst.de)*

Unsettled post-monsoon weather plagued the expedition, but on September 25, from an advance base camp at 4,505m, Cocker, Padman, Worsfold, and I made the first ascent of the highest summit in the sub-range north of the Kankul Khal: Peak 5,301m (a.k.a. Kagbhusandi Parvat). We climbed the mixed northeast face and north ridge at PD+. Kentish and Pinney made the second ascent two days later.

From separate high camps to the east of the Kankul Khal, various members of the team subsequently made first ascents of two other peaks adjacent to Kagbhusandi Parvat. On October 1, Campbell, Padman, and Worsfold climbed Peak 5,201m by its east couloir and north ridge (PD), and on the 7th Pinney and Worsfold climbed Peak 5,120m from the Kankul Khal via a rising traverse of the west face (PD-).

Meanwhile, to the east of the Semartoli Glacier, Cocker, Kentish, Pinney, and I, assisted by two high-altitude Sherpas, established a high camp at 5,010m, then next day, October 2, made the first ascent of Peak 5,515m, located to the north of Peak 5,855m. We climbed a steep, west-facing snow couloir and

[This page, top] John Kentish on the north ridge of Peak 5,515m. The rock tower immediately behind is Peak 5,490m, climbed in 2007, while the large snow peak in the background is Hathi Parvat (6,727m). *Derek Buckle* [This page, bottom] Panorama northeast from the Semartoli Glacier. (A) Hathi Parvat (6,727m). (B) Peak 5,959m. (C) Peak 5,490m (climbed 2007). (D) Peak 5,515m (climbed 2012). (E) Danesh Parvat (5,855m). (F) Oti-ka-Danda (5,780m). *Michael Cocker*

mixed north ridge at AD.

The team is grateful to the Alpine Club Climbing Fund, Mt. Everest Foundation, and Austrian Alpine Club for support. 📷 🔍

DEREK BUCKLE, *Alpine Club, U.K.*

Editor's note: Members of the 2007 expedition climbed a peak they refer to as Danesh (Dhanesh) Parvat (5,490m). This is the rock tower immediately north of Peak 5,515m. Consensus is that the true Danesh Parvat, as marked on the Indian map, is the much larger 5,855m peak to the south. The 2012 expedition also made an unsuccessful attempt to climb Oti-ka-Danda (5,780m) via a couloir on the west face.

Kamet (7,756m), southwest face, Spicy Game. Expeditions to India can be a disaster for morale, if they experience a combination of bad conditions, bad weather, bad local services, and too spicy food. This was the case for the 2009 Groupe Militaire de Haute Montagne (GMHM) expedition to Kamet's neighboring summit, 7,242m Mukut Parvat. [*This ascent was incorrectly reported in* AAJ *2010. On October 2, 2009, six members of the GMHM, Albrieux, Bohin, Giacobi, Jourdain, Pellissier, and Poitevin reached the summit of 7,130m Mukut Parvat East from 6,400m Slingsby's Col, between Mukut Parvat and Abi Gamin/Kamet. This was the first alpine-style ascent, following the route pioneered in 1999 by the Nehru Institute of Mountaineering expedition.*] From their advanced base on the Paschimi (West) Kamet Glacier, they had a good look at the southwest face of Kamet, which they found so steep that looking up at the summit gave them a stiff neck.

For us it was completely different: The only rain or snowfall occurred on the approach. Our staff comprised a cook, a number of porters, all of whom could no doubt climb the 14 8,000ers in a short month, and an excellent sirdar. This allowed us to concentrate totally on our goal, an ascent of the southwest face of Kamet, the highest mountain for which it is possible to get a permit to climb from Indian

[This page] Southwest face of Kamet. (1) The "Indian Couloir," climbed to the west ridge by Indians in 2010 and French in 2012, is hidden but reaches the crest behind the triangular pointed snow pyramid. (2) 1985 Indo-French West Ridge. (3) Spicy Game (2012). (4) South face/ridge descended by the French in 2012, rappelling at the bottom to return to the glacier basin below the face. *GMHM*

[This page] Sébastien Moatti approaching the steep ice runnels of the first day of the ascent of Kamet's southwest face. *GMHM*

soil [*Kangchenjunga from Sikkim is banned for religious reasons, while Nanda Devi and the Nanda Devi Sanctuary remain off limits*].

We placed base camp at 5,300m on the tortuous Paschimi Kamet Glacier. Advanced base was situated on the upper glacier at 5,800m, and from here we could see that the southwest face was in excellent condition.

For further acclimatization Sébastien Bohin, Didier Jourdain, Sébastien Ratel, and I climbed on the west ridge of Mana Northwest (7,092m), spending two nights at 6,300m and reaching 6,500m on this long but objectively safe snow crest first climbed in 1995 by an Indo-Japanese team. It would be a good goal in itself for an expedition. Three days after our descent, and with the weather fair, we made our attempt on Kamet.

All four of us left advanced base at 3:30 a.m. on September 22, and only a few hours later were at grips with vertical ice pitches. We took the easiest route up the nearly 2,000m face, a succession of steep snow traverses linked by good soft-ice gullies (some requiring the leader to haul his pack). We found nowhere flat that was bigger than a magazine, and it took plenty of time and energy to create tent platforms. We took minimal equipment and free-climbed throughout. Our last bivouac was on the south face/ridge at 7,500m, and we reached the summit the following day, our fifth above advanced base, after overcoming unexpected difficulties on the final section. The top was as flat and large as a cricket pitch, but French don't play this game, so we just sat for an hour and appreciated the superb panorama over the Himalaya and Tibetan Plateau.

After another night at our top bivouac, we descended the narrow, hidden, inset south face separating our route from the 2008 line Samurai Direct (Hiraide-Taniguchi) on the southeast face. At the bottom of the south face we rappelled the icefall to the west, descending a labyrinth of stone and seracs, before reaching advanced base in the dark.

A few days later we were on the road to Delhi and the most dangerous part of our visit to India. Restaurants here are Russian roulette, and we often lost, ordering spicy food from an impossible-to-understand menu. We named the route in homage to our tongues, which were burned three times a day by all sorts of pickle. Like climbing mountains, maybe this game is also about pushing your limits. Spicy Game (ED VI/5+ 90°); summit reached September 27. 📷 🔍

SÉBASTIEN MOATTI, *France, with additional information from Didier Jourdain*

Editor's note: Lionel Albrieux, Arnaud Bayol, and Antoine Bletton, also members of the 2012 GMHM expedition, hoped to make an alpine-style ascent of the unrepeated west ridge. In 1985 Balwant Sandhu led a very strong joint Indo-French Army expedition that climbed the left side of the southwest face, overcoming difficulties of UIAA VI and 75° ice, to reach the crest of the west ridge at 6,900m. After a prolonged siege, 13 members reached the summit. It remains one of the hardest first ascents achieved by Indian mountaineers. The route was tried in 2010 by an Indian Army expedition, which accessed the ridge via a large snow couloir further left. Albrieux, Bayol, and Bletton also opted for the "Indian couloir." The trio reached the crest of the west ridge at 6,600m, but problems with their stove and concern that they were perhaps not sufficiently acclimatized prompted them to descend.

EASTERN GARHWAL

Bagini Glacier, unnamed peak, panoramic photo. Cas van den Gevel (The Netherlands) and William van Meegdenburg (Switzerland) climbed to 5,985m on an unnamed peak about 1km east-northeast of their Bagini Glacier base camp (4,510m) while acclimatizing for an attempt on the north face of Kalanka. From here they obtained a magnificent panorama photo of Kalanka, Changabang, Dunagiri, and other nearby peaks. This photograph may be viewed at the *AAJ* website. 📷

SIKKIM

Janak Himal, Dome Kang (7,264m), east-southeast ridge; Domo (7,447m), southeast ridge. Undoubtedly the most significant Himalayan expedition by Indian mountaineers during 2012 resulted in the second ascents of two 7,000m summits, by new routes, in just 12 days climbing above base camp. The venue was the remote Jongsang, a long plateau-like massif, the main summit of which forms the highest triple border point in the world (India-Nepal-Tibet).

The east-southeast ridge, rising above the Jongsang La (6,145m) on the Nepal-Sikkim border, was first attempted in 1983 by Slovenians. That same year a large Indian expedition reported climbing Jongsang, approaching through Sikkim. Details are sketchy, and their claim (to have climbed either the east-southeast ridge or else repeated the original 1930 route on the north face) is now widely discredited. Irish climbers inspected the ridge in 1997, and Spanish climbers reconnoitered it in 2002 and then made two unsuccessful attempts, in 2004 and 2006. Apart from the Indians, the only nation able to get permission to come from the north, all these

[This page] Jongsang Massif from Nepal's Jongsang Glacier. (A) ca 7,350m western top of Jongsang. The main summit and Domo are hidden behind the south peaks, well over 1km across the Jongsang Plateau. (B) Jongsang South Peak II. (C) South Peak I (7,322m). (D) Dome Kang. (1) Southeast face–central couloir to South Peak II (ca 1,000m, Spanish, 2009). (2) Central couloir to South Peak I; Touch of Silence (1,150m, Azman-Markovic, 2000). (3) East-southeast ridge (Indian, 2012). (4) Line descended by Azman after Markovic was killed near South Peak II. *Salvador Garcia-Atance*

parties approached Jongsang from Nepal.

Pradeep Sahoo led a team from Kolkata though Sikkim to the Upper Lhonak Valley, and then onto the Jongsang Glacier leading southwest to the Jongsang La. The expedition established base camp on September 17 at 5,525m (GPS), close to a large lake on the north side of the glacier.

Access to the crest of the east-southeast ridge via the east flanks of Jongsang was barred by steep rocky walls and hanging glaciers. However, two Sherpa finally located a steep gully through these walls. Above, 200m of broken rock at 40-50°, followed by a difficult 200m rock tower—the last part very steep and loose—led to an upper ice field. All this section was fixed.

On the 26th a team of six climbers moved up from Camp 1 carrying four days' food and fuel, and two tents. Over the ensuing days, climbers moved up the ridge and established three higher camps, the highest at 6,874m. On the 29th five climbers reached the 7,257m col (GPS) between Dome Kang and Jongsang, and then split. Ang Dorji, Phurba, and Sahoo set off for Jongsang to the northwest, while Dawa and Mondal headed east for nearby Dome Kang.

Dawa and Mondal left the col at 10:15 a.m., and in 35 minutes reached the top of Dome Kang. Although the official Nepal HMG–Finn map gives Dome Kang (Domekhan) as 7,264m, Mondal suggested he had ascended 30-50m from the col. If the Indian GPS measurements are to be believed, this summit could well be closer to 7,300m.

The Jongsang group followed the knife-edge southeast ridge leading toward Domo (Jongsang's southeast summit) and then on to Jongsang, but decided conditions were too dangerous at that time of day. They returned to the col, and Sahoo waited there while Ang Dorgi and Phurbu descended to Camp 4, collected a tent and several coils of rope for fixing, and then came back up. All three spent a chilly night, then left at 5:30 a.m. on the 30th. In better snow conditions, it took three hours to ascend the ridge to Domo. The only previous ascent of this rounded top had been in 1930 by Günter Dyhrenfurth and Lewa Sherpa, who made the round-trip from Jongsang's main summit in one hour. Average GPS logs on this summit (27°52.692 N, 88°08.371 E) recorded 7,461m.

The three decided not to continue across the plateau to the main summit (7,462m on Finn map) and made a quick descent of the mountain, reaching Camp 1 just after dark. All ropes appear to have been left in place.

LINDSAY GRIFFIN, *Mountain INFO, from information supplied by Pradeep Sahoo, India, and the Himalayan Club*

The Plateau, rare photographic coverage. Harish Kapadia, former editor of the *Himalayan Journal*, had made four trips to Sikkim before May 2012. One prize had escaped him: a visit to the most northerly valley in the state, adjacent to the Tibet border, and known as the Plateau. After the Kangchenjunga Massif, it contains the highest and most beautiful peaks in Sikkim, and was explored by British mountaineers in the early days of Himalayan travel. The latter were generally members of teams returning from Everest, in those days normally accessed from "British India" across the high passes of Naku La or Karpo La, just west of the Plateau. Dr. Alexander Kellas, Wilfred Noyce, Eric Shipton, and Bill Tilman all left their mark. But after the 1962 Indo-China conflict, this area became highly restricted.

The Plateau now holds military installations and is patrolled by the Indian Army. Kapadia, a civilian, was able to gain a rare permit to visit this region, and took even rarer photos of the northern sides of the great peaks. 📷 🔍

LINDSAY GRIFFIN, *Mountain INFO*

[This page] The Gurudongmar peaks from the Plateau to the north: main summit (6,715m) left, and west summit (6,630m). In 1936 Kempson and Shipton reported climbing Gurudongmar via

summit as something else entirely. The main (east) summit was climbed from the northeast in 1991 by an Indian expedition. *Harish Kapadia*

[This page, top] Pauhunri (7,125m) seen from Chholamo Lake (ca 5,000m) to the northwest. When Dr. Alexander Kellas made the first ascent in June 1910 via the obvious snow slopes (possibly behind the left skyline), Pauhunri was the highest mountain yet climbed, a record that would stand until the ascent of Jongsang in 1930. The summit to the right is 7,032m and unclimbed. Farther south of this summit (out of view) lie high tops of 6,911m, 7,037m, 6,915m, and 6,730m, all unclimbed. *Harish Kapadia*

SAHYADRI RANGE

Dhakoba (1,275m), north face, left route. In September veteran climbers from Pune organized a trip with climbers from the "new generation" to stimulate interest in big-wall climbing. The Sahyadri Range, east of Mumbai, is composed of black basalt, and offers innumerable opportunities for rock climbing. The biggest wall is the vegetated 850m north face of Dhakoba. It had only been climbed once, in December 1989, by Pune climbers via a route on the right side. We climbed a new route on the left side over four consecutive days in early January 2013. The total length of our climb was around 1,100 (21 pitches to 6b+/6c).

December and January are the best months for climbing in the Sahyadri, and as the wall faces north we were cool the whole time. Our only problem was active honeybee disturbance: This lasted two hours every morning, and during that time we simply had to cover ourselves and stay calm.

SAMIRAN KOLHE, *India*

[This page, bottom] On the first ascent of the left route on Dhakoba north face. *Samiran Kolhe*

NEPAL

DHAULAGIRI HIMAL

Churen Himal West (7,371m), southwest face to southeast ridge, attempt. The high and remote massif of Churen Himal has three summits: Churen Himal West, Central, and East. All are given the same height. In October an Italian expedition climbed the right side of the southwest face of Churen Himal West to reach the crest of the southeast ridge, then continued upward for a short distance to a small top of ca 7,000m.

The Italian team climbed the prominent spur on the face first attempted in 1983 by Gustav Harder's German expedition, and then in 1984 by an Irish expedition. The Italians fixed ropes on the spur, making Camp 2 at 5,800m. They climbed the remaining 1,200m at TD+, generally 45-70° ice, but with one pitch of UIAA IV+/V-. Marco Camandona, François Cazzanelli, and Emrik Favre reached the small top at 7,000m on October 15 and christened their climb Princess Cecile Line, after the name of Camandona's granddaughter.

After all had rested in base, Camandona, Adriano Favre, Alain Marguerettaz, and Sete Sherpa set off on October 19 to attempt to reach the main summit. There was also an audacious possibility of continuing further, over the tops of Churen Himal Central and East. That evening Favre decided to descend. Marguerettaz followed suit before dawn next morning, leaving the remaining pair to attempt the summit. At around 4 a.m. they heard cries for help, and on descending found that Marguerettaz had fallen into a crevasse and broken a femur. The team managed to rescue the stricken climber, who was evacuated by helicopter to a hospital in Kathmandu. 📄 📷

LINDSAY GRIFFIN, *Mountain INFO*

PERI HIMAL

Himjung (7,092m). Koreans Ahn Chi-young and Kim Chang-ho made the first ascent, via the southwest face, of one of the few remaining unclimbed 7,000ers in Nepal for which it is possible to obtain a permit. There is no known previous attempt. After an initial attempt thwarted by poor weather, they climbed the face up and down in two days from advanced base at 6,050m. Fourteen pitches plus some simul-climbing led to a crevasse bivouac at 6,770m. Next day they simul-climbed to the summit and downclimbed and rappelled their route. The difficulties were rated 5.10+ WI4 M6. A full account appears earlier in the *AAJ*. [*Editor's note: A splendid panorama photo of the Peri Himal range, looking generally north from Manaslu, can be found with the Himjung story at the AAJ website.*]

MANASLU HIMAL

Simnang Himal (6,251m), south-southeast face. On October 23 Sergey Bublik and Mykola (Nicolay) Shymko made the first ascent of Simnang Himal via an alpine-style climb directly up the steep and difficult south-southeast face. Simnang Himal, formerly referred to as P2, lies immediately

southeast of Manaslu across the Pungen Glacier. P1, P2, and P3 (west to east) are points on the long eastern ridge of Ngadi Chuli (Peak 29, 7,871m). The only distinct, and impressive, summit is also the highest: Simnang Himal (100m lower on Google Earth than the official HMG-Finn altitude).

None of these points had known previous attempts until spring 2001, when P2 was brought onto the permitted list mid-season. Ukrainians Mistislav Gorbenko, Vadim Leontiev, Sergei Pugachov, and Mykhaylo Zagirnyak, were part of a larger expedition that season that made the first ascent of the southeast face and east ridge of Manaslu. Their secondary goal was to climb a virgin summit and name it Peak Ukraine, to celebrate 10 years of the country's independence. They established a camp on a 5,200m col below the east ridge of P2 and made six trips to this col before being granted permission to climb. The knife-edge ridge proved too difficult, so the four gave up and climbed a lower nearby top, which officially they would later refer to as P2, and dub Peak Ukraine. Later Gorbenko went a little way up the Lidanda Valley, south of Simnang Himal. He saw an impressive face, was not sure on which peak it lay, but felt it worthy of future inspection.

In 2004 Ukrainians were back, this time in the shape of Sergey Bublik, Vitali Dobrovik, Sergey Kovalev, Alexander Lavrinenko, and Orest Verbytskiy. They approached the east ridge of true Simnang Himal from the Lidanda Glacier, and all but Dobrovik climbed the crest to a foresummit (east top), estimated to be around 6,200m, but still a long way from the main summit.

In 2007 Gorbenko and Vladimir Moglia led a small team to attempt Himalchuli from the Lidanda. They also made an alpine-style attempt on the southwest face of Simnang Himal and reached a high point of 5,950m on this difficult route, before bad weather and lack of time forced a retreat.

In 2012, Bublik and Shymko had difficulty accessing the valley. They were threatened with a ridiculous financial levy in order to progress further than the Lidanda monastery. Pretending to phone their embassy, and waving ice axes while they did so, they eventually were offered a "bargain price," though this could only be achieved by leaving accessories such as tables, chairs,

[This page] Simnang Himal (6,251m) from Lidanda Glacier to south-southeast. (1) Ukrainian 2007 attempt. (2) Redpoint (2012). (3) East Couloir (2012 descent). (4) Ukrainian 2004 attempt, as far as east top. *Mykola Shymko*

and cooking utensils at the monastery.

On October 19, after establishing an advanced base at 4,800m on the Lidanda Glacier, they set off for the south-southeast face of Simnang Himal. Bublik led the first day, taking the pair to a good campsite protected by overhangs. Shymko led the second day, on which they completed the most pitches. On the third day, during which they climbed complex rock sections with poor pro, they got a forecast for bad weather. By this time, having climbed through vertical ice and overhanging granite, they decided that the easiest escape was upward.

The weather came in that night, making the next day a struggle. They had to sacrifice their dream of a totally free climb and use aid in order to progress. That night they stopped well above 6,000m but were unable to find a space big enough to erect the tent. It was a grim bivouac, but in a few hours next morning they had reached the summit in clear weather. They then spent eight hours rappelling the east couloir, and were back at base camp that evening. The route has been named after their sponsor: Redpoint (1,250m, 6c+ A3 M6 WI6).

ANNA PIUNOVA, *mountain.ru, and* MYKOLA SHYMKO, *Ukraine*

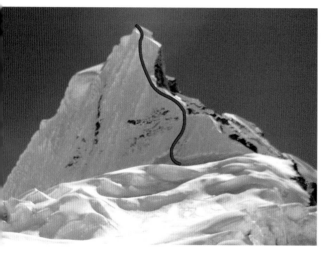

ROLWALING HIMAL

Pt. 5,766m, west face and north ridge; Langmoche Ri (6,552m), northwest ridge. In November, Tino Villanueva and I (USA) spent the month making seven first ascents in Rolwaling. Five of these were water ice and mixed climbs above the main Rolwaling and Yalung valleys. We also repeated several previously established ice climbs. Maximum difficulties were WI5 M6.

We also climbed a likely new route on the west face of Pt. 5,766m, a small peak more or less on the watershed ridge between Chugimago (6,258m) and the Yalung La (5,310m), its south ridge running gently into the broad snow slopes between Chugimago and Ramdung (5,930m).

On November 14 we shouldered eight days food and fuel and, leaving the village of Na, headed up the Drolambo Glacier to attempt the unclimbed north ridge of Tengi Ragi Tau (6,938m). It took two days to reach the ca 5,890m col below Langmoche Ri, a peak that must be traversed to access the north ridge of Tengi Ragi Tau. Next day we made the first recorded ascent of Langmoche Ri via its northwest ridge. The ca 650m route had sustained pitches of 80° X s'nice and two overhanging cornices. On the summit high winds and low temperatures prevented our continuation toward Tengi Ragi Tau. [*This expedition was supported by an AAC Mountaineering Fellowship.*] 📄 📷

ALAN ROUSSEAU, *AAC*

[This page] Northwest ridge of Langmoche Ri, seen from the vicinity of the col south of Pimu. Descent was made by rappelling the face on left. *Alan Rousseau*

Lunag Group; Peak 5,777m, Awesome Show, Great Job!; Peak 5,855m, north face couloir, second ascent; Peak 6,478m, northeast face, attempt. Chris Wright and I read about the Lunag Massif in a feature article by Joe Puryear in *AAJ 2010*. Thanks to his and David Gottlieb's photographs, we found several exciting possibilities: Our objectives would be Little Lunag (6,492m), Lunag III (6,795m), and Lunag IV (6,781m). However, as we approached our base camp in

November, it became obvious that the lines we had identified were not in condition, and were not looking to be so anytime soon. Only the high peaks and northern aspects had acceptable alpine climbing conditions. We received similar information from Chad Kellogg, who was returning from his solo attempt on Lunag I and a solo second ascent of Jobo Rinjang. After hearing Chad's account of "combat zone" rockfall on southern exposures, we turned our focus to the shaded north and northeast faces nearby: Peak 5,777m, Peak 5,855m, and Peak 6,478m.

As a warm-up and acclimatization route we headed for the north face couloir of Peak 5,777m, situated directly south of our base camp near the Lunag Glacier. The peak was climbed in 2009

[This page, top] Peak 5,777m with the line of Awesome Show, Great Job! The Americans descended east along the left skyline (scramble), and there was evidence that parties had climbed the right skyline and descended the same way as the Americans. *Geoff Unger/Chris Wright* [This page, bottom] Northeast face of Peak 6,478m. (1) French attempt in 2010, the northeast face to southeast ridge. (2) The line claimed to have been climbed by a French-Nepali-Swiss team in 2009. (3) Unger-Wright attempt. Their bivouac was at the high point. *Geoff Unger/Chris Wright*

by Schaffter's party (*AAJ 2010*) and again in 2010 by French climbers, who made a north-south traverse (*AAJ 2011*). Our chosen line followed a steep ice smear that led to much easier névé and mixed ground. We named the route Awesome Show, Great Job! (350m, WI4 M3).

As Chris struggled with a chest infection, I headed out to a neighboring peak located west of Peak 5,777m, and labeled 5,855m on the Schneider map. I'd received information from David Gottlieb that a 600m ice chimney led up the north face, and a Swiss team had completed its first ascent a few weeks prior, rating it AI4. The route was obvious when standing beneath the face, and I made the second ascent, and first free solo.

We had heard of a possible ascent of Peak 6,478m (referred to by Schaffter as Jobo LeCoultre, see *AAJ 2010*). Given this information, we decided to choose a line on the northeast face to the right of their route, climbing more directly toward the summit. Initial snow slopes gave way to 60m of WI3 before easing. Soon the face steepened significantly and the snow thinned, leaving a veneer of sugar snow over hard, old alpine ice. After moving together most of the day, we roped up for seven pitches of ice that led to a bivouac below the headwall at ca 6,150m. Unfortunately, frozen toes that did not rewarm overnight forced us to descend next morning, short of establishing a new route on the peak.

This expedition was made possible by the Copp-Dash Inspire Award. Additional thanks goes to David Gottlieb for his beta and support throughout. 📷

GEOFF UNGER, *AAC*

Editor's note: Two other expeditions climbed in the Lunag Range last autumn. Stéphane Schaffter and a Swiss team were back to attempt the southeast ridge of Jobo Rijnang (6,778m). Schaffter first attempted this line in 2009, fixing ropes to 6,000m (AAJ 2010). In 2012 his team found the terrain too stone-swept and dangerous to attempt after the dry summer/autumn. They also made an attempt on the northeast side of Peak 6,478m, but were thwarted by poor snow conditions; details of the exact line are lacking. Afterward, members of the Swiss team (Mathieu Campergue, Xavier Carrard, Jerome Gottofrey, Philippe Mailhot, and Pierre Morand) climbed the north face of what they refer to as Sengjya North (5,757m; 5,855m Schneider map). They climbed a prominent couloir left of center on November 1, naming it Et Vous Croyez les Femmes (600m, 10 pitches to the ridge, D+ 85°). This is the route that Geoff Unger repeated. He descended east from the summit, as most likely did the Swiss.

Also in the area were David Gottlieb and Chad Kellogg, who planned to attempt unclimbed

[This page] The north face of Sengjya North showing the Swiss route, Et Vous Croyez les Femmes, repeated shortly afterward, solo, by Geoff Unger. *Geoff Unger/Chris Wright*

Lunag I (6,895m). However, Gottlieb was ill and unable to take part in any climbing. Kellogg made an unsuccessful solo attempt, retreating in the face of serious objective dangers. He then made a remarkable second ascent of Jobo Rinjang via the south face, for much of the way following the same route climbed in 2009 by Gottlieb and Joe Puryear. Kellogg climbed the face in a little under eight hours, then descended to his advanced base on the glacier in a round trip of 13 hour 22 minutes.

MAHALANGUR HIMAL

KHUMBU SECTION

Kyashar (6,770m), south pillar, Nima Line. In November Tatsuya Aoki, Yasuhiro Hanatani, and Hiroyoshi Manome made the long-awaited first ascent of the south pillar of Kyashar (a.k.a. Peak 43).

After establishing base camp in the village of Tangnag (ca 4,300m, and only a couple of hundred meters below the start of the pillar), the three Japanese acclimatized with an ascent of Mera Peak, then left on November 6 for their attempt on the pillar. Following the Houseman-Stone line (see below), they climbed 17 pitches up the initial rock buttress to a bivouac at 5,200m. Although the climbing was not too difficult (5.8/5.9), they found the rock to be extremely loose. Next day they climbed three pitches through the rock band above (5.9) to reach a shoulder and the hanging

[This page] Kyashar from the Hinku Valley to the southwest. (1) West ridge (Broderick-Frank-Normand, 2003; the team moved left at ca 6,400m and reached the summit via the west face). (2) Southwest face, Ramro Chaina (Doudlebsky-Holecek, 2005; the climbers stopped on joining the west ridge). (3) French attempt in 2011 (Détrie-Labbre-Para). High point quoted as 6,350m, but seemingly lower (4) South Pillar attempt (Doudlebsky-Holecek, 2008). (5) South Pillar: Nima Line (Aoki-Hanatani-Manome, 2012). (H1) High point of Houseman-Stone attempt, 2010. (H2) High point of French attempt. *Andy Houseman*

glacier in the middle of the route. Crossing this, they climbed five pitches on the upper pillar (5.8) and bivouacked at 5,800m.

Day three saw them climbing a further seven pitches on rock (5.10a on the fourth pitch) to reach a wall of snow they dubbed the Slide. Overcoming only half of this that day, they bivouacked at 6,100m. On day four they finished the Slide and a section of mixed terrain above (six pitches, with three or four leads graded 5.8 and M5). They reached the start of a snow arête and bivouacked at 6,350m.

Their fifth day proved to be the most taxing. The crux of the entire route was the five-pitch arête. It took a whole day to cross this section, which featured feather-like, unconsolidated snow up to 80° and was completely impossible to grade. They made a bivouac that night at 6,500m, perched atop a snow mushroom.

[This page, top] Last section of rock band below the seracs on Kyashar headwall. *Yasuhiro Hanatani* [This page, bottom] Kyashar, day five. A foreshortened view of the crux snow arête, with the granite headwall and capping seracs visible above. *Hiroyoshi Manome*

Directly above lay a very steep granite headwall. Next morning the three outflanked this by making a 60m rappel left and climbing two pitches up and left at 5.9 and M5, then two more pitches of steep, solid ice to reach the summit ridge. They were taking photos from the top of Kyashar at 4 p.m.—only the second known party to do so—after which they descended the west ridge to a bivouac at 6,250m. On their seventh day they reached the col at the base of the west ridge, between Kyashar and Kusum Kanguru, negotiating four difficult pitches. All that was left was to continue down to Tangnag, where they arrived at midnight. [*The west ridge/west face was climbed in 2003 by Sam Broderick, Andi Frank, and Bruce Normand to make the first official ascent of the mountain.*]

The autumn was particularly cold, but the route was not affected by the strong winds that plagued other teams in the region, and the climbers benefited considerably from warm sunshine. They named their climb Nima Line (*nima* means "sun" in Nepali; 2,200m, ED+ 5.10a M5).

Prior to their attempt the ridge had been tried at least six times. Three of these were made by Czech alpinist Marek Holecek. In 2001 he climbed for 60 hours with David Stastny to reach the snow shoulder below the upper pillar at ca 5,600m. He was back in 2005 with Jan Doudlebsky. This time the south pillar wasn't on, but the two climbed a new line on the southwest face to join the west ridge at 6,500m, from which point they descended. The same pair returned in 2008 and climbed the southwest flank of the south pillar at WI6 and M7 to reach the shoulder, whereupon Doudlebsky's inflamed tendons dictated retreat.

In 2010 it was the turn of Andy Houseman and Tony Stone. This pair found the southwest flank bare of ice, so they climbed through the rock buttress forming the base of the ridge. It culminated in three long, very loose pitches at around British HVS. The two retreated after gaining the start of the upper pillar at 5,700m. Houseman returned in 2011 with Nick Bullock, but dire weather stopped them getting to grips with the route, and a subsequent attempt on the unrepeated west ridge also failed. Later in the year it was the turn of the French, as reported below. 📷 ▶

From information supplied by HIROSHI HAGIWARA, *Rock and Snow, Japan*

Kyashar (6,770m), south pillar, attempt. In October 2011 Chamonix guides Mathieu Détrie, Pierre Labbre, and Jérôme Para made a spirited attempt on the south pillar, reaching the crest by a previously unclimbed line. Between October 24 and 27, they climbed ca 1,200m up the southwest face before retreating. The returned to base camp five days after leaving, having reached a point on the pillar far higher than any previous party. The climbing had been good, ED in standard, and with the rock often of fine quality. The route recalled the north face of the Eiger, with many traverses. ▤

LINDSAY GRIFFIN, *Mountain INFO*

Various ascents. While there is no suggestion that the following routes are new, they are previously unrecorded, and took place during the past decade. Bare details are published here to assist future climbers:

On Chumbi (6,859m, just south of the Tibet border, between Hunchi and Pumori, with the broad west face rising out of the Gyubanare Glacier), a 1,100m route was climbed on the right side of the west face, leading to the crest of the south ridge at ca 6,500m (D+, with bivouacs at 6,100m on ascent and descent).

On Point ca 6,250m, a small top on the long east-northeast ridge of Melanphulan (6,573m), the 800m north face (TD) above the upper Nare Glacier has been climbed.

[This page, top] This image, used in *AAJ 2010*, shows (1) the north face of Peak ca 6,250m (800m, TD); (2) the approximate line of various attempts made on the north face of Melanphulan, though there is no known complete ascent to the summit. Probably the best effort, ca 50m below the summit ridge, was achieved in 2000 by Wojciech Kurtyka and Erhard Loretan [*AAJ 2011*], who graded their climb TD+. *Krzysztof Starek* [This page, bottom] A foreshortened view of the unclimbed north face of Peak 41 in very dry conditions, showing the 2012 attempt that reached the east ridge. This is the unclimbed north top; the main summit is behind and well off-picture to the left. *Rob Greenwood*

On Peak 6,214m (Schneider map), directly south of Melanphulan, the 1,000m south-southeast spur and south ridge (D+ UIAA III+ 65°) rising out of the Hinku Shar Glacier has been climbed. On Hongu (6,764m), there has been an ascent via the 1,200m south ridge (D).

LINDSAY GRIFFIN, *Mountain INFO*

Peak 41 (6,648m), north face, attempt. In October Jack Geldard and I made an unsuccessful attempt on the north face of Peak 41, a steep snow, ice, and mixed wall that had never been tried before. We shared base camp (4,800m) in the Hongu Valley with Nick Bullock and Andy Houseman, who were attempting Chamlang. It was consistently cold during our stay, never getting above freezing at base camp and often dropping to –10° to –15°C overnight.

We first acclimatized on an attractive ridge opposite Chamlang, reaching a height of 5,500m, and then by making a visit to West Col (6,200m), where we slept the night. Our attempt on Peak 41 followed a couloir on the left side of the north face. After 500m, wind slab was replaced by unconsolidated snow, and making any progress at speed was difficult. When we eventually arrived at the crest of a small ridge, we decided to pitch the tent.

Next morning we set off toward the east ridge above. After more time-consuming and increasingly dangerous climbing, with sugar snow becoming so thin my pick placements went through to shale, I reached the east ridge and looked up. My heart sank: It was a Jenga puzzle of breeze-blocks and shale. The cold weather and strong wind had stripped most of the snow. Had I continued, I likely would have killed Jack, who was simul-climbing below. Game over. The only problem was finding an anchor safe enough to rappel from, and I eventually used a Bulldog ice piton, hammered into shale.

Back at the bivouac site we discussed alternatives. There was a possible line out right that would take us to a considerably higher exit onto the east ridge, where things might be better. But it looked much harder, and given our lack of food, fuel, and time, we retreated.

ROB GREENWOOD, *Alpine Club, U.K.*

Hunku (6,119m), possible first ascent; Chamlang (7,321m), north face, attempt. Post-monsoon in Nepal was frustrating, to say the least, with five weeks of the most stable weather that Nick Bullock and I have ever experienced. However, we got completely shut down on a direct line up the unclimbed north face of Chamlang by high winds at altitude.

After 10 days acclimatizing in and around the Hongu Valley, a trip to the West Col (6,200m) on Baruntse, and another to just over 6,000m on Chamlang's west ridge, we stashed gear below the face and returned for our attempt a few days later, during the first week of November. The face appeared to be in perfect condition, with steep névé and one-swing placements. The weather was good, and we felt well acclimatized. But though we were sheltered low on the face, we began to get hammered by spindrift and we could see massive plumes of snow blowing above us, just where we'd be digging in for the night. It didn't look inviting. We decided to descend, call our attempt a reconnaissance, and wait for a good forecast and lull in the wind.

It never came, and over the next three weeks our forecasts gave a minimum wind speed of 70 kph at 6,000m, and over 100 kph above 7,000m. As it blew straight across the face, and the temperature was -20°C or below, we felt the risk was unjustifiable.

[This page] Hunku from the north, with the line of ascent marked. *Andy Houseman*

During one day when there was something of a lull, eager to get something done, we made a possible first ascent of 6,119m Hunku, north-northeast of Peak 41. [*Brought onto the permitted list in 2002, Hunku appears to have had no official ascent prior to 2012.*] As you walk up the Hongu Valley, below the east face, Hunku looks like a pile of choss. However, halfway along, like an oasis in the middle of a desert, a continuous broad snow couloir leads directly to the summit. Fueled by the hope we would find névé similar to that experienced on Chamlang, we left base camp at 5 a.m. After a two-and-a-half-hour approach and a further hour floundering through deep, unconsolidated snow, we reached the first steep section and, thankfully, bomber névé.

The climbing wasn't technical, just really fun—the way it should be. A couple of short steeper bits led to a final fluted section where we belayed one ice pitch to avoid bad snow. Flutings led straight to the summit and a stunning panorama. The couloir was around 600m and D—think a shorter, easier version of the Swiss Route on the north face of Les Courtes. We descended from ice threads and, lower down, rock gear. Sixteen hours after leaving base camp, we were back. With strong winds still forecast at altitude, we made the decision to bail a week early, and started our four-day trek back to Lukla. 📷

ANDY HOUSEMAN, *Alpine Club, U.K.*

[This page, top] Partial panorama from the summit of Hunku. (A) Peak ca 6,450m at the end of Baruntse's south-southeast ridge. (B) Makalu II (7,678m). (C) West Col (6,135m). (D) Makalu (8,481m) with west face/ridge pointing toward camera. (E) Hongu (6,764m; Pt. 6,770m Schneider Map). This peak has certainly been climbed by the south ridge at D. (F) Hongku Chuli (6,833m, formerly known as Pyramid Peak and thought to have been climbed). (G) Chamlang East (7,290m). (H) Chamlang Central (7,235m). (I) Point 6,440m. (J) Chamlang Main (7,321m). *Andy Houseman*
[This page, bottom] Chago Ridge from south. (A) Chago Lho II. (B) Chago Lho I. (C) Chago Lho III. (D) Chago. (E) Point 6,723m. (F) Chago Shar La. (G) West face of Makalu II. (H) Chago Glacier. *Lindsay Griffin*

MAKALU SECTION

Chago Ridge, south-north traverse. From May 5-7, 2011, during an acclimatization phase as members of a mostly Slovenian expedition attempting Makalu, Steve House and Marko Prezelj traversed the entire Chago ridge from Peak 6,170m to the col before Makalu II's northwest ridge.

On the first day they left the 4,800m base camp, walked up the Barun Glacier, and climbed the south ridge of Peak 6,170m, above the old normal base camp at the foot of Makalu's west ridge. This first, largely rocky, summit is sometimes referred to as Chago Lho III. They continued north to 6,320m Chago Lho I (II is off on a spur to the west), and then onward over the less distinct twin summits of Chago Middle (6,650m, south; 6,768m, north; both first climbed in 1980 by Roger Baxter-Jones, Georges Bettembourg, Ariane Giobellina, and Doug Scott), to Chago (6,893m, first climbed in 1954 by Michael Ball from Hillary's expedition). From here they went down the east-southeast ridge, over Point 6,723m, to the Chago Shar La (6,588m), where the Chago Glacier rises to meet the frontier ridge. The pair made a first bivouac between Chago Lho III and I, and a second a little past Chago Middle. They consider it a long, classic ridge climb with wonderful views, and if snow and ice conditions are good the technical difficulties are low. 🞕

LINDSAY GRIFFIN, *Mountain INFO*

JANAK HIMAL

Janak (7,040m), west face. Young Slovenians Nejc Marcic and Luka Strazar, who received a 2012 Piolet d'Or for their fast and minimalist first ascent of the west face of K7 West, made the second ascent of Janak via a new route up the 1,400m west face. It took them only two days, October 21-22, to complete the round trip from their advanced base.

After setting up base camp in Lonak, on the normal trekking route to Kangchenjunga north-side base camp, they made an extended and arduous journey north to establish an advanced base on the rarely visited Chijima

[This page] The 1,400m west face of Janak rising from the Chijima Glacier. The line of Modri Dirkac and bivouac site are marked. The Stremfelj-Zalokar route comes in from the right, at the foot of the rock band below the bivouac site. In 2006, at approximately the same point as the marked bivouac, Stremfelj and Zalokar found an excellent crevasse in which to erect their tent for the night. The 2012 team was not so lucky. *Luka Strazar*

Glacier, west of the peak. From here they first attempted unclimbed Lashar II (6,803m), gaining valuable acclimatization but unable to summit due to poor conditions. It was now time for Janak's unclimbed west face.

Luka Strazar takes up the story: "It looked totally different than the photo. We knew that mountains tend to be different from what we see in pictures, but it still surprised us. Our planned line did not look feasible due to poor snow conditions, so we had to choose something a little less direct. Sometimes you have to adapt to the situation.

"We started up the face at 1 in the morning. Our approach across the glacier had been quick, because the footsteps of our reconnaissance trip a few days previously were still visible. On the lower part of the route we climbed unroped up easier terrain and did a lot of complaining about how cold it was. Then we had pitches of steeper climbing, and on one crux section I wished I had done more stretching during the preceding days. Due to low temperatures the ice was really hard and shattered easily. It proved annoying, and never really improved from bottom to summit. We slanted right, and after a total height gain from the glacier of ca 1,050m, reached the crest of the southwest pillar, where we joined the top section of the route climbed in 2006 by Andrej Stremfelj and Rok Zalokar. And it was here we bivouacked.

"'Nejc, do you see any crevasses? No? But why not—there should be one around this spot. Shit, where are we going to sleep?'

"Daylight was already fading, and we were forced to dig a bivouac site into steep snow and ice. The final product wasn't a masterpiece, but it proved relatively warm. I even managed a little sleep; Nejc counted stars all night.

"On the second day we still had enough energy to push the remaining 350m to the summit. A freezing morning and rising wind didn't help our cold feet, so our complaining started on schedule. After a long traverse and a few mixed pitches, which seemed to last ages, we arrived at a col just beneath the summit. We left sacks and ropes, and, often crawling because of the strong wind, reached the top. The view was amazing and the subsequent rappels went smoothly, enabling us to reach our advanced base at around midnight."

The climbers named the ca 1,400m route Modri Dirkac (Blue Racer) and reported difficulties to 80° and M4.

Information supplied by Luka Strazar *and* Zdenka Mihelic, *Alpine Association of Slovenia*

[This page] Nejc Marcic on the lower part of Janak's west face. *Luka Strazar*

CHINA

XINJIANG

CENTRAL TIEN SHAN

South Chulebos Massif, Peak ca 5,861m, ascent and tragedy. On July 9 the internationally recognized Chinese alpinist Yan Dongdong was killed in a crevasse fall in the Central Tien Shan. Yan planned to make the first ascent of Chulebos (6,769m), the highest point of a 25-kilometer unbroken crest immediately to the west of the Xuelian Massif (*AAJ 2009*). He decided it should be possible to approach the Chulebos Massif from the south, and with two regular climbing partners, the accomplished Zhou Peng and filmmaker Li Shuang, forced a tortuous route up a long glacier north of Aksu, one valley east of the glaciers that drain the south side of Peak Pobeda (Tomur Feng).

On their fourth day the climbers explored two different cols, from which they found themselves looking down dangerously broken slopes to further long and crevassed glaciers draining north, still some 12 to 15km distant from Chulebos. Discovering a climbable peak close to the more easterly pass, they decided to aim for this as a consolation prize. They spent a full day pioneering a route up snow and ice on the northwest face, and after a bivouac on the summit ridge they reached the top and descended.

At 6:15 p.m. the three had reached 4,400m and had packed up their camp. Only 100m down the glacier, Yan fell unroped more than 20m into a hidden crevasse. Zhou lowered a rope and climbed down, finding Yan to be badly injured and drifting in and out of consciousness. Communication was poor.

Zhou helped to remove Yan's pack, unwedged him, clipped him into a rope, and then climbed out to set up a pulley system. However, Yan apparently began to panic, shouting and gathering up the rope, during which he fell a further five meters into a pool of water. Zhou descended again and managed to attach another rope to Yan, who was now unconscious and breathing poorly. Zhou reascended, but his efforts to extract Yan were to no avail, and after his pulley system stripped the remaining rope, he had no way to descend again. After spending the night by the crevasse, Zhou and Li were unable to detect any sounds from Yan, and surmised that the Chinese mountaineer had died during the night from his injuries.

The peak ascended by the three Chinese was subsequently given the unofficial name of Yan Dongdong Feng (5,861m, 42°03'15" N, 80°23'40" E). See "In Memoriam" in this *AAJ* for more about Yan, one of the foremost figures of modern Chinese alpinism.

BRUCE NORMAND, *China*

ALTAI

Keketuohai National Park, new routes and access. In September, Garrett Bradley, Andrew Hedesh, Aleksandra (Ola) Przybysz, Torsten Treufeld, Li Yuanliang, and I traveled to Keketuohai (local name Koktokay), where we established 30 new routes, most between two and five pitches, but some as

long as eight. Difficulties ranged from 5.5 to 5.12. The most noteworthy were probably Fishy Flip-flops on Waterfall Rock (six pitches then 4th class scrambling, about 5.11a), and the Bundy Route (255m, eight pitches, 5.11+ A2), both of which topped out on some of the bigger walls in the valley. We also climbed Sky Rim, with six pitches up an arête (5.10) followed by 200–250m of low 5th class scrambling, and the five-pitch Jirou Ban Mian (5.12d A3) on Divine Bell. Protection was largely trad, though a few protection and belay bolts were placed.

Access to this area may have been resolved. On arriving in the town of Keketuohai, check in and register with your passport at the main hotel run by the Keketuohai National Park Investment Company. Its name is Keketuohai Jiedai Zhongxin. After this, travel five kilometers to the main park gate and sign a waiver at the main building of the administration center. We were told the park company is eventually going to offer seven-day passes for climbers. On entering the park, you may be asked to show the authorities where you want to climb. The ability to camp, or live in yurts, within the park is uncertain, but might become more relaxed as time progresses. Proof of climbing competence (e.g., AAC membership card) is also required, and any of the

[This page, top] Mike Dobie leading pitch three (5.11) of Eternal Crack on Shepherd's Rock. Shen Zhong/Divine Bell lies on the opposite side of the river, while the closest dome on the left side is Papagu Shan. Pubu Shan is visible just behind it on the same side of the river. *Garrett Bradley*
[This page, bottom] Mike Dobie and Andrew Hedesh on the lower section of the Bundy Route, Papagu Shan. *Garrett Bradley*

above requirements may change. We also gave the administration a code of ethics for new routes, which we ask future climbers to follow. Be sensitive to bolting; it is not encouraged and should be done minimally and professionally. [*Editor's note: The first recorded route in Keketuohai appears to be the two-pitch Unlucky Times, put up during October 2007 by Andy Merriman, who visited the area with his wife and a group of friends living in China. There are now close to 50 routes. Ola Przybysz is writing a guidebook, which will be available online at http://beijingboulders.com/about-2/.*] 📷

MIKE DOBIE, *China*

SICHUAN

SHALULI SHAN

Gangga and Kawarori massifs, reconnaissance. With the political situation sensitive and uncertain in East Tibet, my preferred field of research, I organized a survey team from the Hengduan Mountain Club to visit the West Sichuan Highlands from late September to late October. While there are only about 10 unclimbed summits over 6,000m in this region, countless challenging lower peaks exist. The main objective for Tsuyoshi Nagai, Tadao Shintani, and I was to identify and photograph the little-known peaks of the Gangga and Kawarori massifs. The Gangga group lies just south of the town of Ganzi, and forms the northernmost extension of the Shaluli Shan. Kawarori lies ca 30km southeast of Ganzi and is a sacred mountain in the Gongkala Shan, guarded by Tibetan monks and villagers.

As in the past, we arranged our trip through Zhang Jiyue of Sichuan Earth Expeditions, and he accompanied us. We had unusually bad weather, with only one and a half days of fine conditions during two weeks' travel. The other unusual problem was the restriction imposed on foreigners due to political uncertainty in the region, where intermittent suicides by Tibetan monks have occurred since the spring of 2012. We were only able to travel through officially restricted areas thanks to

[This page, top] The central (and eastern) Gangga Massif seen from the north-northeast. From left to right: Peaks 5,429m, 5,400m, and 5,286m. *Tom Nakamura* **[This page, bottom]** The north face of Peak 5,241m, east of the Zhouda Qu (valley). This peak has a height of 5,641m on the Russian map. *Tom Nakamura*

Jiyue's organizational abilities. I also found the acceleration of highway construction in western China truly amazing.

Only one previous reconnaissance has been made of the Gangga Massif, in 2005 by a Japanese party. However, it did not bring back much useful information. While the mountains are not high (Gangga I is 5,688m, and most summits in the massif lie between 5,300m and 5,500m), there are impressive rock peaks. On September 30 we reached Lazika pass at 4,000m on the Sichuan-Tibet Highway, from where we were able to photograph both Gangga and Kawarori. It was from this pass that British consular officer Eric Teichmann first identified Kawarori in 1918.

On October 1 we entered the Zhouda Qu, a valley south of Ganzi, and ascended to Zhuodana Pass (4,820m), from where we could study the central and southern sections of the Gangga Group.

While peaks in the Gangga remain unattempted, three expeditions have planned to climb Kawarori: a British team in 2005, which approached from the south with a permit from the Sichuan Mountaineering Association (SMA), but was forcibly ejected by local monks; another British team in 2007, which in the end failed to obtain a permit; and a Japanese team in 2011, which gained an official permit from the SMA but was then blocked by a senior official in Kangding. There are two principal peaks, Kawarori I (5,992m) and II (5,928m), each impressive from the north.

TOM NAKAMURA, *AAC Honorary Member, Japan*

Crown Mountain (5,609m PLA map), northwest face and west ridge. On September 3, 2011, Szu-ting Yi (Taiwan), Eric Salazar, and I (both U.S.) made the first ascent of Crown Mountain in the northern Shaluli Shan of West Sichuan. We approached the peak, which is 10km southeast of Xiashe (5,883m), by jeep from Litang, traveling along dirt roads up a rough drainage. We established base camp on the east side of the mountain. The peak is composed of loose volcanic rock and has a couloir splitting the northwest face. We climbed a rotten gully south of the couloir to reach the west ridge, and then followed the crest (mostly third and fourth class, with two pitches of 5.6) to join the last 100m of the couloir, which we followed (50°) to the summit. We descended the same way.

DAVE ANDERSON, *AAC*

Kemailong (5,873m), south ridge, Joining Hands. On October 1, Szu-ting Yi (Taiwan) and I climbed the ca 1,050m south ridge of Kemailong to make the first ascent of this striking granite tower in western Sichuan. [*A photo of this mountain, labeled Peak 5,873m, was first published in* AAJ 2011,

[This page] Kawarori seen from the northwest, close to Ganzi. The twin-summited Kawarori I (5,922m) is to the left; Kawarori II (5,928m) right. *Tom Nakamura*

p. 86. The south ridge faces the camera.]

Our expedition almost ground to a halt in the town of Lamaya, before we reached base camp, when horse packers discovered our climbing equipment. The problem was neither that of permit issues, nor the peak being considered sacred—it was about self-preservation. In 2006 Christine Boskoff and Charlie Fowler disappeared in this region, and before their bodies were discovered in avalanche debris on the slopes of Genyen, Chinese authorities imprisoned several Lamaya horse packers, merely on suspicion that they had somehow been involved with the American's disappearance. Six years later, horse packers were still fearful of helping climbers. To resolve the issue Yi and I wrote, signed, and fingerprinted a "waiver," releasing the horse packers from any responsibility if we failed to return from Kemailong.

At base camp poor weather prevented us from seeing a route up the lower section of the peak, but when the clouds eventually parted, we pieced together a potential approach. Having already spent three weeks above 4,000m, while guiding in the area prior to the climb, we were able to make a quick ascent of a grueling boulder field and establish high camp at 5,200m to the south of Kemailong.

A midnight check revealed stars instead of the usual mist and hail, and at 7 a.m. on October 1 we began climbing three mixed pitches to the saddle at the base of Kemailong's south ridge. Moderate 5th class on the broad crest led upward for 270m, until the ridge narrowed and became more challenging. Featured granite kept the grade below 5.10 for the next four pitches. Above, we simul-climbed for another 360m on ground similar to the east ridge of Wolf's Head in the Cirque of the Towers. Mixed pitches, a false summit, and several rope lengths past a series of snow-covered gendarmes led to the final pitch, a stout overhanging hand crack (5.10) leading to unprotected but easier face climbing.

We summited at 5 p.m., the weather already deteriorating. Gusty winds, hail, and electrical discharges zapped us as we scrambled from the top. We had planned to descend the route, but with all our metalwork humming, we opted for the steep, unknown east face. Heavy snow compounded

[This page, top] The south ridge of Kemailong, showing the line of Joining Hands. *Dave Anderson*
[This page, bottom] Szu-ting Yi leading on the blocky granite of Kemailong's south ridge. *Dave Anderson*

the difficulty of finding rappel anchors on the 700m face, but after several stuck ropes and leaving most of our rack on the 13 rappels, we stumbled into high camp at 1 a.m. on October 2. We named the route Joining Hands (V 5.10 M5), because it was our combined logistical and climbing skills that allowed us to succeed.

This was my third expedition to the Shaluli Shan in the last six years, and I was amazed at the changes. New roads and electrical lines now crisscross this remote region, which had previously been the domain only of nomads and their yaks. Improved roads and new airports have dramatically shortened approach times, but weaving through the bureaucracy, nationalism, and social and cultural diversity of China remains challenging. We would like to thank the AAC for providing financial assistance with a Lyman Spitzer Cutting Edge Award. 📷

DAVE ANDERSON, AAC

DAXUE SHAN

Tatsienlu Massif, Baihaizishan (a.k.a. Tshungpingling, 5,924m PLA map), northwest ridge, attempt; Wupingfeng (5,672m), quasi-winter ascent via north ridge. One of the advantages of living in China is that it gives access to a number of unclimbed, indeed unattempted, peaks. Perusal of Tom Nakamura's *Sichuan's Most Outstanding Unclimbed Peaks* led Simon Moore, Rimon Than, Alex Tomaczynski, and I to Baihaizishan in the Tatsienlu Massif near Kangding. The highest summit in the range, Lamo-she (6,070m), and three other peaks had previously been climbed (*AAJ 2011*), while Baihaizishan had received one attempt, in 2010 by the late Yan Dongdong. The rest appears to be completely unexplored. We found that even the local yak herders had not ventured beyond the highest alps.

After paying an exorbitant peak fee and hiring Lenny—the well-known local fixer—and a cook named Banjiu, the six of us, with the help of 12 horses, reached base camp at 3,900m in late November. The weather was great, yaks were numerous, juniper plentiful, and the mountains pristine. Unfortunately, we could now see that our original goal, the west face, was beset by hanging glaciers, blocking access to the summit slopes. It had not snowed since September. Bad ice and aerated sugar snow prevailed.

Instead we turned to the northwest ridge, a spiky crest of rock rising toward a subsidiary snow summit. It looked easy: up the rocks, traverse across the upper snowfield onto the summit ridge, and Bob's your uncle. We acclimatized with a bit of exploration, set up an advanced base on a small col at 4,400m, packed enough for a three-day trip, and set off up the ridge.

It proved amazing, like Skye in winter but without the rain. There were pinnacles, knife-edge crests, snowfields, and a series of seeming dead-ends that always provided a way onward. The wild, tangled summits of western Sichuan and Tibet, and the peaks of the fabled Minya Konka range, gradually came into view as we ascended. We dug out small snow platforms for tents just below the crest, at ca 5,300m, and next morning set out for the summit. At ca 5,500m we were brought to a halt by a gaping cleft in the ridge, unseen from below. Overhanging rock ahead and right, and sugar snow over steep slabs to the left, put an end to our hopes.

Back at base camp, where nighttime temperatures were now dropping to -22°C, we decided to attempt the peak to our north, Wupingfeng, which at the time we thought unclimbed. After a difficult traverse that involved a Scottish III gully, an overnight camp, a massive moraine, and a crevassed glacier, we made a high camp and set off next morning in a howling gale.

[**This page**] Baihaizishan from the west. The November 2012 attempt followed the left skyline ridge as far as an unseen cleft just below the first snow-dome top (Haopingling, 5,864m). The peak right of Baihaizishan is Tshienpingling (5,612m). *Duncan Francis*

We gained the north ridge and followed it over hard névé, ice, and outcrops of solid granite to the summit ridge, where we were exposed to the full force of the wind. We reached the top on December 3. Sadly, little over two months later, Rimon died in an avalanche in the Cairngorms. [*Editor's note: This was the fourth ascent of Wupingfeng. The north ridge was first climbed in October 1996 by Americans Mark Carter and Steve Must.*]

DUNCAN FRANCIS, *China*

Minya Konka Range, Melcyr Shan (5,910m), west face; Stifler's Mom, west face and north ridge. Mirko Breckner, Max Dünsser, Dario Haselwarter, Reinhard Hones, Felix Sattleberger, and Uli Steiner, young climbers from the Deutscher Alpinverein (German Alpine Club), and David Göttler as leader, spent October in the Tshiburongi Valley of the northern Minya Konka Range. Base camp was at 4,000m in the main valley below the entrance to the Tshiburongi. An intermediate camp was placed halfway up the glacier at ca 4,600m, and an advanced base toward the head at 4,950m.

After two weeks in the area, the team was acclimatized, mountain conditions were good, and a forecast sent from Innsbruck predicted several days of dry if windy weather. On October 15, Breckner, Dünsser, Göttler, and Steiner left advanced base and moved up to the ca 5,400m col at the head of the glacier, below the west face of Peak 5,910m. Here, the wind was so strong that tents beneath an overhanging rock wall had to be anchored by Abalakovs and pitons.

At 4 a.m. the following day the tent fabric finally stopped flapping, and just after dawn the team began its ascent of the west face. Above an entry pitch, a 300m snow/ice gully led to a broken area, where they had to traverse right. The terrain now became steeper and the ice thinner. Rock peg belays were left for the rappel descent. The last pitch, led by Göttler in worsening weather, was a tricky rock climb, but at 1 p.m. the team was hoisting Tibetan flags on the 40cm-wide summit. A five-hour rappel descent through snowfall and strong winds led back to camp, where they spent the night before returning to base. The 16-pitch route was named Nubiline (WI4 M5), and the peak was called Ueba (in Chinese) or Melcyr Shan. Later Göttler and Hones climbed a six-pitch variation start, You Happy, We Happy (WI5), but did not continue up the parent route.

On October 22, Breckner, Haselwarter, and Hones reached the summit of the rock tower to

the north of Melcyr Shan, after a previous failed attempt by Haselwarter, Hones, and Sattleberger. They called this Stifler's Mom, after the part played by Jennifer Coolidge in the comedy *American Pie*. The steep west buttress of this summit was attempted in 2009 by a French team (*AAJ 2010*). The Germans had also thought about this line, but the cold, windy weather put them off. Instead they climbed a long, broad snow couloir to reach the crest of the rocky north ridge, and continued up this to a bivouac at ca 5,650m, the only spot on the narrow crest where they could pitch a small tent. At 10 a.m. all three squeezed onto the summit, and two days later were safely back at base camp. They named their route 1989 Steps Toward Heaven (UIAA VI M6). 🔍

From information supplied by Max Dünsser, David Göttler, and Salman Mitha, Germany

QIONGLAI MOUNTAINS

SIGUNIANG NATIONAL PARK

Abi (5,694m), southeast ridge. Marion Poitevin, Christian Trommsdorff (French), and Gugu and Li Zhongli (Chinese) climbed Abi as a joint venture involving the French Groupe de Haute Montagne and the Chinese Mountain Development Institute. (*Climbs in the Daogou Valley and on Daogou peak, reported elsewhere in this section, also were part of this collaborative effort.*) These four summited Abi by the southeast ridge, finding signs of a previous ascent (700m, D+ M5). As reported in *AAJ 2011*, Abi has been climbed by Chinese mountaineers several times from the southeast and southwest. Prior to their visit to the Siguniang region, the team climbed together at the sandstone cragging area close to Liming.

LINDSAY GRIFFIN, *Mountain INFO, information supplied by Christian Trommsdorff, France*

[This page] Looking southeast toward the head of the Tshiburongi Glacier. (1) 1989 Steps Toward Heaven, to the summit of (A) Stifler's Mom. (2) 2009 French attempt on west buttress. (3) You Happy, We Happy. (4) Nubiline, to the summit of (B) Melcyr Shan (5,910m). *Pascal Trividic*

Daogou Valley, Peak 5,062m, Rising Wind Horse Flag, and possible first ascent of peak; Peak 4,970m, east ridge; Shark's Fin (5,086m), south face to east ridge (not to summit). In August 2010, Li Yue and I spent 10 days exploring five different side branches of the Shuangqiao Gou. In late July 2011, I returned with Ye Feng, Wu Peng, and Gong Xiaorui and spent another 10 days walking up the Shuangqiao and then around the northern part of the range, before making base camp at 4,100m in the Daogou, where we were joined by Zhang Yunping. On August 7 we summited unnamed Peak 5,062m on the ridge that rims the north side of the valley, running southeast from Potala Shan and Eagle Peak (and forming the watershed between the Daogou and upper Changping). We climbed the left side of the southwest face in 13 pitches. The first third was in a groove line, the second face climbing, and the final third on a

ridge. Nearly all the climbing was less than 5.7. We started at 3 a.m., took three and a half hours to reach the base, and then climbed for five and a half hours to the summit. We rappelled the route and were back on the ground at 5 p.m. We named the route Rising Wind Horse Flag (650m of climbing, IV 5.9+). There was loose rock in the initial groove, but generally the granite was very good. We heard rumors that the peak might have been climbed by the Japanese Yoshiaki Seno, via a solo ascent up the center of the southwest face. However, we saw no sign of rappel anchors.

After a rest day Ye Feng, Zang Yunping, and I made the first ascent of Peak 4,970m. This lies on the continuation of the ridge running southeast from Peak 5,062m and is situated ca 2km north of Daogou West (5,422m, Brown-Thomas, 2006). It took more than three hours to reach the foot of the east ridge, which we climbed in six pitches to the summit (350m of climbing,

[This page, top] Looking northwest from near the top of Peak 5,062m. (A) Unclimbed Peak 5,240m. (B) Unclimbed Peak 5,180m. (C) Potala Shan (5,428m, climbed from the far side in 2003 by Andrej and Tanja Grmovsek). *He Chuan* **[This page, bottom]** South face of Shark's Fin showing line climbed by Chinese in October 2011. American and rumored Japanese routes are on the other side of the peak. *He Chuan*

IV 5.9+). There was no evidence of a previous ascent. In our two visits to the region we spied more than 20 enticing granite peaks with dozens of potential lines, from alpine rock routes to big walls.

In October 2011, Wu Peng, Gong Xiaorui, and I returned to the valley for another attempt on Shark's Fin, which lies on the watershed ridge between Peaks 5,062m and 4,970m. We had tried a line in 2010 and retreated just above 4,900m. After waiting 24 hours for the wall to dry, we started from camp at midday on the 5th, opting for a single push due to the uncertain weather. We carried down jackets and an emergency blanket but no other bivy gear. From 2 p.m. to 1 a.m. the following morning we climbed 11 pitches, after which we decided to wait until sunrise on tiny ledges; there was no sleep that night. Above, 20m without protection and some easy moves got us to the east ridge, ca 50m below the summit. We could see a runner left by the Americans who almost made the first ascent from the opposite side. [*In 2010, Chad Kellogg, John Dickey, and Dylan Johnson climbed the northwest arête from the Changping Valley and traversed below the summit block to the narrow east ridge, where they were stopped 25m below the top by steep, unprotectable granite. They carried no bolt kit. See* AAJ *2011*]. We retreated from this point and got back to camp at 4 p.m. on October 6. This was an awesome line with 600m of climbing at V 5.10b: clean granite, good natural protection, no pegs or bolts. 🔳

HE CHUAN, *China*

Daogou (5,466m), northwest face. On October 24 and 25, Jérôme Para and I made the first ascent of the ca 700m northwest face of Daogou (the higher and easterly of the two Daogou peaks). On the 23rd, it took nine hours to walk from the main Shuangqiao Valley west of the peak to the bottom of the face, where we bivouacked. Next day we climbed unroped up 150m of easy snow slopes to reach the crux pitch, 50m of steep thin ice that we rated WI6 R. The pitch above also was not easy (WI5/5+), but then a broad couloir of deep snow led to a bivouac at ca 5,000m. On the 25th we started early, taking just one rucksack. We followed a long couloir with easy ice steps to the large rock barrier below the summit. We climbed this in 10 mixed pitches up to M5+. From the summit we made a rappel descent of our route, reaching the base of the mountain the same night. [*Editor's note: The only known previous ascent of Daogou took place in 2005, when Chad Kellogg, Joe Puryear, and Stoney Richards climbed the south face, approaching from the Changping Valley to the east* (AAJ *2006). The lower Daogou West has had two ascents.*]

DAMIEN TOMASI, *France*

[**This page**] From southwest face of Peak 5,062m, looking down Daogou Valley to Daogou West (5,422m) and, behind and to the left, Daogou (5,466m). *He Chaun*

[This page, left] Northwest face of Daogou showing the 2012 French ascent. *Damien Tomasi*
[This page, right] Jérôme Para leading the crux pitch on day one. *Damien Tomasi* [This page, bottom] Pomiu from the southwest showing the line, and bivouac sites, of the Western. (B1) is on the ascent. (B2) is on the descent, a more direct line being rappelled below this point. *He Chuan*

Mt. Pomiu (a.k.a. Celestial Peak, 5,413m), southwest face and south-southwest ridge, The Western; south-southwest ridge, alternative start. In late July, Ye Feng, Zhang Yunping, and I climbed a new line up the southwest face to reach the south-southwest ridge. It was an enjoyable and yet tormenting 52 hours, as we were hit by various calamities. On the approach one of our guides fell into a treacherous river, and once at base camp we had to wait out prolonged rain and sleet before making the ascent. We took two rucksacks, which were carried by the seconds, some basic emergency bivouac gear, seven liters of water, and a stove.

After 16 hours of uninterrupted climbing we had reached the top of the 23rd pitch. It was now 3 a.m. on the 29th, and raining. We sat on a ledge until sunrise, and then climbed three more pitches to the summit, which we reached at 9 a.m. We named our line the Western (1,400m, VI 5.10a). We climbed 14 new pitches on the southwest face, and a further 12 on the south-southwest ridge, more or less following the upper section of the route first put up in 2005 by Luo Erjia, Luo Rijia, and Su La.

On the first rappel a rock the size of a plate hit my leg. The scenes from *Touching the Void* entered my head, but the bone was not broken; I was able to continue, albeit in some pain. We were forced to make a second bivouac near the point where our route left the ridge, and we subsequently had great difficulties rappelling down our line, as the ropes caught repeatedly in cracks.

In September, Zheng Chaohui and Li Yuan climbed the mountain via the south-southwest ridge. They followed the ridge more or less directly from its foot, between the 2005 Luo Erjia–Luo Rijia–Su La start up the left flank, and the 2005 Liu Xinan–Qiu Jiang on the right. The two set up base camp (4,500m) on the 5th with the help of two porters, and left next day at 9 a.m. They reached the top at 2 p.m. on September 7, and regained base camp at noon on the 8th, having rappelled Liu Xinan's line in the lower section. The weather was good and Zheng had previous experience on the route, having climbed the ridge to 5,280m in 2009, looking for a missing climber. Zheng and Li Yuan climbed ca 1,600m up to 5.9+. They left one bolt as a rappel anchor.

HE CHUAN, *China*

Mt. Pomiu, previous unreported ascents and history. Pomiu was first climbed in October 1983 by Ted Vaill's American team, via a fairly direct line up the south face (5.10c, fixed ropes). Liam Lahr, Eric Perlman, and Alan Steck reached the summit, followed a day later by Robert Schneider, Brock Wagstaff, and Pete White (*AAJ 1984*). Two years later American Keith Brown reported climbing the southeast ridge, solo over three days. He rappelled the east face (*AAJ 1986*). The third ascent was made in August 2005 by Chinese Luo Ergia, Luo Rijia, and Su La. They began from Pomiu Lake way to the northwest, and made a long traverse below the west face, eventually climbing up to the crest of the south-southwest ridge (left of the original route), which they followed to the summit. A few days later Chinese Liu Xinan and Qiu Jiang climbed the right flank of the south-southwest ridge to reach the crest at a similar point to the previous team, after which they followed more or less the same route to the summit.

The fifth ascent was made by Russians (Kolesov, Shelkovnikov, and Sherstnev) in 2007. From February 9 to 19, they followed a significant new line up the east face, probably the first major winter ascent in this region.

Americans John Dickey, Toby Grohne, and Jesse Huey made the sixth ascent in September 2010 by a new route. The three climbed the ca 1,100m northeast ridge in around 10 hours, simul-climbing all but one 5.10 pitch. They spent extra time re-leading some pitches for Dickey's camera. They rappelled the east face, reaching their high camp after a 22-hour round trip.

A month later the peak received its seventh ascent by Russians Evgeny Bashkirtsev and Denis Veretenin, who made the second ascent of the southeast ridge over three days (1,500m of climbing). Maximum difficulties were 6c, but the pair stated that in perfectly dry conditions most of the climbing would not be extreme. The 2012 Chinese ascents, recorded above, mark the eighth and ninth of this notable rock pyramid.

LINDSAY GRIFFIN, *Mountain INFO*

[**This page, left**] Largo's Route on the north-northeast face of Pt. ca 5,600m. *Thomas Vialletet*
[**This page, right**] Christophe Dumarest during the first ascent of Largo's Route. *Thomas Vialletet*

Pt. ca 5,600m, north-northeast face, Largo's Route. On November 5, Christophe Dumarest and I made the probable first ascent of Pt. ca 5,600m at the end of the southwest ridge of Chang-gou (a.k.a. Lara Peak, 5,700m). This rocky summit is situated immediately north of Siguniang North at 31°07'29.00" N, 102°54'04.32" E (Google Earth). From a camp at 4,500m, above the Changping Valley, we first acclimatized by climbing a nice ridge close to camp, following it to 5,000m. From here we saw an attractive gully on Pt. ca 5,600m and decided to leave some gear at the end of the ridge and descend to camp for the night.

Next morning we made an early start, walked up to 4,900m, collected our gear, and climbed a 200m mixed section (M5 maximum) to reach a small notch in the northwest spur. From here we traversed a steep snow slope across the north-northeast face to reach the base of the gully. The first pitch of the gully proved to be the crux: very committing, quite runout, and a steep mixed snow/ice section. Above, it was still sustained and hard to protect, but the climbing was excellent. We completed five or six pitches of 60m before reaching the summit ridge, where a final 50m rock section of 5c led to the top. On the summit we estimated we were 100m to 150m below the top of Chang-gou. We rappelled the gully using a mixture of pitons, nuts, and jammed knots as anchors. We named our 800m line Largo's Route (ED- WI6 M5 X 5c).

THOMAS VIALLETET, *France*

MIN SHAN

Xiao Xuebaoding (5,440m, Chinese map; 5,443m, GPS), northeast ridge. On May 3 Karim Adouane (France), Jon Otto (USA), Su Rongqin (a.k.a. Asu, China), and I made the first known ascent of Xiao Xuebaoding (32°38'29" N, 103°53'16" E,), a peak we referred to as Little Xuebaoding, the second highest in the Min Shan. In the absence of detailed, up-to-date maps we mainly relied on GPS to

[This page] During the ascent of the northeast ridge of Xiao Xuebaoding. The mountains in the background, part of the Min Range, are unnamed and unclimbed. *Linda Eketoft Collection*

traverse a rugged landscape of gorges, rivers, and dense bamboo forest to a base camp at 4,000m. The weather throughout was unpredictable, with rain, hail, and snow that led to total whiteouts. After a few days of acclimatization, we set up an advanced camp at 5,000m. Winds were strong, temperatures low, and routefinding challenging. Having waited two days in our tents for a storm to pass, we made a summit attempt with only one day's provisions remaining.

We left camp at 4 a.m. on May 3, climbing up to the northeast ridge. Conditions were difficult, with loose, waist-deep snow releasing from the mountain. Ropes were fixed on certain sections. A mixture of frozen scree, ice, rock, and loose snow made the ascent exhausting. We reached the summit at 11 a.m.; the route was around D 5.6 WI3 M4. After returning to our high camp we navigated the terrain southwest, crossing crevassed glaciers and the hidden Tibetan valleys of Mafeng, eventually reaching connecting roads leading to Songpan, where our expedition ended.

Linda Eketoft, *Sweden*

Editor's note: The highest peak in this area, 5,588m Xuebaoding, which lies about six kilometers to the northwest, may have first been climbed in 1986 by an expedition from the Himalayan Association of Japan. However, the ascent was disputed by a second expedition from the HAJ, which claims to have made the first ascent in 1991. The 1992 AAJ reported that, also in 1991, another Japanese party, the Sagama Family Alpine Club, led by Kazuo Yamagagishi, made the first ascent of Xao (or Xiao) Xuebaoding (5,440m) via the southwest face. However, through the kind assistance of Tom Nakamura and Kinichi Yamamori, this is now known to be incorrect. Immediately south of the marked name Xao Xuebaoding (no height quoted) on the map in A Guide to Mountaineering in China *lies the subsidiary top 5,026m. It was this that the Japanese climbed, thinking it was the named peak. Recent updated Chinese maps mark both this summit and Xiao Xuebaoding. The Min Shan is the most northeasterly massif in Sichuan, situated directly north of Chengdu.*

YUNNAN

HENGDUAN MOUNTAINS

Baima Xueshan, first ascents. In 2012 I set up Summit Outdoor School, a nonprofit organization providing free courses to Chinese villages, outdoor, and university clubs. Our aim is to train local people to become guides or instructors in their mountains, and in order to keep the instructional level of our own staff high, each year we will try to climb for three weeks in a remote area. In October 2012, after we finished a training course on Mt. Haba (Haba Xueshan, 5,396m) with local villagers, the Summit Outdoor School instructors went to Mt. Baima.

The Baima Xueshan massif ("Baima Snow Mountains") is situated in Deqen County, not far to the south of Meili Xueshan (Kawagebo, 6,740m). It lies close to and west of the Yunnan-Tibet Highway, where it runs northwest from Zhongdian to Deqen. The mountains, which rise to over 5,400m and contain many steep peaks above 5,000m, lie in the Mt. Baima Reserve. Until now it has not been possible to climb there legally, though there have been unauthorized attempts by Chinese and foreign parties. We talked with authorities from the Baima Reserve and secured permission to stay in the region for a long time, in order to acclimatize and properly reconnoiter the mountains, so we could climb multiple routes.

In three weeks we made five first ascents: Duochubomubadeng (5,466m) by Near at Hand (1,000m from glacier, III AI2 M3 40° snow, Li-Zhao); Unnamed Peak (5,288m) by Miss Zhu's First Ascent (800m from glacier, III AI2 M2+ 50° snow, Huang-Jiang-Li-Zhao-Zhu); Unnamed Peak (5,295m) by Regards for Freedom (800m from glacier, III 5.8 M3 40° snow, Li-Zhao); Unnamed Peak (5,250m) by Storm is Always Followed by Sunshine (800m from glacier, 5.9 M5 50° snow, Sun-Song); and Zhalaqueni South Summit (5,420m) by Road of Progress (700m, 5.9 M4 50° snow, Sun -Tuo).

[Editor's note: In 2006 the Jing brothers (China) attempted the main summit of Zhalaqueni (a.k.a. Zhalachoni Feng, 5,429m) by a route on the right side of the face, reaching 5,200m. The same line had been attempted in 2002 by a pair of foreign climbers. This summit eventually received a Chinese ascent in 2013; see report in this section.]

We also talked with the head of the Baima Reserve about setting up the right mode of adventure tourism, which would protect this beautiful region and help the economy of the local community. 📷

SUN BIN, *China*

Baima Xueshan, Zhalaqueni (5,429m). Li Yuan, Zhang Xiaohui, and Zheng Chaohui made the first official ascent of the north summit of Zhalaqueni, reaching the top on January 27, 2013. The three spent three and a half days climbing directly up the east face by a new line they named Excavator

[This page] The east faces of the Baima Xueshan. (A) Duochubomubadeng, (B) Peak 5,288m, (C) Peak 5,295m, (D) Peak 5,250m, and (E) Zhalaqueni South Summit. Routes of 2012 ascents are shown. To the right of (E) is Zhalaqueni main summit. *Sun Bin*

[This page] The east face of Zhalaqueni. (1) Road of Progress, to the South Summit. (2) Jing brothers attempt in 2006 on main summit. (3) Excavator, climbed in the winter of 2013. *Sun Bin*

(1,300m, WI4+ AI3+ M5). Over the last 10 years approximately nine teams have tried unsuccessfully to reach this summit, though one unauthorized ascent is reported.

Climbing in alpine style, the three started from base camp at 4,095m on the January 24, making their first camp at 4,857m. Immediately above lay challenging deep snow, then several pure water ice pitches and harder mixed ground. Camp 2 was placed at 5,127m. On the third day they spent 12 hours climbing less than 300m. Thin ice and broken rock provided the mixed crux at AI3+ and M5. The final camp was at 5,407m, where they had a bad sitting bivouac, enduring frost nip to the fingers. On the morning of the fourth day, 150m up the northeast ridge led to the summit. They descended to the site of Camp 2 that night.

Winter provides the most stable climate in this region. The summit day was windless but savagely cold.

ZHENG CHAOHUI, *translated by Huang Jiyun and supplied by Ma Demin, China*

LAOJUN SHAN NATIONAL PARK

Traditional rock climbing. Activity at the newly developed sandstone trad climbing area close to the town of Liming has increased: There are now close to 200 routes, both single and multi-pitch, from 5.6 to 5.13. However, the area still holds vast potential; over seven valleys remain untouched, and walls reach 240m in height. In June the area's foremost activist, American Mike Dobie, completed the first route in the park to top out on a high wall and involve a walk-off descent. The eight-pitch Back to the Primitive, climbed with Sarah Rasmussen, will go at 5.11+. Some of the belays have bolt anchors. Pitches five and seven have yet to be climbed free, though the second pitch was freed by Dobie at 5.11c/d. There are three possible starts, the nicest probably the one-pitch Lollipop (5.9, FA Andrew Hedesh, FFA Rasmussen). The climb finishes up an airy arête, and the walk-off should not take more than one and a half hours.

In October the area was the venue for what has been billed as China's first trad climbing festival, an event jointly sponsored by the North Face and Black Diamond. Around 200 people from many different countries took part. Chinese activists, most of whom are sport climbers, are taking to naturally protected routes with great enthusiasm. Visit www.junshanclimber.com for current information on the area.

Dobie and friends have also been active in exploring the potential for rock climbing and bouldering in southwest Sichuan, and an 82-page guidebook is now available to the Dao Cheng area (Ruba Chaka Village, Haizishan Preserve), called *Southwest Sichuan: A Partial Guide to Bouldering and Climbing*. While most of the guide documents the extensive high-altitude bouldering in the region, also included is Tuarshan, an alpine rock venue north of Haizishan Preserve and east of the Dao Cheng–Litang highway. Early in 2012, Dobie made a solo visit to this area, where summits rise to 5,000m, and climbed a few spiky rock peaks, one of which had a 5.6 crack on the summit tower. He notes great potential for multi-pitch routes on various granite faces.

From information provided by MIKE DOBIE, *China*

[This page, top] Mike Dobie on Faraway Corner (5.11) at Liming. *Eben Farnworth* [This page, bottom] View of about half the valley that has seen the most development in Laojun Shan. Back to the Primitive climbs the central buttress in eight pitches. *Mike Dobie*

TIBET

Central and southwest Tibet, various ascents. In the course of geological field research on the India-Asia collision zone, members of our University of Arizona Geosciences team have climbed several non-technical peaks, some of which would only be legally available to those with research permits.

In 2012 we climbed an unnamed 6,164m summit at 29°54.971' N, 84°52.795' E, in the group of peaks immediately northeast of the Loinbo Kangri Range. Locally known as the Linzhou Range, it is designated on the Russian 1:200,000 topographic map of the region as the Kanchun Kangri. From a camp in the main valley, which we reached by Land Cruiser, we walked eight kilometers northeast up a side valley to place a high camp at 5,800m, at the toe of the ice sheet that blankets the west face of 6,164m. (This peak is located just south of Pt. 6,251m on the Russian map.) The upper reaches of this valley hold four beautiful, dry alpine glaciers, which appear to be in rapid retreat.

On June 26 Barbara Carrapa, Ryan Leary, and I climbed directly up the icy west face, which was easy 35-40° névé with patches of ice, arriving on the summit at 8 a.m., just in time to catch first light igniting the upper reaches of Loinbo Kangri (7,095m). The fourth member of our party, Matt Dettinger, climbed solo on loose rock up a 6,087m rocky sub-summit on the ridge southwest of our top (29°54.774' N, 84°52.392' E). The only other recorded climb in this range is Pt. 6,044m, a dry peak on the northwest side of our approach valley, climbed in 2006, solo, by Oliver von Rotz.

During previous fieldwork in central Tibet, in 2004, Paul Kapp and I climbed an unnamed 6,258m summit in the Muggar Kangri Range (shown on Technical Pilot Chart TPC G-7C). This remote range contains three clusters of 6,000m peaks, and is well seen north of Dagze Co, a sizable lake north of Nyima. Located at 32°17.624' N, 087°23.287' E, the peak is 58km north-northeast of Nyima. A slightly higher summit to the north could easily be reached from this point.

During our 2005 field season in the Kailash region of southwestern Tibet, Paul Kapp and I

[This page] Northern Loinbo Kangri Range at first light, seen from high on the route toward Peak 6,164m in the Linzhou Range. (A) Phola Kyung (6,530m, first ascent 2006). (B) Peak 6,230m (first ascent 1998). (C) Loinbo Kangri (7,095m, first ascent 1996). (D) Peak 6,340m (first ascent 1994). *Ryan Leary*

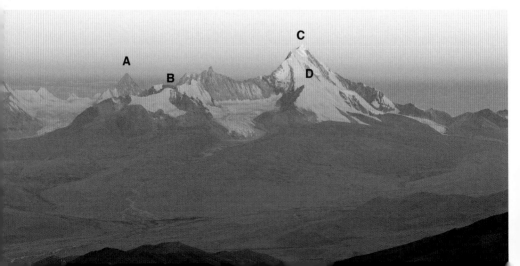

climbed an unnamed 5,781m summit at 31°37.910' N, 79°59.506' E in the Ayi Shan while collecting samples of granite and snow. This obscure peak (more or less north-northeast of Kamet on the Indo-Tibet border) is located near the main road that leads west across the Ayi Shan into the Zhada basin, where the 10th century Guge ruins are located. The climb was a long scramble up snowy, shattered-granite terrain. Again, this region is legally accessed only with research permits.

In June 2007, Paul Kapp and I ascended the long gorge shaped like an inverted question mark leading from the south shore of Lake Manasarovar into the heart of the Gurla Mandhata massif. We made camp after six hours' walk, 750m northeast of Namarodi Co. The big U-shaped canyon is flanked on both sides by an imposing array of 6,000m summits, all of which are dwarfed by the immense east face of 7,694m Gurla Mandhata. On the 14th we ascended a fine, south- and east-trending, corniced snow ridge directly to an unnamed 6,085m summit (30°26.518' N, 081°28.525' E). This region is desolate and wild, with no obvious signs of human activity. ◙

[This page, top] A rarely seen view of Gurla Mandhata (7,694m) from the east. *Peter Decelles* [This page, bottom] Looking east from the valley north of Loinbo Kangri at the Linzhou Range after fresh snowfall. (A) Peak ca 6,080m (Russian map). (B) Peak 6,251m (Russian map). (C) Peak 6,044m (GPS). (D) Peak ca 6,080m (Russian map). (E) Peak 6,164m (GPS). (F) Peak 6,087m (GPS). The last two were climbed in 2012. *Lindsay Griffin*

BORNEO

Mt. Kinabalu, extremely difficult sport climbs at altitude. In the winter of 2011, Yuji Hirayama sat down with James Pearson and me at our annual meeting at the North Face to discuss expedition ideas. Yuji proposed a trip to Mt. Kinabalu (4,095m) in Borneo, Malaysia. He showed us a photo of a 100-meter, overhanging thumb of granite near the summit, filled with perfect holds. This easily convinced us to go, even if we only tried this one route. According to Yuji, there was plenty more to be done.

I didn't really know what was in store. I had done plenty of high-altitude bouldering in Colorado, but only for daylong trips. Our base camp on Mt. Kinabalu would be the Sayat Sayat Hut at 3,668m. Here we would stay for 17 nights, with limited electricity and water, no TV, shower, Internet connection, cell reception, or washer and dryer (just to list a few everyday essentials). The nighttime temperature averaged –7°C. Our mission, along with the French climber Caroline Ciavaldini and filmmaker Chuck Fryberger, was to develop new routes in the area, both challenging and easy. Mt. Kinabalu is famous for guided hikes up Low's Peak (the highest point in Malaysia) and a high-elevation via ferrata. Rock climbing was still a new concept, and that is where we came into play. An abundance of easy routes would attract people to learn how to climb (through guides, of course).

In 2003, Yuji had come close to completing a two-pitch project on Oyayubi Peak. The first pitch is 5.13a climbing for 65 meters, delivering you to a hanging belay. Yuji thought the 35-meter second pitch felt like 5.14d, depositing you on top of the thumb feature. The climbing is resistant, broken down into a 13d intro to a strenuous rest, a six-move V10/11 boulder problem, and an endurance 5.13d finish. Oyayubi is at nearly 4,000m, and after just a few minutes of climbing, the pump started to kick in. Yuji had to learn how to control his breathing and heart rate to prevent this. He spent a week acclimatizing on "easier" routes, before attempting his main goal, and on June 19 he completed the first ascent of Pogulian Do Kododuo (5.14d).

A day later, Yuji had another vision on the West Donkey's Ear formation. The line was 40 meters long and slightly overhung. It began with eight bolts of technical 5.13c, leading into an overhanging dihedral rest. From here, the climbing becomes much more bouldery. Yuji was able to figure out most of the moves on the lower boulder problem, but not the rest. There was speculation that the upper moves might not go. One night at the hut, Yuji and Chuck suggested I try, considering my bouldering background. I was hesitant at first. But sending a technical arête that I had previously bolted (Enter the Void, 5.14b) gave me enough confidence for a recon mission on the project.

The lower half went well, and after a few attempts I was able to link the first crux moves and

[Previous page] Daniel Woods climbs the extremely technical Enter the Void (5.14b) on Mt. Kinabalu. *Shinji Mitsubori* [This page] Woods on Tinipi (5.15a) at over 4,000m. *Shinji Mitsubori*

go on to the two-move second crux. I had to take a right-hand sidepull, paste my feet on minuscule foot chips, do a long lock-off to a left-hand, two-finger sloping crimp, place my right heel next to my right hand, lock off, and do a powerful crossover to a right hand flat edge. The distance between these moves was large. I could do them individually, but linking them was another story. I left it at that and moved onto the final crux. This involved mini-compression between slopers, gaining two small crimps, and finishing with a downward dyno to a jug. I was able to figure out the beta and connect the dots. To my surprise, the project seemed possible. All that remained was a technical 5.12b/c slab to the top. Overall, the boulder section broke down into 13 moves of V10, two moves of V11, and 10 moves of V10. Resting was not possible between these sections.

The next day, starting from the bottom of the route, I fell two times on the final boulder problem. Climbing so hard at 4,055m made it difficult to breathe, and caused cramps in my legs and forearms. Yuji advised me to use slow, deep breaths to control my heart rate, which helped a lot. Two days later I came back. When I arrived at the dihedral rest, mist started to roll in, but luckily it lasted just a few minutes. Everything clicked this burn, and Tinipi (5.15a, "dream" in Malay) became a reality. I thank Yuji for giving me an opportunity to try his creation. He later tried the route and was unable to put together one of the moves. He will be back!

James spent three days on an incredible double-arête compression route, with very precise and technical climbing, before making the first ascent of Excalibur (514c), one of the coolest lines I have seen. Caroline bolted and climbed Apuri Manan (5.13d), with a very tough double dyno at the end, and Alanga, a three-pitch 5.13d. In total, we bolted 20 new routes, leaving a good spectrum of grades for people to play on.

The trip was monumental. I think we all had to adapt to the difficulties the mountain presented us. Once we understood, our dreams were made possible.

DANIEL WOODS, *USA*

BOOK REVIEWS

EDITED BY DAVID STEVENSON

Buried in the Sky: The Extraordinary Story of the Sherpa Climbers on K2's Deadliest Day. Peter Zuckerman and Amanda Padoan. W.W. Norton, 2012. 285 pages. Hardcover. $26.95.

The Time Has Come: Ger McDonnell, His Life and His Death on K2. Damien O'Brien. The Collins Press, 2012. 188 pages. Paperback. $29.95.

Welcome, dear reader, to another chapter in our favorite publishing market category: forensic mountaineering literature! Both these books concern the famous (infamous?) 2008 tragedy on K2, in which 11 climbers died. The formula is simple: hybridize a traditional climbing narrative with a deadly force of nature. Then look through the wreckage for good guys to exalt and villains to excoriate.

In *Buried by the Mountain* the good guys are the climbing Sherpas and Pakistani high-altitude porters, and the deeds of the sahibs are in the background. This role reversal touches a guilty nerve in the climbing community. Few readers of the AAJ, I'll wager, have returned from Himalayan expeditions entirely satisfied that they treated the locals fairly, from porters to liaison officers. I sure haven't.

Zuckerman and Padoan make a commendable effort to liberate "high altitude workers" from the anonymity of their servile position. There are rich biographical portraits and excellent anthropological insights. Though but a sideshow in the overall disaster, the treatment of Shaheen Baig, 39, vividly dramatizes what it means on a dangerous mountain when one kind of life is worth more than another. Shaheen, working for a Serbian team, is chosen leader to set ropes on the Bottleneck on summit day. Pulmonary edema strikes him violently in the early morning at Camp 2. Lungs gurgling and paralyzed, certain that he will die soon, he radios to the cook, Nadir Ali, and asks to be left on the mountain. But Nadir, a devout Muslim, sees this as a direct command from Allah to go to the rescue. His attempts to raise alarm in camp are cold-shouldered, so he sets off alone. He passes three descending climbers and they too decline to help. After 12 hours of continuous climbing, Nadir reaches Camp 2, zaps a comatose Shaheen with dexamethasone, and drags him down the mountain and out of the shadow of death. When later asked about the three descending climbers who refused to help, Nadir replies that they were doubtless weak and nursing ailments of their own. Would they have helped if Shaheen were Australian, say, and not Pakistani? "I don't want to answer that aloud," he replies. "They don't work for us. We work for them and I want to keep working for them. They pay good salaries. Most of them are good people, and we need them to keep coming back to Pakistan, so please don't make them look bad."

Heroic action often is born from disaster, and another hero on K2 that season was Gerard "Ger" McDonnell, very likely the last of the 11 to die. *The Time Has Come* memorializes the life of the first Irishman to make it to the top of K2, relates his previous climbing adventures, introduces us to his wonderful family from Kilcornan in county Limerick, his love of Irish music (he played percussion with a bodhrán), his Catholic piety, his Samaritanism, his bonhomie. From the anecdotes and testimonials of climbing partners and Ger's diary, there emerges a picture of a fine individual.

The core of the book is what happens in the hours preceding his demise. Ger, 37, an Everest summiteer, was one of two non-Dutchmen on the eight-man K2 Norit team. Because of delays in setting up fixed ropes in the Bottleneck and the Traverse, and slow progress by a Korean team in the lead, it is not till 4 p.m., 12 hours after setting out from Camp 4, that the majority of the climbers work through these key obstacles. Even with hours of further climbing to the summit, the Korean, Norwegian, and Norit teams go ahead, trusting to get there just before dark, which they do, at 6:40. On the descent the leader of the Norit team (Wilco van Rooijen), Ger, and an Italian, Marco Confortola, run out of strength and willpower and are benighted at around 8,400 meters, despite urgings from Sherpas to climb down. At first light, Wilco charges downhill and passes two Koreans and a Sherpa, tangled in fixed rope and hanging upside down, pretty close to death. When Ger and Marco later come upon this sight, they devote no fewer than three hours in an attempt to rightside these men, without success. Whereupon Ger wordlessly climbs up toward the anchors in further attempts, and Marco heads down.

In Marco's view, expressed in highly fractured English, and subsequently reported in the first newspaper accounts, Ger was disoriented and hypoxic to the point of irrationality. But evidence indicates Ger had almost certainly reached the anchors, lowered the entangled bundle and freed the three men, and that they had subsequently started down the mountain, Ger following, when all were wiped out by serac fall. The story arc is familiar: man leaps off sea cliff in attempt to save drowning child; both are swept out to sea.

Both authors have one-paragraph caveats about the credibility of their reconstructions. Zimmerman observes that: "Survivors of the Death Zone have imperfect recall, and the media maelstrom makes recovery—and accuracy—elusive." But they press forward undeterred. Forensic mountaineering literature cannot exist without basically denying the vast evidence from high-altitude psychological and physiological research.[1] These books are shaped by a few conjectural language bridges over lacuna and aporias. And often the final narratives, as with the McDonnell story, are pitted with illogicalities and papered-over disconnects.

Neither of these books is particularly timely. It's been five years since the K2 disaster, and three years since the publication of Freddie Wilkinson's very competent *One Mountain Thousand Summits,* which gave generous consideration to Sherpa perspectives and to the probability that McDonnell acted as his family believes. In the normal course of publishing, belated factual differences or reinterpretations don't merit entire books. But forensic mountaineering lit is different. In this market niche it appears that any climbing misadventure with a high body count can be disinterred again and again.

JOHN THACKRAY

---

1 There are dozens of citations in the medical literature on brain damage, psychosis, cognition impairment, persistent memory loss, neuropsychological impairment, lost psycho-motor ability, and mental efficiency at high altitudes.

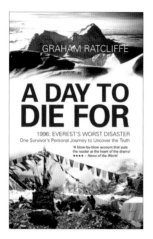

A Day to Die For 1996: Everest's Worst Disaster, The Untold True Story. Graham Ratcliffe. Mainstream Publishing (U.K.), 2011. 322 pages. Color photos. Paperback. £11.99.

The title refers to May 10, 1996, and what so many people have come to call the "*Into Thin Air* accidents" on Mt. Everest. Graham Ratcliffe was part of a team aiming for the top on May 11 that year, which means he was on the South Col for the tragic evening of the 10th.

As a longtime Everest guide, I consider myself familiar with the tragedy, although I've never been particularly fond of arguing its details, its heroes, and its supposed villains. My view is that one should understand the accident so as not to repeat it—while also respecting the privacy of those involved and not sensationalizing the misfortune of others. Given that bias, I was pleased that Ratcliffe began with non-tragic circumstances.

In 1995 Ratcliffe makes the top on one of the earlier commercial expeditions to succeed from Tibet. He then decides to go for Everest's summit again in 1996, and it occurs to him that he could be the first Brit to make it up twice, and the first to summit from both sides. Hard to quibble with such a lofty and ambitious goal, but I'll admit that I was a little shocked that he presents it all as a done deal to his wife just a few months before the spring trip—this after convincing us that his wife and two daughters are a priority in his life. I cringed to read: "She knew only too well that trying to talk me out of it would be tantamount to cruelty. As she put it, 'It would be like caging a wild animal asking you not to go.' "

Ratcliffe and his teammates are in the storm on the South Col that key night, unaware of the awful circumstances playing out around and above them. The next morning they descend the Lhotse Face before the disaster is apparent. I, for one, was convinced that his team had their hands full and they might be excused for not wandering around in the stormy night to check on others, presumably well-guided and fat on resources.

Ratcliffe, while understandably disturbed and saddened by the tragedy, is not ready to let go of his climbing goals in its wake. He learns the game of self-promotion and sponsorship and keeps trying for the top of Everest. He gets up in 1999, beating other Brits to the goal, as he'd hoped, but it is a rough climb. At this point in my read I was slightly worried, since Ratcliffe had reached the end of his climbing narrative but my Kindle showed plenty more book.

He begins an obsession with 1996. That's his word—obsession—and it seems quite accurate. He feels guilt at not helping those in peril on the mountain. And somehow, this transforms to anger. Ratcliffe seems inclined to entertain conspiracy theories and begins to believe very strongly that other teams had access to weather forecasting in 1996, and that Rob Hall and Scott Fischer urged his team to change their attempt from the 10th to the 11th so as to avoid crowding, but without warning them that this would put them in the path of an oncoming storm. I concur that it is interesting to put all the weather data together again, and see that it adds up to a storm, but that is not the same thing as knowing exactly what synopsis the team leaders had in their hands in the lead-up to the big climb.

The second half of *A Day to Die For* is repetitive and circular by its very nature. It becomes a book about writing a book, and so it gets tedious. Ratcliffe's transformation to muckraking investigative reporter is a slow process. He doesn't seem to know how to get the information he wants, so we suffer along with him for years, poring through accounts of the tragedy and then eventually hitting up survivors and meteorologists for answer after answer in his quest. The "Aha!" moments and a few revelations do come, but they don't seem all that revelatory.

The things that Rob Hall and Scott Fischer allowed to interfere with their judgment in May of 1996 have been explored already, many times. I don't buy Ratcliffe's stated rationale for going there again. One begins to suspect that his guilt and sadness turned to anger over the years because he was left out. The clients and guides and leaders and Sherpas involved all became boldface names in our climbing world. They wrote books and articles and made movies—and they didn't consult Graham Ratcliffe or ask his opinion, because it wasn't his epic.

As I hinted at earlier, perhaps I'm predisposed as an Everest guide to not like a book that hammers Everest guides. And in the interest of full disclosure, I even take a small, unnamed beating in the book for my part in putting out "tasteless" pictures of George Mallory's body upon its discovery. Ratcliffe rightly believes that Mallory's descendants had feelings that should have been respected. Not unlike the families and friends of Scott Fischer and Rob Hall, I'd venture. Ratcliffe's venom for those dead and alive is righteous, but then at the end he says he feels a lot better for getting it all out there. So there's that. And hey, now he is in with the boldface names in the continuing saga of the May 1996 tragedy. I'll accept that writing such a book was good therapy for Graham Ratcliffe. Unfortunately, reading *A Day to Die For* is not terribly therapeutic for the rest of us.

DAVE HAHN

On Top of the World, The New Millennium: The Continuing Quest to Climb the World's Highest Mountains. Richard Sale, Eberhard Jurgalski, and George Rodway. Snowfinch Publishing (U.K.), 2012. 248 pages. Color and black-and-white photos. Hardcover. £30.

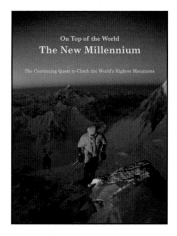

As the world "continuing" in its subtitle suggests, *On Top of the World* is a sequel, in this case to Richard Sale and John Cleare's immensely thorough, useful, and beautifully illustrated *Climbing the World's 14 Highest Mountains: The History of the 8,000-Meter Peaks* (The Mountaineers, 2000). Its predecessor tells the stories of these peaks up to 1999; *On Top of the World* summarizes that previous history and carries it forward through 2011. Both belong in any serious collection of books on the subject of high-altitude Himalayan mountaineering.

Each chapter is devoted to an 8,000-meter peak, in the order they were first ascended, and a concluding chapter speculates on the future of Himalayan mountaineering. A rich collection of photos illustrates main routes for each mountain and highlights climbs. The chapter on Everest, as expected, includes more than its share of mountaineering stunts (first snowboard descent included), plus accounts of busy summit days (with 597 climbers getting to the top in 2007 alone). Also included are important new routes established since 2000, including one on the north face by a Russian expedition in 2004, and on the southwest face by a Korean team in 2009.

Some of the most interesting climbs and accounts are in the chapters devoted to the more obscure high peaks. Gasherbrum I (Hidden Peak) had its first ascent in 1958 by an American team led by Nick Clinch. It wasn't climbed again until 1975 when Reinhold Messner and Peter Habeler established a new route to the summit. Many new routes went up on the mountain between that second ascent and 1990, but for nearly two decades thereafter, the mountain was relatively neglected by cutting-edge mountaineers. But in 2008 Russians Victor Afanasiev and Valery Babanov, climbing alpine-style, put up a new route on the mountain's southwest face, notwithstanding a falling rock screaming into their tent (a wince-inducing photo of Afanasiev's bloody, bandaged head helps illustrate the story.) Bloody head and all, on the very next day Afanasiev and Babanov summit.

As Sale notes in his introduction, literally thousands of climbers have successfully climbed one or another 8,000-meter peak over the past six-plus decades, which might suggest that such a climb is no longer a big deal. What that number obscures is the fact that the overwhelming majority of those climbs have been restricted to only two of the 14 8,000ers: Everest, which owes its popularity to being the highest peak, and nearby Cho Oyu, which attracts legions of climbers due its relative ease of approach and ascent. Most of the others have been summited, as of the end of 2011, by only a few hundred climbers each—Annapurna, the first to be climbed, by fewer than 200.

MAURICE ISSERMAN

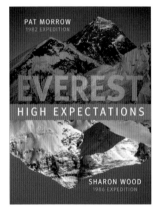

Everest: High Expectations. Pat Morrow and Sharon Wood. Bungalo Books (Canada), 2012. 142 pages. 140 color photos. iPad only. $9.95.

Frankly, I don't—how shall I put this delicately?—give a damn about Everest or its literature. In fact, *Everest: High Expectations* is the first book about Everest I ever paid for.

I bought it for the ultimate challenge: to test my new iPad. *Everest: High Expectations* may be the first climbing book to employ Apple's new iBooks Author book-design technology, and I wanted to see what it looked like. Perhaps you have no more interest in book-design software than I do in Everest base-camp shenanigans, but the resulting work is still worth every Loonie. The Canadian publisher, Frank Edwards of Bungalo Books, coined the term "coffee-tablet book" for photo-heavy creations viewed on a tablet. I love this term—and this book.

Back in the early 1980s most Everesters were elite climbers, often sponsored by their home nations. Canadians were late to the Everest game, but they were no less prideful. In *Everest: High Expectations*, Pat Morrow relates the story of the mountain's first Canadian ascent (1982), while Sharon Wood tells her tale of the first ascent by a North American woman, who also happens to be Canadian (1986). Their reporting is well worth reading, especially if you're not familiar with Everesters who place their own ice screws. In Morrow's case, my crusty cynicism melted in the face of the month-long approach hike (this was pre-Lukla airstrip), multiple deaths under multiple avalanches, and Morrow's dumpster diving on the South Col for half-empty oxygen tanks.

But these stories, good as they are, are not why I bought the book. I bought it to watch what happens when I flip my iPad sideways and back again. And to see how a "book" displays full-screen slideshows. To hear sound recordings of walkie-talkie conversations as I read. To click a link and watch Monty Python's classic "Hairdressers on Everest." In short, I bought this book for style over substance. But I ended up delighted with both.

Frank Edward's term "coffee-tablet book" perfectly describes *Everest: High Expectations*. It's a feast for the eyes, the effect nothing short of spectacular.

As far as I can tell, there are just two downsides to books created with iBooks Author. First, you can only buy and read them on an iPad (not even an iPhone will do, nor laptop or desktop of any stripe). Second, all those photos and videos take up a lot of space—a fat 275 megabytes for *Everest: High Expectations*. Fortunately, the book is also stored in Apple's cloud, so you can delete it from your iPad when you're done, and download it again whenever you want—it's the digital equivalent of putting a dead-tree coffee-table book back on the shelf. Whether you come for the words, the pictures, or just to see what new media can do, this book is top of the world.

JOHN HARLIN III

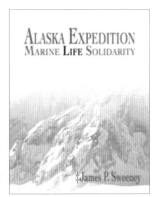

Alaska Expedition: Marine Life Solidarity. James P. Sweeney. VP & D House, 2012. Softcover. 300 pages. $19.95.

Jim Sweeney's *Alaska Expedition: Marine Life Solidarity* exposes the underbelly of alpine climbing: failure, fear, severe injury, and a series of mistakes capable of amplifying into scenarios that might have been woven by Jack London or Robert Service. Natural fury completely beyond any human influence has ended many lives in the mountains. But not Sweeney's. Through luck, fortitude, toughness, and his and his partner's perseverance, he survived to relate this complex and entertaining tale.

Sweeney and partner Dave Nyman were attempting Mt. Johnson's Elevator Sahft in the Ruth Gorge when a huge snow mushroom collapsed and crushed Sweeney: femur broken, hip displaced, feverish nightmares on hand. Any assistance would be from six people without any useful experience in the mountains: a crash-landed private pilot and his pregnant wife (the Nivers) and four who had flown in for what turned into a weather-extended weekend at the Sheldon Mountain House. All six were over three miles from Sweeney's accident, and all are only peripheral to his eventual survival. But Sweeney weaves them in, and they become at least an entertaining sub-story. They certainly affected Nyman's decisions and his heroic role in the incident.

Throughout this story of pluck and rescue, readers go on sweeping side-trips though intensely autobiographical sketches. Sweeney vividly describes his thoughts and actions through bouts with pain, fear, delirium, and solitude.

Joe Simpson's *Touching the Void* is one measure for stories of survival in the alpine zone. Those who've read it will relish reading *Marine Life Solidarity* and comparing the mistakes, tensions, and ultimate survival. Sweeney's tale bares much more of his psyche and how raw, exposed, and defenseless it became during his ordeal. The story is what it is, but Sweeney's perspective, written fairly long afterward, has aged better than many scotches over the same period. What really goes on in the mind when survival is threatened and the body is battered? This book lets us know.

CARL TOBIN

The Storms of Denali. Nicholas O'Connell. University of Alaska Press, 2012. 295 pages. Hardcover. $23.95.

Many writers of climbing fiction invent their own mountains. Not Nicholas O'Connell. Drawing upon his own ascent of Denali, he gives us a vivid—and appropriately chilling—picture of this coldest of North American peaks. "As the angle of the slope steepened, the air grew thin, the sky blue-black, and the full moon appeared as close and brilliant as a newly minted coin. It seemed like we were leaving the earth behind and climbing into outer space." The descriptions are not always so poetic, but realistically gritty: "I found nothing attractive about the climbing. I simply bashed my way up it, pulling on gear, driving in pitons when I needed to, slogging my way up."

O'Connell's characters are not attempting merely Denali, but a new route, really a major variation, on its forbidding south side. His detail—landmarks, logistics, gear, food—confers credibility on the narrative. Yet O'Connell faces a familiar problem: How to employ technical terms for a general audience? Thus we are told what a 5.10 is and how jumars work. Once past these obstacles, O'Connell uses his climbing terms smoothly.

Denali throws everything in its power against its challengers. There are crevasse falls, avalanches, rock fall, incipient pulmonary edema, and the inevitable storm. The climbers endure personal conflicts, bad judgment, ambition, and fear—all the pleasures of a serious expedition.

With his characters, O'Connell is less successful than with their environment. The four climbers are largely generic, and their copious dialogue does not well differentiate them. The principal two are Wyn, single-minded in his ambition, and John, strong but conflicted about leaving his wife and child behind. John's lack of depth is notably regrettable, as he is the narrator. He, and thus we, see relatively little of Lane and Al, the second rope team. Once O'Connell has to let John overhear their conversation in a neighboring tent to tell us what they are really feeling. An omniscient point of view might have served the novel better.

Like many an expedition, this book starts slowly. It does, however, generate considerable excitement as the climb goes higher and dangerous decisions are made under stress. Here we have the real thing: exaltation, suffering, and other consequences of trying something this hard with a group that never really becomes a team.

STEVEN JERVIS

Fiva: An Adventure That Went Wrong. Gordon Stainforth. Golden Arrow Books (U.K.), 2012. 210 pages. Black-and-white photos. Paperback. $16.95.

Remember your first really frightening climbing epic? When the day's outcome, even your own survival, seemed perilously uncertain? If you long for those experiences, I suggest you take a memorable plunge into *Fiva: An Adventure That Went Wrong.*

Climbing accidents and ordeals are instigated in numerous ways. "Wrong place at the wrong time" and "self-inflicted by inexperience" are two popular causes for mountain disasters. *Fiva* stems from the latter. When at 19, English climber Gordon Stainforth convinces his twin brother and primary climbing partner, John, to try their biggest challenge yet—the 5,000-foot alpine rock route Fiva on Store Trolltind, the tallest peak in Norway's Romsdal region—their life-and-death scene is set. Oh, and one more thing. It's July 1969, and Apollo 11 is about to blast off for the moon.

Space exploration was high-tech, but climbing tech wasn't. Harnesses hadn't happened. "Waistlines" (British for swami belts) were 24 feet of quarter-inch hemp, and the era's most popular nut was a famed proto-stopper called a MOAC, its name an abbreviation of Mountain Activities. Who knew? In reading this tale you'll also learn the difference between the terms "graunchy" and "thrutchy"—and which slang designates the most awkward moves. Repetitive analogies, however, to pinned insects and dangling marionettes could positively have been whittled down.

The twins commence their ambitious ascent. Having "a rather exaggerated assessment of [our] climbing ability," trying to follow a vague guidebook description, the pair soon pass the point of no return. Then the first accident seals their fate. John and Gordon Stainforth are to be commended for daring to revisit, four decades onward, the scene of their youthful, near-fatal folly, and for so skillfully reconstructing and reweaving the timeline of events, dialogue, and emotions of their climb. Funny how you never forget it when your lack of judgment comes within a hair of killing you!

Playful, absorbing, and highly recommended, *Fiva* transports the reader back to an innocent age when any climb was possible.

"I didn't know any better. I was 19!
We'd never tackled a big mountain route!
We're going to succeed!
Or are we?"

ED WEBSTER

Wind from a Distant Summit: The Story of New Zealand's Leading Woman Mountaineer. Pat Deavoll. Craig Potton Publishing (N.Z.), 2010. 263 pages. Softcover. NZ$40 ($33).

Heralding from the same province in New Zealand, I became aware of the remarkable Pat Deavoll in the late 1980s, through the University of Canterbury Canoe Club. Even in her first year of kayaking Deavoll became legend, but boating was a passing fancy and receives only a mention in her first book, *Wind from a Distant Summit*. Published in New Zealand, perhaps it appeals mainly to a reader familiar with the vagaries of cloud, wind, and storm in the Southern Alps. Here, teenage Deavoll discovers her life passion among serrated peaks, glaciers, and open grasslands. A passion that, even now, burns fiercely after 35 years.

After recounting her early and extensive forays into the New Zealand Alps, Deavoll journeys deep into the Himalaya in the early 1980s with her husband, Brian. On a shoestring budget and always hungry, they explore the range, carrying enormous packs in a time when Himalayan trekking was not yet the fantasy of many. After two years of travel, Deavoll returns and a dark funk plagues her off and on in the ensuing decades. Climbing provides the escape from depression, and she seeks harder routes, honing her skills to a world-class level. She journeys into the steep: Grade 6 ice routes in Canada, heady grit (her favorite rock), and increasingly technical routes at home. Her 50th birthday in 2009 passes unannounced as she makes a solo first ascent of the 2,600-meter south face of Karim Sar (6,180m) in Pakistan.

Wind from a Distant Summit also explores deeper reasons for climbing, and Deavoll is honest about her doubt and fear. Her historical research shows real passion for India and Pakistan— their mountains have given her so much. Chapters examining partnership and loss, depression, participation of women in the sport, and the moral dilemmas of holidaying in poor regions of the world reveal a woman whose depth of caring reaches far beyond mere pursuit of high places. Pat questions her motives but can never turn away. The mountains are her path.

Contemplate the tenacity of this middle-aged hardwoman. Despite a titanium knee and reconstructive ankle surgery, Deavoll still seeks unclimbed peaks in remote ranges. She breaks her back rock climbing in February 2010 yet sets off to the unclimbed west face of Vasuki Parbat in India that same September. Four days before she leaves, her home city, Christchurch, is wracked by a 7.1 earthquake. On Vasuki, she realizes that continuing the cold and severe climb is beyond her. She spends two days retreating alone on a 5.5mm haul line as her partners, Malcolm Bass and Paul Figg, continue on an ascent named "one of the best Himalayan climbs of the decade."

"I've given away long-term partners and a marriage, a permanent home and financial security to pursue what I'm just beginning to accept has been my only path. There have been defeats and failures, but anyone who climbs mountains will have failures; I accept this now. It's the journey and the trying that matter; the heart that goes into the attempt rather than the summit."

ANNA KEELING

Going Up: Tales Told Along the Road to El Capitan. Joe Fitschen. Whole Tone Press, 2012. 421 pages. Hardcover. $29.

Now in his 70s, Joe Fitschen has worked unsparingly to give us this account of his life. The work is both an autobiographical tale of youth and a history of that exciting first extended decade of modern climbing: postwar to 1960. His style is anecdotal to its very core.

Fitschen reveals the principal players in their odd, unsteady youth. It is fun to take in a wobbly Robbins, Frost, Powell, Kamps, Pratt, and other paragons from the period, many well-known still today. Some of the text is eclectic minutiae, but some rewards us with the glistening bones of our history.

The players in this tale are growing up in 1950s Southern California and later Berkeley. After the second ascent of the Nose with Robbins, Frost, and Pratt in 1959, the book ends, leaving the desperate ascent of Mt. Watkins and those fierce climbs in the Kichatnas and everything afterward, nearly 50 years worth, out of its arc. Fitschen soon heads off to a conventional life. One does wonder what happened "after the Nose" and why he ended up a dedicated New York City dweller. The reader becomes attached to this author by then and doesn't get the reward of seeing how his life turns out. It's a tale of youth, surely, but could use some denouement.

Fitschen's style is understated, low key. A jazz horn player, his writing is largely untinged by the frequent accents and passions one sees in more dramatic climbing accounts. One need only consider Gervasutti or Terray for contrast, or an even more dramatic example, St. Exupery. But Fitschen is happier avoiding terror, grimy anxiety, and vigorous or rude appetite. Even on his long hike out of virginity, the anecdotes are allowed to border on dispassionate formula and are barely amusing for lack of sharper treatment or emphasis.

When the youths escape their various life predicaments to go climbing, they reach personal liftoff. Mostly all of this early climbing is understated, as many of those old routes remain among the world's most important climbs. Fitschen recounts them, step-after-step, well worn, somewhat in the friendly standup genre of old-fashioned Sierra Club writing.

Some have said that mountaineering and climbing literature is a particularly loathsome form of travel writing. Fitschen knows this peril and frequently develops anecdotes that he believes are telling a deeper story, creating some descriptive intimacy. He wants to show that many climbers then were not the imagined paragons of manhood and cultural leaders of a vast and mobilizing era so much as they were quiet, hermitic, and privately stymied, perhaps even wounded, young men who, with great and novel motivation, established a kind of small, loose, even private brotherhood that mattered to no one else at the time. But then because of the day, talent, resources, zeitgeist, and unforeseeable future, they grew wings in the most amazing way.

This is a good long read, worth it. I think it easily surpasses Robbins's recent autobiographical volumes, but could borrow from their greater enthusiasm and open wonder. There are 31 black-and-white photos, some never seen before. Photo reproduction is not terrific; they are small too, and there should be closer, larger imagery of the young Fitschen and company. Fitschen has his dignity like anyone else, and it seems he has held back, considering his emotional intelligence and human experience are remarkably high. The text is viable and rich enough to hold a reader but might have brought us further with more passionate and imaginative descriptive efforts, even in his task as chronicler.

PETER HAAN

Cold Wars: Climbing the Fine Line between Risk and Reality. Andy Kirkpatrick. Mountaineers Books, 2012. (First edition: Vertebrate Publishing, U.K., 2011.) 270 pages. Softcover. $18.95.

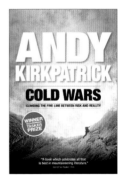

Cold Wars is the second of Kirkpatrick's two Boardman-Tasker prize-winning books. The first, *Psychovertical*, was about "a man who is struggling against the wall, against himself, but who wins through. The story a hundred thousand word answer to the question: 'Why do you climb?'" *Cold Wars*, Kirkpatrick tells us in his preface, "asks a different question: 'What is the price?'"

Cold Wars also literally begins where *Psychovertical* ends, after Kirkpatrick's solo of the Reticent Wall on El Capitan in 2001. Between books he has made it down the trail and finds himself in the Yosemite Lodge cafeteria where he runs into (duh!) climbers, including Leo Houlding ("his skills as a climber touched by magic") who introduces him to Pep Masip, also a veteran of the Reticent. Masip has just backed off his solo attempt of Native Son, citing exhaustion following his 34-day ascent of Amin Brakk. Masip shifts the conversation to domestic life and leaves Kirkpatrick with these words: "Climbing is like a lover, and your wife knows this. Whenever you are together, no matter how much you love your family, your thoughts are only of your lover, of climbing." Though this is a climbing book through and through, those words are never far from its center.

One thing I like about a book like Kirkpatrick's: It's a first-person narrative, so you know the guy manages to keep himself alive long enough to finish it. If his threshold for risk is ratcheted high, his threshold for suffering is even higher.

The climbs themselves are, oddly, not particularly memorable. Kirkpatrick's telling is. He is not interested in first ascents, nor is he of the currently fashionable fast-and-light school of alpinism. As a climber he's a plodder, steady and determined; an aid-specialist in an era of free climbing. As a writer he's self-deprecating, introspective, and hilarious, also dyslexic. Both his writing and his climbing call for persistence above all else.

On the Dru: "All our hard work, the climbing, two walk-ins, all of it for nothing. The portaledge was destroyed, all our bivy gear gone, darkness all but upon us.

" 'Don't worry,' I said, 'It's not as bad as it looks.' "

And, one page later, he and Ian Parnell are upward again, for the third time in a week, toward a successful second ascent of the Lafaille Route, in February.

If Kirkpatrick did not make good on his promise to show us "the price," the climbs themselves would be well worth reading. But in fact, he does make good on that promise, not only invoking the specter of death—Lafaille, Jules Cartwright, the brother of an unnamed partner—but in depicting the price paid among the living. He devotes a considerable amount of the book to his relationships with his children and his father. His father, a climber himself, abandoned his family when Kirkpatrick was quite young, a fact that the boy does not seem to hold against him. Despite being away from home for long periods of time and risking his life, Kirkpatrick is determined to be present for his own children.

In one of the parenting chapters, Parnell is preparing for some epic or another while Kirkpatrick carries his son on his shoulders, the kid holding on to his ears to steer him right or left.

Throughout the book Kirkpatrick wonders why he can't do enjoyable climbs and seems to resent the friends-turned-guides who have learned to ski. In the book's final chapter there he is: skiing with his children above Chamonix. He tells his daughter: "I like the end… when it's over and I'm human again. And I can see the magic."

And the price? In his opening acknowledgments he mentions that his wife, Mandy, for whom he has written the book, is "noticeable by her absence" from it. In the biographical note she is also conspicuously absent from this closing sentence: "He lives in Sheffield with his two children."

For introspection and suffering Kirkpatrick can't be bested. Indeed, he shows us the magic he's seen. His writing deserves a large audience. I hope he's around to keep us entertained, and thinking, for a very long time.

DAVID STEVENSON

IN MEMORIAM

EDITED BY DAVID WILKES

Note: Many of these articles have been edited for length. The full-length tributes are available to read at the AAJ website: aaj.americanalpineclub.org.

BJØRN-EIVIND ÅRTUN, 1966–2012

On February 7, 2012, my good friend and best climbing partner, Bjørn-Eivind Årtun, was killed along with his partner, Stein-Ivar Gravdal, while attempting a new big-wall mixed climb on Kjerag, a seaside wall in southwest Norway. A large block of rock came loose and crushed them both. The futuristic line they were attempting, as well as the fantastic big-wall ice and mixed climb they had established on Kjerag in 2009, Strandhogg, were indicative of Bjørn's extremely high skill level and creative dreams. A photographer by profession, he was an artist whose creativity could also be applied to extreme alpine projects. I think that Bjørn will be remembered in the way that Mugs Stump is often remembered: a true visionary, who was carrying alpinism to the next level.

Bjørn made a big impact in the world of hard alpine climbing in a short time. In addition to his exceptional ice and mixed climbing exploits in Norway, Bjørn climbed the north buttress of Mt. Hunter in a single push in 2009, and climbed a new route on the southeast face of Mt. Foraker in a single push in 2010. Bjørn made several trips to Patagonia, where the best of his many successes was Venas Azules, a futuristic ice and mixed climb on the south face of Torre Egger, established just a few weeks before his death.

I first met Bjørn in 2007, at the Niponino bivouac below Cerro Torre. From our first conversations I knew that Bjørn was a special person. We finally climbed together in Alaska in 2009; it was such an enthusiastic and successful trip that we returned the next year. Bjørn, the big dreamer, had no fear and limitless motivation, and on several occasions I have him to thank for convincing me to try, when my inclination was to be more hesitant. It is impossible not to make connections between Bjørn's big dreams and fearless approach and his tragically early passing. Bjørn was not a reckless climber, but the level to which he was taking his climbing was inevitably rife with risk.

In addition to a community of friends and climbing partners, Bjørn parts with his daughter, Iben, who was 12 years old at the time of his death. From endless tent-bound conversations enduring Alaskan storms, I know that Bjørn loved Iben more than anyone else on Earth. I am deeply sorry for Iben's loss, and I hope that she may live like her father, with endless enthusiasm, beautiful dreams, and the skills and motivation to turn them to reality.

COLIN HALEY

BEAN BOWERS, 1973–2011

I remember when it started, with a cryptic message from a friend in Ridgway, Colorado: "Have you talked to Helen or Bean in the past few days?" I hadn't. But I had spoken with Bean the day after Christmas, when he fessed up and told me that he had broken his femur while skiing and was in the hospital after surgery. I called back later and had the talk of why we live, and how risk is part of our lives, and that these things happen. This was not the first time that Bean had called me with medical issues. They came in waves, mixed between his exploits and his nine lives of living on the edge while passionately exploring the mountains.

After I received the message, I called Helen, Bean's wife. I had to stop driving and sit still while she told me what had happened after the surgery on Bean's leg. I sat in the van in tears, saddened by the news and impact on my good friend. About eight days after his surgery, Bean woke in the night with a headache that resulted in him being taken to the hospital by ambulance. For Bean to call an ambulance for a headache was monumental, given his tenacity and grit. His stories are legend: tales of falling through lake ice on an approach in Patagonia, a 100-foot fall on Torre Egger—the list is long.

A diagnosis of a brain tumor followed, and that was the tip of the proverbial iceberg. He had tumors in many places. I spoke with him briefly in the haze of his course of treatment. What can you say to a man who was in his prime, kicking ass and living his life just the way he envisioned, only to be given a kick in the ass after he was kicked in the balls? He was only 38, and in those years he had accomplished much and touched many lives.

I remember all the good, the humility of watching Bean's grace as he climbed, and the power in those arms on steep limestone. We tried to ski the Grand once, and the weather and conditions were horrendous, so that after we reached the top of Tepee col and the snow was still bulletproof and dangerous, we just laughed and called it a day. There were loads of good days with him, and I revel in the knowledge that I can call him my friend and brother.

ALAN ORAM

HARVEY CARTER, 1932–2012

Legendary Colorado climber Harvey T. Carter died in March at the age of 81 from prostate cancer. Harvey started climbing in the late 1940s in Colorado Springs, where his mother and father were professors at Colorado College. Over the years he did more than 5,000 first ascents. Of course, Harvey's definition of a new route included any section of a route that hadn't been climbed, including variations, direct starts, direct finishes, and boulder problems. Harvey also had a longtime subtle competition with his friend Fred Beckey to see who could do the most first ascents.

I like to note that Harvey, who was a staunch climbing traditionalist his whole career, ironically created the first sport climbing area in the United States by hammering fixed pitons into holes drilled in the soft sandstone at the Garden of the Gods, a city park in Colorado Springs. Many of those original drilled pitons, all soft-iron Army angles, are still used by climbers at the Garden.

Harvey, with his background in sandstone climbing, did many first ascents in the canyon country surrounding Moab, Utah, as well as on the Navajo Reservation and on Shiprock in northern New Mexico. In 1962 Harvey did the first ascent of the Priest near Moab, and then the next day made the second ascent of Castleton Tower, which Layton Kor and Huntley Ingalls had climbed the day before. He also made the first ascents of all the major towers at the Fisher Towers near Moab, except for the Titan.

Besides having a world-class climbing career, Harvey was also an expert skier. He worked on the Aspen Ski Patrol from 1957 to 1979, and later tried to create a downhill ski area on some property behind Pikes Peak that he owned. Besides all his first ascents, part of Harvey Carter's legacy is *Climbing* magazine, which he founded in 1970.

He was a curmudgeon, a traditionalist, and a bit cranky, but Harvey was always a climber. Rest in peace my friend.

STEWART GREEN

HERBERT WILLIAM CONN, 1920–2012

Credit: Beth Wald

On February 1, 2012, the climbing and caving world lost a quiet and unassuming pioneer and role model. Herb Conn passed away in the heart of the Black Hills, in the same bed he had shared with Jan, his wife of nearly 68 years.

Herb and Jan Conn are inextricably linked with the pioneering of rock climbing and caving, especially in the Black Hills of South Dakota. Their rock climbing lives began in 1942, during World War II. Although Herb wasn't drafted, he was declared "Essential Personnel" and was employed in Washington, D.C., by the Department of the Navy. On Sundays, the Conns began accompanying adventurous friends to Carderock. Herb later wrote, "We are everlastingly grateful to Washington climbers for corrupting us, for convincing us that climbing and exploring rocks and caves are more important than steady jobs and raising a family."

On a trip to climb Devils Tower, the couple visited the Needles in the Black Hills. Impressed with the huge potential to climb and explore in relative solitude, they purchased land as close to the spires as possible. They climbed in the mornings, and during the afternoons began laying up stone, fashioning a front wall and roof to a concavity on a small cliff—the Conncave became their home in 1949 and they stayed ever since. With no electricity or running water, they lived a happy life off the grid.

I didn't know any climbers in 1966, when I was just starting out as a rock climber. Someone told me of a guy named Conn, who lived near Custer and was "a mountain climber and had climbed all the Needles." As we arrived at the Conncave, Herb exuberantly loped up to the car, and he and Jan kindly and with much patience answered myriad questions. For a quarter, I purchased one of Herb's pamphlet guides to climbing in the Needles. Herb gave me a sack with a half-dozen registers that had blown off various summits, which hikers had found and somehow returned to him. He suggested I put them back up. It took me years to gain the boldness and skills necessary to return them all.

Over the years I received numerous impeccably typed letters from Herb, which were filled with friendly encouragement. The way Herb lived was a shining example of how I wanted to live my own life. I'll be forever grateful that he was a mentor.

PAUL PIANA

BILL FORREST, 1939–2012

A legend of the Colorado climbing scene, Bill Forrest died of a heart attack on December 21, while snowshoeing on Old Monarch Pass with his wife and outdoor partner of 26 years, Rosa. He was 73. Forrest began technical climbing while serving three years in the infantry in Germany. After completing his education in the 1960s, he founded Forrest Mountaineering in Colorado, churning out inventions that would become a staple of Boulder's high-end climbing shops, not to mention many of our climbing racks.

Forrest came up with a fiberglass wall hammer and ice tools with interchangeable picks, the swami belt with adjustable leg loops, the daisy chain and shock-absorbing quickdraws, copperheads, and Tritons, those all-in-one pieces for belaying, rappelling, and protection. Later he became a designer and tester for Mountain Safety Research and won awards for his snowshoe designs.

He did the first solo ascent of the Diamond on Longs Peak in 1970. Then, in May 1972, he and partner Kris Walker put up the first ascent of the Painted Wall in the Black Canyon of the Gunnison, taking nine days to establish a 26-pitch route up Colorado's largest cliff. In July 1979 he made the first ascent of Uli Biaho Tower in Pakistan with the powerhouse climbers Ron Kauk, John Roskelley, and Kim Schmitz, putting up the first Grade VII by Americans.

Friends, many of whom turned out for his memorial service in his adopted hometown of Salida, Colorado, remember his kindness and decency, his generous advice as a mentor for others, his restless spirit of innovation and adventure, and that he wasn't easily ruffled.

Forrest told *Climbing* magazine in 2011 that his best product ideas came "from seriously participating in the activity. When you love the activity—and live it—the ideas flow."

JOHN HEILPRIN

MAURICE HERZOG, 1919-2012

As the evening shadows gathered on June 3, 1950, the chances seemed slender that 31-year-old French climber Maurice Herzog would see the next morning, let alone his 93rd birthday. At about 2 p.m. that afternoon, he and Louis Lachenal, climbing without oxygen, had been the first two people ever to reach the summit of an 8,000-meter peak, Nepal's 8,091-meter Annapurna. But now, exhausted, hypoxic, and with his hands freezing after he lost his gloves, Herzog stumbled down the mountain behind Lachenal, into darkness and a gathering snowstorm.

Maurice Herzog was born in Lyon, France, on January 15, 1919, into a mountain-climbing family. He was a student when the Second World War broke out in 1939, and in 1944-'45 fought with the French Resistance in the Alps. After the war he joined a French tire company as an executive. Herzog was a talented amateur climber, although by no means in the front ranks of French alpinism. But in 1950 the Federation Française de la Montagne appointed him leader of the first major postwar French expedition to the Himalaya.

After their success on Annapurna, the climbers returned to France as national heroes, but paid a stiff price for their achievement. Lachenal lost all of his toes to frostbite, Herzog both his toes and his fingers. While recuperating in the year that followed, Herzog wrote the most successful expedition book of all times, titled simply *Annapurna* in its English edition, selling over 11 million copies.

In his later life, Herzog held a number of government posts, including minister for youth and sport under Charles De Gaulle, and mayor of Chamonix. He was also a member of the International Olympic Committee. In the past decade, several books questioned his judgment on Annapurna on that June day in 1950. He was accused of subsequently downplaying the role of other members of the expedition, especially that of Lachenal. But, unquestionably, Herzog's acceptance of a higher level of risk than was common on previous expeditions to 8,000-meter peaks ushered in what is sometimes called the Golden Age of Himalayan mountaineering. Herzog died at his home in Neuilly-sur-Seine, France, on December 14, 2012.

MAURICE ISSERMAN

BEN HORNE, 1980-2012

The climbing world lost one of its most inspirational climbers when Ben Horne died while descending from a first ascent in Peru, in July, with Gil Weiss. Ben grew up in Virginia and went to college at Rice University in Houston, where he excelled in academics as well as in being a student leader. After college, Ben discovered his true love for the mountains while living in Kyrgyzstan, culminating in a solo ascent of 7,000m peak Khan Tengri.

Upon returning to the U.S., Ben enrolled in the economics Ph.D. program at UC-San Diego and climbed frequently in the Sierra Nevada. Some of Ben's most notable climbs in the region include a first winter ascent of the Evolution Traverse, as well as the full Palisades Traverse. His athleticism extended beyond the mountains, as he trained for and competed in some of the most grueling races around the country, including the Badger and Leadville 100-mile trail runs.

To us, Ben Horne was a friend, an incredibly strong climbing partner, and an inspiration. He not only had enough positivity and athleticism to achieve his own goals—he had enough to share and inspire others.

PULLHARDER ALPINE CLUB

DALE JOHNSON, 1931–2012

In the introduction to his autobiography, Dale Johnson quoted Christopher Morley: "There is only one success: To be able to spend your life in your own way." This philosophy was a cornerstone of Dale's approach to life, guiding the roles he played not only in the mountains, but also in business.

From his earliest years as a climber, Dale was a leader. As Pat Ament put it in one book, the young Boulderite "would help bring Colorado climbing into the modern age." One of Dale's first ascents was the Northwest Overhang of the Maiden in Boulder's Flatirons in 1953, on which he decided the possibility of falling would be worth the gamble. When a piton pulled, he fell and…nothing happened. Such acceptance of falling was unprecedented at the time.

Dale continued his string of first ascents with the south face of the Matron and the Redguard route in Eldorado Canyon. In 1957, he added the Jackson-Johnson route on Hallett Peak. He climbed many of the great Alpine peaks, and in 1963 he organized an expedition to the Peruvian Andes for 40 Colorado Mountain Club members, leading them up two 20,000-foot peaks. The CMC later recognized Dale's ambition and commitment by presenting him with their highest honor, the Ellingwood Mountain Achievement Award. He also donated money to help build the American Alpine Club headquarters in Golden, Colorado.

In 1958, Dale partnered with Gerry Cunningham to form Gerry Mountain Sports; Dale managed Gerry's first retail store in Boulder. The two came together at a time when the outdoor industry as it is known today did not exist. They farmed out sewing for their backpacking and climbing equipment to home-based seamstresses. In 1965, Johnson left Gerry to develop the company he would eventually name Frostline Kits, helping customers construct their own jackets, tents, and sleeping bags on their home sewing machines. Thirteen years after Frostline's inception, Dale sold the company to Gillette, the razor blade company. He was 48. From then on, his full-time focus would be wilderness travel and flight. He observed in his later years, "As I've grown older, I've required more wilderness, not less."

Throughout his climbing life, many of Dale's most significant ascents were with his family, starting with climbs in Europe with his wife and 9-year-old son Brad. In 1974, when he was 43 and Brad was 19, they teamed to climb Mt. Kenya, where they shared leads as equals. A long 17 years later saw Brad taking Dale up Island Peak in Nepal and the north face of Quitaraju in Peru. Dale fielded falling ice at the bergschrund, along with the requisite exhaustion by days' end—all routine features of alpine climbing. The difference was, he was 64. Now Brad was the lead guide.

Dale Johnson passed away in Boulder on February 23, 2012. Brad was at his side.

BRAD JOHNSON *and* ERIC MING

ANN DODGE MIDDLETON, 1928–2012

Annie outdid her renowned father, Joe Dodge, as a mountaineer, and I believe that if she had not kept such a full plate with demands of wife, mother, and grandmother, she might have had time to develop her dad's oratorical experience as well. Joe was well known as the Appalachian Mountain Club's huts manager, with a distinguished career at New Hampshire's Pinkham Notch. Annie arrived with her dad's great qualities and devotion to the area, but she stood all on her own too. Annie worked in all parts of the AMC hut system, packing supplies, cooking, guiding, and managing, and served as the hut master at the AMC's Pinkham Notch hut.

She could also ski much better than her old man. She was a professional ski instructor, taught skiing for the Hannes Schneider Ski School at Cranmore Mountain, and was even a member of the U.S. Ski Team. Indeed, Annie's stiffest competition on the slopes came from her brother, "Brookie" Dodge, who developed the "two-pole turn" and was a member of the 1952 and 1956 U.S. Winter Olympic teams.

After marrying Jack Middleton, one of the most prominent members of the New England legal community, and an active outdoorsman and mountaineer as well, Ann made many fine ascents throughout New Hampshire, the western United States, Canada, Europe, Mexico, Ecuador, Africa, and Nepal. She was a life member of the Appalachian Mountain Club and a member of the American Alpine Club.

Annie and Jack established their own camp in 1987 on Loon Lake in Freedom, New Hampshire, and it was gradually adorned with impressive trophies of the Middletons' ventures to Africa and elsewhere. Returning from the Wild West to the North Country, where we had all misspent so many pleasant days, my entire family was always made welcome, so long I brought along sufficient Laphroaig single malt and T-bones.

The remaining Middletons have a lot to be proud of in their departed matriarch. May her swash never buckle!

WILLIAM LOWELL PUTNAM

ROGER PAYNE, 1956–2012

Roger and I first tied in together in 2002 at the base of a huge unclimbed ridge in Arizona's Grand Canyon. Our friendship was thus forged on an alpine-like ridge deep in a ditch in the desert (*AAJ 2003*). Two years later Julie-Ann Clyma, Roger's wife, joined us for another long new ridge route, this time on the great south face of Mont Blanc. The final few hundred meters of the descent involved hiking down the very same slope on Mont Maudit that gave way nine years later, on July 12,

burying Roger under a vast tonnage of snow that also killed his two clients and six other people.

A great light was extinguished under that awful slab. Roger shined with a brilliance that should have burned a hole right through the snow. Never has a death crushed me more than his. It hardly seems possible. Not Roger. Poor Julie-Ann. Theirs was one of the finest relationships I've been privileged to witness.

Every year after Roger and Julie-Ann married brought another expedition together: Peru, Nepal, China, Tibet, India, Pakistan, Kazakhstan, and Alaska. While they would each climb independently when the occasion warranted, mostly they were a team, on the mountain and off. From 2004 on they focused on Sikkim, with annual climbing trips leveraged with efforts to develop international tourism that would help the local people and their economy. Roger's involvement with international development began in the early 1990s, when he and Julie-Ann combined the installation of village micro-hydro projects with attempts on K2 and Broad Peak in Pakistan.

Roger's off-mountain career revolved around climbing. In 1989 he became the National Officer for the British Mountaineering Council, and six years later its general secretary (executive director). In both roles he orchestrated huge changes at the organization, including developing international climbing competitions. His experience with competitions served him well when he became the UIAA's first "sports and development director." He left the UIAA in 2005 to devote himself full-time to guiding.

Conversations with Roger were always as bright as the mountain air outside his living room in Leysin, Switzerland. He'd often recite a few lines of memorized poetry. Year after year, there was one passage I was sure to hear, from Geoffrey Winthrop Young, and we'd toast it with a clink of our glasses:

"What if I live no more those kingly days?
their night sleeps with me still.
I dream my feet upon the starry ways;
my heart rests in the hill.
I may not grudge the little left undone;
I hold the heights, I keep the dreams I won."

JOHN HARLIN III

JACK ROBERTS, 1952–2012

Jack Roberts, a mountain guide and guidebook author best known for desperate first ascents in Alaska, died on January 15, 2012, while climbing Bridalveil Falls, near Telluride, Colorado. Jack was almost 60 years old when he fell, which speaks volumes of his passion and skill over a long career.

Jack began climbing in Los Angeles, making the progression from the boulders of Stoney Point to the multi-pitch routes of Tahquitz Rock and on to the big walls of Yosemite. He first gained attention on the spectacular direct aid routes of El Capitan, accompanying Hugh Burton on the second ascents of El Capitan's Shield and Zodiac, and the second ascent of Cosmos with Rob Muir.

Roberts was still an alpine apprentice in 1977 when he and I met in Chamonix and teamed up for the north face of Les Droites. A week later, he and Steve Shea climbed a direct route up the 700-meter north couloir of the Dru. On this trip he met a British climber, Simon McCartney, and they became fast friends, exchanging visits between their homes in London and Santa Monica.

In 1978, Roberts and McCartney set their sights on the unclimbed north face of Mt. Huntington. Provisioned to take four days, they made the first ascent and first traverse of the mountain in nine, overcoming leader falls, injuries, frostbite, and days without food. *Mountain* magazine hailed it as "a major step in alpine-style ascents."

Roberts moved to Colorado in the early 1980s, and made the first ascents of numerous ice and mixed routes. He used his vast local knowledge to publish a guidebook to ice climbs, and his guiding business similarly focused on ice and alpine climbing. It was in Boulder he met Pam Ranger, a schoolteacher with a matching love of outdoor adventure. Friends would comment on how, in the later years of his life, Jack seemed remarkably at peace, and Pam was the reason. That they were soul mates could not be more apparent.

After the first ascent of the north face of Mt. Kennedy, with Jack Tackle, Roberts wrote of looking back at the route they'd just climbed and feeling "the warm glow of success building in my stomach." I expect that Jack had that same warm feeling of accomplishment and pride when he looked back on an extraordinary life.

RICK ACCOMAZZO

GIL WEISS, 1983–2012

Gil Weiss died with Ben Horne in July while descending from Paclaraju Oeste in the Cordillera Blanca, after establishing a new route. Gil was a key member of the informal, San Diego–based Pullharder Alpine Club. Originally hailing from Queens, New York, Gil attended college at George Washington University in Washington, D.C., majoring in English. After finishing college, Gil moved to San Diego where he began climbing. His first alpine route was the Swiss Arete on Mt. Sill in 2007.

Climbing became his passion, and when he moved to Boulder, Colorado, in 2008 he continued to document his adventures via the Pullharder.org blog. His adventures included three seasons in the Cordillera Blanca, big-wall climbs such as the Shield on El Capitan, Half Dome in a day, long free routes such as Bienvenidos a mi Insomnio in Cochamó, Chile, and numerous alpine climbs in Rocky Mountain National Park, including a new line on Arrowhead which he named after his mother, Deborah, who passed away following a battle with cancer in 2009.

More important than his climbing resume was Gil's wit, generosity, free spirit, and open heart, which won him loyal friends all around the world. While Gil's physical presence may be gone, his spirit lives on, and we will be reminded of him every time we swing a tool, embark on a runout, or strike the "Pullharder" pose for a photograph.

PULLHARDER ALPINE CLUB

YAN DONGDONG, 1984–2012

Yan Dongdong, one of China's leading alpinists, died in July in a crevasse fall while descending from a peak in the Tien Shan. Dongdong's accident occurred while doing what he loved the most, namely putting up a technical route on a completely unknown and unclimbed mountain in a remote part of China. (*See Climbs and Expeditions: China.*)

Infectiously enthusiastic for the mountains and for climbing, Dongdong was known for his tireless work ethic and for a cheerful and friendly demeanor, never fazed by the less comfortable aspects of alpine-style climbing. Aged only 27, his short but spectacular climbing career began in 2002 at China's Qinghua University. His position as captain and later advisor of the Qinghua mountaineering club led to his selection for the Olympic torch team, and he was among the climbers on the summit of Everest in May 2008. This experience, which he later called his worst ever in the mountains, contributed to his embracing alpine-style climbing. He became well known in China for his "free mountaineering'" adventures, pushing the boundaries both of regulations and of technical difficulty.

Dongdong's biggest climbs included hard lines on Siguniang (2009), Reddomain, and Jiazishan (both 2011), all with regular partner Zhou Peng, as well as the first ascent of Wuse Shan (2010) and the first winter ascent of Nojinkangsang, a 7,000m peak in Tibet (2010), both with leading female alpinist Li Lan. For the Siguniang climb, he and Zhou were awarded an honorary Piolet d'Or, in recognition not only of their climbing achievement but also of the significance of this route for Chinese alpinism and alpinists.

As a member of the North Face China athlete team, he and Zhou broke another boundary by becoming the first successful privately sponsored alpine climbers in China. With an excellent command of English, he translated English-language books on mountaineering and modern alpine climbing for the Chinese audience, interfaced extensively with foreign climbers, and wrote about his adventures in blogs, climbing magazines, and journals for both domestic and international audiences. Thus he truly inspired many people with his love of the mountains.

BRUCE NORMAND

MICHAEL J. YBARRA, 1966–2012

The eldest of three, Michael was the consummate big brother: self-assured, protective, and always the leader. From an early age he exhibited superior intellect and a desire for adventure. Michael was full of boundless energy and always mischievous.

Threaded throughout all of his endeavors was a sense of unparalleled drive and passion, whether in his intellectual achievements or his outdoor adventures. Despite Michael's unassuming manner and humor, he was a successful journalist and author as well as a serious climber. Michael spent years researching and writing his award-winning book *Washington Gone Crazy: Senator Pat McCarran and the Great American Communist Hunt* (Steerforth, 2004). An equal amount of meticulous study went into the climbing arc of his life: from endless months practicing, taking lessons, and attending clinics, to careful planning and preparation for his expeditions.

At a dinner in Yosemite on September 28, 2012, which would have been his 46th birthday, his friend Rosa Tran told me she once asked Michael how he became so proficient at ice climbing. His reply: "I spent every day for three months practicing." Classic Michael.

In addition to the physicality of climbing, the problem-solving skills it required appealed to him, and it also provided a sense of community. Michael was a seeker, and the transcendent quality he found in nature filled his soul. He truly loved the outdoors and sought to convey this to a broad audience in his articles as the extreme sports correspondent for *The Wall Street Journal*.

Though my family and I miss him profoundly, there is comfort in the knowledge that Michael's last few days were spent with friends, and in the mountains from which he derived such sublime happiness. We hope the spirit of this wonderful man—whom we call a son, brother, uncle and friend—is soaring in the very mountains that he loved so much.

SUZANNE YBARRA

NECROLOGY

Boris Avdeev	Dale L. Johnson	Steve Romeo
Diana C. Dailey	Ann D. Middleton	Gil Weiss
Bill E. Forrest	Theodore Nicolai	Michael Ybarra
Richard M. Gnagy	Roger Payne	
Ben Horne	John J. Roberts	

CLUB ACTIVITIES

EDITED BY FREDERICK O. JOHNSON

Alaska Section. We dedicated the summer of 2012 to designing and installing a solid-waste dehydrating system for the Snowbird Hut outhouse. Several passive systems were integrated into the outhouse design, including urine separation, passive solar, and continuous air movement to dry solid-waste matter. The lightened matter then can be removed from the outhouse less frequently to be transported off the mountain. This new design combination will provide insight to others with the problem of handling human waste at higher elevations. Cindi Squire has been invited to present a poster about this design at the Sustainable Summits Conference in Talkeetna in September 2013.

The Alaska Section has received an incredible amount of positive feedback about the Snowbird Hut. Users have sent thanks and many beautiful pictures. This is the reward for all the hard work our volunteers put in to make this hut a reality. A plaque at the hut, which was dedicated in August 2011, says it all: "This hut is dedicated to adventurous backcountry users who love and live in the outdoors. Please preserve it for the future and include it in your adventures now!"

HARRY HUNT *and* CINDI SQUIRE, *Co-Chairs*

Sierra Nevada Section. In 2012 the section pulled off another full slate of "Climb-munity" gatherings, which continue to be popular and well attended. These included a January ice-climbing weekend in Cold Stream Canyon, near Truckee; a May rock-climbing weekend at Pinnacles National Monument; a June weekend at Donner Summit; our much-loved Pinecrest event in September with Royal and Liz Robbins and Tom Frost; the Yosemite Facelift cleanup in September; and the ever-popular Holiday Dinner in Berkeley. The latter was highlighted by an outstanding multi-media presentation by AAC Past President and 2012 Piolets d'Or winner Steve Swenson, whose show focused on his 30-plus years of climbing in the Karakoram.

The section's conservation activities included hosting a weeklong stewardship project with the National Park Service in Tuolumne Meadows in August, and hosting the Fall Highball Craggin' Classic in Bishop. With over 200 attendees, we and our friends in the AAC Southwest Section contributed over 400 volunteer hours in the Buttermilks, including trail delineation, revegetation, campsite inventory, and graffiti removal. At the climbers' reception, hosted by New Belgium Brewing, over $2,000 was raised for Western Region Live Your Dream Grants.

We continued to sponsor year-round free coffee with climbing rangers every Sunday morning in Yosemite. Yosemite Committee Chair Linda McMillan and her husband, Tom McMillan, also led free Saturday-evening slideshows in Yosemite as part of the climbers' interpretive program, generating further goodwill and exposure for the club. New to the calendar this year was a sponsorship of the Meyers Climbing Festival and Bouldering Competition in Lake Tahoe.

KAREN ZAZZI, *Chair*

Southwest Section. We had four main events in 2012 and also met frequently at Cal Tech for programs such as the Reel Rock Film Festival and the Banff Film Festival tours, sponsored by the Cal Tech Alpine Club. On March 23 the section participated in a service project at Happy Valley campground in Joshua Tree, during which 200 new plants were put in the ground, watered, and protected in wire cages. Thanks to Bernadette Reagan for arranging the project. On June 2 the section helped sponsor the second annual Idyllwild Climbers Festival. Volunteers were treated to coffee and pastries in the morning, after which they worked on the three trails to Tahquitz and Suicide. The day ended with a raffle that raised money for the Idyllwild Climbers Alliance. The section also helped sponsor the Fall Highball in Bishop, which included a work party at the Buttermilk area and a great fundraiser for the regional Live Your Dream grant program.

Finally, we hosted a holiday dinner at Taix French Restaurant in Los Angeles, featuring a slideshow and film by Mark Richey on the first ascent of Saser Kangri II. With the assistance of a no-host bar and appetizers, about 60 people enjoyed visiting with old friends and making new ones. In addition to Mark's excellent presentation, there was a silent auction that raised $1,000 for the section. Thanks to Regional Coordinator Jeff Deikis for his help with this event, along with Chris Savage, Tony Yeary, and Jim Pinter-Lucke for organizing the dinner, and Claudia Pinter-Lucke for her assistance at the dinner.

JIM PINTER-LUCKE, *Chair*

Arizona Section. In our inaugural year as an independent section, we worked with Regional Coordinator Jeff Deikis to achieve a solid start. We initiated a series of communications with club members and created a Facebook presence, and on March 31 AAC members joined the Arizona Mountaineering Club for its 48th birthday celebration at Pinnacle Peak Park. Climb-and-Brew events were held in April in Tucson, Phoenix, and Flagstaff. On April 22, a Play in the Arizona Snow Day was held on Mt. Humphreys. Members also met to climb at Jack's Canyon, Oak Creek Canyon, Mt. Lemmon, and the McDowells, among other places. Some outings were set up so AAC members could meet local climbing guidebook authors, including Eric Richard-Fazio, who led a Mt. Lemmon outing on August 12. Several social events also were held. A screening of Reel Rock films and an audience-choice film night occurred in Flagstaff. A gear swap was held in Phoenix in conjunction with the Arizona Mountaineering Club. Section members also assisted with an AAC-supported stewardship day at Le Petit Verdon, south of Flagstaff, in August, and a post-fire stewardship day at Jack's Canyon in November.

ERIK FILSINGER *and* JEFF PAUL SNYDER, *Co-chairs*

Utah Section. Utah, the home of many world-class and historically important climbing areas, has finally seceded from the Northern Rockies Section and become, drumroll please, the Utah Section. In 2012 our efforts focused on conservation. On August 18 and 19, the section teamed up with the Salt Lake Climbers Alliance, the Jeep Access Fund Conservation Crew (Jeff Young and Jason Kaplan), and the Forest Service's Joseph McFarland for the Ruth Lake Crag Day in the Uinta Mountains. Ruth Lake's crags are situated at 10,000 feet and are very popular with climbers trying to beat the summer heat in the valleys below. AAC members helped eliminate social trails in this fragile alpine environment, harden soggy footways, and replace an especially steep and loose section of trail with a stone staircase that will stand the tests of time. All this hard work was followed by a BBQ sponsored by the AAC. Over 30 volunteers participated.

October 13 and 14 brought Jim Donini's Annual Indian Creek Trail Days. The Jeep Access Fund crew, Rocky Mountain Field Institute, and 70 volunteers showed up for a weekend of climbing, hard work, and BBQ. Much thanks to the Western Slope Section for sponsoring this event. Meanwhile, an AAC Cornerstone Conservation Grant to the Salt Lake Climbers Alliance will ensure the existence of seasonal latrines at Joe's Valley for the next two years.

Jewell Lund of the Utah Section was the recipient of the Northern Rockies Live Your Dream Grant, and she and Kim Hall went and sent in the Wind Rivers. "It's going to eat me!" is a quote from Lund's trip report. For details, you'll have to read the report at the AAC's Inclined blog (inclined. americanalpineclub.org).

BLAKE SUMMERS, Chair

Front Range Section. This was my first year as chair after the untimely demise of the previous chair, Chris Pruchnic, in a climbing accident in Rocky Mountain National Park. Although the time and commitment of this position sometimes seem daunting, the rewards—tangible and intangible—are worth the effort. I hope to foster a greater sense of community in our region.

On very short notice, about 100 members attended an event with Fred Beckey coinciding with the release of his book, *Fred Beckey's 100 Favorite North American Climbs.* Fred gave a slideshow and signed numerous copies of his book, as well as members' personal guidebooks and climbing paraphernalia. Chris Warner presented "Surviving K2" at the Boulder Patagonia Store to a standing-room-only crowd. He pointed out that only 15 Americans have summited K2, and three of them were in the room (one being our very own Phil Powers).

In July we hosted 12 women from the Alpine Club of Iran along with their 10 American hosts. After a day in Boulder, the women traveled to Estes Park, where they stayed at the Colorado Mountain School hostel. One group ascended Flattop Mountain, another clipped bolts at Jurassic Park, and others got a crack-climbing clinic at Lumpy Ridge. Next they decided to ascend the highest peak in Colorado, Mt. Elbert. At their Lakeview campground base camp, the Iranian women began an impromptu singing and dance session, which honored their feelings of liberation from being in the mountains. On the summit they unfurled an AAC banner and the Iranian flag to honor the bond between the two countries. The last day was spent in Eldorado Canyon, climbing and hiking. At a send-off cookout at Neptune Mountaineering in Boulder, members of the Front Range community had a chance to mingle with the group and learn more about Iranian climbing culture. We were grateful for the opportunity to bond with these women who share our passion for the mountains.

CAROL KOTCHEK, Chair

Great Lakes Section. Three-hundred and thirty-seven participants were greeted with extremely mild temperatures and a lean ice year at the 2012 Michigan Ice Fest over the first weekend of February. Participants traveled from as far as Kentucky and Colorado to Munising, Michigan, to enjoy the climbing at Pictured Rocks National Lakeshore. On Friday, Roger Strong thrilled the crowd with slides and a video from his days as a crab-fishing captain on the Discovery Channel's "Deadliest Catch," along with tales of climbing icebergs, ice routes in the Northwest, and the story of a serious ski accident. After a long day of climbing on Saturday, everyone converged upon Sydney's for free beer provided by La Sportiva. The evening's first presentation featured Vince Anderson, who spoke about the direct new route he and Steve House pioneered on the Rupal Face of Nanga Parbat. The final presentation was by Ice Fest favorite Barry Blanchard. A fantastic storyteller, Barry reminisced about past climbing partners, including Kevin Doyle and Guy Lacelle, really hitting home on what makes a special climbing partner and friend.

After the shows we introduced Sommer Edwards and Izabella Tancredi as the 2012 Sue Nott Scholarship winners. Down Wind Sports created the Sue Nott Scholarship to introduce young females to the sport of ice climbing. Sommer and Izabella were selected from the largest group of girls ever to submit applications, and were provided with free entry to the Ice Fest and the Women's Intro-To-Ice Course. Over the weekend we signed up 31 new members to the AAC and the Access Fund, and exposed hundreds of first-timers to the sport of ice climbing.

In the fall our section and Down Wind Sports hosted CLIMB UP 2012!, a four-day event on the south shore of Lake Superior. On Thursday, September 27, a group of climbers representing the AAC, the South Superior Climbing Club, and the Upper Peninsula Climbers Coalition met at Slugs Bluff, outside Palmer, Michigan, for a crag cleanup and dedication of new signs welcoming climbers to Slugs Bluff. On Friday, climbers congregated at Silver Mountain, just south of Keweenaw Bay, and were blessed with incredible climbing weather and peak fall colors. That night we gathered at Northern Michigan University in Marquette for a presentation by Bo White, who has recently climbed in Tajikistan and is planning a trip for club members in August 2013. Kurt Smith then entertained us with a perspective on his storied climbing career. On Saturday the crew headed to the local crag, the AAA Wall, for climbing, camping, and a bonfire party!

On November 10, Planet Rock of Ann Arbor hosted the Reel Rock film tour for a huge crowd of climbing enthusiasts. The Great Lakes Section was represented with a booth (conveniently next to the keg). A big thanks goes out to Planet Rock, and specifically to Christopher Lemon, for hosting the film and giving some big shout-outs to the AAC.

BILL THOMPSON, *Chair*

New England Section. In February our section helped the International Mountain Climbing School sponsor the 19th annual Mt. Washington Valley Ice Fest in North Conway, New Hampshire. On Friday night, Will Gadd showed his short film, "Ice Revolution." Saturday's après-climbing party at IME found Rick Merritt and Nancy Savickas passing out wine and AAC information, and a silent auction benefited both the Ice Fest and the AAC's Live Your Dream Grants for Northeast climbers.

In March the section's 16th annual benefit dinner in Boston included one slideshow by Kurt Diemberger and another by AAC members Freddie Wilkinson, Mark Richey, and Steve Swenson about their first ascent of Saser Kangri II in the Indian Karakoram.

For the first time, we held our annual summer BBQ at the base of Cathedral Ledge, where climbers joined the fun after climbing on North Conway's legendary granite. At the fall BBQ, a 90 percent chance of rain kept some away, but a hardy few showed up at the soggy base of Cathedral and enjoyed the grill and good company.

During the summer, Boston-area members held a couple of Bouldering and BBQ after-work evenings at Hammond Pond, organized by volunteers including Justin Walsh, Sarah Arsenault, Michael Coote, and Sam Streibert. We also joined forces with the Rumney Climbers Association, the U.S. Forest Service, and the Access Fund to support several "Coffee with a Ranger" programs in the parking lot at Rumney, New Hampshire, during busy summer weekends. This gave climbers a chance to talk to rangers and local climbing activists about land stewardship issues at these popular cliffs. Finally, Chad Hussey hosted our fifth annual "It Ain't Over Til It's Over" cragging day in Connecticut in early November.

NANCY SAVICKAS, *Chair*

Metro New York Section. If you mention "New York Section" in AAC circles, people will invariably associate it with our annual black-tie dinner. While the definition of "black tie" has evolved over the last 33 years to include forms of attire scarcely acceptable years ago, the purpose of the dinner has not changed: to reunite committed climbers in an elegant setting, with fine food and wine, and to celebrate the brotherhood of the rope among generations old and new. In addition, the November event has raised significant sums over the years to help fund the AAC Library, the *AAJ*, and most recently the climbing grants program. Thanks in great part to some spirited bidding engineered by our dynamic auctioneers, Steve Schofield and Dee Byers, we were able to establish a special fund enabling young climbers to live their dreams. This fund is being named after our dear member Clif Maloney, who perished on Cho Oyu in 2009.

The keynote speaker at this year's dinner, held November 10 at the Union Club, was Arlene Blum, best known for her groundbreaking and successful women's expedition to Annapurna in 1978, and more recently for her pioneering efforts as a biochemist to ban toxic flame-retardant chemicals in children's sleepwear and other textiles. Mark Richey gave a short but absorbing presentation that had the audience on the edge of their seats as his small team conquered Saser Kangri II, then the second-highest unclimbed peak in the world.

Apart from our dinner, the section had a large number of indoor and outdoor events in 2012, including winter and spring Adirondacks outings, both held in excellent conditions for the large contingent who journeyed from Manhattan and environs. Of note during the year were slideshows by Kurt Diemberger, Majka Burhardt, Donn Healy, and a film program and reception at the Polish Embassy celebrating the feats of the indomitable Polish climbers of the 1980s. In May we were treated to a special showing of the spectacular images of Mario Colonel, the noted Chamonix photographer and guide, at a reception hosted by Jeffrey Cohen in his Village home.

In the summer we joined forces with the Rubin Museum to cosponsor both a kids' Everest program inside the museum as well as a series of four dramatic Hollywood film showings that drew sellout crowds. Among the films featured was "K2," introduced by AAC Executor Director and K2 climber Phil Powers. Ted Vaill gave us an insider's view of "Lost Horizon-Shangri La," having done extensive research and organized an expedition to Shangri La's likely location in Szechuan Province.

In December, about 30 members gathered for a winter hike of Breakneck Ridge in the Hudson Highlands, followed by a reception at the Galligans. Over the years, Chris and Mim have proved to be the kindest and most generous of hosts in their house in Garrison.

Finally, my thanks to our dynamic group of volunteers, whose enthusiasm and hard work made all the above possible. Visit our section website (nysaac.blogspot.com) for recent section news, photos, and coming events.

PHIL ERARD, *Chair*

Mid-Atlantic Section. The Mid-Atlantic Section participated in the AAC's 2012 membership drive at two New Jersey climbing gyms. Michael Feldman manned a table at the Gravity Vault in Chatham, while Barry Rusnock greeted climbers at the New Jersey Rock Gym in Fairfield. Because of Michael and Barry's efforts, the section added 10 new members that evening.

Members gathered August 4 for a day of multi-pitch climbing at the Delaware Water Gap National Recreational Area, along with Simon Carr, Blue Ridge Section Chair. We gathered afterward at the Deer Head Inn for cocktails, followed by a Haitian dinner at the Zen Safari in Delaware Water Gap. On October 6 the section hosted its Second Annual Allamuchy Top Rope Social and Oktoberfest Dinner. The Top Rope Social was held at the Main Wall crag in Allamuchy Mountain State Park, New Jersey, some 50 miles west of New York City, where climbers challenged themselves on many crag classics. About 15 members then attended the Oktoberfest Dinner at the well-known Black Forest Inn in nearby Stanhope.

I would like to thank the AAC staff, including Sarah Garlick, the Northeast Regional Coordinator, for their support. We look forward to continuing our efforts to build a strong AAC community in the Mid-Atlantic area.

BARRY RUSNOCK, *Co-chair*

Southern Appalachian Section. In 2012 the section enjoyed a record number of local AAC events, from informal climbing-video nights and first-aid and climbing safety classes to full-on banquets. Let it be said at the outset that all of these events were possible only through the commitment of many AAC volunteers and local business partners. Our thanks to all!

Responding to a disturbing incidence of climbing accidents in the southern Appalachian region, most recently the death of a 19-year-old climber while rappelling at a crag in North Carolina, the section committed to the development and ongoing delivery of free public clinics designed to promote safer rappelling practices. This project was led by Danny McCracken and Aram Attarian, and the first clinic was held in November. Led by Patrick Weaver, Danny, and Aram, the clinics are taught by AMGA-certified instructors from the Appalachian Mountain Institute of Pisgah Forest, North Carolina. By January 2013, seven sold-out clinics had been delivered across North Carolina, with over 80 participants attending. More clinics and venues are in the pipeline, with the goal of reaching 200 climbers by year-end 2013.

In March and November, Danny McCracken taught Wilderness First Aid classes featuring significant customization to focus on climbing accident scenarios. Class pricing was designed to incentivize participants to join the AAC rather than pay higher tuition. In July, at a backyard barbecue in Raleigh, the section welcomed Lisa Hummel, the new Regional Coordinator for the Southeast. Forty members, guests, and local AAC partners enjoyed a slide presentation by John Bragg, AAC Director of Community Programs. Love the Lycra, John!

The entertainment highlight of the year was the visit of prominent alpinists Janet Bergman and Freddie Wilkinson for three AAC events in October. Janet and Freddie presented "Karakoram Frontiers: A Season of First Ascents" to enthusiastic audiences in Raleigh and Winston-Salem. Janet also hosted a well-received event for AAC women. Our thanks to Mountain Hardwear, Great Outdoor Provision Co., and the Triangle Rock Club for supporting their visit.

The 8th Annual Eastern North Carolina AAC Get Together was held December 8 at the home of the section chair in Raleigh. The featured speakers were Roger Putnam, recipient of a 2012 AAC Research Grant, who presented his work on mapping the geology of El Capitan, and Jeff Witt, visiting Exum guide, who presented a tutorial on the climbing routes of Aconcagua.

DAVID THOENEN, *Chair*

INDEX

COMPILED BY RALPH FERRARA & EVE TALLMAN

Mountains are listed by their official names. Ranges and geographic locations are also indexed. Unnamed peaks (e.g., Peak 2,340) are listed under P. Abbreviations are used for some states and countries, and for the following: Article: art.; Cordillera: C.; Mountains: Mts.; National Park: Nat'l Park; Obituary: obit. Most personnel are listed for major articles. Expedition leaders and persons supplying information in Climbs and Expeditions are also cited here. Indexed photographs are listed in bold type. Reviewed books are listed alphabetically under Book Reviews.

INTERNATIONAL GRADE COMPARISON CHART

THIS CHART IS DESIGNED TO BE USED WITH THE AMERICAN ALPINE JOURNAL TO HELP DECIPHER THE DIFFICULTY RATINGS GIVEN TO CLIMBS

SERIOUSNESS RATING:

THESE OFTEN MODIFY TECHNICAL GRADES WHEN PROTECTION IS DIFFICULT

R: POOR PROTECTION WITH POTENTIAL FOR A LONG FALL AND SOME INJURY

X: A FALL WOULD LIKELY RESULT IN SERIOUS INJURY OR DEATH

YDS=YOSEMITE DECIMAL SYSTEM; UIAA=UNION INTERNATIONALE DES ASSOCIATIONS D'ALPINISME; FR=FRANCE/SPORT AUS=AUSTRALIA; SAX=SAXONY; CIS=COMMONWEALTH OF INDEPENDENT STATES/RUSSIA; SCA=SCANDINAVIA; BRA=BRAZIL

NOTE: ALL CONVERSIONS ARE APPROXIMATE

YDS	UIAA	FR	AUS	SAX	CIS	SCA	BRA	UK	
5.2	II	1	10	II	III	3			
5.3	III	2	11	III	III+	3+			D
5.4	IV-/IV	3	12		IV-	4			VD
5.5	IV+		13		IV	4+			
5.6	V-	4	14		IV+	5-		4a	S
5.7	V/V+		15	VIIa		5			HS
5.8		5a	16	VIIb	V-	5+	4/4+	4b	VS
5.9	VI-	5b	17	VIIc		6-	5/5+	4c/5a	HVS
5.10a	VI	5c	18	VIIIa	V	6	6a	5a	E1
5.10b	VI+	6a						5b	
5.10c	VII-	6a+	19	VIIIb		6+	6b		E2
5.10d	VII	6b	20	VIIIc	V+		6c		E3
5.11a	VII+	6b+		IXa		7-	7a	5c	
5.11b		6c	21	IXb		7	7b		
5.11c	VIII-	6c+	22	IXc	VI-	7+	7c	6a	E4
5.11d	VIII	7a	23						
5.12a	VIII+	7a+	24	Xa		8-	8a		E5
5.12b		7b	25		VI	8	8b		
5.12c	IX-	7b+	26	Xb		8+	8c		
5.12d	IX	7c	27				9a	6b	E6
5.13a	IX+	7c+	28	Xc		9-	9b		
5.13b		8a	29				9c		
5.13c	X-	8a+	30	XIa		9	10a	6c	E7
5.13d	X	8b	31		VI+		10b		
5.14a	X+	8b+	32	XIb			10c	7a	E8
5.14b		8c	33			9+	11a		
5.14c	XI-	8c+	34	XIc			11b	7b	E9
5.14d	XI	9a	35				11c		E10
5.15a	XI+	9a+	36	XIIa		10	12a		
5.15b	XII-	9b	37		VII		12b		E11
5.15c	XII	9b+	38	XIIb			12c		